KU-709-733

BUSINESS BASICS

Marketing

Askham Bryan College
LIBRARY BOOK

PUBLISHING

First edition 1995
Third edition September 2000

ISBN 0 7517 2130 1
(previous edition 0 7517 2121 2)

British Library Cataloguing-in Publication Data

A catalogue record for this book is available from the British Library

Printed in England by DACOSTA PRINT
35/37 Queensland Road, London, N7 7AH
(0207 700 1000)

Published by

BPP Publishing Limited

Aldine House, Aldine Place

London W12 8AW

www.bpp.com

All our rights reserved. No part of this publication may be reproduced,
stored in a retrieval system or transmitted, in any form or by any means,
electronic, mechanical, photocopying, recorded or otherwise without the
prior written permission of BPP Publishing Limited.

© BPP Publishing Limited 2000

CONTENTS

Contents

PREFACE

BUSINESS BASICS are targeted specifically at the needs of:

- Students taking business studies degrees
- Students taking business-related modules of other degrees
- Students on courses at a comparable level
- Others requiring business information at this level

This *Marketing* text has been written with two key goals in mind.

- To present a substantial and useful body of knowledge on marketing at degree level. This is not just a set of revision notes – it explains the subject in detail and does not assume prior knowledge.

- To make learning and revision as easy as possible. Each chapter:

    - Starts with an introduction and clear objectives
    - Contains numerous activities
    - Includes a chapter roundup summarising the points made
    - Ends with a quick quiz

    And at the back of the book you will find:

    - Multiple choice questions and answers
    - Exam style questions and answers

The philosophy of the series is thus to combine techniques which actively promote learning with a no-nonsense, systematic approach to the necessary factual content of the course.

BPP Publishing have for many years been the leading providers of targeted texts for students of professional qualifications. We know that our customers need to study effectively in order to pass their exams, and that they cannot afford to waste time. They expect clear, concise and highly focused study material. As university and college education becomes more market driven, students rightly demand the same high standards of efficiency in their learning material. The BUSINESS BASICS series meets those demands.

BPP Publishing
September 2000

Titles in this series:

Accounting
Law
Quantitative Methods
Information Technology
Economics
Marketing
Human Resource Management
Organisational Behaviour

> You may order other titles in the series using the form at the end of this book. If you would like to send in your comments on this book, please turn to the review form following the order form.

HOW TO USE THIS STUDY GUIDE

This book can simply be read straight through from beginning to end, but you will get far more out of it if you keep a pen and paper to hand. The most effective form of learning is *active learning*, and we have therefore filled the text with exercises for you to try as you go along. We have also provided objectives, a chapter roundup and a quick quiz for each chapter. Here is a suggested approach to enable you to get the most out of this book.

(a) Select a chapter to study, and read the introduction and objectives at the start of the chapter.

(b) Next read the chapter roundup at the end of the chapter (before the quick quiz and the answers to activities). Do not expect this brief summary to mean too much at this stage, but see whether you can relate some of the points made in it to some of the objectives.

(c) Next read the chapter itself. Do attempt each activity as you come to it. You will derive the greatest benefit from the activity if you write down your answers before checking them against the answers at the end of the chapter.

(d) As you read, make use of the 'notes' column to add your own comments, references to other material and so on. Do try to formulate your own views. In economics, many things are matters of interpretation and there is often scope for alternative views. The more you engage in a dialogue with the book, the more you will get out of your study.

(e) When you reach the end of the chapter, read the chapter roundup again. Then go back to the objectives at the start of the chapter, and ask yourself whether you have achieved them.

(f) Finally, consolidate your knowledge by writing down your answers to the quick quiz. You can check your answers by going back to the text. The very act of going back and searching the text for relevant details will further improve your grasp of the subject.

(g) You can then try the case studies at the end of most chapters, the multiple choice questions at the end of the book and the exam style questions to which you are referred at the end of the chapter. Alternatively, you could wait to do these until you have started your revision – it's up to you.

Further reading

While we are confident that the BUSINESS BASICS books offer excellent range and depth of subject coverage, we are aware that you will be encouraged to follow up particular points in books other than your main textbook, in order to get alternative points of view and more detail on key topics. We recommend the following books as a starting point for your further reading on *Marketing*.

In addition to the books and articles listed below, it is recommended that students regularly read a quality newspaper such as *The Times*, and one of the trade magazines such as *Marketing Business*.

Aaker, D A, *Strategic Marketing Management*, 1988

Adcock, Bradfield, Halborg and Ross, *Marketing Principles and Practice*, 1998, FT Pitman Publishing

Ansoff, H I and McDonnell, E J, *Implementing Strategic Management*, 2nd edn, 1990, Prentice Hall

Ansoff, H I, *Corporate Strategy*, 1975, Pelican

Assael, H, *Marketing: Principles and Strategy*, 1990, The Dryden Press

Baker, M J, *Marketing: An Introductory Text*, 1996, Macmillan Business

Baker, M J, *The Marketing Book*, 3rd edn, 1994, Butterworth-Heinemann

BARB, *Guide to the Broadcasters' Audience Research Board*, 1993, BARB

Boston Consulting Group, *The Product Portfolio*, Perspectives, August 1990

Cannon, T, *Basic Marketing: Principles and Practice*, 1992, Cassell

Clifton, P, Nguyen, H and Nutt, S, *Market Research: Using Forecasting in Business*, 1992, Butterworth-Heinemann

Howard, J A, and Sheth, J N, *The Theory of Buyer Behaviour*, 1969, Wiley

Kotler, Philip, Armstrong, Gary, Saunders, John, Wong, Veronica, *Principles of Marketing – European Edition*, 1996, Prentice Hall

Kotler, P, 'Diagnosing the marketing takeover', Harvard Business Review, Nov-Dec 1965

Kotler, P, *Marketing Management: Analysis, Planning, Implementation and Control*, 6th edn, 1988, Prentice Hall

Lancaster, G and Massingham L, *Essentials of Marketing*, 2nd edn, 1993, McGraw Hill

Levitt, T, 'Exploit the product life cycle', Harvard Business Review, Nov-Dec 1965

Levitt, T, 'Marketing myopia', Harvard Business Review, July/August 1960

Martin, C and McDonald, M, *Marketing: An Introductory Text*, 1995, Macmillan

Mercer, David, *Marketing*, 2nd edn, 1996, Blackwell Business

Morden, A R, *Elements of Marketing*, 3rd edn, 1993, D P Publications

Nader, R, *Unsafe at Any Speed*, 1973, Bantam

Oliver, G, *Marketing Today*, 3rd edn, 1990, Prentice Hall

Oliver, N, *JIT: Issues and Items for the Research Agenda*, 1991

Rice, C, *Consumer Behaviour: Behavioural Aspects of Marketing*, 1993, Butterworth-Heinemann

Schiffman, L and Kanuk, L, *Consumer Behaviour*, 1991, Prentice Hall

Smith, P R, *Marketing Communications: An Integrated Approach*, 1993, Kogan Page

Webster, F E and Wind, Y, *Organizational Buying Behaviour*, 1972, Prentice Hall

Wilmshurst, J, *The Fundamentals and Practice of Marketing*, 3rd edn, 1995, Butterworth-Heinemann

Wood. L 'The end of the product life cycle?', *Journal of Marketing Management*, vol. 6, 1990

Zelthaml, Parasuraman and Berry, *Delivering Quality Service: Balancing Customer Perceptions and Expectations*, 1990

Chapter 1 :
THE MARKETING CONCEPT

Introduction

Marketing can be thought of as a philosophy for business organisations. It is also a functional area of management located within a departmental structure. The marketing concept means putting the customer first. In practice, this consumer orientation should permeate every part of a business if it is to succeed. The theory of marketing is based on the 'marketing mix' variables of product, price, place and promotion which will be discussed throughout this text. This chapter aims to give an overview of the marketing concept. It will also investigate the organisation of marketing within the company structure but first we will review the historical development of marketing.

Your objectives

In this chapter you will learn about the following.

- (a) The history and development of marketing

- (b) What is meant by marketing and the marketing concept

- (c) Why organisations need a marketing oriented strategy

- (d) The elements that make up the 'marketing mix'

- (e) How marketing activities are managed and organised within a marketing department

- (f) How the marketing department fits into the organisation as a whole

NOTES

1 HISTORY OF MARKETING

Marketing grew out of trade and exchange. When a society becomes capable of producing a surplus (that is, more than is necessary for subsistence), this can be traded for other goods and services. In early societies this trade was direct, using a barter system, exchanging goods for other goods. As societies develop, trade takes place using an agreed medium of exchange, usually money.

Production before the industrial revolution was usually fragmented, small scale and aimed at local customers. During the industrial revolution production became organised into larger units. Towns grew bigger and trade increased as people became more dependent on buying goods rather than producing these goods themselves. Producers and the markets to which they sold became geographically separated from each other, rather than confined to small localities. Before the industrial revolution buyers had direct contact with sellers and so producers knew their customers' needs and wants. Later, when buyers lived some distance from producers, it became necessary for producers to find out what products buyers wanted and what product attributes were desired.

Activity 1

In February 1995 Tesco launched its Clubcard scheme which awards points for sums spent over a minimum amount. The points can later be turned into money-off vouchers. Is this just to encourage people to spend more or, in the light of what you have just read, does it have other purposes?

Mass production techniques increased the number and types of goods on the market. Increased productivity also reduced unit costs. With new cheaper products on offer, demand was such that until very recently many business problems centred on production and selling rather than marketing, since it was more important to produce enough of a product to satisfy strong demand than to think about 'customer needs'.

This was exacerbated in the UK because of its historical pre-eminence in industry and trade. Great Britain dominated world trade up until the First World War when other countries emerged to compete. The United States, Japan and Germany took much of Britain's share in the market for manufactured goods. Present-day UK businesses have to compete effectively. Marketing enables them to identify customer needs and to find products that satisfy those needs.

Production is no longer the main problem facing business concerns. Indeed, for most products and services, it is excess supply rather than excess demand which is the problem. In these circumstances, the focus has switched from 'how to produce enough' (supply factor) to 'how to increase demand' (demand factor). Marketing techniques have been developed as a result of this switch in orientation.

Initially, mass marketing techniques were applied to selling fast-moving consumer goods such as washing powder, toothpaste and groceries, although these were relatively unsophisticated. Subsequently, marketing methods have been applied to industrial goods and, more recently, to services. Marketing techniques have grown in importance as competition and consumer choice have increased. Marketing methods are seen as a means of competing with rivals.

Services and industrial markets are only now becoming marketing orientated. However, what is marketing orientation? The next section aims to answer this question and to discuss the marketing concept in more detail.

> **Activity 2**
>
> If you walk into your local chemist, or a supermarket, you will notice anything up to 20 different brands of toothpaste on sale. Why do you think there are so many?

2   THE MARKETING CONCEPT

There are many definitions of marketing. Here we will consider three which will provide insight into how marketing is used in practice.

Definition

> Marketing is the management of exchange relationships.

This emphasises the role of marketing in relating to the world outside the organisation. All relationships between the organisation and the outside world, especially when they relate to customers, need to be managed. The organisation will be judged by customers, suppliers, competitors and others according to their personal experience. How often have you been put off an organisation by the manner of a telephone operator, or the tone of a receptionist's voice? These contacts are vital in creating a positive image for the organisation with customers and the public.

Another definition is that of the Chartered Institute of Marketing.

Definition

> Marketing is the management process which identifies, anticipates and supplies customer requirements efficiently and profitably.

This definition emphasises the wide scope of marketing, ranging from initial identification of customer needs by means of research, right through to eventual, profitable satisfaction of those needs.

Definition

> Marketing is concerned with meeting business objectives by providing customer satisfactions.

This definition is important because it stresses the importance of the customer and, more particularly, customer satisfaction. When people buy products or services they do not simply want the products, they also want the benefits from using the products or services. Products and services help to solve a customer's problems. It is the solution to these problems that customers are buying.

Activity 3

When people buy the products listed below, what problems or types of problems are they trying to solve?

(a)   Lawn mowers
(b)   Life insurance
(c)   A particular model of car

A market orientated organisation will have the following features.

(a)   A commitment to meeting the needs of customers more successfully than the competition

(b)   A structure and processes of operation which are designed to achieve this aim. It is not sufficient that the company employs a marketing manager or has a market research department. All the company's activities must be co-ordinated around the needs of the customer when making decisions about what to produce and, subsequently, how and where the product or service is to be made available.

Underlying all this is the belief that a market orientation is essential to the long-term profitability of the company.

In summary the marketing concept has three elements.

- Customer orientation
- Co-ordination of market led activities
- Profit orientation

Activity 4

How might a profit orientation undermine attempts to co-ordinate market-led activities?

The activities and philosophy of market orientated companies contrast sharply with production orientated and sales orientated organisations.

Definition

A production orientation may be defined as the management view that success is achieved through producing goods of optimum quality and cost, and that therefore, the major task of management is to pursue improved production and distribution efficiency. A sales orientation is the management view that effective selling and promotion are the keys to success.

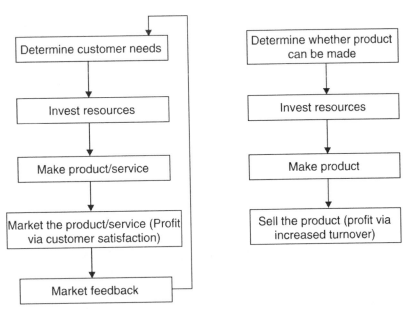

Figure 1.1 Comparison of marketing orientation with production orientation

2.1 Customer orientation

The truism that 'without customers, you don't have a business' remains the logic for maintaining a customer orientation. Satisfying customers' needs at a profit should be the central drive of any company.

In contrast to following a market orientation, however, many companies adopt a sales orientation. Here, the tendency is to make the product first and then to worry about whether it will sell. Underlying this philosophy is a belief that a good sales force can sell just about anything to anybody.

Theodore Levitt distinguishes between sales and marketing orientations in terms of the place of the customer in the marketing process.

Definition

> Selling focuses on the needs of the seller; marketing on the needs of the buyer. Selling is preoccupied with the seller's need to convert his product into cash; marketing with the idea of satisfying the needs of the customer by means of the product and the whole cluster of things associated with creating, delivering and finally consuming it.

The marketing concept suggests that companies should focus their operations on their customers' needs rather than be driven solely by the organisation's technical competence to produce a particular range of products or services, or by a belief in the sales force.

If new products and services are developed that do not meet customer requirements, the result will be the need for an expensive selling effort to persuade customers that they should purchase something from the company that does not fit their purpose.

If the organisation has got its marketing right, it will have produced products and services that meet customers' requirements at a price that customers accept. In theory, at least, little or no sales effort will be needed.

Activity 5

Quality Goods makes a variety of widgets. Its chairman, in the annual report, boasts of the firm's 'passion for the customer'. 'The customer wants quality goods, and if they don't get them they'll complain, won't they? We haven't had any complaints, so the customers must be happy!'

Is this a marketing orientated firm?

2.2 Co-ordinating marketing activities

A true marketing orientation requires a co-ordinated marketing effort. This covers market research to identify customer needs, market-led product development, sales promotion and advertising to ensure that customers know of the existence of the product and its benefits, effective distribution and delivery to ensure availability, and market-based pricing.

Marketing orientated companies consequently need the following organisational characteristics for an integrated marketing effort.

(a) Marketing functions are identified (market research, product-market planning, advertising and promotion, sales and distribution) and co-ordinated under a single executive.

(b) Direct, formal communications are established between the marketing function and executives responsible for development, design and manufacturing, and finance. This ensures direct linkage between market needs and production decisions.

If marketing effort is directed at making long run profits the whole organisation clearly benefits. In the short term, however, many companies will set sales-maximising objectives for the sales force. High sales, of course, do not necessarily guarantee high profits.

If the sales force is directed solely to maximise sales volume, then it may wish to reduce prices or attempt to offer speedier delivery. There will be a greater incentive to reduce prices and disrupt planned production at the cost of overall profitability. Under these circumstances there is likely to be frequent and unhelpful conflict between production and sales departments with an inevitable loss of customer service.

However, when the sales force is motivated to maximise profit rather than sales, it will only wish to make extra sales if this is profitable for the company. The impact on profits will be taken into account before offering a price cut. Similarly, the costs of disrupting production will be considered when deciding whether or not to make a delivery promise that would involve rescheduling production of the next batch of the product.

Marketing performance must be judged by profit and return on investment – not by volume of sales. The wider implications of marketing decisions must be recognised. If sales are an end in themselves, conflicts with the production departments are almost inevitable.

Top management must ensure that the marketing department and in particular the field sales force are clear about the objective of increasing corporate profits.

Using profitability as the benchmark for performance also acknowledges the role of the market place as the ultimate arbiter of success.

2.3 The marketing concept in practice

The term 'marketing' has only entered general use since the 1960s. Before that, most companies had a sales department but not a marketing department. The increasing use of 'marketing' rather than 'sales' in job titles does not necessarily mean that all such companies are becoming more marketing orientated.

Even though the marketing concept, with its attempt to match goods to consumer needs, is widely accepted, there will always be a need for a persuasive sales force. The need to convince the customers that they should buy the company's products arises because it is highly unlikely that their needs can be exactly satisfied. Also, they may not be aware of the needs which the product satisfies. The sales force will therefore have to overcome the following problems.

(a) The organisation is unlikely to be the only potential supplier. It will therefore be necessary to convince customers to buy from the company and not from a competitor who may also have attempted to match the customers' needs and wants.

(b) Customers may need to be reassured about the benefits of owning or using the company's product or service. In industrial markets buyers will require evidence that technical specifications and appropriate industry standards are met.

(c) It may not be feasible to meet the exact requirements of each specific customer. When mass production techniques are targeted at the average customer's requirements, it may be that no individual's needs are actually satisfied.

(d) Customers' requirements might have changed since market-led production decisions were made. In markets for basic commodities, customer requirements are stable over considerable periods. Other markets are very dynamic and consumer needs change quickly. Markets subject to rapid changes in taste or fashion, such as clothing, leisure and entertainment, are particularly prone to rapid obsolescence.

The sales force's effort will be more successful if products and services meet market needs. A market-led approach will make what is on sale more acceptable to customers. Salespeople are no longer left trying to persuade potential buyers to change their perceptions of what they need. More productive activities such as developing leads, providing better customer service and identifying changes in customer requirements (to which the organisation needs to respond) can be pursued.

All good sales presentations are customer orientated. Instead of merely cataloguing a series of product features, the intelligent salesperson concentrates on promoting the benefits that will be derived from the company's product or service. The DIY enthusiast is not necessarily interested in the technical specification of a power drill's electric motor. Whilst this might be the pride and joy of the company's research and development team, the customer is only really interested in finding a solution to a range of DIY tasks – for a way of getting a series of 5mm holes to fix some brackets, for example. The good salesperson will ensure that the potential purchaser is assured that using the product will provide the particular benefits sought. In industrial markets such benefits might include the cost reductions that can be gained using the company's products, the reliability of deliveries and product quality.

NOTES

> **Activity 6**
>
> What went wrong in the following cases?
>
> (a) Company A printed 10,000 T-shirts bearing the legend 'England – World Cup 1994'.
>
> (b) The marketing literature for Company B's new toaster proudly proclaims that it has a 2kw element heating to a temperature of 300°.
>
> (c) Company C, which makes electronic personal organisers, has a stand in the computer department of W H Smith's.

We will now consider the strategic issues facing the market orientated organisation.

3   MARKETING ORIENTATED STRATEGY

So far, our consideration of the marketing concept has concentrated on tactical issues – the day to day marketing activities of a company. At this level, it is possible to argue that under certain circumstances a sales orientation might be preferable. After all, people do buy things that they have little need of. A particular company may have a charismatic sales force, but lack any skill to comprehend or respond to customer needs. Such a company may well be profitable operating a sales orientation, but find it difficult and costly to change towards a customer-needs focus.

3.1   Marketing myopia

On the longer term consequences of ignoring market needs, however, the case for adopting a marketing orientation appears to be overwhelming. Theodore Levitt's seminal article 'Marketing myopia' appeared in the Harvard Business Review in July-August 1960, arguing that a market orientation should determine the longer term strategic direction of companies. If managers perceive the company's business solely in technical and production terms, products will be perceived according to their physical properties. In an industry where competitors probably share similar technical competences, everyone will appear to produce similar products.

Levitt's argument is that there are clearly large numbers of growth markets derived from society's needs, but the industries that serve these needs at a particular time may well decline in the face of competition if another industry's new technology better matches the growing market's needs.

Levitt illustrates his argument with examples of vision blinkered by the production concept of competing for business in a particular industry. The following question is posed.

EXAMPLE: AMERICAN RAILWAYS

Q   Why did the American Railways not respond to the airlines and trucking companies that eventually took away the railroad's passenger and freight business?

The railways certainly had the available capital reserves to respond to this competition, built up over the years that 'rail was king'. The infant businesses that grew to be Pan Am, TWA and the national carriers struggled for their early existence. Levitt provides the following answer.

A They let others take customers away from them because they assumed themselves to be in the railroad business rather than in the transportation business. The reason they defined their industry wrongly was because they were railroad oriented instead of transportation oriented; they were product oriented instead of customer oriented.

The railway industry went into decline even though the transportation market continued to grow by leaps and bounds. By adopting an 'industry focus' the railways did not take on the new enterprises which they did not see as being any part of the railroad business.

Not all North American railways took such a 'myopic' stance. Canadian Pacific saw its role in the transportation market clearly, expanding into trucking, shipping and airlines, later moving into telecommunications and telex to adopt the most suitable technology for transporting data.

The strategic message is clear. A marketing orientation focuses on the needs of the customer. If these needs change, or a better technology emerges that more closely attends to these needs, the company will be responsive; such events are its business. Responding to such changes is the only way for the company to survive. The marketing concept, as the basic philosophy that underpins corporate strategy, is therefore widely accepted.

Activity 7

Another often-quoted example of this phenomenon is the US movie industry, which reacted with hostility to the development of television. Analyse this reaction along the line suggested by Levitt's example and try to identify its shortcomings.

EXAMPLE: GENERAL MOTORS

Even if the need to respond to change is accepted, adherence to a production orientation can produce costly mistakes. In the late 1950s and early 1960s the American car market was under threat from import penetration, with the Volkswagen Beetle making the most significant inroads.

General Motors (GM), the largest American motor manufacturer, reacted in a way which betrayed the production orientation followed by the company. GM's four main 'badges', used to segment the market place, are:

- Cadillac – the super luxury market
- Pontiac – the executive range
- Buick – middle range
- Chevrolet – value for money and young driver segment.

The physical product characteristics of a VW Beetle might include the following.

- Small (by US standards)
- Rear engined
- Air-cooled engine (therefore noisy)
- Minimal instrumentation

BPP
PUBLISHING

NOTES

This was the product to which GM was losing sales. Chevrolet, the corresponding wing of the company, set about making just such a product. Naturally, the new small car was to be powered by an air-cooled rear engine and it would have very basic instrumentation. GM were ill-prepared for this venture. The company was under pressure from senior management to produce the new car quickly. The smallest available engine block was a flat six cylinder that was still very heavy for a relatively small car. The new engine also needed to be air-cooled as that was what the customers were buying. To achieve this, Chevrolet mounted a large fan that sat on top of the engine driving air vertically down on to the cylinder heads. To drive this large fan a long fanbelt was added that took the power from the crankshaft via a right angle pulley.

The new car was launched as the Chevrolet Corvair. Its design caused a number of serious problems. The stresses on the fan belt frequently led to either the belt breaking or the bracket holding the right angle pulley fracturing. The car was so noisy that the sound of these mechanical failures could not be heard. Naturally, with minimal instruments the driver could not sense that the engine was now rapidly overheating until, as often happened, the engine either seized or caught fire. To compound these problems, the weight distribution on such a small car with a very heavy rear engine caused difficulties. For safe driving the rear tyres had to be pumped up rock hard whilst the front tyres were kept soft.

After a number of fatal accidents, the consumer activist Ralph Nader produced Unsafe at Any Speed, which recounted the story of the Chevy Corvair. The book made little impact until General Motors, unwisely, sued and lost. Nader was established as the leader of the American consumer movement.

What would have happened if GM had followed a marketing orientation and had attempted to find out why people were buying the Beetle rather than looking at the Beetle's product features? Key consumer benefits might have included:

- Reliability
- Economy
- Affordability
- Ease of parking

The Japanese got this right in the late 1960s and 1970s with models that bore very little physical similarity to the Beetle.

Activity 8

How many brands can you think of today that serve the same purpose and yet bear very little physical similarity?

The marketing concept is not universally supported and has come under strong criticism, as we shall now consider.

3.2 The marketing concept: a critical review

Not all commentators accept that the use of the term marketing rather than selling represents a real shift in basic philosophy. Some suggest that this simply reflects the fact that bringing in revenue is now more complex. It makes sense to use advanced techniques in advertising and market research that were previously unavailable. Others argue that today's 'sophisticated' consumers are more critical and more aware than

PUBLISHING

previous generations. So-called 'marketing techniques' are simply a continuation of the same old process of persuasion in order to sell products.

Approval of the marketing concept is not universal even among those who accept that it represents a real change in philosophy and practice. Thus, the uncritical acceptance of marketing orientation as the established wisdom within both the commercial and academic communities has, itself, been the subject of debate.

There are two main arguments against the influence of the marketing concept.

(a)   Organisations develop a bias that favours marketing activities at the expense of production and technical departments. As a result, insufficient energies go into the development of technical improvements which could offer a more appealing product.

(b)   Secondly, apart from attending to customers' current needs, organisations must focus on future customer requirements. Slavishly focusing new product development on satisfying immediate customer perceptions of what is needed can, the argument runs, stifle real innovation.

Activity 9

Imagine you are a consumer being asked what features you would like to see if you were buying a new television set (a) in the early 1960s and (b) in the new millennium. What is your response?

EXAMPLE: ROLLS ROYCE

In defence of Levitt's views, outlined above, one might consider the case of the collapse of Rolls Royce in the early 1970s. The reason for this failure is well documented. The company was producing a new generation of large turbo-fan jet engines. All three major competitors were producing such engines. The Rolls Royce response was the RB211, which differed from the competitors' engines in its use of advanced carbon fibre technology in its turbine blades. The introduction and development of the new technology turned out to be an extremely costly business. The company chose to show this expenditure as an asset on its balance sheets, rather than writing off development costs against current revenues. Research and development expenses exceeded budgeted levels and Rolls Royce encountered severe cash flow problems resulting in the company's liquidation.

Rolls Royce's focus on engineering excellence is a clear indication of the production orientation. Pratt & Whitney and General Electric appeared to follow a product development strategy closer to a marketing orientation. The demand for the

new types of engines arose from a change in airlines' requirements. The environmentalist lobby against aircraft noise in the late 1960s and 1970s had succeeded in getting restrictions on night flying and regulations covering permitted noise levels from all new civil aircraft. The oil crisis and rising energy prices created the need for greater fuel efficiency. The new generation of wide-bodied jumbo jets created the need for a range of powerful jet engines.

Customers' needs were therefore clearly defined. Airlines needed larger, more powerful, more economical, quieter jet engines. Provided that engines satisfied these criteria then customers would be interested. The Rolls Royce engine was proving to be more

BPP PUBLISHING

expensive largely because it offered a product feature, carbon fibre technology, that airlines did not need. American competitors gave customers what they wanted without having to develop a new metallurgical competence. As airlines became aware of teething problems with the carbon fibre turbines, this product feature actually impeded sales of the engine.

Rolls Royce did not completely ignore market conditions. All companies have to take risks, but the RB211 project was so expensive that failure inevitably jeopardised the company's future. It may have been that the company's history of engineering excellence produced too great a bias towards production and too little concern for marketing realities. The Rolls Royce case illustrates the need for a balanced view. Whilst the technical competence and manufacturing skills of companies are important, technical excellence should not take precedence over customer needs.

General Electric, one of Rolls Royce's major competitors, made its commitment to the marketing concept as long ago as 1952.

(The marketing concept) ... introduces the marketing man at the beginning rather than at the end of the production cycle and integrates marketing in each phase of business. Thus, marketing, through its studies and research, will establish for the engineer, the design and manufacturing man, what the consumer wants in a given product, what price he is willing to pay, and where and when it will be wanted. Marketing will have authority in product planning, production scheduling, and inventory control, as well as in sales distribution and servicing of the product.

(1952 Annual Report: US General Electric Company)

Activity 10

What would be the effects of introducing a marketing approach to a charity?

We shall now consider the marketing mix and its interaction with market forces.

4 THE MARKETING MIX

4.1 The four Ps

The marketing mix consists of four variables, the four Ps of product, price, place and promotion. These four variables are the heart of a marketing plan. They are highly interactive, however: a decision relating to one variable is very likely to have an effect on other elements of the mix. A highly co-ordinated approach is needed if the company is to arrive at the most effective blend of factors.

The marketing function is concerned with identifying and analysing markets: understanding how consumers are motivated and how they behave in those markets as well as identifying groups of consumers which are of particular interest to the business. To build the link between the business and its customers requires the development of an appropriate marketing mix. The four Ps may be elaborated on as follows.

Product/service	Price
Features	Price level
Quality	Credit terms
Brand	Discounts
Packaging	Allowances
Durability	Trade-ins
After-sales service	

Promotion	Place
Advertising	Channels of distribution
Personal selling	Intensity of coverage
Merchandising	Location
Publicity	Stockholding
	Freight/insurance

Activity 11

In the spring of 1981 Hammerite, the all-in-one rust proofing paint, ran a highly successful advertising campaign. Timing was immaculate, the advertisements in both national press and the DIY magazines coinciding exactly with a break in the winter weather. All over the country avid home improvers prepared to go out into the garden to repair the ravages that the British winter had wrought on swings, iron gates and the like.

The problem was that the campaign was too successful and demand outstripped supplies available. Dealers rapidly stocked out and rather than lose a sale, recommended other products.

Try to analyse this failure in terms of the marketing mix.

The four Ps of the marketing mix are often described as 'the controllables', to distinguish elements of marketplace operations that an organisation can influence as opposed to those that are beyond its control. 'Uncontrollables' include competitors' actions, government policy, general economic conditions and so on. The Hammerite example, however, was caused by factors that should have been entirely within the organisation's control.

4.2   Market forces

Definition

The concept of a marketing mix, sometimes known as the marketing offer, was first used by Professor Neil Borden of Harvard Business School in 1965, who summarised the concept of the marketing mix as:

A schematic plan to guide analysis of marketing problems through utilisation of:

(a)   A list of the important forces emanating from the market which bear upon the marketing operations of an enterprise;

(b)   A list of the elements (procedures and policies) of marketing programmes.

Borden formulated a check list of the market forces bearing upon the marketing mix, changes in any one of which should lead to a review of the marketing mix and adjustments to take account of new market conditions.

These market forces are as follows.

(a) The motivation of consumers, their buying habits and their attitudes towards products or services in the market.

(b) Trade motivation and attitudes, trade structure and practices.

(c) Competition analysis requires answers to the following questions.

(i) Is this based on price or non-price actions?

(ii) What choice is available to customers in terms of products, price and service?

(iii) What is the relation between supply and demand?

(iv) What is the company's size and strength in the market?

(v) How many firms operate in the market?

(vi) Is market power becoming more or less concentrated?

(vii) Are there any substitute products or services?

(viii) Are competitors developing new products, pricing strategies or sales promotions?

(ix) Are competitors' attitudes or behaviour changing?

(x) How is the competition likely to react to any of the company's proposed plans?

(d) Government controls over the following.

(i) Products (for example, government standards – BSI, prohibitions and health and safety legislation).

(ii) Pricing (for example, on government contracts, measures to control inflation).

(iii) Competitive practices (for example, referrals to the UK Competition Commission, EU rulings on fair competition, USA Sherman anti-trust legislation).

(iv) Advertising and promotion (for example, restrictions on advertising tobacco, gambling and alcohol, limits on the advertising spend on ethical drugs, cooling-off periods after signing contracts for personal loans).

Borden's original (very broad) formulation of the marketing mix includes market forces which are not under the control of the company, and management's response to changes in the company's marketing activities.

As we have seen, the current, most common, definition of the marketing mix concentrates on the variables under the firm's control that the marketing manager manipulates in an attempt to achieve tactical marketing objectives.

4.3 Three more Ps

Some commentators have argued that at least three other 'Ps' also exist and are of particular relevance to service industries.

(a) People. Inclusion of 'people' in the marketing mix reflects the fact that the consumer's perceived quality of a service depends heavily on those giving the service.

(b) Processes (for example, ease with which loan application forms can be completed if they are well designed).

(c) Physical evidence (for example, logos, uniforms, branch or shop layout).

4.4 The three Cs

The four Ps of the marketing mix have long been a feature of the literature on marketing. More recently, the 'three Cs' or 'strategic triangle' identified by Kenichi Ohmae in The Mind of a Strategist have been recognised. Ohmae's book is primarily concerned with strategic planning, but his theories can be applied to marketing. By the three Cs, Ohmae means the three main players in the construction of a business strategy.

- The company itself
- The customer
- The competition

On this view, the task of a strategic planner is to match the company's strengths to the customer's needs more effectively than the competition can do.

5 MARKETING AS A BUSINESS FUNCTION

To see, first of all, how marketing fits into business operations as a whole, we will consider three essential systems: distribution, information and the flow of influence.

5.1 The distribution system

In exchange for payment, goods and services flow from producers to customers through a distribution system. This system has a large number of components, such as credit terms, delivery, insurance, price/discounts/margins and storage.

The distribution system can be long or short. Customised industrial goods are often supplied direct from producers to customers. When international trade is involved, a longer distribution system may involve importers, exporters, agents, wholesalers and retailers.

The distribution system may be owned by the producer or may be independent. So, for example, a building society's distribution system is its branch network. This is a short system. On the other hand, a producer of low value plastic toys may export them in the first instance using a freight forwarder. The overseas buyer may be a wholesaler who then sells to shopkeepers who finally sell to the end consumers. This is a long system.

Customers may be final consumers of the product or service or they may be organisational buyers who in turn are producers of other goods and services for which the purchased item is a component.

5.2 The information system and the USP

Information flow is essential in marketing. Before a customer orientated firm makes and supplies goods or services, it will want to ensure that they meet customers' needs. If distributors are independent, the producer also needs to be aware of their needs. The producer needs a flow of information from its market and distribution system. This information should then be used by the firm to construct its product (or service) offering, expressed as a bundle of customer satisfactions.

The flow of information from the producing firm to its market is called a marketing flow. The elements of this marketing flow are price information, product/service information, promotion/advertising information, distributor information and selling information. Together these make up the marketing mix for the product or service. The art of marketing is to blend these elements into a unified whole which presents the market with a clear, distinctive product, which offers something different from its rivals. This clear overall message is the product's USP: its unique selling proposition (USP).

5.3 Flow of influence

Business flows do not operate in isolation. Each part of the process has influences on it.

(a) The actions of producers and distributors are influenced by competitors. Each competitor is striving for competitive advantage, trying to get ahead of its rivals.

(b) Customer behaviour is influenced by a whole range of factors. People are members of groups and organisations and they may be influenced by cultural, social, psychological and practical factors.

To obtain an accurate picture, the whole business system must be considered within its environment. It may be influenced by the following.

(a) **Political and legal factors**, for example, employment legislation, advertising laws, legislation affecting sales and purchasing and credit controls.

(b) **Economic influences**, for example, income levels, employment levels, the rate of inflation and growth rates in the economy.

(c) **Social influences**, for example, friends and family, fashions, politics, and political influences such as voting intentions and attitudes to the EC and the Commonwealth.

(d) **Technological influences**, for example, information technology, new forms of leisure, robotics and computer aided manufacturing/design (CAM/CAD).

These PEST factors (from the initials of each type of factor) will be dealt with in more detail in the next chapter.

5.4 What is the scope of marketing?

The table below shows a list of the types of marketing decision. This is a 'typical' list for a 'typical' organisation. Different organisations operating in different markets will have different organisational structures and so will depart from this list.

Marketing decision	Policies and procedures will be needed relating to:
Product planning	Product lines to be offered – qualities, design, detailed contents etc
	The markets in which to sell – to whom, where, when and in what quantity
	New product policy – research and development programme
Branding	Selection of trade marks and names
	Brand policy – individual or family brand
	Sale under private brand or unbranded
Pricing	The level of premiums to adopt
	The margins to adopt – for the trade, for direct sales

Channels of distribution	The channels to use between company and consumer
	The degree of selectivity among distributors and other intermediaries
	Efforts to gain co-operation of the trade
Selling personnel	The burden to be placed on personal selling
	The methods to be employed (1) within the organisation and (2) in selling to intermediaries and the final consumer
Advertising	The amount to spend – the burden to be placed on advertising
	The copy needed for (1) product image desired, (2) corporate image desired
	The mix of advertising – to the trade, through the trade to customers
Promotions	The burden to place on special selling plans or devices directed at or through the trade
	The form of these devices for consumer promotions, for trade promotions
Servicing	Providing after sales service to intermediaries and to final consumers (such as direct mail offers)

It can be claimed that marketing involves every facet of the organisation's operations. It can be argued that the philosophy of a customer orientation, central to marketing, is a central business function which is a prerequisite to success. It is easy to get carried away with this argument and thus to understate the role of finance, production, personnel and other business functions. The marketing department's conviction that customer orientation is all-important can lead to conflict with other departments.

A survey in 2000 by the Chartered Institute of Marketing discovered that the marketers of today consider the following issues to be of top importance.

See chapter

•	New media/e-commerce	3
•	Customer satisfaction	7
•	Customer loyalty	7
•	Relationship marketing	7
•	Databases and marketing segmentation	6
•	Marketing's interaction with other departments	1

In the next section we will explore the central activities of marketing management.

6   MARKETING MANAGEMENT

Marketing management involves analysis, planning and control.

(a)   **Analysis**

A marketing orientation begins and ends with the customer. Analysis in marketing management involves identifying the customers and discovering why they buy the product and whether they are satisfied with it, having bought it. This process includes market research which is covered in more detail in a later chapter. The process can include quantitative analysis (How many customers? What is our market share? How many competitors?) and qualitative analysis (Why do people buy? What are their motivations, attitudes, personality?).

In sophisticated companies, market information is integrated into a marketing information system which can be used by managers in making marketing decisions. Decision support systems use such information to develop effective marketing decision making.

(b)   **Planning**

Marketing management also uses the information from marketing analysis to develop the organisation's marketing response – the strategic marketing plan.

The strategic marketing plan will involve:

(i)   Identification of selected target markets

(ii)   Forecasting future demand in each market

(iii)   Setting the levels of each element of the marketing mix for each target market

(c)   **Control**

The third main component of marketing management is control of the ways in which the marketing plan is implemented. Control involves setting quantifiable targets and then checking performance against these targets. If necessary, remedial action is taken to ensure that planned and actual performance correspond.

Marketing organisation within a company's organisational structure involves a range of problems.

Activity 12

A customer contacts your company and asks whether it can make a completely silent washing machine. This is not possible with current technology. What is your reaction?

6.1   The development of marketing departments

Although every organisation is different, common patterns appear in the structure of organisations. Current departments of marketing are widely thought to have evolved from sales departments. Traditionally all marketplace issues would have been the responsibility of a sales director who would typically report direct to senior management. Marketing orientation was probably absent. At this point, the organisation would usually have been production or sales orientated. When the need for a marketing orientated approach became more apparent a marketing director might appear in parallel to the sales director, each having a distinct functional department.

Marketing departments have generally replaced sales departments in organisational structures as business philosophy has changed. With fuller recognition of the marketing approach to business, sales and marketing may become a single department, with sales as a sub-group within marketing as opposed to marketing being a sub-group within sales.

The marketing department plays a key role in co-ordinating marketing activities. The marketing manager has to take responsibility for planning, resource allocation, monitoring and controlling the marketing effort. In order to ensure that the marketing effort has maximum effectiveness, this co-ordinating role is crucial, involving co-ordination of marketing efforts for different products in different markets as well as ensuring that individual marketing campaigns are themselves co-ordinated and consistent. As such, the marketing function tends to be thought of as a staff management function with a co-ordinating role, rather than as a line management function.

6.2 Organising marketing departments

The organisational role and form of marketing departments will continue to vary. There is no one format which can be described as 'best' or 'most effective'. The existing organisational structure, patterns of management and the spread of the firm's product and geographical interests will all play a part in determining how it develops. Whatever the format, the marketing department must take responsibility for four key areas.

- Functions (promotion, pricing etc)
- Geographical areas
- Products
- Markets

These four areas of responsibility will provide insight into how the different forms of marketing department may arise.

Activity 13

Why bother to learn about the organisation of the marketing function?

Functional organisation

The department is headed by a marketing director who is responsible for the overall co-ordination of the marketing effort. A number of functional specialists such as a market research manager and a sales manager are found in the second tier of management and they take responsibility for all related activities across all products and markets. This format has the benefit of great simplicity and administrative directness. It allows individuals to develop their particular specialisms, but also imposes a burden on the marketing director who has to co-ordinate and arbitrate activities to ensure the development of a coherent marketing mix for elements of the product range.

With a limited product portfolio, the burden on the marketing director may not be a problem. As the range of products and markets expands, however, it will tend to become less efficient. There is always the danger that a particular product or market may be neglected because it is only one of many being handled by a single manager who will find it difficult to play a specialist role for all products.

Geographical organisation

This is an extension of the functional organisation. Responsibility for some or all functional activities is devolved to a regional level, through a national functional manager. This type of organisation is more common in firms operating internationally where the various functional activities need to be broken down for each national market or group of national markets.

Product-based organisation

Definition

> In a product-based organisation, product managers are responsible for specific products or groups of products. This approach is likely to be particularly appropriate for organisations with a very diverse or very extensive range of products.

The individual product manager develops plans for specific products and ensures that products remain competitive, drawing on the experience and guidance of functional managers. The product manager is effectively responsible for all the marketing activities relating to a particular product group and consequently needs skills in promotion, pricing and distribution. This approach allows the individual product managers to develop considerable experience and understanding of particular product groups and as such may be effective within a rapidly changing competitive environment. Because they have to undertake a variety of functional activities, the danger is that they will become 'jacks of all trades and masters of none'. In spite of this, the product-based approach is becoming increasingly important because the benefits of managers with expertise related to specific product groups is seen to outweigh the costs associated with a loss of functional specialisation.

Market management

Definition

> Market management is a variant on the product management structure. Instead of individual managers taking responsibility for particular products they will instead take responsibility for particular markets.

When an organisation sells a variety of different products into particular markets, the understanding of the product is perceived to be slightly less important than the understanding of the market. Managers with knowledge and experience of a particular market are more valuable.

Matrix management

Definition

> Matrix management can be thought of as an integration of the product and market management approaches.

In an organisation dealing with a variety of products in a variety of markets the product-based approach requires managers to be familiar with a wide variety of different markets, while the market-based approach requires managers to be familiar with a wide variety of products. In either case, however, expertise may not be fully or efficiently utilised. The matrix-based system combines the two. One group of managers deals with markets and another deals with products. The market managers take responsibility for the development and maintenance of profitable markets while the product managers focus on product performance and profitability. The system involves these being interlinked. Each product manager deals with a variety of market managers and each market manager deals with a variety of product managers.

Although this system may seem to resolve the dilemma of choosing the best form of organisation for a marketing department, it presents certain problems. It is extremely costly, employing large numbers of managers. There are also possible conflicts between product and market managers to consider and, particularly, the issue of who should take responsibility for certain activities. Should the sales force be product- or market-based and who should take responsibility for pricing?

Divisional marketing organisation

As well as the organisation of marketing within a unitary organisation, there are many organisations where the larger product groups are developed into separate divisions (what is often called a multi-divisional or 'M' form organisation). These divisions will have a high degree of autonomy but ultimately are responsible to a head office. Here, marketing activity will often be devolved to divisional level (see below) although some marketing decisions will naturally remain the responsibility of corporate headquarters. The extent of corporate involvement can vary from none at all to extensive. There is no optimum level of corporate involvement; however, corporate involvement will tend to be more extensive in the early stages of the organisation's development when the divisions are individually quite weak, and decline as divisions strengthen.

6.3 Relationship with other departments

The table below shows potential conflicts which can arise between the marketing department and other departments in the organisation. This can only be a partial list and is intended as a warning of potential dangers. The top management of the organisation needs to take a strong line on any conflicts which arise and to ensure that departmental heads have clear instructions as to the organisation's priorities.

Summary of organisational conflicts between marketing and other departments		
Other departments	**Their emphasis**	**Emphasis of marketing**
Engineering	Long design lead time Functional features Few models with standard components	Short design lead time Sales features Many models with custom components
Purchasing	Standard parts Price of material Economic lot sizes Purchasing at infrequent intervals	Non-standard parts Quality of material Large lot sizes to avoid stockouts Immediate purchasing for customer needs
Production	Long order lead times and inflexible production schedules Long runs with few models No model changes Standard orders	Short order lead times and flexible schedules to meet emergency orders Short runs with many models Frequent model changes Custom orders

Business Basics: Marketing

Other departments	Their emphasis	Emphasis of marketing
	Ease of fabrication	Aesthetic appearance
	Average quality control	Tight quality control
Inventory management	Fast moving items	Broad product line
	Narrow product line	Large levels of stock
	Economic levels of stock	
Finance	Strict rationales for spending	Intuitive arguments for spending
	Hard and fast budgets	Flexible budgets to meet changing needs
	Pricing to cover costs	Pricing to further market development
Accounting	Standard transactions	Special terms and discounts
	Few reports	Many reports
Credit	Full financial disclosures by customers	Minimum credit examination of customers
	Lower credit risks	Medium credit risks
	Tough credit terms	Easy credit terms
	Tough collection procedures	Easy collection procedures

Source: Philip Kotler, 'Diagnosing the marketing takeover', *Harvard Business Review*, Nov–Dec 1965

A continual problem is the relation between research and development (R&D) and marketing. This has already been touched on in this chapter in the context of objections to the marketing concept.

(a) Part of the problem might be cultural. To the marketing department, the R&D department may seem filled with boffins; to the R&D department, the marketing department may seem full of wideboys. Furthermore, the R&D department may have an academic atmosphere, as opposed to a commercial one.

(b) Part of the problem might be organisational. If R&D consumes substantial resources, it would seem logical to exploit economies of scale by having it centralised.

(c) Finally, marketing work and R&D work differ in many important respects. R&D work is likely to be more open-ended than marketing work.

Nonetheless, there are good reasons why R&D should be more closely co-ordinated with marketing.

(a) If the firm operates the marketing concept, then the 'identification of customer needs' should be a vital input to new product developments.

(b) The R&D department might identify possible changes to product specifications so that a variety of marketing mixes can be applied.

Activity 14

This is a question that you can discuss in class, or perhaps even write an essay on, based on what you have learned in this chapter.

The phrase 'the customer is always right' was introduced into the retail trade in the 1930s by H Gordon Selfridge, who founded the department store that still bears his name. 'Whatever the true rights and wrongs of the situation, it was to be assumed that the customer was always right.'

Do you think Selfridge was ahead of his time, or was his concept not the same thing as the 'marketing concept'?

Chapter roundup

- In this first chapter we have looked at the marketing, sales and production orientations and discussed why the marketing orientation has gradually come to be accepted as the most appropriate and the most likely to be successful.

- Although the marketing concept is accepted, at least in principle, by a large number of UK organisations it is important to remember that many others have a sales or production orientation. Even among those that claim to be marketing orientated, the reality may not always match the aspiration.

- The marketing mix is a schematic plan to guide analysis of marketing problems. The four elements in the mix are product, price, promotion, place. Each of these has a chapter to itself later in this book. Three more Ps have also been suggested: people, processes and physical evidence.

- We have seen how the marketing orientation has resulted in increased importance for the marketing department, and we have looked at ways of organising the marketing function in an organisation and at the relationship of marketing with other parts of the organisation.

Quick quiz

1   Why did mass production lead to the development of the marketing orientation?

2   Give three definitions of marketing.

3   What is a sales orientation? How does it differ from a market orientation?

4   Why might sales maximising objectives result in lower profit margins?

5   Where did General Motors go wrong in developing the Chevy Corvair?

6   What are the two main arguments against the marketing concept?

7   List the four Ps and elaborate upon what each P entails.

8   List the market forces bearing upon the marketing mix.

9   What is a USP?

10   What are the advantages of functional organisation for a marketing department?

11   What are the disadvantages of matrix management?

Answers to activities

1   Tesco wanted to 'say thank you to customers' and recreate the kind of relationship that existed between consumers and local shops half a century ago. The latter point is the important one. Tesco can build a sizeable database of customers' names, addresses and shopping habits. It can exploit this by, say, targeting its own-brand baked beans at customers who are known to purchase branded beans; find out more about why one family buys its wines and spirits from the supermarket and another does not.

Not all companies agree that this is a worthwhile exercise. Asda has never had a loyalty card, and in 2000 Safeway abandoned its loyalty card scheme to concentrate more upon local promotions and price offers.

2   This is an example of how the problems facing firms have changed. Production of toothpaste is not a problem: there are many different manufacturers in the market. The problem now is to get the customer to buy your toothpaste rather than the next one. One approach is to focus on the differences between one toothpaste and another. Emphasis on such differences is one of the reasons for the proliferation of brands.

3   (a)   is fairly straightforward. The gardener is trying to get a task done (mowing the lawn), presumably with the minimum of effort and at economical cost.

(b)   is more complicated. The purchaser of life insurance may be trying to remove a feeling of financial insecurity, or to fulfil a duty of providing for dependants. There may be more immediate problems involved; for example, taking out life insurance is often a pre-condition of getting a mortgage.

(c)   is in some ways the trickiest of all. Although there are some simple facts involved (the need to get from A to B cheaply and conveniently), there are also subtle points of self-image and status in the choice of a particular model of car.

4   The production function might try to increase profits by reducing costs. The marketing function might try to increase profits by emphasising the quality of the product. Lower costs and higher quality might not be achievable.

5   No. A mere absence of complaints is not the same as the identification of customer needs. The firm, if anything, has a product orientation.

6   Think about (a) and (b) for yourself, in terms of what you have read in the paragraphs preceding this exercise. For (c), where in Smith's might have been a more appropriate location for the stand?

7   No solution is given here. You should do the analysis for yourself.

8   Mass-produced branded goods all tend to look like the brand leader these days. We could not think of any examples that are significantly different in appearance, though there are often small differences in features. Do you think this makes things easier for the consumer or more difficult?

9   Two suggestions (you should have come up with more) are colour in the 1960s (now taken for granted) and a remote control now (essential to the

average couch potato, but unlikely to have entered people's minds as a possibility in the 1960s).

10   (a)   The reasons for the organisation's existence ('what business are we in?') should be expressed in terms of the 'customer'.

       (b)   Marketing research should be used to find out:

           (i)   Who needs help, and in what ways, and how satisfactory is the current help provided

           (ii)   Where funds should be raised, and what the best approaches should be

           (iii)   Which political figures are susceptible to 'lobbying' and how such lobbying should best be conducted

       (c)   'Target markets' would be identified for charitable acts, fund-raising and influencing.

       (d)   The charity might also wish to promote an image to the public, perhaps by means of public relations work.

       (e)   The management of the charity will be aware that they are in competition for funds with other charities, and in competition with other ways of spending money in trying to obtain funds from the public. It should organise its 'sales and marketing' systems to raise funds in the most effective way.

11   By not fully co-ordinating their marketing activities, the benefit of Hammerite's promotion went to the competition because the marketing mix between promotion and place elements was not properly balanced. Hammerite's distribution could not support the promotional policy that was in operation.

12   First, establish the demand for completely silent washing machines. If demand is sufficiently widespread it is worth trying to address the problem. However, you must find out, by talking to customers, what the real problem is – perhaps that the sound travels to other rooms and wakes the baby or annoys the neighbours. There may well be product modifications, or add-on products, that can minimise this problem.

13   Because co-ordination of the efforts and activities of different parts is so frequently a problem, even in small organisations. An example may help. Kodak reorganised its group structure with the aim of shortening lines of communication, ensuring that functions such as research and development, marketing and customer service were better co-ordinated, simplifying the management of customer accounts and encouraging sales representatives to listen more closely to customers' needs. The formation of Kodak Office Imaging brought together businesses which previously operated as distinct units, sometimes even in competition with each other. Now customer databases have been merged and only one Kodak sales rep will call on customers in future instead of two, apparently resulting in enormous new sales opportunities.

14   No solution is given here. You must reach your own conclusions.

Further question practice

Now try the following practice questions at the end of this text.

Multiple Choice Questions: 1–10

Exam Style Question: 1

Chapter 2 :
THE MODERN MARKETING ENVIRONMENT I

Introduction

An organisation must understand its environment if it is to exploit changing market conditions, the essence of a successful marketing strategy. The micro environment includes all factors which impact directly on a firm and its activities in relation to a particular market in which it operates and also any internal aspects of the organisation which influence the development of a marketing strategy. The macro environment is concerned with broad trends and patterns in society as a whole which may affect all markets, but will be more relevant to some than others. Careful monitoring of the macro environment can enable an organisation to identify opportunities for and threats to its business and will enable it to adopt a proactive rather than a reactive approach in the action it takes.

The macro environment is large and complex. We shall look in some detail at the ways in which economic factors, at home and abroad, social and cultural factors within families and larger groups, and legal and political considerations, can all affect the marketing of goods and services.

Your objectives

In this chapter you will learn about the following.

- (a) Features of the business environment that influence marketing strategy
- (b) Economic factors that impinge on marketing activities
- (c) How social, cultural and legal factors affect customer behaviour and their implications for marketing

1 MARKETING AND THE BUSINESS ENVIRONMENT

1.1 The micro environment: the market environment

The nature of the market environment is outlined in the diagram below.

Definition

> The market environment comprises all aspects of a market which affect the company's relationship with its customers and the patterns of competition.

Its importance should not be underestimated, not only because it has a major impact on the operation of a business, but also because business can, in part, control and change it. Suppliers, distributors, consumers, competitors and interest groups have all been identified as key elements of the market environment.

Understanding the interactions and the behaviour of these groups enables the firm to use its marketing strategies to encourage loyalty, obtain preference from suppliers/distributors, and influence what competitors do and what consumers think. Equally, through the development of corporate image, it can influence the way the business is perceived by various interest groups. Understanding of and reactions to the market environment can be a key factor in ensuring longer term competitive success.

The micro environment

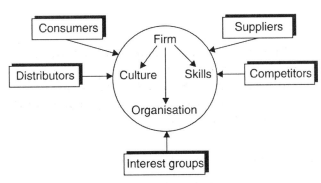

Figure 2.1 The micro environment

We will now consider each of the key elements of the market environment in turn.

Suppliers

Organisations need information about the number, size and bargaining strength of their suppliers. This includes their ability to guarantee regular supplies, stable prices and quality.

Distributive network

Although the nature and structure of the distributive network is generally treated as a marketing mix variable which can be controlled by an organisation, it is also part of the market environment. There are few instances where a market is so new that there are no existing distribution systems. Normally these systems are in place and they will impose constraints on what an organisation can do, partly because of consumer familiarity with existing systems and partly because of the degree of market power held by the distribution network. For example, in the UK food industry the decisions taken by food manufacturers are heavily influenced by the market power of the large supermarket chains. This power is often criticised by pressure groups, such as those representing farmers who argue that they sell their meat to the supermarkets at far lower prices than those eventually charged to supermarket customers.

Activity 1

Try to think of industries where a highly developed and visible distribution network exists.

Consumers

Understanding consumers is clearly of considerable importance when developing a marketing strategy. As we shall see later, it bears on many aspects of marketing decisions.

Competition

Marketing as an aid to establishing a competitive position in the market place has already been stressed. Any organisation must develop an awareness and understanding of its competitors, their strengths and weaknesses and the essence of their strategic approach.

Interest groups

Finally, any analysis of the market environment must accommodate the role of interest groups (sometimes referred to in marketing literature as 'publics'). These are groups whose opinions and attitudes may affect the success or otherwise of a business. An understanding and awareness of the attitudes of these groups will enable the business to consider how best to present itself to them.

1.2 The micro environment: the internal environment

The internal environment is where the firm can exercise greatest control and should possess the greatest knowledge. The internal capabilities of the organisation are a key factor in generating marketing success. The analysis of the internal environment rests on an understanding of the nature of the corporate culture – the attitudes and beliefs of personnel at all levels. Strategies appropriate for an organisation with a culture orientated towards rapid innovation and risk-taking may be quite different from those available to a company orientated towards high quality and an exclusive image, or those pursued by an organisation which sees itself as a low risk market follower with a reliable and traditional product range.

An understanding of the strengths and weaknesses of the structure of the company and of the personnel within the company is equally important. Internal structures may be changing to reflect the increased pressures of a competitive market place.

Marketing audits help an organisation (and the individuals involved in the planning process) to understand the internal environment.

Definition

> A marketing audit is simply a systematic analysis and evaluation of the organisation's marketing position and performance.

It may cover all activities which are either directly or indirectly connected with the marketing function, or it can simply focus on specific products/markets or specific marketing functions. Further distinctions may be drawn between audits at the corporate level, at the divisional level or at the level of the product/market.

The audit will focus on all the relevant marketing activities, but the following may be singled out as being of particular importance.

Marketing capabilities

The audit considers in which aspects of marketing the company may be considered to have particular strengths and weaknesses. We may want to know the following.

- How flexible/responsive is the organisation of the marketing department?
- What is the company's image/reputation?
- How strong are particular product lines?
- What is the extent of brand loyalty among customers?

Although these assessments are subjective, they are important because they will often form the basis of future marketing campaigns.

Performance evaluation

This involves comparing the actual achievements of marketing with what was expected.

- Are sales meeting forecasts?
- Is the message being communicated to the target group?
- Is the product reaching consumers?

This evaluation will identify weaknesses and strengths of current marketing campaigns and processes which can then be modified for this product and for products in the future.

Competitive effectiveness

This focuses on the source of an organisation's competitive advantage. Analysis requires understanding competitors, the markets they are targeting and the particular features they use to their advantage, and how the product is differentiated from competitors'.

There are a number of tools available for marketing audits. Note that the marketing audit should be systematic, should canvass a wide variety of opinions and is frequently based on data gathered by questionnaire surveys.

1.3 The macro environment

The macro environment can be described in terms of four key components: political/legal, economic, social/cultural, and technological (PEST factors). The diagram below shows these factors.

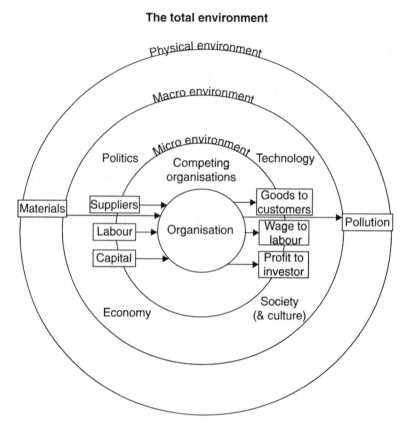

Figure 2.2 The macro environment

1.4 The organisation in the international trading environment

We will now look at the PEST factors in greater detail, starting with those that constitute the economic environment.

PEST (political, economic, socio-cultural and technological) factors are held to be the main issues in the domestic environment and the same factors hold for a firm's international exposure. International factors affect:

- An organisation in its domestic environment
- An organisation's activities abroad (by definition)

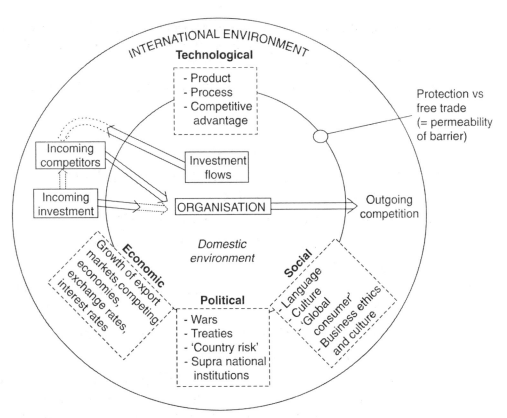

Figure 2.3 International influences on the organisation's domestic conditions

The diagram demonstrates the following.

(a) In times of increasing free trade, firms (unless they have overwhelming competitive advantages in their national markets) can expect incoming competition. That said, the possibility of competing abroad is also available. Take the oil industry for example. American-owned oil firms compete in the UK.

(b) Investment flows can also go two ways. A firm can attract investment from overseas institutions. Competing firms from overseas can receive investments from domestic institutions. For example, non-UK banks have paid large sums to acquire UK stock brokers and investment firms. British firms invest in overseas companies.

(c) The barrier between the domestic environment and the international environment may be penetrated, depending on the following.

(i) The product (for example, UK national newspapers do not compete abroad, although their owners might have overseas interests, as national newspapers are very culture-specific)

(ii) The relative openness of the market for the product or of the economy as a whole. This influences the seriousness of threats from incoming competition and opportunities for overseas activity.

(d) Political factors

(i) Political conditions in individual overseas markets (for example, package tourist firms and Zimbabwe) or sources of supply (for example, risk of nationalisation)

(ii) Relationships between governments (for example, UK exporters and investors were worried that Anglo-Chinese disputes over Hong Kong would damage their trade with China)

(iii) Activities of supra-national institutions (for example, EU regulations on product standards)

(e) Economic factors

(i) The overall level of economic activity

(ii) The relative levels of inflation in the domestic and overseas market (as inflation affects your prices)

(iii) The exchange rate, regarding its actual level and stability

(iv) The relative prosperity of individual overseas markets

(f) Social and cultural factors

(i) The cultures and practices of customers and consumers in individual markets

(ii) The media and distribution systems in overseas markets

(iii) The differences of ways of doing business

(iv) The degree to which national cultural differences matter for the product concerned (a great deal for some consumer products, for example, washing machines where some countries prefer front-loading machines and others prefer top-loading machines, but less so for products such as gas turbines)

(v) The degree to which a firm can use its own 'national culture' as a selling point ('Marks and Spencer's ... quintessentially British products, such as crumpets, pies and sliced white bread ... [are] helping to make Paris the second biggest store in Marks and Spencer' – *Financial Times*)

(g) Technological factors

(i) The degree to which a firm can imitate the technology of its competitors

(ii) A firm's access to domestic and overseas patents

(iii) Intellectual property protection (for example, copyright, patents), which varies between different countries

(iv) Technology transfer requirements (some countries regard investments from overseas companies as learning opportunities and require the investing company to share some of its technology)

(v) The relative cost of technology compared to labour

We shall be looking at technological factors in more detail in the next chapter.

Activity 2

Tommy's Toys Ltd manufactures model cars and trucks, which are normally battery driven. The firm has not gone into exporting very much because of the trouble caused by different product standards and requirements. What are the consequences of the single European market?

BPP
PUBLISHING

2 THE ECONOMIC ENVIRONMENT

2.1 Economic factors

You will often hear reports of politicians discussing the state of the economy. We all know that this is supposed to be important, but unfortunately vague terms like 'recession' don't give us much useful information. They certainly don't give business people enough information to decide what to do. We need much more precise measures of how the economy is doing. These can then be identified as the economic factors which affect businesses and set their economic environment. For example, the rate of inflation is both a measure of how the economy is doing and an important factor for most businesses: if costs are rising, a business must either raise its own prices or save on costs in order to maintain profits. We will therefore identify a number of key measures, and look at why they are important for businesses.

The rate of growth

The rate of growth of the economy is the rate of increase in total economic activity. It can be measured using the gross national product, which is (roughly) the total amount of goods and services made in a year. For example, if a country has only one product, cars, and in year 1 it makes 1,000 cars and in year 2 it makes 1,200 cars, the rate of growth is 20%. The rate of growth matters to businesses because the faster the economy grows, the better off people become and the more they will buy. People can also change what they buy. For example, they might buy more cars and fewer train tickets, because they prefer private transport. This could have a knock-on effect: the demand for driving lessons might increase while the demand for sandwiches at stalls in railway stations might fall.

The rate of inflation

This is the rate at which prices are rising. Businesses must take account of how their costs might increase, what wage rises they might have to pay and the extent to which competitors might increase their prices.

Quite apart from general inflation, the prices of certain raw materials may go up or down dramatically, having a direct effect on some businesses. For example, the price of crude oil has fluctuated sharply in the past 30 years, affecting not only the price of petrol but also the price of all goods transported by road or sea.

The level of unemployment

The number of unemployed people is particularly important for consumer markets and the retail sector. If people are out of work, they will not spend much in the shops.

Businesses may also be interested in who is unemployed, if they are looking for new workers. Some businesses need workers who already have special skills, or who can be trained quickly. If most of the unemployed are unskilled, this may make recruitment difficult.

Interest rates

Most businesses borrow money, either as overdrafts or as long-term loans. If a business wishes to expand, perhaps buying a new factory and machinery, it may need to take out a large loan. If interest rates are low, this may be easy. If, on the other hand, interest rates are high, it may be too expensive and the expansion plan may have to be abandoned. High interest rates can even drive a business to bankruptcy, if it can no longer afford the interest payments on its existing borrowings.

Taxation levels

Taxation levels and the nature of taxes can greatly affect businesses and their customers.

The opposite of taxes is subsidies, when the government hands out money to new businesses, businesses in poor areas and so on. Businesses who might be eligible are obviously directly affected by the level of subsidies.

The level of personal saving

If people earn money, they can either spend it or save it. If they spend it, businesses get the benefit straightaway through making sales. If they save a large part of their incomes, businesses may suffer in the short term. However, savings are ultimately invested, and make capital available for industry to expand.

The balance of payments

This is a measure of whether the country is exporting more than it is importing (a surplus) or the other way round (a deficit). If the UK has a surplus, this will tend to make the pound worth more, so that imports become cheaper. This will help businesses which import, for example a UK dealer in Japanese televisions. A deficit will have the reverse effect.

How other countries are doing

If a company exports to, for example, Australia, it is likely to do well if the Australian economy is doing well: Australians will have more money to spend on its output. This in turn will depend on Australian inflation, unemployment, interest rates and so on.

International barriers to trade

Some countries set up barriers, such as customs duties on imports, so as to make it difficult for foreigners to sell goods into the country. On the other hand, groups of countries can set up free trade areas such as the European Economic Area, and remove trade barriers within the area.

Activity 3

Think about a company which makes personal computers and give one way whereby each of the above economic factors may affect the company.

Some of the economic factors we have looked at tell us a lot about a business's local environment, for example the town it is based in. Some tell us more about a business's country. And some are only really important when we look at the whole world.

We will now look at examples of economic factors in action at each of these three levels.

2.2 Levels of environment

The local economic environment

A business's local environment is most likely to have a big impact on its prospects if it is a retail business. A shop will only do well if there are customers in the town with money to spend. The most important local factor is likely to be the unemployment rate. A major industrial closure, for example of a coal mine, can destroy shops in the area. On the other hand, the opening of a new factory can bring prosperity to all businesses.

The national economic environment

The national environment affects practically all businesses. Growth, inflation, unemployment, interest rates, taxation rates and the level of personal saving are all relevant. Another factor which affects long term national economic prospects is the make-up of the population. In some countries the retired population is increasing faster than the working population, because people are living longer but having fewer children. This may mean that economic growth will slow down, because too small a proportion of the population is making things to sell.

Note that these national economic factors are things which an individual business, even a very big one, can do little or nothing about.

The world economic environment

World economic factors include the balance of payments and exchange rates, the performance of other countries' economies and international barriers to trade or free trade areas. Businesses may be affected by these things directly, if they import or export goods. They may also be affected indirectly, if they buy from an importer or sell to an exporter. For example, a printer may work only for UK publishers and may buy paper only from UK paper makers, but the paper makers will buy their raw material, wood pulp, from Sweden where the trees are grown. If the pound falls in value against the Swedish Krona, the price of wood pulp will go up in pounds and the printer will have to pay more for paper. This in turn may put up the price of books in bookshops, affecting the number of books sold and the shops' profits.

The economic state of the world as a whole is often held to be responsible for the performance of individual countries.

Activity 4

Do you feel that the UK economy is doing well or badly at the moment? What are the good signs and what are the bad signs? Are there any big problems looming in the years ahead?

The impact of some changes can be dramatic. Consider, for example, the UK's departure from the European Exchange Rate Mechanism (ERM) in 1992 and the subsequent fall in value of the pound against many other currencies. This provided a welcome boost to UK companies who were major exporters, because it made their goods cheaper to overseas markets. On the other hand it increased the price of imported raw materials, pushing up domestic inflation. The recent strength of sterling has been bemoaned by manufacturers. Now a business buying large items of machinery from Germany, for example, may sign a contract in 2000 for goods to be delivered and paid for in 2002. If, in the meantime, the pound falls in value against the Mark, the goods will be more expensive than expected. Businesses can protect themselves against such risks, but the protection costs money.

BPP
PUBLISHING

NOTES

> **Activity 5**
>
> Can you think of any other way a company may attempt to overcome the various economic problems that arise from world trade?

*Social and cultural factors are another important **PEST** factor in the external environment for a marketing business. To some extent they interact with economic factors.*

3 SOCIAL AND CULTURAL FACTORS

3.1 Society

People on the whole are social animals. Most of us come into contact with others fairly frequently. Society provides the framework for human behaviour and conduct. Underpinning this is a set of attitudes and beliefs. We know that if we want to be accepted by others, we should behave in certain ways. For example, when a group of friends are drinking in a bar, it is normal for them to take it in turns to buy drinks for each other. If you accept drinks from other people but never buy any in return, you will not be popular! This example of a round of drinks reflects deeper attitudes about sharing.

> **Activity 6**
>
> Think of five recent advertisements which play on social attitudes.

When a business is taking account of social influences, it should consider the following aspects.

    (a)   Norms and values, such as sharing. Families influence people strongly.

    (b)   Lifestyles, for example the young, free and single lifestyle or the middle-aged lifestyle. These are often influenced by the media.

    (c)   The influence of peer groups. These are groups of people of your own age, status and so on, whom you tend to mix with. There is often pressure to conform, to be like your peers in your choice of clothes, restaurants and so on.

> **Activity 7**
>
> To what extent does marketing mould society, as opposed to society influencing marketing? You may wish to consider the impact of Sunday shopping, global brands such as Coca-Cola, and the targeting of computers at the young.

3.2 Demography

Definition

> Demography is the study of population characteristics and population trends. It is about how many people there are, how old they are, the proportions of men to women and how the population is spread across the country.

Demographic factors affect what consumers are likely to want, and the quantities they will want. For example, if the population comprises mostly young adults, demand for baby care products may be high. When planning for the future, an organisation should consider the following factors.

(a) The rate of growth or decline of the national population.

(b) Population changes in particular regions.

(c) The age distribution of the population, both nationally and regionally. This will not only affect what people want. It will also affect what people can afford to buy, both individually and as a whole. If a country has a high proportion of retired people, who are not productive, the overall standard of living may be low.

(d) Where people live (cities, small towns or the countryside), whether people live alone or in families and so on. This will affect where goods should be sold.

Activity 8

Consider the following figures for the United Kingdom, which are in millions of people.

Age	1971	1981	1991	1993	2001
Under 16	14.2	12.5	11.7	12.0	12.4
16-39	17.5	19.7	20.4	20.3	19.7
40-64	16.7	15.7	16.6	16.8	18.3
65-79	6.1	6.9	6.9	6.2	6.8
80 +	1.3	1.6	2.1	2.3	2.6

What are the main trends? What are the main implications for organisations in (1) the health care sector and (2) the manufacturing sector?

When we look at a country's population, it is often helpful to use a standard classification of people and households. There are several such classifications. The idea is that people in one class will behave in similar ways, particularly in the things they buy. There are some informal categories which we use in everyday speech, such as yuppie (young upwardly mobile) and dinky (double income no kids yet): the formal classifications into groups are simply extensions of this idea, meant to cover the whole population.

An early example, which still has some uses, is the socio-economic grouping originally developed by the UK Registrar General. It is as follows.

NOTES

EXAMPLE: REGISTRAR GENERAL'S SOCIO-ECONOMIC GROUPINGS

A: Managerial and professional, such as lawyers and company directors

B: Intermediate managerial and professional, for example teachers and managers

C1: Supervisory and clerical staff, for example foremen and shop assistants

C2: Skilled manual workers, such as electricians

D: Semi-skilled and unskilled manual workers, such as cleaners and machine operators

E: People not working, for example pensioners

A much more elaborate classification is ACORN, which stands for A Classification of Residential Neighbourhoods. This classification is useful because where someone lives is very often a good guide to their lifestyle. You can see the ACORN classifications in Chapter 6.

The 2001 UK census is planning to use a new categorisation system, reflecting recent changes in the UK population. Chief among these is the increased role of women in the workplace.

New social class	Occupations	Example
1	Higher managerial and professional occupations	
1.1	Employers and managers in larger organisations	Bank managers, company directors
1.2	Higher professional	Doctors, lawyers
2	Lower managerial and professional occupations	Police officers
3	Intermediate occupations	Secretaries/PAs, clerical workers
4	Small employers and own-account workers	
5	Lower supervisory, craft and related occupations	Electricians
6	Semi-routine occupations	Drivers, hairdressers, bricklayers
7	Routine occupations	Car park attendants, cleaners

There are other groupings that are based upon the status of the household and what stages people have reached in their lives. These are called family life cycle (FLC) analyses. Here are two examples.

Dynamic entity

Stage 1	Bachelor / Spinster	Young single people not living at home
Stage 2	Newly Married Couples	Young couples with no children
Stage 3	Full Nest 1	Young couples with youngest child under 6 years old.
Stage 4	Full Nest 2	Older couples with dependent children
Stage 5	Empty Nest 1	Older couples with no children at home, household head in employment
Stage 6	Empty Nest 2	Older couples with no children at home, household head retired
Stage 7	Solitary Survivor	In employment
Stage 8	Solitary Survivor	Retired

Leisure

Stage 1	Solo	Young, single people
Stage 2	Homebuilders	Young couples, maybe married, childless
Stage 3	Learner parents	Couples with young children below 10 years old
Stage 4	Practised parents	Couples with older children. Youngest 10–15 years old.
Stage 5	Free again	Typically over 55 years old, no children at home.

Activity 9

What use could a housebuilder make of family life cycle analysis, and information on the number of people at each stage in the cycle, in planning the types of houses to build?

It is important to remember that the model of the family life cycle shown in the tables displays the classic route from young single to older unmarried. In contemporary society, characterised by divorce and what may be the declining importance of marriage as an institution, this picture can vary. It is possible and not uncommon to be young, childless and divorced, or young and unmarried with children. Some people go through life without marrying or having children at all. Individuals may go through the life cycle belonging to more than one family group. At each stage, whether on the classic route or an alternative path, needs and disposable income will change. Family groupings are, however, a key feature of society.

There has been some criticism of the traditional FLC model as a basis for market segmentation (see for example, Rob Lawson, 'The Family Life Cycle: a demographic analysis', *Journal of Marketing Management* (Summer 1998).)

(a)   It is modelled on the demographic patterns of industrialised western nations - and particularly America. This pattern may not be universally applicable.

(b)   As noted above, while the FLC model was once typical of the overwhelming majority of American families, there are now important potential variations from that pattern, including:

(i)	Childless couples	-	because of choice, career-oriented women and delayed marriage
(ii)	Later marriages	-	because of greater career-orientation and non-marital relationships: likely to have fewer children
(iii)	Later children	-	say in late 30s. Likely to have fewer children, but to stress 'quality of life'
(iv)	Single parents	-	(especially mothers) because of divorce
(v)	Fluctuating labour status	-	not just 'in labour' or 'retired', but redundancy, career change, dual-income etc
(vi)	Extended parenting	-	young, single adults returning home while they establish careers/financial independence; divorced children returning to parents; elderly parents requiring care; newly-weds living with in-laws
(vii)	Non-family households	-	unmarried (homosexual or hetero-sexual) couples
		-	divorced persons with no children
		-	single persons (mainly women, or older products of delay in first marriage)
		-	widowed persons (especially women, because of longer life-expectancy)

An alternative or modified FLC model is needed to take account of consumption variables such as:

(a) Spontaneous changes in brand preference when a household undergoes a change of status (divorce, redundancy, death of a spouse, change in membership of a non-family household)

(b) Different economic circumstances and extent of consumption planning in single-parent families, households where there is a redundancy, dual-income households

(c) Different buying and consumption roles to compensate/adjust in households where the woman works. Women can be segmented into at least four categories - each of which may represent a distinct market for goods and services:

- Stay-at-home homemaker
- Plan-to-work homemaker
- 'Just-a-job' working woman
- Career-oriented working woman

Age structure

The age structure of the population is of particular concern to planners and business organisations. In 1951, 10% of the population were over 65. This will rise to nearly 20% by 2021. Here are some trends for the age structure.

Age	2021 est %	2011 est %	Projected % change 1991–2011	1991 %	1981 %	% change 1981–1991	1961 %	% change 1961–1991
Under 16	19.5	20.1	(1)	20.3	22.2	(8.5)	24.8	(18%)
16–39	30.5	30.0	(15)	35.2	34.9	0.8	31.4	12%
40–64	31.9	33.7	17	28.7	27.8	3.2	32.0	11%
65–79	13.6	11.7	(3.5)	12.0	12.2	(1.6)	9.8	22%
80+	4.5	4.4	21	3.7	2.8	32%	1.9	95%
Rounding		0.1		0.1	0.1		0.1	
Total	100.0	100.0		100.0	100.0		100.0	

It can be seen that, while the working population (those between 16–65, although this does not take into account people in higher education, or the fact that women retire earlier than men) is fairly constant as a percentage, there is a shift in the relative proportion of elderly and young dependants. In 1961, 11.7% (9.8 + 1.9%) of the population were over 65. By 1991 this had risen to 15.7% (12% + 3.7%). The proportion of under 16s in the same period fell from 24.8% to 20.3% of the population. This has been occurring since 1961 and has continued in the 1980s. This shift is important for the following reasons.

(a) The elderly dependants have different needs (for long term health provision, for example) to younger people whose needs are for education and so on. Planners must take this into account when allocating resources for social provision.

(b) The elderly, as a market segment, will be increasingly important, not only because of their numbers, but because they are likely to be increasingly affluent.

The 'mature' market is currently the fastest growing demographic sector in Europe. The sector is complex, and must be segmented and targeted, as with any other market. This targeting may include the following considerations.

- Design and layout of material
- Use of appropriate imagery
- Choice of words and phrasing
- Choice of medium, including the Internet
- Use of direct mail

The '50 plussers' spend the most on cars, holidays, financial products and luxury goods.

(c) The decline in the number of young people will mean that organisations might have to change their recruitment policies or production methods. There will be fewer young people, and more competition for them. However, the fall in young people is more complex than a simple decline. The demographic time-bomb is not quite so marked after all.

(i) In 1971 there were 14.3 million under 16.

(ii) In 1988 there were 11.5 million under 16.

(iii) In 2001 it is projected that there will be 12.6 million under 16, before a slow fall and stabilisation.

The age structure, as with population size generally, depends on the birth rate and the death rate. Importantly, of course, the age structure depends not only on the current birth rate, but on that of previous years. For example, there was reputedly an increase in

the numbers of births immediately following World War II and another, as these 'baby boomers' themselves had children, in the 1960s.

Demography has a big effect on culture, and cultures can influence demography. A mainly young society is likely to have a different culture from an elderly one, and culture influences people's decisions on whether or when to have children.

The next section looks at several cultural issues.

3.3 Culture

Definition

> Culture is the sum total of the inherited ideas, beliefs, values and knowledge that make up the basis of social action.

A society's culture comprises three interdependent elements, as follows.

(a) The ideological system represents the ideas, beliefs, values and ways of reasoning that we accept. For example, most people accept that they have some responsibility not to endanger others through carelessness, and therefore accept (at least in theory) that they should drive carefully.

(b) The technological system comprises the skills, crafts and arts that allow us to make things. Thus one of the most important reasons why our culture today is very different from the culture of 500 years ago is that we have aeroplanes, computers, telephones and so on.

(c) The organisational system is the system which co-ordinates people's efforts. It includes the government, companies, families and social clubs.

Activity 10

The role of the family and religion are two of the main indicators of what a culture is like. What do you think that the other main indicators are?

Businesses must take account of the culture of their society. It will determine what they can sell and how they should sell it. For example, an advertisement containing a shot of a semi-naked woman might be perfectly acceptable in some countries, but will be very offensive in others. Businesses must also pay attention to subcultures, the cultures of groups within a society. The culture of young students will differ from that of middle-aged business managers.

Attitudes to pleasure

Many people have spare money to spend as they choose, and businesses want to attract that money to themselves. There are many different ways in which they can get people to spend on things they do not really need. One approach is to appeal to self-centredness, using slogans such as 'Go on, treat yourself'. Another approach is to emphasise the benefits to others, for example by emphasising that producers of the goods in poor countries are paid a good price for their output. Which approach is best will of course depend on the product, but it will also depend on the culture.

Changes in culture

A business must not simply find out about the state of the culture it operates in, and leave it at that. Culture can change, and businesses need to notice these changes and adapt. For example, while belief in marriage has persisted, the belief that people should marry young has not: women now have careers before they marry, and have children later than they used to.

4 POLITICAL AND LEGAL ASPECTS

4.1 The political environment

Businesses, like everyone else, have to work within the law. Laws are made by Parliament for the good of society as a whole. What laws are made depends on which political party holds power. Therefore the political environment is important to businesses. However, this environment goes further than the election of governments. Although a government will come to power already committed to making certain changes, there are many other things which it might or might not do. Businesses may, either individually or though trade associations, lobby for changes they would like. In the UK, pressure groups have an important role, and businesses can hire professional lobbyists who know how to persuade politicians to do things. Even beyond legislation, businesses must also be aware of general political attitudes. For example, some governments favour free enterprise, while others prefer central control, and even nationalisation of industries. Large businesses and pressure groups may put a lot of effort into influencing such attitudes.

We will start by looking at how political systems can affect businesses.

4.2 Political systems

The UK's political system has been remarkably stable, with no revolutionary changes for over 300 years. Over the same timespan, most European countries have experienced violent revolutions which have seriously disrupted their economies. UK businesses need not worry about revolutions. What they do need to worry about is the risk of dramatic changes in government policy, as one party replaces another in government at a general election. The UK system channels any urges for dramatic change into the voting system, which allows a change of heart by a few voters to change the whole direction of government.

Activity 11

How might a UK car manufacturer be affected by a change of government (to the left or to the right)? You might consider the effect of changed policy towards, say, company cars, road-building, green issues, personal taxation and import restrictions.

Businesses can to some extent get round the problems created by the political system. The most useful thing is to be able to predict the result of a general election, and the likely effect on government policies. Accurate prediction is very difficult, but opinion polls and policy statements by party leaders can help.

A business can go further than prediction and attempt to influence the political process itself. Many large companies contribute money to political parties. They also use political lobbyists to put forward their point of view. Some organisations, such as professional bodies, also retain Members of Parliament as Parliamentary advisors.

Activity 12

Think of one argument for allowing businesses to pay Members of Parliament to act as advisors, and one argument against it.

The political system has a direct impact on the way the economy is run. Three major types of economic system are based on differing amounts of government influence. At one extreme is the planned economy, in which decisions about who makes what, how much is made, where it is sold and at what price, are all made centrally. An example is North Korea. At the other extreme is the free market, where the influence of government is minimal. In between is the mixed economy. This is the most common system, and it is the UK's system.

In a mixed economy the government controls a significant part of the economy. It is the largest supplier, employer, customer and investor. A shift in political policy can change a particular market overnight. For example, the end of the Cold War has been a big problem for weapons makers.

Any business which operates abroad, or which has overseas suppliers or customers, needs to consider the political environment in the countries involved as well as in the UK. In many cases there is no special problem beyond the need to deal with different sets of rules and forms to fill in, because many countries are stable democracies. In some countries, however, one has to consider the risk of revolution, military coup or economic collapse. These can lead to assets being confiscated and debts never being paid. Even in safer environments, there can be problems. If an economy is in difficulties, perhaps suffering high unemployment, foreign businesses are often blamed. The consequence can be unexpected controls on trade. Whole industries, as well as individual businesses, can also be affected by international politics. For example, the deregulation of air travel in Europe and the USA has proceeded very slowly.

One of the main functions of the political process is lawmaking. Businesses and consumers are directly affected by the laws passed, and by the international conventions which governments agree to. We will now look at these legal aspects.

4.3 Legal aspects

Laws can affect businesses in the following different ways.

(a) Dealings with customers can be affected by laws on the sale of goods and services, on advertising and trade descriptions, on product safety and on shop opening hours.

(b) How a business treats its employees is affected by employment legislation and trade union law, largely designed to protect employees' rights. Thus there are strict rules on the dismissal of employees and on equal opportunities.

(c) Dealings with shareholders are affected by the Companies Acts, which lay down how information must be given in published accounts and what dividends may be paid.

(d) The criminal law can affect companies. Some offences can be committed by companies as separate legal persons distinct from their directors and employees.

Some laws apply to all businesses. Others apply only to particular types of business. An example is the Financial Services Act 1986, which affects sellers of insurance, pensions and other financial products.

Changes in laws are often predictable. The proposals may be part of a government's declared programme or part of an opposition party's manifesto. The process of enacting laws in the UK also gives businesses time to plan for proposed changes: there is likely to be a preliminary period of consultation, followed by the Parliamentary process. This process can itself take several months.

Businesses are affected by laws made outside the UK. For example, anyone doing business in the USA must take account of US law. Even a business which has no international dealings must take account of European Union law.

4.4 The European Union

The European Union (EU) comprises 15 countries: Austria, Belgium, Denmark, Finland, France, Germany, Greece, Ireland, Italy, Luxembourg, the Netherlands, Portugal, Spain, Sweden and the UK.

A key aim of the EU is the creation of a single economic area which is as good as a single country for the businesses and individuals in it. The idea is that businesses throughout the EU should be subject to the same laws, and that there should be no barriers to trade within the EU. If you have flown within the EU, you will have noticed the blue exit channel at your destination airport. This is for people travelling within the EU, and reflects the fact that there are no customs controls within the EU. This is of course far more important to a company sending lorryloads of goods abroad than to the average holiday traveller.

The EU has done many things to make the sale of goods in different countries easier, and to allow the free movement of capital and labour. Here are some examples.

(a) Setting common standards on food labelling and hygiene.

(b) Setting common standards for information technology.

(c) Making rules to ensure that when a government needs to buy something, all EU companies have an equal chance to supply and the home country's companies are not favoured.

(d) Liberalisation of capital movements, so that (for example) a UK investor can freely move money to another country and invest it in a business there.

(e) Removing of rules which limited access to financial services. It should soon be possible for insurance companies to sell their products anywhere in the EU.

(f) Ensuring mutual recognition of professional qualifications, so that (for example) a French lawyer can practise in the UK without having to requalify as a UK solicitor or barrister.

(g) Giving all EU citizens the right to work anywhere in the EU.

NOTES

Activity 13

A Japanese electronics company decides to set up a factory in the UK. Can you think of three political and three legal aspects that the company will need to be aware of which will impinge on the company and its products?

The last PEST factor is the technological one. We discuss it in the next chapter in the context of change since this is the area in which the greatest environmental developments are currently taking place.

In this chapter we have looked at factors that have been important aspects of the marketing environment since the Industrial Revolution and the emergence of the consumer society. In the next chapter we will look at factors that have become important more recently and which promise to have increasing impact in the future.

Chapter roundup

- A firm's business environment needs to be considered in terms of particular markets, internal organisational aspects and broad trends in society as a whole (PEST factors).

- Economic factors such as rate of growth, inflation, taxation rates and interest rates, at home and abroad, must be considered when devising marketing plans.

- Social and cultural factors such as demography, family relationships, religion and ideology will all affect consumers' responses to the product; the marketing effort must take account of these factors.

- To a large extent, the macro environment is determined by political and legal factors which the marketer can do little to influence. These factors may produce constraints on marketing activities; on the other hand, they may provide opportunities for new products and services necessary to enable citizens to stay within new laws (smokeless fuels, car seat belts and so on)

- To a large extent, the macro environment is determined by political and legal factors which the marketer can do little to influence. These factors may produce constraints on marketing activities; on the other hand, they may provide opportunities for new products and services necessary to enable citizens to stay within new laws (smokeless fuels, car seat belts and so on)

Quick quiz

1 Draw a diagram illustrating the market environment.

2 What is the purpose of a marketing audit and what particular activities will be scrutinised?

3 List the major economic factors that the marketing manager must take into account.

4 In what ways may the economic factors of another country affect the marketing of a product made in the UK?

PUBLISHING

5   What demographic factor changes would increase the markets for a) comics and b) eye make-up?

6   How can the marketing manager of a charity use the public's desire for pleasure to raise funds?

7   What are the three main types of economic system?

8   List three ways in which EU law has affected the marketing environment.

Answers to activities

1   There are of course many possibilities: the food industry (grocer's shops and supermarkets); motor cars (the network of motor dealers); mortgage lending, postal services (post office branches); and so on.

2   (a)   Tommy's Toys Ltd can expect more competition.

(b)   Tommy's Toys Ltd will find it easier to compete in Europe as there should be a convergence of product standards.

(The single European market is extremely significant for business. If you are based in the UK the Department of Trade and Industry can provide further information).

3   The rate of growth will determine the number of computers sold: if people have more money, and new businesses are being created, then sales should be good. The rate of inflation will affect costs, the price which can be charged and the profits made. The level of unemployment will affect demand: unemployed people are not likely to buy computers. Interest rates will determine the amount the company has to spend on financing its activities. If customers borrow money to buy computers, interest rates may also affect the willingness of customers to buy. The balance of payments will affect the exchange rate, and this in turn will affect the cost of imported components and revenue from export sales. International barriers to trade and the state of other countries' economies will affect export sales.

4   You will reach your own conclusions from your discussion.

5   A company may decide to open up a factory or offices overseas. Motor manufacturers have done this very successfully in order to gain advantages of low wage rates, taxation and get round import controls.

6   Your answer will depend on what advertisements you have seen recently, but food and drink advertisements often centre on happy gatherings of families or friends. BT advertisements also centre on family and friends as do those for package holidays.

7   You will reach your own conclusions from your discussion.

8   In all groups except the 16-39 years olds, growth is predicted. The number of retired people will continue to rise with a marked growth in the 80 plus age group. The health care sector will be faced with an ageing population, but also with some growth in the child population. Child medicine and care of the elderly are likely to be the main areas for the sector to concentrate on.

9   A housebuilder will look at the size of the family unit. The response to trends toward single households, couples deciding to have children later and people living longer has been to build smaller housing units, for example one bedroom starter homes, and sheltered housing.

BPP
PUBLISHING

10   Other main indicators of culture are language, education and material possessions.

11   You will reach your own conclusions from your discussion.

12   An argument for allowing MPs to be paid advisors is that they will spend time on the work, in addition to their normal duties, and that time should be paid for. An argument against allowing payment is that MPs may spend too much time working for whoever pays them the most, and may ignore their duties to their constituents.

13   Examples of legal aspects which would impinge upon the company are health and safety laws, employment law and planning regulations. Examples of political aspects are grants for companies in certain areas of high unemployment, tax policy and relations between Japan and the UK (and EU) generally.

Further question practice

Now try the following practice questions at the end of this text.

Multiple Choice Questions: 11–14

Exam Style Question: 2

Chapter 3:
THE MODERN MARKETING ENVIRONMENT II

Introduction

Developments in technology, affecting all aspects of life, are happening at an ever increasing pace. Products that could probably not have been imagined by many people 20 years ago – such as the digital camera – are now available. The rapid appearance of completely new products, and obsolescence of those thought essential only a few years ago, presents a special challenge to marketing.

The marketing concept is being increasingly affected by ecological issues. In the past there has been a tendency to regard business activities as antithetical to the concept of 'green-ness', but now it is being recognised that the two are complementary. This is having a profound impact on marketing practices.

Quality has become increasingly important for managers in every part of modern business organisations. In Europe and the USA this has been generated by the success of Pacific Rim economies. Many have argued that the central tenet of Japanese business philosophy has been the ability to produce high quality goods closely in tune with the needs of the target market. It is now widely recognised that quality of goods or service relative to major competitors is the single most important factor in an enterprise's performance.

Your objectives

In this chapter you will learn about the following.

(a) How technological issues can affect marketing

(b) The impact of the Internet and e-commerce

(c) The concerns of the green movement, their impact on marketing, and the marketing response

(d) The basic principles of Total Quality Management and its marketing implications

1 TECHNOLOGICAL ISSUES

Technology is strictly the use of tools to make new things. It depends on knowledge which now often comes from scientific research and can be 'high tech', for example the use of micro chips. However, technology can also be 'low tech', for example child-proof tops on medicine bottles.

An invention is the product of research and development. Innovation is making commercial use of an invention.

Of all of the environmental factors technology is the most challenging for the marketing manager. Change is rapid, and a company which makes the right decisions early can get a big advantage over its competitors. To stay ahead, companies need effective research, planning and marketing of new products. In some cases, if a new product is late, it may barely sell at all because better products have become available in the meantime. This has happened with personal computers: there would be little point in launching a new range of computers with 486 processors now that the more powerful Pentium processors are widely available.

The need to market the right technology at the right time and to consider all the relevant factors is illustrated by domestic video systems. Initially, consumers could choose between the VHS system or the Betamax system. In the end VHS won, not because it was technically better nor because it was available sooner, but because the promoters of VHS ensured that lots of films were available on video in the VHS format. This was important to many consumers, who wanted to be able to rent films to watch at home.

Digital cameras, which take still pictures but record them electronically instead of on film, are now available. Pictures taken on them can be loaded into computers and manipulated (for example changing colours or merging two pictures).

Technology can drive some companies out of business, or at least force them to change their products completely. For example, the market for mechanical typewriters is now much smaller than it was, because computers with word-processing packages are so cheap. This is an example of the impact technology can have on the marketing environment, which we will now look at more closely.

Activity 1

Why have electronic personal organisers (such as those made by Psion) not destroyed the market for ring-bound organisers (such as Filofaxes)?

1.1 The impact of technology

Technology can affect businesses in the following ways.

(a) The types of products that are made have changed. In consumer markets we have seen the emergence of personal computers, compact disc players and palm held televisions. Satellite TV, received via dish or cable, is now commonplace. Industrial markets have seen the introduction of sophisticated new machines run by microchips.

(b) The manufacture of products has changed. Robots are now used in many factories, for instance.

(c) The quality of products has improved with the use of automatic testing equipment that takes away human error.

(d) The way in which goods and services are delivered to the customer has changed. For example, automatic teller machines are now the main route by which people get cash from their banks. Home shopping is also becoming easier and more widespread.

(e) The availability of goods has improved. The flow of goods can be monitored by the use of computerised point of sale equipment such as bar-code readers in shops. This information can be used to re-order goods automatically when stocks are low, and also to gather marketing information.

(f) Large scale databases to monitor customer behaviour are now possible. The Barclays Bank group of companies have access to a database of over 20 million potential customers and can closely monitor the individual members of its market. Direct mail can be sent to the right people instead of to everybody.

(g) Technology has significantly changed the way people work. Computers are used not only to create documents and to store and process data, but also to communicate using electronic mail (e-mail). Many people can now work at home and be linked to their employers electronically.

Activity 2

There are now far more mobile telephones than there were five years ago, and a very high proportion are used for private, rather than business, purposes. What impact has this technology had on people's lives? How might the technology be developed further?

Activity 3

Look at the direct mail that you or your family have received during the past few months. How do you think the senders obtained your names? How relevant are the products or services to you? Do you think that the senders have any idea of how old you are, of how much money you have or of your lifestyle?

1.2 Technological change

The effects of technological change can include the following.

(a) A fall in costs. The most dramatic example is data processing costs. The cost of working out how much a customer owes, or working out an employee's pay is now about 0.2% of what it was 40 years ago.

(b) Improved quality, especially in the area of customer service. If, for example, a customer telephones with an enquiry, that customer's details can be called up on screen straightaway. The customer does not have to wait while their file is found.

(c) New products and services. For example, telephone subscribers can now get itemised bills.

(d)   Easier access to products and services, for example home shopping by computer, use of the Internet to access information, shops and books.

Activity 4

Think of a company which you know something about. How has it changed over the past few years in response to new technology? How might it have to change over the next few years?

As technology has become more complex and the pace of technological change increases, so concern for the rights of the consumer has also become greater. The consumer has a right to be treated fairly in situations where power may seem to reside only in the big corporations marketing goods and services.

2   THE INTERNET AND E-COMMERCE

The Internet links computer and computer networks world-wide. These are linked together enabling users to search for and access information provided by others.

The World Wide Web is the multimedia element which provides facilities such as full-colour, graphics, sound and video.

2.1   Current uses

At the time of writing, the scope and potential of the Internet have not yet been fully achieved or even visualised. Its uses already embrace the following:

(a)   **Dissemination of information** - generally free of charge.

(b)   **Product/service development** - through almost instantaneous test marketing.

(c)   **Transaction processing** - both business-to-business and business-to-consumer.

(d)   **Relationship enhancement** - between various groups of stakeholders, but principally (for our purposes) between consumers and product/service suppliers.

(e)   **Recruitment** and job search - involving organisations worldwide.

(f)   **Entertainment** - including music, humour, art, games and some less wholesome pursuits!

What is different about the Internet and e-commerce?

There are several features of the Internet which make it radically different from what has gone before.

(a)   It **challenges traditional business models** - because, for example, it enables product/service suppliers to interact directly with their customers, instead of using intermediaries (like retail shops, travel agents, insurance brokers, and conventional banks).

(b)   Although the Internet is global in its operation, its benefits are not confined to large (or global) organisations. **Small companies** can move instantly into a global marketplace, either on their own initiative or as part of what is known as a 'consumer portal'. For example, Ede and Ravenscroft is a small outfitting and tailoring business in Oxford: it could easily promote itself within a much larger 'portal' called OxfordHighStreet.com, embracing a comprehensive mixture of other Oxford retailers.

(c)   It offers a **new economics of information** - because, with the Internet, most information is free. Those with Internet access can view all the world's major newspapers and periodicals without charge.

(d)   It supplies an almost incredible **level of velocity** - virtually instant access to organisations, plus the capacity (at least theoretically) to complete purchasing transactions within seconds.

(e)   It has created **new networks of communication** - between organisations and their customers (either individually or collectively), between customers themselves (through mutual support groups), and between organisations and their suppliers.

(f)   It stimulates the appearance of **new intermediaries** plus, correspondingly, the disappearance of some existing ones. Businesses are finding that they can cut out the middle man, with electronic banking, insurance, publishing and printing as primary examples.

(g)   It has led to **affiliate programmes**. For example, a university can put its reading list on a website and students wishing to purchase any given book can click directly through to an on-line bookseller such as Amazon.co.uk. The university gets a commission; the on-line bookseller gets increased business; the student gets a discount. Everyone benefits except the traditional bookshop.

(h)   It **promotes transparent pricing** - because potential customers can readily compare prices not only from suppliers within any given country, but also from suppliers across the world.

(i)   It facilitates opportunities for very **high levels of (apparent) customer intimacy** between service suppliers and their clients because each client can believe that he or she is receiving personalised attention.

EXAMPLE: EGG AND THE INTERNET GENERATION

In October 1998, the Prudential launched Egg, which within 6 months had reached its initial five year target of attracting £5 billion in savings. At one year old it was the UK's leading Internet financial brand.

Covering savers, homebuyers and borrowers, Egg's services were made available seven days a week, 24 hours a day, by telephone, post and Internet. Its first home loan was processed in 48 hours. Over the next nine months, the brand was developed to cover travel insurance, email and credit cards. Its market leading Egg Savings Account now only uses the Internet for account applications.

Research has shown that by the year 2013 two out of three financial products will be sold by electronic methods.

2.2   **Growth of the Internet**

It is estimated that over 50% of households in the USA will have Internet access by the year 2001, with the figure rising to just under 60 per cent by 2002. In the UK, with a growth rate fuelled by Freeserve, the comparable figures are 32 per cent and 40 per cent respectively. In mid-2000 it appears likely that by 2002 there will be at least 15 million UK Internet users. The UK growth will be fuelled by:

(a)   Many UK households have multiple Internet access points, through both parents and children.

(b)   Changes in the telecoms market are likely to mean that Internet connection time will become much cheaper, if not free.

(c)   Digital TV will permit the Internet to be accessed without the necessity for purchase of a personal computer. This in turn will widen the market place for the Internet to encompass those in the lower socio-economic categories who are more likely to subscribe to cable or satellite TV companies.

(d)   Web-enabled mobile phones are already on the market. The recent emergence of WAP (Wireless Application Protocol) is allowing the use of mobile phones for a wide range of interactions with the web. Already, NatWest Bank has a joint venture with Orange to develop a mobile phone that has links to the bank using WAP.

(e)   For many, the preferred Internet interface is not the PC but the PDA (Personal Digital Assistant) . In the USA and more recently in the UK, there are already several wireless-based PDAs being used to link investors to stock market information.

(f)   Post Office Counters are actively exploring the use of kiosks for a wide variety of applications, to include e-commerce in rural outlets.

A critical factor in the long-run expansion of the Internet is its use today by children, the adult consumers of tomorrow. In early 1999, more than three million children under 17 in the UK used the Internet, an increase of 12 per cent over the previous six months - and a staggering 17 per cent of children have made on-line purchases with the aid of their parents' credit cards!

2.3   Electronic commerce

Electronic commerce is the latest example of the impact of technology on global markets.

Definition

Electronic commerce (e-commerce, e-business, e-biz) can be defined as using an electronic network to speed up all stages of the business process, from design to buying, selling and delivery. The process is fairly familiar between companies, but less so between retailer and customer.

The internet is the sum of all the separate networks (or stand-alone computers) run by organisations and individuals alike. (It has been described as an international telephone service for computers.)

'The internet offers efficient, fast and cost effective email, massive information search and retrieval facilities. There is a great deal of financial information available and users can also access publications and news releases issued by the Treasury and other Government departments.

To access the internet you require a microcomputer, a modem and the services of an internet provider.

One of the main uses of the internet is for the sending and receiving of email. This has become a popular method of communication for companies of all sizes.

The main advantage of email is the speed of delivery; messages are delivered within a few seconds and take no longer to travel to Moscow than to Manchester. Messages can be sent to multiple addresses, they can contain images, sound and computer files in addition to the text.'

Certified Accountant, August 1997

Electronic commerce in the sense of customer buying via the Internet has had a slow start, in the UK at least. There are many factors contributing to this, one of the chief ones being people's concern about the security of on-line transactions. However, a massive increase in e-commerce is on the way according to some forecasts. Here are some figures on European usage.

	UK	France	Spain	Germany	Sweden
% of companies with web sites	51	25	16	48	54
% of companies selling via the net	9	3	9	9	10
Value of goods sold online 1999 (£m)	5,300	3,400	400	3,600	700
PC penetration at home (% of population)	37.3	26.6	27.4	35	64
Online penetration (% of population)	26.3	8.7	10.5	16.2	41
People with internal access (millions)	12.5	5.21	3.91	11.2	3.63
Mobile phone penetration (% of consumers)	34.8	28.5	31.4	24.5	55.2
% internet users who shop online	25	10	9	36	33

(Source: *Connectis, March 2000*)

The London Chamber of Commerce predicts that by 2001, e-commerce will account for 5% of all worldwide sales, worth £20 trillion. Cheaper personal computers will help to boost the trend, as have free internet access services, such as Dixons' Freeserve.

EXAMPLE

The phenomenon of e-commerce is not just the domain of the large firm. Jack Scaife, a Yorkshire family butcher in the UK, uses the Internet to sell black pudding and bacon all over the world. The Internet can give the smallest business the same global reach as

BPP
PUBLISHING

the largest. Indeed it has been found that the best websites belong to small firms. Larger firms such as the big car manufacturers are adopting e-commerce at a much slower pace, with websites that are little more than promotional material rather than venues for direct selling. To quote an example, an article in PC Week online found that Exxon's website consisted largely of job advertisements and a download of the Tiger mascot. For now, the leaders in this area remain books, electronics, catalogues, food and CD sellers. Many big companies are, however working on business-to-business e-commerce projects that consumers never see.

Electronic commerce draws businesses, suppliers and customers closer together, enabling collaboration on design, pinpointing of consumer demand and sharpening of marketing strategies. It opens markets for 24 hours a day.

Governments are major players in the market for goods and services. Public purchasing accounts for 11% of European GDP. The European Commission has set a target of 25% of public procurement to be done via e-commerce by 2003. The UK government wants 25% of its services available on-line by 2001.

E-commerce is not restricted to the major industrialised nations represented in the US, Europe and Japan. It is predicted that Latin American countries will spend $8 billion a year on-line by 2003. Sales of computer equipment here in 1998 reached $22 billion. There are still hurdles to be overcome, such as finding secure methods of on-line payment and bureaucratic customs procedures, coupled with expensive Internet access fees. Three quarters of all money spent on the Internet in Latin American countries is currently sent to overseas companies, predominantly in the US. Many UK technology firms are desperate for new markets and the region is therefore vital.

Companies going on the Internet must have regard to local culture and tastes. It has been found that most attempts by Internet retailers in the US to target other countries consist mainly of translating an existing website into the relevant native language. Companies who want to compete more effectively must take account of varying regional characteristics.

In early 1999 the UK government unveiled a new legal framework for e-commerce, designed to boost public confidence in using the Internet. This has become enshrined in the Electronic Communications Act 2000. Among other proposals, the courts are to be allowed to recognise electronic signatures as legally binding. The aim is to make the UK one of the easiest places to do 'e-biz' in the world. The US administration is also seeking to encourage the development of the 'digital company', pushing for greater access to the Internet for small US firms and the developing nations.

E-commerce can reduce expensive sales and distribution workforces, and offers new marketing opportunities.

Distribution

The Internet can be used to get certain products directly into people's homes. Anything that can be converted into digital form can simply be uploaded onto the seller's site and then downloaded onto the customer's PC at home. This is contributing to a process called disintermediation.

Marketing

Besides its usefulness for tapping into worldwide information resources businesses are also using it to provide information about their own products and services.

For customers the Internet offers a speedy and impersonal way of getting to know about the services that a company provides. For businesses the advantage is that it is much cheaper to provide the information in electronic form than it would be to employ staff to man the phones on an enquiry desk, and much more effective than sending out mailshots that people would either throw away or forget about when they needed the information.

For many companies this will involve a rethink of current promotional activity.

EXAMPLE

Peapod.com is an online supermarket and one of the more sophisticated recorders and users of customers' personal data and shopping behaviour. With over 100,000 customers in eight US cities, Peapod's website sells groceries that are then delivered to customer's homes. a list of previous purchases (including brand, pack size and quantity purchased) is kept on the site, so the customer can make minor changes from week to week, saving time and effort.

Peapod creates a database on each shopper that includes their purchase history (what they bought), their online shopping patterns (how they bought it), questionnaires about their attitudes and opinions, and demographic data (which Peapod buys from third parties). A shopper's profile is used by the company to determine which advertisement to show and which promotions/electronic coupons to offer. Demographically identical neighbours are thus treated differently based on what Peapod has learned about their preferences and behaviours over time.

Shoppers seem to like this high-tech relationship marketing, with 94% of all sales coming from repeat customers. Manufacturers like it too. the more detailed customer information enables them to target promotions at customers who have repeatedly bought another brand, thereby not giving away promotion dollars to loyal customers.

Collecting information about customers

People who visit a site for the first time are asked to register, which typically involves giving a name, physical address and post code, e-mail address and possibly other demographic data such as age, job title and income bracket.

From the initial registration details the user record may show, say, that the user is male, aged 20 to 30 and British. The website can respond to this by displaying products or services likely to appeal to this segment of the market.

2.4 Possible strategies

There are four possible strategies that a company may adopt towards e-commerce.

(a) **Do not sell products through the internet at all,** and prohibit resellers from doing so. Provide only product information on the internet. This may be an appropriate strategy where products are **large, complex and highly customised,** such as aircraft manufacturing.

(b) **Leave the internet business to resellers** and do not sell directly through the internet (ie do not compete with resellers). This can be appropriate, for instance, where manufacturers have already assigned exclusive territories to resellers.

(c)   The manufacturer can **restrict internet sales exclusively to itself**. The problem with this is that most large manufacturers do not have systems that are geared to dealing with sales to end users who place numerous, irregular small orders.

(d)   Open up internet sales to everybody and **let the market decide** who it prefers to buy from.

If the decision is made to enter into e-commerce a new e-business needs support and long-term commitment from high-level management. Ideally such a project should be 'sponsored' by the chief executive or a board-level director.

A report from Andersen Consulting points to huge differences between the US and European attitudes towards electronic commerce. It has been said that Europe is around 12 to 18 months behind the US in terms of technological and business development of the Internet. Although 82% of the 300 European executives interviewed recognise the strategic importance of e-commerce, only 39% are doing anything about it. Even within Europe, there a variations in Internet and e-commerce adoption.

Whereas US industrialists are working hard to keep government regulation out of e-commerce, European businesses want to bring governments in so that rules can be created. The contrast could hardly be more extreme.

The point being missed is that e-commerce is not a distinct marketplace in itself: rather, internet technology has created new tools that businesses can use, if they choose, to broaden their markets. E-commerce brings big changes, creating opportunities for some, threats for others; it may affect commerce in ways akin to the discovery of new trade routes or the invention of faster modes of transportation - broadening trade horizons and creating, in some fields, truly global markets, products and services.

A 1999 survey by Booz Allen & Hamilton and the Economist Intelligence Unit, involving 600 executives, sought views on the strategic significance of the Internet. The results indicated a much greater awareness of the Internet and its potential to transform business than many previous studies had suggested.

(a)   Over 90 per cent said the Internet would reshape business markets within two years.

(b)   61 per cent believed the Internet would help them to achieve business goals.

(c)   30 per cent said the Internet had already forced them to overhaul their existing business strategies.

(d)   On the other hand, only 28 per cent had seen any profits from the Internet, and nearly 70 per cent did not expect to see a return on their Internet investment until the year 2001.

Most observers and experts agree that a successful strategy for e-commerce cannot simply be bolted on to existing processes, systems, delivery routes and business models. Instead, management groups have, in effect, to start again, by asking themselves such fundamental questions as:

- What do customers want to buy from us?
- What business should we be in?
- What kind of partners might we need?
- What categories of customer do we want to attract and retain?

Effective, competent and acceptable customer service through the Internet is a combination of the following factors:

Chapter 3: The modern marketing environment II

NOTES

Factor	Comment
Rapid response time	If the website is not fast, the transient potential shopper will simply click on to another. These 'fickle' visitors to a website will only allow around five to eight seconds: if the site has not captured their attention in that time-frame, they will move elsewhere.
Response quality	The website must be legible, with appropriate graphics and meaningful, relevant information supplied. Generally speaking, website visitors are not interested in the company's history and size: they are much more concerned about what the company can offer them.
Navigability	It is important to create a website which caters for every conceivable customer interest and question. Headings and category-titles should be straightforward and meaningful, not obscure and ambiguous.
Download times	Again, these need to be rapid, given that many Internet shoppers regard themselves (rightly or otherwise) as cash-rich and time-poor.
Security/Trust	One of the biggest barriers to the willingness of potential Internet customers actually to finalise a transaction is their fear that information they provide about themselves (such as credit card details) can be 'stolen' or used as the basis for fraud.
Fulfilment	Customers must believe that if they order goods and services, the items in question will arrive, and will do so within acceptable time limits (which will generally be much faster than the time limits normally associated with conventional mail order). Equally, customers need to be convinced that if there is a subsequent need for service recovery, then speedy and efficient responses can be secured either to rectify the matter or to enable unsatisfactory goods to be returned without penalty.
Up-to-date	Just as window displays need to be constantly refreshed, so do websites require frequent repackaging and redesign.
Availability	Can the user reach the site 24 hours a day, seven days a week? Is the down-time minimal? Can the site always be accessed?
Site effectiveness and functionality	Is the website intuitive and easy to use? Is the content written in a language which will be meaningful even to the first-time browser (ie the potential customer)?

3 ETHICS AND CONSUMERISM

The importance of customer care has been acknowledged as a result of the growth of consumerism. A number of consumer rights have been recognised, including the following.

(a) The right to be informed of the true facts of the buyer-seller relationship, such as the following.

    (i) The true cost of loans (APRs must now be published in any advertisement for loans)

    (ii) Truth in advertising (watchdog bodies vet any advertisement and consumers can complain about advertisements to the Advertising Standards Authority).

(b) The right to be protected from unfair exploitation or intrusion. Consumers' trust in organisations must not be abused. For example, the sale of mailing lists to third parties can lead to consumers receiving vast quantities of 'junk' mail.

(c)   The right to a particular quality of life. This right is focused increasingly on environmental protection, making suppliers aware of the implications of their actions on the eco-system, and the quality of water, air etc.

Suppliers need to take careful note of these consumerist pressures to maintain a good image and reputation with customers and other important publics. This may militate against aggressive marketing tactics. The need to consider the best interests of customers should be paramount in a marketing strategy. The long-term view is necessary rather than attempting to maximise short-term profits.

Activity 5

What factors do you think are important in determining the bargaining power of buyers?

Technological developments are often seen as causing problems such as increased pollution and waste of natural resources. These factors affect everyone, not just the consumers of particular products. 'Green issues' are concerned with the whole planet, its populations and natural systems.

4   THE GREEN ENVIRONMENT

4.1   Green concerns

The modern green movement, although arising from concerns over pollution and overpopulation which are centuries old, was given major impetus by studies carried out in the 1970s into the effects of massive economic growth on the finite resources of the Earth. The possible consequences were underlined by disruptions in the supply of oil and other raw materials caused by wars and economic conflicts. Initial predictions of impending disaster failed to produce a significant change in public opinion and policy making on green issues was largely stalled.

From the mid-eighties onwards, however, a series of ecological disasters (the emission at the Union Carbide plant at Bhopal, India, the Chernobyl nuclear reactor accident in the USSR, the Exxon-Valdez oil spill in Alaska, and the torching of the Kuwaiti oil fields at the end of the Iraqi invasion) reawakened public concern and sparked general public fears about environmental dangers. Other factors contributing to increased 'green consciousness' included scientific reports about the state of the North Sea, the forests of Central Europe and the droughts which afflicted several regions, all of which were linked to environmental damage caused by modern industry.

The end of the cold war led to a search, on the part of the media and the public at large, for a substitute threat to the safety of the world in place of nuclear war. Scientific progress also enabled us, for example, to measure the hole in the ozone layer which had long been suspected. Pressure groups, agencies and prominent individuals began to play a part in bringing these issues to the public attention.

Fast air transport and new satellite communication systems give media such as television and newspapers fast access to, and rapid dissemination of information from, countries affected by environmentally-linked disasters, such as the Ethiopian famines. Events in countries in Eastern Europe, South America and Asia can be transmitted internationally, almost instantly, with the same technology. Such media coverage has elevated general concerns about common dangers and conflicts which threaten our environment. Consumers are aware of the importance of green issues. Products and services, and the ways in which they are marketed, are changing to reflect this growing consumer awareness.

Activity 6

It is the year 2095 and you and almost everyone you know are vegetarians. You are having a dinner party and your significant other is getting into a flap because one of the guests has told you she is a carnivore. Neither you nor your partner have ever cooked meat before.

If this scenario comes true what does it mean for the marketing of meat? Analyse the situation in terms of a framework like the four Ps.

Try to imagine a world where green issues predominate (glance over the next few pages for ideas). Then see if you can fill out the dinner party preparation scenario with further details. This is ideally carried out as a group Activity, so you can share ideas.

Against this background the green movement has gained momentum and is having an increasing effect on the practice of marketing.

4.2 The green movement

The green movement is concerned with human beings' relationship to the environment. A major focus of this is concern about the damage to nature and living things which has come about as a consequence of exploitation of natural resources and modern ways of living. This is expressed through philosophical ideas.

- Stewardship and paternalism
- Humanism
- Conservationism
- Environmentalism
- Animal rights and welfare
- Pacifism

A major concern is with the study of ecology.

Definition

Ecology is concerned with all the varieties of plant and animal life and the relationships between them, and between these life forms and their environment.

Major themes of this way of thinking include the following.

(a) The environment is a 'web' of complex interconnected living (biological) and non-living (physical) systems.

(b) Everything, including pollution, goes somewhere into this 'web'.

Askham Bryan College
LIBRARY BOOK

BPP PUBLISHING

(c)   Nature has an inherent equilibrium or 'balance'.

    (d)   All exploitation of nature which upsets this balance will ultimately have a cost.

4.3 Which environmental issues will impact upon marketing practices?

Among the environmental issues which are likely to be seen as relevant to businesses are the following.

    (a)   Resource depletion may influence business operation by reducing the availability of raw materials through damage to soil, water, trees, plant-life, energy availability, mineral wealth, animal and marine species.

    (b)   Genetic diversity may not seem immediately important for business, but in fact the development of many important new varieties of plants and animals, and of medicines and the new bio-technology which enables commercially valuable materials of all kinds to be synthesised, depends crucially on the availability of wild species from which genetic resources can be drawn. In the development of high-yield and disease-resistant crop plants, for example, wild species are a critical resource.

    (c)   Pollution concerns are at the centre of most worries about the environment.

        (i)   Businesses are finding themselves under more and more pressure to curtail the impacts of their activities on the water table, the rivers and the oceans. Concern over the quality of drinking water, to which this has been linked, has generated a massive increase in the size of the bottled water market in the UK.

        (ii)   The quality of air has been much discussed, owing to the effect of motor vehicle exhaust – clearly this could have a bearing upon distribution policies.

        (iii)   Concerns about the pollution of land, through landfill policies and the long-term damage wrought by industry upon the land it occupies, are all likely to require some government and business policy changes over the next few years.

        (iv)   Noise pollution is also likely to become more important and this could have far reaching impacts on the operation of many businesses.

In order to take action to remedy these problems, the polluter pays principle was adopted by the OECD in the early 1970s. It aims to relate the damage done by pollution involved in the production of goods and services to the prices of those goods. The intention is to deter potential polluters by making it uneconomic to produce goods and services which also create pollution. The principle has been broadly accepted and has been a major factor in reaction to major pollution incidents, such as large-scale oil and chemical spills. The costs of road transport, however, do not as yet reflect the amount of air and noise pollution caused by vehicles.

Acid rain

Acid rain, which has been linked to large scale damage to forests throughout northern Europe and acidification of water supplies and of fish-bearing lakes and rivers, has generated massive bills. The bills involved and the impacts on the natural environment and agricultural systems are so large that political pressures to constrain the effects of industrial production have increased enormously.

NOTES

The ozone layer

Similar alarms have been expressed about ozone depletion, which is caused by the CFC group of chemicals. Alternatives to CFCs are being developed to act as solvents in the electronics industry, and coolants in refrigerators. The use of CFCs for blowing polystyrene foam used as insulation by the building industry has been banned in some countries and is being phased out in many others. Even where products containing CFCs are legally available, consumers may refuse to buy them. This has speeded up the development of replacements.

Waste

Waste is causing just as much alarm, whether it is nuclear waste from power stations or industrial or domestic waste in landfill sites or water systems. There is increased legislation by governments to control waste disposal. New international agreements, arrived at by governments concerned, for example, about the effects of waste dumping on marine life and on beaches also lead to domestic legislation.

Climatic change

Climatic change, involving the effect of excess carbon dioxide in the atmosphere, is still debatable in terms of its actual effects in producing 'unnatural' weather. Potentially, the consequences could be profound, with average temperatures increasing and sea levels rising, with disastrous effects on agriculture and flooding of low lying areas. In the event, great changes would be necessary, including new types of agricultural practices, different areas of habitation and tourism, as well as modification to the production processes and consumption patterns which have been identified as contributory factors. Undoubtedly, laws would be enacted in a wide range of business and marketing related areas to enforce such restrictions as were thought appropriate.

Energy resources

Concerns about energy resources and about the environmental impacts of energy usage are related to the concern over climatic change. Some of the energy sources used at the moment are yielding far less of their potential than seems possible – coal, for example, typically yields only 40% of its potential when burned to produce electricity. Energy saving programmes are under way in most of the countries of the developed world, involving the development of more efficient industrial equipment, and projects such as combined heat and power systems serving neighbourhoods or industrial plants. New energy efficient products are also being developed. Legislation which would penalise the use of certain scarce or potentially wasteful energy sources – for instance, a carbon tax – may well encourage the demand for energy efficient products.

Recycling

This practice is already widespread and the demand for products and packaging made from recycled materials, or from materials which lend themselves to recycling, is increasing steadily. Car manufacturers such as Mazda and Citroen are using plastic components to reduce vehicle weight and are recycling used components.

Animal welfare

In addition to these concerns about the impact of production and consumption on the environment, there are also concerns about animal welfare. The mistreatment of animals in food production and concern about the inhumanity of certain kinds of animal husbandry techniques have produced a strong reaction among consumers. Vegetarianism

BPP PUBLISHING

is increasing in the UK and this has reduced the demand for meat, amongst other changes. There has also been an impact on the sales of cosmetics and other products in which animals are used in product testing.

Related to this, there have been a whole series of food scares, some of which have been related to the ways in which food is produced. Concerns about food safety and dietary health are closely linked to concerns about the use of chemicals and drugs in intensive husbandry and crop production, as well as the forms of feeding which have been employed. The scare over 'mad cow disease' has been linked to the use of recovered proteins from waste meat products in the production of animal feed.

Activity 7

Some argue that the concerns of 'vigilante consumers' – consumers who are not just interested in the products or services they buy but the behaviour of the company behind the brand and the way the product or service is developed – are becoming integral to corporate decision making.

Examples of the impact of such movements include Levis' decision to issue global sourcing guidelines setting out new terms of engagement with suppliers and retailers, excluding those operating in countries with 'oppressive' regimes, and Premier Beverages fair trade initiative of selecting plantations on social and environmental criteria and placing the 'Caring for tea and our tea pickers' logo on all Typhoo tea packaging.

To what extent are you aware of such initiatives and to what extent are you influenced by them in your own purchasing decisions? Can you think of, or find, other examples?

Concerns about all the above factors are having an increasing impact on the business environment and the ways in which businesses operate within society.

4.4 Green pressures on business

Pressure for better environmental performance is coming from many quarters. Consumers are demanding a better environmental performance from companies. In recent surveys, it has been demonstrated that around three-quarters of the population are applying environmental criteria in many purchase considerations.

Green pressure groups

Groups have typically exerted pressure through three main types of activity.

(a) Information based activities: gathering and providing information, mounting political lobbies and publicity campaigns.

(b) Direct action: varying from peaceful protests and the semi-legal activities of organisations such as Greenpeace through to the environmental terrorism of more extreme organisations.

(c) Partnership and consultancy: groups here aim to work with businesses to pool resources and to help them improve environmental performance.

Employees are increasing pressure on the businesses in which they work for a number of reasons – partly for their own safety and partly in order to improve the public image of the company. People do not like to work for companies with poor reputations.

Legislation is increasing almost by the day. Growing pressure from the green-influenced vote has led to mainstream political parties taking these issues into their programmes. Most countries now have laws to cover land-use planning, smoke emissions, water pollution and the destruction of animals and natural habitats.

As we have seen, part of this increased pressure is coming from the media. Large scale disasters and more technical, less dramatic issues such as global warming have become common themes for newspaper and television stories, and have generated very widespread public awareness of the issues concerned.

Central to green philosophy is the idea that businesses have moral and ethical responsibilities to society as a whole – not just their customers. It is assumed that in the long run, behaving responsibly will be in the best interests of the businesses concerned, enabling them to flourish in the long term.

4.5 Social responsibility and sustainability

Green marketing is founded on two main ideas: one is a response to and responsibility for the community. The other is sustainability – the idea that we must be aware of the need for resources to be marshalled and monitored so that the environment can continue to provide natural resources and absorb and recycle the waste products of human consumption.

Social responsibility is based on two ideas.

(a) **The moral and ethical responsibilities of businesses**

Businesses must exist within and depend upon a society. While businesses control many of the resources available to society, the majority of the population actually contribute to the production of wealth, and justice demands that they share in its benefits. On the other hand, society should not be asked to solve and pay for those problems which businesses cause, without help from those businesses, which have a moral obligation to assist in their solution. Businesses and business people are also socially prominent and must be seen to be taking a lead in addressing the problems of society.

There are three contrasting views about the responsibilities of the corporation.

(i) If the company creates a problem, it must fix it (eg Exxon)

(ii) The multinational corporation has the resources to fight poverty, illiteracy, malnutrition, illness etc. This approach disregards who actually creates the problems.

(iii) The third perspective says that companies already discharge their social responsibility simply by increasing their profits and thereby contributing more in taxes. If a company was expected to divert more resources to solve society's problems, this would represent a double tax.

(b) **The benefits to business of 'enlightened self-interest'**

In the long term, a business concern over the possible damage which may result from some of its activities will safeguard the interests of the business itself. In the short term, responsibility is good for the image of the company – it is a very valuable addition to the public relations activities of a business. In addition, as pressure for legislation grows, 'self regulation' can avoid potentially disadvantageous legal restrictions.

Definition

> Sustainability involves developing strategies so that the company only uses resources at a rate which allows them to be replenished in order to ensure that they will continue to be available, while at the same time emissions of waste are confined to levels which do not exceed the capacity of the environment to absorb them.

In relation to the development of the world's resources, policies based on sustainability seek the following.

- To pursue equity in the distribution of resources
- To maintain the integrity of the world's ecosystems
- To increase the capacity of human populations for self-reliance

EXAMPLE

Some business leaders have made a case for becoming ecologically and socially sustainable:

- 'Institutions that operate so as to capitalise all gain in the interests of the few, while socialising all loss to the detriment of the many, are ethically, socially and operationally unsound ... This must change.' Dee Hock, Founder, President and CEO Emeritus of Visa International, the credit card organisation.

- 'Far from being a soft issue grounded in emotion and ethics, sustainable development involves cold, rational business logic.' Robert B Shapiro, Chairman of Monsanto, the US multinational.

- 'The gap between rhetoric and reality is increasing. I would tell multinationals they have to watch out ... they are much more vulnerable because they have to be accountable to the public every day.' Thilo Bode, Executive Director of Greenpeace.

- Explaining his company's forays into renewable energy and enhanced support for the communities where it does business: 'These efforts have nothing to do with charity, and everything to do with our long-term self interests ... our shareholders want performance today, and tomorrow, and the day after.' Sir John Browne, CEO of British Petroleum/Amoco.

BPP PUBLISHING

Activity 8

Roy Brooks was an estate agent in Kensington who became famous in the 1950s and 60s for insanely honest property advertisements such as these.

'This DESIRABLE RESIDENCE has everything – dry rot, a settlement, filthy decor, running cold water – sometimes where it was intended ...'

'So-called garden with possibilities – best solved by saturation bombing'

'Back bedroom suitable only for dwarf or placid child'

'A fussy purchaser would presumably have the gaping hole in the top bedroom ceiling – open to the sky – repaired'

'The gdn looks horrible but so would you if you'd been neglected for 20 yrs'

More recently Gerald Ratner of Ratners Jewellers said in an after dinner speech that his company's earrings were cheaper than a prawn sandwich from Marks and Spencer and probably did not last as long.

Do you think it would be in the interests of manufacturers or customers to adopt this approach to marketing? Discuss this in class if possible, and design your own insanely honest advert for something that you have bought recently.

---

5 GREEN MARKETING

5.1 Four Ss

Getting marketing's four Ps (price, place, promotion and product) right leads to profit, according to orthodox ideas. Green marketing by contrast insists that the mix must be evaluated in terms of four Ss.

- Satisfaction of customer needs

- Safety of products and production for consumers, workers, society and the environment

- Social acceptability of a product, production and the other activities of the company

- Sustainability of the products, their production and the other activities of the company

A successful green marketer needs:

(a) To understand the consumer's wants and needs

(b) To understand the environmental issues which are relevant to the company, customer, products and market environment

(c) To evaluate the degree to which green product attributes fit consumer needs

(d) To match price to consumer demand

(e) To develop strategies which identify and effectively meet consumer needs and competitor challenges in relation to green issues

(f) To promote the flow of environmentally-related information on consumers and product/service performance throughout the company

---

Activity 9

You are the product manager of Anti-Zit, a facial cleanser. You receive a phone call claiming that an entire consignment of Anti-Zit, now in the shops, has been contaminated by animal welfare activists who believe – wrongly – that the product is tested on animals. Due to controls that are known to be operating effectively it is highly unlikely in reality that more than a few bottles have been tampered with.

The media have the story already. What practical action should you take and how should you deal with media questions?

5.2 Principles of green marketing

There is an apparent contradiction between the reduction in consumption which lies at the heart of the idea of green marketing, and the extra consumption which has been the primary aim of marketing as previously conceived. However, green marketing begins from the premise that marketing as such is not environmentally unfriendly. There is a view that products and services will necessarily become greener as consumers become more aware of the need to counter the effects of environmental degradation and to develop sustainable management strategies.

A number of barriers have to be overcome.

(a) Costs are likely to be incurred when developing new products and services.

(b) Technical and organisational barriers have to be overcome in developing, for instance, practical applications of green energy sources, and in reshaping organisations and their workforces into new ways of carrying out their work roles and promoting new attitudes to their jobs.

(c) At the moment, many of the problems which will need to be addressed are highly complex, and there seem to be conflicts between the various alternatives available. How do we choose between fuels which create acid rain and those which produce atomic waste? What about the human consequences of dismantling environmentally unfriendly industries in areas where there are no alternative sources of employment?

(d) Many of the policies pursued by a particular enterprise will have implications for the environment in countries beyond national boundaries.

(e) Changes which promote beneficial effects, for example on the ozone layer, may well have no visible effects and may be resisted as a consequence.

(f) The fact that problems are generally created, and have to be treated, over a relatively long time scale also creates difficulties in promoting policies and mobilising groups to implement them.

One of the main problems faced by those seeking to implement these green policies is the lack of certainty about the nature of the problem, about the effectiveness of the remedies proposed, and about the reactions of the publics towards which the policies are ultimately directed.

In some cases, companies have introduced supposedly environmentally-friendly policies and products simply as a means of paying a token allegiance to the idea, or to try to garner extra sales from the gullible. One possible consequence of this is moral fatigue: as with other issues in the past, the public may become disenchanted with the whole idea, or sceptical about claims to greenness which are made, in various ways, by almost every manufacturer or service provider.

5.3   A model of the green marketing process

The green marketing process requires the matching of those internal variables which the company can control with the 'green' strictures of the operating environment which the commercial decision-maker faces. Like conventional marketing, green marketing needs to deal with a blend of internal and external factors. Peattie (1992) describes these as internal and external 'green Ps' (that is, the green equivalent of the four Ps) to be used as a checklist to diagnose how well the company is succeeding in living up to targets for green performance.

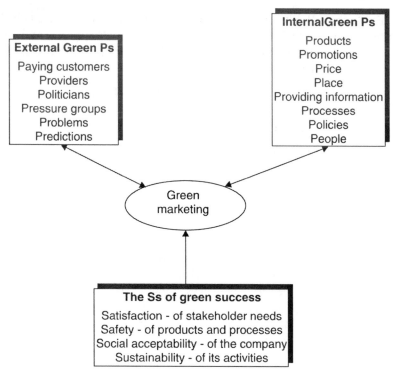

Figure 3.1 'The Green Marketing Process'

Analysing the process

Inside the company, marketers need to attend to the following 'internal green Ps'.

(a)   Products. A green audit needs to look at how safe products are in use, how safe they are when disposed, how long they last and what are the environmental consequences of materials used in manufacturing and packaging the product.

(b)   Promotion. Using green messages in promotion. Establishing standards of accuracy and reliability.

(c)   Price. Prices set for green products must reflect differences in demand; price sensitivity is also an important issue.

(d)   Place. How green are the methods by which distribution takes place?

(e)   Providing information. This needs to be related to internal and external issues bearing on environmental performance.

(f)   Processes. Energy consumed, waste produced.

(g) Policies. Do they motivate the work force? Are there policies to monitor and react to environmental performance?

(h) People. Do they understand environmental issues and how the company performs in relation to these issues?

Outside the company, a different set of factors needs to be addressed. These might be referred to as 'external green Ps'.

(a) Paying customers. What are their needs in relation to green products and services? What information are they receiving about green products?

(b) Providers. How green are suppliers of services and materials to the company?

(c) Politicians. Public awareness and concern over green issues is beginning to have a strong influence on the legislation which appears, and this directly affects the conduct of business. A modern organisation must make this part of its concerns.

(d) Pressure groups. What are the main issues of concern? Which groups are involved and what new issues are likely to concern them?

(e) Problems. Which environmental issues have been a problem for the company, or part of the area in which it works, in the past?

(f) Predictions. What environmental problems loom in the future? Awareness of scientific research can be strategically vital.

(g) Partners. How green are my allies? How are business partners perceived? Will this pose problems?

Resistance to green marketing within many companies is likely to remain strong. It may be necessary for marketers to internally market ideas for these changes. New products, new communications strategies and messages, new 'clean' plant and technology, new appointments of staff skilled in these areas, and very broad changes in organisational culture will all have to be 'sold' to powerful individuals and groups within organisations. The internal politics of business organisations need to be taken into account by green practitioners.

Green marketing needs to be incorporated in the present policies of the company and in the way in which it plans and acts far into the future. It is necessary to institutionalise the ideas and to change the culture of the company.

(a) Building a basis for understanding by setting up frameworks for disseminating information

(b) Formulating systematic plans for the implementation of green marketing

(c) Setting aside resources

(d) Requiring demonstrations of managerial commitment

(e) Encouraging participation and contributions throughout the company

(f) Sustaining an internal public relations programme which creates a healthy response to green ideas

> **Activity 10**
>
> Environmental matters are often in the news. Over (say) the next month, cut out items from (good) newspapers or make notes from any relevant TV or radio items or programmes which are concerned with environmental matters. Consider the implications for the marketing function of the business, government department etc concerned.

Concern for the quality of the environment has been matched by increasing concern with the quality of products and services themselves. The two are related in that good quality control reduces waste.

6 THE QUALITY MOVEMENT

6.1 Quality issues and marketing

The quality movement grew from the general alarm which spread throughout Europe and the US during the 1980s as previously successful manufacturing industries failed, while Japanese cars and electronic goods prospered. Japanese takeovers of failing western companies, and turnarounds based on the application of new managerial practices, underlined the urgency of understanding what this new approach involved, and how it could be applied here in the UK.

In the past, quality has been approached by looking at processes of manufacturing and reducing the variability and waste which such systems can produce by using control systems, and introducing methods of checking to assure quality and reliability. The aim is to remove faults and substandard work.

More recently, approaches to quality developed in Scandinavia and the USA have emphasised the importance of marketing, particularly for the service industries. This approach insists that quality should only be seen from the perspective of the customer, since the customer is the only judge of what is to count as quality. In keeping with the most recent writing on quality systems in general, this services-marketing perspective is entirely appropriate for manufactured goods companies, breaking the inertia of a production-based philosophy.

The principles of Total Quality Management are an amalgam of the ideas of three main thinkers: W Edwards Deming, Joseph M Juran and Philip B Crosby. Each has their own version of how quality can be achieved.

6.2 Deming

Definition

> The foundation of the Deming system is the improvement of products and services by reducing uncertainty and variability in the design and manufacturing processes through an unceasing cycle of product design, manufacture, test and sales, followed by market surveys to gain feedback, after which the cycle begins again with re-design.

Deming saw variability as the chief cause of poor quality, with failure to adhere to the original specifications in manufacturing producing product failure, and inconsistent service frustrating customers and damaging the firm's reputation.

According to Deming, higher quality leads to higher productivity which in turn produces long term competitive strength. The Deming Chain Reaction says that fewer mistakes mean lower costs and higher productivity, because work does not have to be redone. This has obvious implications for the success of a company.

The Deming Chain Reaction

Improve quality

↓

Decrease costs

↓

Improve productivity

↓

Increase market share

↓

Stay in business

↓

Provide more goods and more jobs

Deming produced an accessible methodology which incorporated ideas in the famous table of 14 Points for Management. These embody what he saw as the principles which lead to quality.

Deming's 14 Points for Management

1   Create and publish to all employees a statement of the aims and purposes of the company or other organisation. The management must constantly demonstrate their commitment to this statement.

2   Learn the new philosophy.

3   Understand the purpose of inspection.

4   End the practice of awarding business on the basis of price tag alone.

5   Improve constantly and forever the system of production and service.

6   Institute training.

7   Teach and institute leadership.

8   Drive out fear, create trust. Create a climate for innovation.

9   Optimise toward the aims and purposes of the company the efforts of teams, groups, staff areas.

10   Eliminate exhortations for the workforce.

11   (a)   Eliminate numerical quotes for production. Instead, learn and institute methods for improvement.

      (b)   Eliminate MBO (management by objectives). Instead, learn the capabilities of processes and how to improve them.

12   Remove barriers that rob people of pride and workmanship.

13   Encourage education and self improvement for everyone.

14   Take action to accomplish the transformation.

Deming's work remains controversial, since it calls for fundamental and sweeping changes in organisational culture and attacks some of the traditional shibboleths of management, such as MBO. It has, however, been highly influential.

EXAMPLE: FORD'S GUIDING PRINCIPLES

- Quality comes first. To achieve customer satisfaction, the quality of our products and services must be our number one priority.

- Customers are the focus of everything we do. Our work must be done with customers in mind, providing better products and services than our competition.

- Continuous improvement is essential to our success. We must strive for excellence in everything we do; in our products, in their safety and value; and in our services, our human relations, our competitiveness and our profitability.

- Employee involvement is our way of life. We are a team. We must treat each other with trust and respect.

- Dealers and suppliers are our partners. The company must maintain mutually beneficial relationships with dealers, suppliers and our other business associates.

- Integrity must never be compromised. The conduct of our company world-wide must be pursued in a manner that is socially responsible and commands respect for its integrity and for its positive contributions to society. Our doors are open to men and women alike without discrimination and without regard to ethnic origin or personal beliefs.

Activity 11

As a way of gaining familiarity with the issues under discussion try to match up Ford's principles with Deming's Points.

6.3 Juran

Juran believes, with Deming, that lack of quality leads to competitive failure and huge costs and that the only remedy for this is new thinking about quality which includes all levels of the management structure. The top level, he affirms, is particularly in need of training on the importance of management for quality.

While Deming proposes fundamental cultural changes which strike at the very core of every organisation, Juran aims to fit his quality program into a company's current strategic planning with the minimum risk of rejection. Employees, he states, speak different languages in the different levels of an organisation and this must be taken into account. While top managers speak the language of dollars, workers speak the language of things, and middle managers must be able to speak to both and mediate between them.

NOTES

Definition

> Juran defines quality as 'fitness for use'.

There are four components to quality, according to Juran.

(a) Quality of design: focusing on market research, the product concept and design specifications.

(b) Quality of conformance: technology, manpower and management.

(c) Availability: reliability, maintainability and logistical support.

(d) Field service: promptness, competence and integrity.

Activity 12

The boss of Acme Umbrellas Ltd believes that customers want robust umbrellas, so he makes one entirely out of aluminium apart from some gold decoration. 'It is a bit heavy, I suppose', he says, showing an example. 'But it's perfectly made, look at the gold pins and look at the flawless finish. Why don't people want it?'

6.4 Crosby

P H Crosby describes his system in two sets of principles, the 'absolutes of quality management' and the 'basic elements of improvement'.

Absolutes of quality management

(a) Quality means conformance to requirements, not elegance

Crosby insists that quality is a series of requirements which must be clearly stated. It can then be communicated and measured to see if it has been achieved. These measurements will establish the presence or absence of quality. Absence of quality is a nonconformance problem or an output problem. How requirements are set is a managerial issue.

(b) There is no such thing as a quality problem

Problems arise in specific departments and must be identified by those departments. Both quality and problems are created in specific departments and are not the province of a specific 'quality' department within the organisation.

(c) There is no such thing as the economics of quality; it is always cheaper to do the job right first time

Quality is free. Nonconformance costs money.

(d) The only performance measurement is the cost of quality

The cost of quality is the expense of nonconformance. While most companies spend almost 20% of their revenue on quality costs, a well run quality management programme can reduce this to less than 3%. A major

PUBLISHING

part of the programme involves measuring and publicising the costs of poor quality, to focus managerial attention on this problem.

(e)   The only performance standard is zero defects

Zero defects is a performance standard, with the theme 'do it right the first time'. This means concentrating on the prevention of defects rather than finding and fixing them.

'Basic elements of improvement', the other aspect of his system, includes three themes.

(a)   Determination, or the commitment of management to this process

(b)   Education, which involves transmitting the absolute standards to the members of the organisation

(c)   Implementation, which should clearly specify how quality is to be established within the organisation

This has proved a popular approach because it emphasises behaviour processes within organisations. At the same time, it does not stipulate what a programme will involve in fine detail. As a consequence, it can be fitted alongside existing corporate strategies and tailored to the enterprise involved.

Systems within the business to achieve and maintain high quality standards are only half the story. Marketing is concerned with relating quality to customer satisfaction.

7   QUALITY AND CUSTOMERS

7.1   Total Quality Management: the marketing implications

As the discussion of the main quality gurus demonstrates, such agreement as exists on the definition of what quality involves refers to customer needs.

Definition

To deliver quality is to identify and produce what customers need.

There is, recognisably, a close connection with the core of the marketing concept: to identify and meet customer needs at a profit.

7.2   Total quality and total customer orientation

A customer orientation, seeking to satisfy the customer, is pursued in marketing by recognising that customers buy 'the sizzle, not the steak' – products are bought for the benefits they deliver; how customers can use the product to accomplish the things they want to do.

Feigenbaum (1983) identifies Total Quality Management (TQM) directly with the customer.

Definition

> TQM is defined as the total composite product and service characteristics of marketing, engineering, manufacture and maintenance, through which the product and service in use will meet the expectations by the customer.

What constitutes a 'quality product or service' must, it seems, be related to what the customer wants. Indeed, quality would have no commercial value unless it delivered customer benefit, since the key reason for aiming to produce quality products is to derive extra sales by establishing competitive advantage through tangible and generally perceived superiority in particular product or service features. All the gurus would agree that the customer must be the final arbiter of the quality which a product possesses.

Activity 13

In class, pick three or four different products. Each member of the class should write a list of five features that they would want to find in a high quality version of each product. Then compare your lists.

From a marketing point of view, then, quality is in the eye of the consumer. If quality is meeting the requirements of the consumer, then it should be recognised that throughout and beyond all enterprises, whatever business they are in, is a series of 'quality chains'.

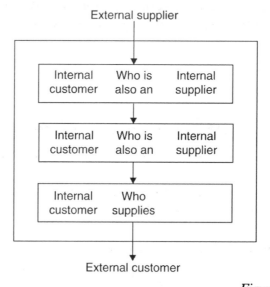

Figure 3.2 The quality chain

John Oakland (1989) argues that meeting customer requirements is the main focus in a search for quality. While these requirements would typically include aspects such as availability, delivery, reliability, maintainability and cost effectiveness, in fact the first priority is to establish what customer requirements actually are. If the customer is outside the organisation, then the supplier must seek to set up market research to gather this information and to relate the output of their organisation to the needs of the customer.

Internal customers for services are equally important, but their requirements are seldom investigated. The quality implementation process requires that all the supplier/customer relationships within the 'quality chain' should be treated as marketing exercises, and that each customer should be carefully consulted as to their precise requirements from the product or service with which they are to be provided. Each link in the chain should prompt the following questions, according to Oakland.

Of customers

- Who are my immediate customers?
- What are their true requirements?
- How can I find out what the requirements are?
- How can I measure my ability to meet the requirements?
- Do I have the necessary capability to meet the requirements?
  (If not, then what must change to improve the capability?)
- Do I continually meet the requirements?
  (If not, then what prevents this from happening, when the capability exists?)
- How do I monitor changes in the requirements?

Of suppliers

- Who are my immediate suppliers?
- What are my true requirements?
- How do I communicate my requirements?
- Do my suppliers have the capability to measure and meet the requirements?
- How do I inform them of changes in the requirements?

It should be noted that this focus on the customer does pose a number of problems.

(a) **Quality is subjective**

   (i) If quality is relative to customer expectations, it cannot be measured in an absolute sense.

   (ii) Different customers will want, need or expect different things from the same product-type.

(b) **Quality is distinctive**

Product differentiation and highly segmented modern markets mean that the precise requirements of a particular market segment will produce an equally precise and differentiated definition of quality.

(c) **Quality is dynamic**

Expectations, and therefore definitions of quality, are highly dynamic: they change over time as a consequence of experience. A ratchet effect is highly likely, so that expectations will rise relatively easily, but will rarely and very reluctantly fall.

If quality is the outcome, marketing research techniques are very clearly the main instruments through which this problem can be solved. A widely used technique is gap analysis.

7.3 Quality and gap analysis

Parasuranam et al (1985) have applied 'gap analysis', developed within the services marketing field, to the realisation of quality in manufacturing and product marketing.

Definition

> Gap analysis involves focusing on the potential gaps between identification, interpretation, specification, delivery and reaction to services. Customer satisfaction – satisfying the customer's needs in the delivery of a quality product or service – occurs when these are matched, and the gaps are minimised. Dissatisfaction (a poor quality product or service) occurs when these gaps are broad.

Parasuranam and his colleagues concluded that a key differentiating feature of service quality is that it is judged by the consumer not simply on the outcome of the service (what the service is intended to deliver) but also on the way in which the service is delivered.

7.4 Quality gaps

Gap analysis proposes that customer perceptions of the quality of a product or service are determined by the degree to which they believe it meets their expectations. These expectations are created from a variety of inputs. These would include physical aspects, service elements and other cues available.

Gap analysis sets out to measure levels of satisfaction, or dissatisfaction, to identify the source of dissatisfaction when it occurs and to eliminate it. The central issue is how customer expectations develop; what are the sources of unrealistic or inappropriate requirements?

What expectations are raised partly depend on the way in which the organisation treats the customer. A company which is product-orientated starts with its own beliefs about what the customer expects and creates a specification to guide the production or creation process. The product or service which is delivered in this case reflects the company's perceptions of quality, rather than the customer's.

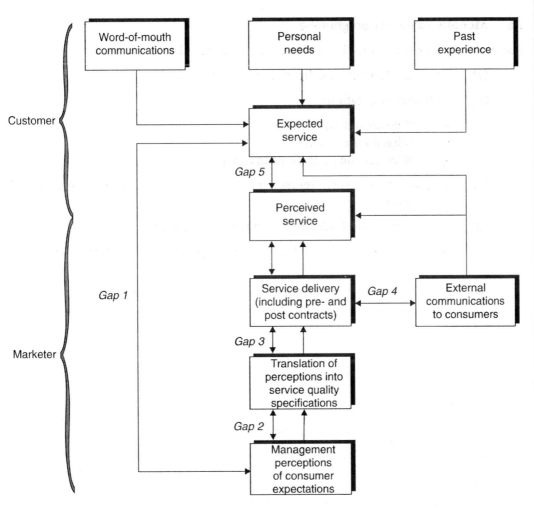

Figure 3.3 Quality gaps in the service system

(Adapted from: Zeithaml, Parasuraman, Berry,
Delivering Quality Service, 1990)

The major factors which determine customer expectations and perceptions with regard to service quality are as follows.

- Word of mouth communications
- Personal needs
- Past experience

The 'gaps' which can cause dissatisfaction are between:

- Customer expectations and marketers' perceptions
- Marketers' perceptions and (service or product) quality specifications
- Quality specifications and delivery
- Delivery and external communications
- Perceived service/product and expected service/product

A marketing orientation to a quality programme starts from the identification of what the customer expects. This is quite likely to be varied and the key to using this idea is to gather marketing intelligence using appropriate methods and to make this information available, in an appropriate and usable form, to managers within the organisation.

Once customers' requirements have been researched and understood, the information obtained needs to be applied within the business.

NOTES

7.5 Mounting a quality programme

Successful programmes typically involve a number of key characteristics.

(a) Total involvement: a culture change is involved.

(b) Customer orientation:

- Who are our customers?
- What do they want?
- What are the obligations involved?

(c) Quantified processes: measurement is critical to monitor progress and improvement.

(d) Commitment and leadership from top management.

(e) Strong process control (for example, systems being implemented and strictly observed).

(f) External customer objectives are given the highest priority.

Activity 14

You have just overheard the following conversation. The Board of a company are in a meeting and they are having a 'full and frank exchange of views' (that is, a blazing row).

Chairman: Ladies and gentlemen, please....

Marketing director: No, he's said quite enough. Customers are our department, and all this TQM nonsense is just another, yes another example of those jargon-spouting boffins and bodgers in production trying to encroach on my turf! I do need resources. I don't need white-coated robots criticising the angles at which I fix the paper clips on to my reports!

Chairman: Ladies and gentlemen, please....

Production director: No, she's said quite enough. Marketing people couldn't give one hoot, let alone two, about quality and we all know it's quality that sells the goods. Remember, when we had to abandon our solar powered torch? State of the art, state of the art that was, and did they try and sell it? Did they?

Chairman: Ladies and gentlemen, please.....'

Finance director: 'No, they've both said quite enough. If all we get out of TQM is pointless rows like this, I might as well go back and count some more beans. At least it's meaningful and relaxing.

Chairman: Ladies and gentlemen! No, you've all said quite enough. I don't think any of you have grasped the point. I'd better get another management consultant in with a better flipchart.

What insights do each of the above characters have into TQM?

Chapter roundup

- Environmental issues have become more important over the last 10-20 years, with the emergence of the green movement and green economics. Environmental issues will have a direct and indirect impact on both marketing practices and on businesses in a more general sense.

- Environmental protection is now a key strategic issue and businesses need to set up environmental management systems.

- Green marketing practices must overcome a variety of barriers. A new 'green' orientation is required in obtaining marketing information, in marketing planning and in creating a green marketing process.

- The heart of quality programmes is the need to define, research and respond to customer need. This is the marketing orientation at work. Quality programmes complement this core element with the formulation of systems which ensure sustained and consistent delivery of the desired processes and products. Further, their insistence on commitment from all parts of the organisation, on monitoring and measurement to check that the systems are working, and the requirement that the very top management should provide leadership on these issues, aims to take this consumer-driven approach to the very heart of management philosophy.

Quick quiz

1 What environmental issues will impact upon marketing practices?
2 Define 'sustainability'.
3 What are the 'four Ss' of the green marketing mix?
4 Draw a model of the green marketing process.
5 List Deming's 14 Points for Management.
6 Explain the components of Juran's definition of quality.
7 Define total quality management.
8 What quality gaps cause dissatisfaction?

Answers to activities

1 Electronic personal organisers are much more expensive than most ring-bound organisers, and some people do not like using very small keyboards.
2 You will reach your own conclusions from your discussion.
3 Your name might have come from a list sold by another business you have had dealings with, from a membership list of an organisation you belong to, even from a telephone directory. The senders probably know something about you, if only the type of area you live in.
4 Your answer will depend on the company you have chosen. For example, a retailer might now user EFTPOS (Electronic Funds Transfer at Point of Sale); a firm might use the Internet for promotional purposes.
5 Just how strong the position of buyers will be depends on a number of factors.

(a) Whether the buyer's purchases represent a substantial proportion of total sales by the producer. If they do, the buyer will be in a strong position relative to the seller.

(b) Whether the buyer's purchases from the industry represent a large or a small proportion of the buyer's total purchases. If most of a buyer's supplies come from a single industry, the buyer will be in a weaker bargaining position than if only a small proportion did so.

(c) Whether switching costs are high or low. (Switching costs are a barrier to entry.)

(d) Whether the products supplied by the industry are standard items and undifferentiated. Suppliers may try to increase their bargaining power over buyers by creating a strong brand image. Thus, a supermarket chain may feel obliged to stock leading brands of a product because its own customers might expect to find these brands in any supermarket.

(e) Whether the buyers make low profits. A buyer who makes low profits will be forced to insist on low prices from suppliers.

(f) The threat that buyers might take over sources of supply, if suppliers charge too much.

(g) The skills of the buyer's purchasing staff, or the price-awareness of consumers.

(h) The importance of product quality. When product quality is important to the buyer, the buyer is less likely to be price-sensitive, and so the industry might be more profitable as a consequence. For example, although the Ministry of Defence may wish to keep control over defence spending, it is likely as a buyer to be more concerned that the products it purchases perform satisfactorily than with getting the lowest price possible for everything it buys. As a consequence, profitability in the defence industry is likely to be high.

6 You should refer back to chapter 1 if necessary to help you consider all aspects of the four Ps. You might also consider how PEST factors will affect the situation.

7 You should have little trouble finding examples because every aspect of a product is affected by environmental issues – how it is made, what is made of, how it gets to the customer, what it is used for, what is the effect of its use, and how it is disposed of. 'Green' issues have affected the product itself ('ozone-friendly', 'dolphin-friendly'), its packaging (recyclable), its price (organically-produced vegetables are more expensive, for example), and its promotion (Anchor Butter promotes its product using images of happy cows in lush pastures).

8 You might have made the points that Ratners' trading worsened following Mr Ratner's unguarded comments (though it was already in difficulties); that consumers want to believe that the purchase decisions that they make are good ones; but that it is undoubtedly in the interests of consumers that advertising should be honest; that to be 'honest' about a product might genuinely be to sing its praises if it is a really good one. There are many other points to make.

9 Hushing it all up and doing as little as possible is definitely not the answer in any crisis, as many organisations have found to their cost. Be

completely open and give out as much information as possible to reassure the public that they are not at risk.

Briefly, the extent of the contamination, if any, should be ascertained. If it is not possible to demonstrate beyond doubt that the bulk of the consignment is uncontaminated (if tamper-proof bottles are not used, for instance) it should be entirely withdrawn from the shops and consumers should be asked to return bottles that have been sold already. The media and perhaps the public should be invited to inspect the company's testing facilities and, if security allows, the control procedures that are in place should be demonstrated. As long as the product and the company's practices are spotlessly clean the threat can be turned into an opportunity.

12   The design quality is poor, in that it does not meet customer requirements in an appropriate way. The umbrella is, however, perfectly made, so its conformance quality is high.

14   The chairman has got the gist. They all miss the point as to the nature of TQM. The marketing director has a point in that TQM does imply a blurring of functional boundaries, but the marketing director ought to be pleased that, if TQM is implemented, the marketing concept will be brought into product design. The production director still has not grasped the concept. His idea of quality is 'technical excellence' not fitness for use. The finance director ought to care, as TQM has meaningful cost implications. The row is not pointless: at least the issue is being discussed, which is a beginning.

Further question practice

Now try the following practice questions at the end of this text.

Multiple Choice Questions: 15–20

Exam Style Question: 3

Chapter 4 :
BUYER BEHAVIOUR

Introduction

The study of human behaviour is a huge subject and we shall only be scratching the surface of it in this chapter. Nevertheless basic knowledge about what makes people behave in the way they do is clearly essential if the marketer is to understand and satisfy the customer's needs. We shall be looking mainly at motivational, cultural and sociological influences and we shall consider a model of consumer buying behaviour.

You should also appreciate that there are certain differences between the behaviour of an individual who decides to buy, say, a new car, and the behaviour of an organisation that decides to buy a new car. Again we shall consider the influences that operate in this situation and consider some models of organisational buying behaviour.

Finally, markets are increasingly global markets. National and cultural differences may make it impossible to sell your product in the same way to all the different people you want to reach. We shall consider to what extent marketing can be standardised across the world and look at some of the factors like taboos, symbolism and language that need to be taken into account.

Your objectives

In this chapter you will learn about the following.

    (a)   The influences that shape a consumer's behaviour, and their importance to achieving marketing objectives

    (b)   The particular features influencing organisational buyers

    (c)   The importance of national differences and similarities

1 INFLUENCES ON CUSTOMER BEHAVIOUR

It is important that each customer who deals with an organisation is left with a feeling of satisfaction. This outcome is important since it can lead to increased purchases and/or to a willingness to pay higher prices and thus to higher profits. If customers are satisfied they may:

- Buy again from the same supplier
- Buy more of the same item or of more expensive items
- Advise their friends to buy from the supplier

Making a purchase necessarily involves taking a risk. Everyone likes to get value for money, but the risk in buying a new product or buying from a new supplier increases the risk of dissatisfaction. It is important that the supplier helps to reduce this risk for new customers so that they are more likely to become regular customers.

Customer loyalty is important for several reasons.

(a) It means that customers will support the supplier when times are hard, making it difficult for competitors to attract them away from their favoured supplier.

(b) Regular customers provide regular and reliable income and turnover.

(c) It is possible to build rapport with customers over time which helps the supplier understand their needs more easily, thus making the sales process more straightforward.

(d) Customer loyalty is a source of goodwill and will enhance the supplier organisation's image. It can be a source of very potent advertising in that loyal customers may recommend the supplier to their friends or colleagues.

Customer dissatisfaction is the reverse of customer loyalty in the sense that it may dissipate established goodwill and can adversely affect the company image. The added complication is that bad news travels faster than good news. It is easier by far for new customers to be put off by a negative recommendation than for a company to attract new customers with positive recommendations. Understanding customer behaviour can be a major help in effective marketing management. However, there are many influences on customer behaviour and so the outcome in terms of purchasing decisions can be very difficult to understand from a rational viewpoint. Emotional and rational influences intertwine and lead to purchases which can seem illogical even to the buyer. We are all purchasers, and even organisational buying is conducted by individuals who have their own preferences and preconceptions which still affect them in the work environment.

We will now consider influences on customer purchasing decisions, namely needs, motives, culture, socio-economic groups, family and other reference groups.

1.1 Needs

There are many classifications of need. The simplest is to split needs into two main types.

(a) Physiological needs concern physical well-being and include needs for food, drink, warmth, sex and sleep.

(b) Psychological needs concern emotional or mental well-being and include needs for belonging (to groups), acceptance (by those regarded as important) and affection (of others).

We are born with these needs. In addition, we learn other psychological needs as we grow in society. These are secondary or learned needs and include the following.

- Appreciation (by others)
- Respect (by others regarded as important)
- Recognition (of accomplishments)
- Achievement

> **Activity 1**
>
> What has all this got to do with marketing? According to economists, purchasers (a) behave rationally, and (b) spend money in order to maximise utility. Try to think of examples where this economic approach appears inadequate to explain a purchasing decision.

1.2 Motives

Definition

> Motives sit between needs and action. A need motivates a person to take action.

Motives are derived from needs. The differences between needs and motives are as follows.

(a) Motives activate behaviour. Being thirsty (need) causes (motivates) us to buy a drink (action). If the need is sufficiently intense, we are motivated to act.

(b) Motives are directional. Needs are general but motives specify behavioural action. A need to belong may lead to a motivation to join a badminton club.

(c) Motives serve to reduce tension. Essentially people aim to be in an equilibrium state. This aim is known as the concept of homeostasis. If we are too cold, we are motivated to reduce the tension in our bodies that this causes by seeking a source of warmth. If we are not accepted by those we regard as important, we aim to reduce the tension this causes by seeking to change our behaviour so as to gain acceptance by those we value. This tension is also known as dissonance. When it exists, we aim to reduce it.

Definition

> Dissonance is the tension that exists when there is a perceived gap between a person's current situation and the situation they would prefer to be in.

For example, dissonance may arise when an item is purchased which does not give satisfaction. The buyer may feel that he has not 'done the right thing'. This tension has to be reduced. The buyer may convince himself that he has bought the right thing by rereading the sales brochure or revisiting the sales people who sold it to him.

Alternatively, he may get rid of the item and reduce the tension in this way. Importantly, what remains is likely to be a negative image of the supplier.

Activity 2

Have you ever bought something on impulse or been talked into buying something that you were not quite convinced that you needed? Try to remember how you reconciled yourself to the purchase.

1.3 Culture

Motives arise from needs and can lead to purchasing actions. However, motives do not tell us how consumers choose from the options available to satisfy needs. Other influences are clearly at work.

Culture represents a group's common interests. It is about values and characteristic ways of living in a society. Culture varies widely and has many influences as shown in the following lists.

The impact of culture

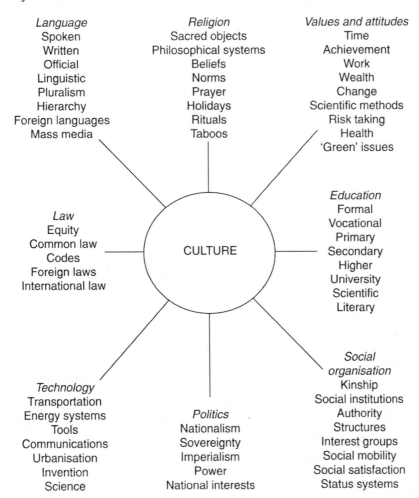

Fig 4.1 Influences of culture

Culture varies between countries but also within countries (subculture). Not only do we have restaurants in the UK offering ethnic food (such as Chinese or Indian) but within the UK there are certain (although declining) regional differences in the food we eat – lava bread in Wales, lardy cake in the West and potato bread in Northern Ireland being examples.

Language differences raise obvious marketing implications when brand names have to be translated, often leading to entirely different (and sometimes embarrassing) meanings in the new language.

Cultural differences raise many purchasing issues influencing every facet of life.

- What is bought (style, colours, types of goods/service)?
- When are things bought (for example, is Sunday shopping approved of)?
- How are things bought (bartering, haggling about price)?
- Where are things bought (type of retail outlet)?
- Why are things bought (influence of culture on needs and hence motives)?

1.4 Socio-economic groups

Marketing interest in socio-economic groups stems from the observable fact that members of specific groups have similar lifestyles, beliefs and values which can and do affect their purchasing behaviour.

Socio-economic classification is very commonly used in marketing and market research in the UK, despite its somewhat simplistic basis. More sophisticated measures of socio-economic group membership have been devised. An example is the ACORN system (A Classification of Residential Neighbourhoods).

Further, more sophisticated classifications based on socio-economic groups have been developed which add the person's activities, interests and opinions to the analysis. These analyses (known as psychographics) enable the identification of specific clusters of individuals who share similar activities, interests and opinions and hence, by association, purchasing behaviour. The 'He Man' cluster of young, aggressive, sporting men is one psychographic group. This group is a target group for lager advertising and sportswear, for example.

1.5 Family

Family background is a very strong influence on purchasing behaviour. It is in family groups that we learn how to be members of society and how to behave in different settings. Having learnt, it is difficult to forget. Family influences remain strong through the rest of our lives.

In the UK family structure is changing. There are more single person and single parent households as the divorce rate has increased and as the population ages. There are now more single person households of young unmarried people than of older widows/widowers. The traditional nuclear family of husband, wife and two children beloved of TV advertisements actually represents a small proportion of all families.

The family is important in purchasing behaviour because it is often a 'purchasing unit' with one member (the buyer) buying on behalf of all members (users) but others in the family influencing the decision (influencers). Joint husband and wife purchasing decisions for major items are common.

Activity 3

These terms are taken from Kotler's identification of the following participants in the buying process.

(a) The initiator – who suggests the idea.
(b) The influencer(s) – anyone with a say in the decision.
(c) The decider – who finally takes the decision.
(d) The buyer – who actually makes the purchase.
(e) The user – who consumes the product.

Suppose your own family (or any other family if you prefer) was considering the purchase of a family saloon from a motor dealer. Identify the people who would fill the Kotler roles above.

1.6 Other reference groups

The family is a reference group in that in marketing decisions it is used as a reference point. Socio-economic groups are also reference groups in this sense. The immortal phrase 'keeping up with the Jones's' is a useful reminder of a further point: that other groups to which a person belongs or aspires to can be strong influences on purchasing and other behaviour. Examples abound. Yacht clubs are synonymous with a particular style of dress (club blazer, for example) whereas working men's clubs conjure up different but no less potent images (such as the cloth cap). Different marketing approaches by suppliers are necessary for each type of reference group.

1.7 Other influences on customer behaviour

There are other influences on customer behaviour in relation to suppliers.

(a) **Economic influences**

- Income
- Occupation
- Career prospects
- House type

(b) **Social influences**

- Family
- Socio-economic group
- Culture
- Reference groups
- Education

(c) **Psychological influences**

- Needs
- Motivation
- Personality
- Attitudes

(d) **For organisational buyers: organisational influences**

- Company needs
- Inter-departmental rivalries
- Performance
- Buying committee/purchasing officer.

To get a better idea of how these factors can influence purchasing behaviour, we will continue by considering the major steps in the purchasing process.

1.8 How do people buy?

People buy not because they want the product/service in itself but because they want to solve problems they have. These problems to be solved are rooted in the lifestyle of the buyer and are influenced by the factors we have discussed in this chapter.

There is an identifiable buying process which consumers follow through, either consciously and logically or, more often, unconsciously and intuitively. This can be summarised as a model with the following steps.

- Problem recognition
- Information search
- Evaluation of alternatives
- Purchase decision
- Post-purchase evaluation

The first stage in the process is **problem recognition**. The buyer must recognise a need and be motivated to solve it. A difference exists between the customer's desired state and his or her actual state, and this difference (dissonance) is sufficiently large to persuade the customer to act in order to solve the problem. The recognition, by the customer, of a problem (a need for a particular type of product or service) will be affected by the individual's personal characteristics, social position and relationships, economic circumstances and psychological make up.

The second stage involves an **information search** which can be used in the decision making process in order to solve an identified problem. Many sources of information exist and typically the more complex the problem, the more information will be sought. Sources of information include the following.

(a) Memory: if the purchase to be made is of a type which has been made before, then past experience is a potent influence.

(b) Family: reference may be made to past purchasing behaviour by the family unit. A child who has left home, for example, may buy the brands familiar from home.

(c) Friends: especially if a friend is a 'significant other', someone whose view on a particular type of product is respected (for example, a car enthusiast or a hi-fi buff may be approached because their views on car or hi-fi purchases are valued and seen as independent, and hence highly potent in influencing behaviour). Pharmacists are often asked to recommend patent medicines by mothers, a fact recognised by suppliers who try to convince pharmacists to recommend their brand.

(d) Sales brochures

(e) Visits to sales outlets

(f) Watching/listening to/reading advertising messages

(g) Consumer advice sources, such as Which? magazine

The process of collecting information regarding the possible purchases which could be made in order to generate a solution to a particular problem may be internal, based on past experience of a product/service, or may simply take the form of brand loyalty. Equally, though, the customer may undertake external searches, collecting information from manufacturers, distributors, other users, consumers' associations and so on.

Purchasers are at their most receptive to advertising messages at this stage. How to recognise and influence purchasers who are at this stage is an important decision, and making sure persuasive information is available is a key task.

The third stage is to identify alternative solutions and to **evaluate each option**. This process may be as quick and simple as looking at competing brands on a supermarket shelf or it may take months if the purchase is important and the criteria are complicated (such as buying a car). Based on the evaluation of alternatives, the consumer will make a choice to buy, selecting that product which has the most satisfactory performance in relation to the evaluative criteria.

How the options are evaluated will involve both rational and emotional considerations. For example, a car can be evaluated on rational criteria such as price, economy, range of extras and performance but also on emotional criteria such as style, colour, image and personality.

The prime task for suppliers is to get their product on to the customer's shortlist of options.

The fourth stage is the **purchase decision**. The customer will see this decision as finding a solution to the problem he or she has identified. It is important that suppliers also take this view and thus express all communications to customers in terms with which the customer can identify.

Based on the evaluation of alternatives, the customer will make a choice to buy, selecting that product which seems to have the most satisfactory performance in relation to the evaluative criteria. In the absence of sudden or unexpected changes in the customer's circumstances or in the market place, the purchase decision will lead to actual purchase. It is of course possible that the decision will be not to buy or to postpone purchase until a later date.

The process does not end with the purchase decision. Buyers **reappraise** their decision.

Activity 4

Why is this post-purchase reappraisal important for marketers, given that the sale has already been achieved?

1.9 The perception of quality

People evaluate products on the basis of certain informational 'cues' or indicators. Some of these cues are characteristics of the products themselves (intrinsic cues), but some (extrinsic cues) are external factors associated with the product – price, brand name, promotion, display etc. A combination of these cues goes into the perception of a product's quality or value.

Intrinsic cues include the size, colour, smell, taste, feel and functional effectiveness of the product itself. Consumers tend to believe that their evaluations of product quality are based on these objective, physical cues. Indeed, they tend to want to believe it, because the buying decision is more readily justifiable on such a basis. However, the physical characteristics chosen as an indicator of quality may actually have little direct relevance.

(a) People claim to prefer the taste of certain brands (of cola-flavoured drink, or margarine, say) to that of others – yet blind tastings show that this discernment is not reliable.

Business Basics: Marketing

(b)   People associate the attributes of quality with irrelevant intrinsic cues – like the colour of biscuits or toothpaste, or the feel of the packaging.

Activity 5

You will certainly have read of the efforts manufacturers take to ensure that the 'intrinsic cues' give the right message. Can you think of examples?

Extrinsic cues are brought to bear on quality evaluations, especially if the consumer has no direct experience of the product.

Price is a particularly interesting extrinsic cue. People perceive price to be related to quality, and it has even been shown that consumers may evaluate differently identical products with different price tags! In the absence of other more influential cues such as brand or shop image, price acts as a surrogate indicator of quality: there is a positive price/quality perception. Some products are therefore priced deliberately highly to position them as 'premium' or 'quality' brands: consumers may be suspicious of brands that are 'cheap'.

(a)   Stella Artois beer has been marketed as 'reassuringly expensive'.

(b)   Various brands (of beer, coffee, dishwashing liquid) have been positioned as 'costing a bit more', but 'worth the difference' because of their superior quality.

(c)   However, given experience with a product, or familiarity with a brand name, price is a less important indicator of quality, and highly-priced brands which do not bear out expectations of quality difference can be negatively perceived: 'I'm not paying more for Brand X – it doesn't taste any different to this cheaper/own brand one!'

1.10   Perceived risk

Definition

Perceived risk is the uncertainty that consumers face when they cannot foresee the consequences of their purchase decisions.

Any purchase decision involves some risk, and to the extent that risk is perceived by the consumer, it will influence his or her decision.

Perceived risks are of four kinds.

(a)   **Functional** – will the product do what 'they' say it will, and what I want it to do? Is there a better one?

(b)   **Financial** – will it be worth its cost? Am I getting a good deal on it? Ought I to spend this money?

(c)   **Physical** – is it difficult or dangerous to use, or environmentally unfriendly?

(d)   **Social/psychological** – will the family/friends/Jones's approve of it? Will I be embarrassed if it fails, or is the 'wrong' one? Will I feel good about it?

PUBLISHING

The extent to which an individual perceives any of these risks to be present depends on a number of factors.

(a) Personality and past experience: some people are high-risk perceivers, risk-averse and wanting to 'play safe', while others are low-risk perceivers, preferring to 'live dangerously' in the choices they make. People learn about risk from experience: 'once bitten, twice shy'.

(b) The product: buying a car or a fitted kitchen is more high-risk than, say, buying a book or a set of cookware.

(c) The situation: ordering by mail or telephone is riskier than buying something in a shop. Choosing something in your own time is perceived as less risky than having to make up your mind in front of a door-to-door salesman.

(d) Culture: some cultures are more risk-sensitive than others, because of attitudes to money, status, the environment or whatever. Marketers cannot take for granted the effectiveness of their risk-reduction strategies in one country, if they want to apply them to another.

Consumers handle risk in various ways, according to the type and degree of risk they perceive. Typical strategies – which marketers may support with their own efforts – include the following.

(a) Gathering more information from product users and other trusted people. Marketers can help this process by encouraging word-of-mouth reports (or simulating them in a promotional message: 'I always buy...', 'I wouldn't swap my ... for anything else'). Endorsements and consumer reports are perceived as 'unbiased' sources of reassuring information, but advertisements and sales force presentations may also be directed at overcoming specific doubts.

(b) Loyalty to a tried and trusted brand, avoiding the risky situation of trying something new and unknown. This is most common for products like shampoos and detergents.

(c) Trust in a well-known, established and/or 'best selling' brand name/image. Such a brand has been positioned as dependable, high-quality or whatever, and appears as a 'safer bet': 'x is well-known for its quality', or 'two million people can't be wrong' (yes they can, but few people perceive the logical flaw).

(d) Trust in the price/quality relationship. The expensive brand is often assumed to be the best.

(e) Trust in the image/reputation of the retail outlet. If they have no experience of the product, but have positive experience of the shop in which it is being sold, consumers may trust the judgement of the shop – especially if it also gives them the option of returning the product, or getting after-sales service.

Marketing organisations can also offer reassurance in the form of: guarantees and warranties, offering money-back for fault or dissatisfaction; free trials, samples or periods of 'home approval'; publicity for awards and official approvals gained; certificates of laboratory testing; qualification for British Standard or similar quality 'marks'.

Activity 6

Can you think of some examples of these reassurances?

We have now considered influences on customer behaviour and introduced one type of model of the purchase process. More complex models have been devised, which take more variables into account.

1.11 Models of customer behaviour

The use of models for buying behaviour is an attempt to express simply the fundamental elements of a complex process. Such models try to express the interrelationship of those variables which are significant in influencing the outcome of a purchase motivation. Their aim is to help marketing managers to understand the buying process so that they may use a marketing strategy which is most applicable to the specific situation.

Thus the simple model discussed in section 1.8 attempts to simplify and clarify the purchase decision process by showing it as a series of sequential steps. This type of model is useful to the marketing manager in trying to influence the process. For example, advertising and promotional activity is aimed at the information search stage and after-sales service is aimed at the post-purchase evaluation stage.

The other major type of model is the theoretical model which tries to show the interrelationship between the various behavioural and economic factors which are involved. The aim is to give the marketing manager a better understanding of the buying process. On the next page is an example of a well known theoretical model, the Howard-Sheth model of consumer behaviour.

The Howard-Sheth model has a number of elements.

(a) **Inputs**

Information inputs about the alternative services available include both rational and emotional elements. Thus, the interest rate structure information for a particular type of savings account at a bank or building society (rational or factual data) can be an input, as can the customer's reaction to the organisation's logo (emotional or irrational factor).

(b) **Behavioural determinants**

These elements (covered earlier in this chapter) include the existing predispositions of the purchaser which have been influenced by culture, socio-economic group, family and personality factors, amongst others. This element will have a larger role for big or otherwise significant purchase decisions.

(c) **Perceptual reaction**

Information from inputs is not accepted at face value but interpreted. For example, an individual is likely to value information more highly if it has been actively sought than if it has been passively received (from TV advertisements for example). The credibility of information varies according to the credibility of the source, perceived authority and content of the information. The customer will filter out information which is thought to be unimportant or which lacks credibility.

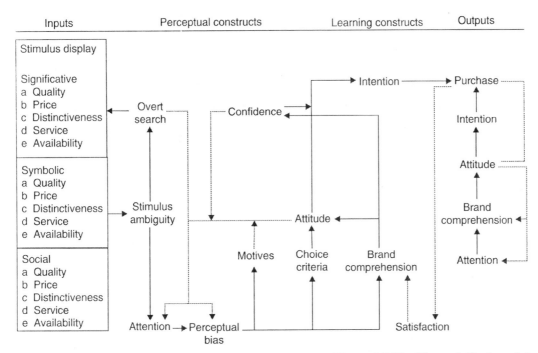

Figure 4.2 The Howard-Sheth model

(d)   **Processing determinants**

These are the factors affecting how the information gathered is evaluated. They include motivation (based on perceived needs), the available satisfactions relevant to the purchase motivation and the individual's past experience of the supplier's services. The individual will also have some judgmental criteria with which to evaluate the alternatives. These personal criteria are clearly vital in the process. Organisations can use market research methods to try to identify these criteria so as to try to influence the individual.

(e)   **Inhibitors**

There are external constraints on actual or potential purchase behaviour. For example, for the purchase of a car, constraints could include the following.

- The rate of interest charged for a loan
- Legal constraints on credit terms
- The price of petrol and performance criteria of different models of car
- Time constraints, such as the duration of a special offer

(f)   **Outputs**

The outcome of the complex process of interacting elements may be a purchase decision, a decision not to buy or a decision to delay buying.

The Howard-Sheth model has a number of advantages over other models.

(a)   It has been validated for practical examples of purchases.

(b)   It indicates the complex nature of the buying process.

(c)   It emphasises the need for marketing managers to analyse the satisfactions which customers seek in relation to the purchase of goods or services.

(d)   It emphasises the need to gain a clear understanding of individual purchase motivations.

(e)   It points to the importance of external constraints on the process.

(f)   It suggests that customer satisfactions occur on a number of levels and in a number of forms at the same time. For example, both rational and emotional satisfactions are likely to be sought.

The Howard-Sheth model can help the marketing manager to obtain useful and practical insights into customer behaviour. Like other such models, however, it is not an infallible guide. In particular, its predictive power is obviously limited.

People buying on behalf of their organisations are influenced by factors beyond those which determine the behaviour of individuals buying for themselves or their families, with their own money. We look at organisational buyers next.

2   FEATURES OF ORGANISATIONAL BUYER BEHAVIOUR

All organisational buying decisions are made by individuals or groups of individuals, each of whom is subjected to the same types of influences as they are in making their own buying decisions. However, there are some real differences between personal and organisational buying decision processes.

(a)   Organisations buy because the products/services are needed to meet wider objectives: for instance, to help them to meet their customers' needs more closely. However, as individuals do not buy products and services for themselves but for the benefits they convey, it could be argued that both are forms of derived demand.

(b)   A number of individuals are involved in the typical organisational buying decision. Again, a personal buying decision may involve several family members, for example, and so may not be very different in some cases.

(c)   The decision process may take longer for corporate decisions: the use of feasibility studies, for example, may prolong the decision process. Tendering processes in government buying also have this effect.

(d)   Organisations are more likely to buy a complex total offering which can involve a high level of technical support, staff training, delivery scheduling, finance arrangements and so on.

(e)   Organisations are more likely to employ buying experts in the process.

There are many examples of different types of organisational buying behaviour ranging from simple reordering (for example, of stationery supplies) to complex purchasing decisions (such as that of a consortium to build a motorway with bridges and tunnels, for example). Although it is difficult to identify a useful overall categorisation scheme there are common features which can be discussed.

(a)   Who buys? Is it an individual or a committee? What is the job title of the buyer? Who influences the process?

(b)   How does the organisation buy? Are there discernible stages in the buying process?

(c)   Why does the organisation buy? What are the factors which influence the decision process and what is the relative importance of these factors?

> **Activity 7**
>
> It is sometimes said that one distinction between an organisational buyer and a consumer is that the latter is less likely to act in a completely rational way. What exactly do you think this means, and do you believe it is true?

2.1 Complexity of organisational buying

One system of categorisation for corporate buying decisions, devised by Howard and O'Shaughnessy, is based on the complexity of organisational buyer behaviour. They identify three categories.

(a) Routinised buyer behaviour. This category is the habitual type, where the buyer knows what is offered and is buying items which are frequently purchased. It is likely that the buyer has well developed supplier preferences and any deviation in habitual behaviour is likely to be influenced by price and availability considerations.

(b) Limited problem solving. This category is relevant to a new or unfamiliar product/service purchase where the suppliers are nevertheless known and the product is in a familiar class of products, for instance a new model of car in a company fleet.

(c) Extensive problem solving. This category relates to the purchase of unfamiliar products from unfamiliar suppliers. The process can take much time and effort and involve the need to develop criteria with which to judge the purchase, for example the construction and refurbishment of new offices where previously buildings were looked after by managing agents.

2.2 Large organisational buyers

An extra dimension in the organisational buying process occurs where the customer involved actually or potentially represents a significant proportion of the total sales of the supplier. For marketing purposes the relationship between the supplier and the large customer needs to be managed well. In addition, it is possible that independent intermediaries such as consultants are involved in the process, adding complexity. It is important to identify the dimensions of this complex buyer-seller relationship so that the supplier can try to plan and control the relationship.

2.3 Choosing a supplier

In practice there are two types of dimension to the relationship between organisational buyer and supplier.

(a) Formal dimensions include objectively measurable supplier characteristics such as price, credit terms, delivery speed, documentation and product training.

(b) Informal dimensions include subjectively evaluated supplier characteristics such as technical product responsiveness, producer credibility, perceived sales representative quality and perceived ease of contact.

The reason for making the distinction between formal and informal dimensions is to emphasise the role which marketing can play in the supplier's attempt to influence the interface. In addition, the distinction emphasises the importance of customer service in the supplier's marketing mix.

From a marketing perspective, the role of the sales representative is vital to the supplier. As the human face of the supplier company, the sales representative is a key figure in establishing the relationships between the supplier and the customer.

Just as models of individual consumer buying behaviour have been devised, so have models of the potentially more complex organisational buying behaviour been put forward.

2.4 Models of the organisational buyer behaviour process

A number of models have been devised to try to encapsulate the essence of the organisational buying process. Here we consider two.

Wind's model of industrial source loyalty

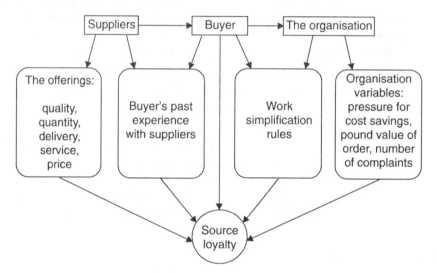

Figure 4.3 Wind's model: a model of industrial source loyalty

This model stresses source loyalty: in other words, the tendency for customers to continue to rely on the same supplier unless there are good reasons not to do so. These reasons are classified by Wind as:

(a)   The offerings and dimension of the relationship with the customer

(b)   The past relationship with the supplier

(c)   Organisational variables such as the degree of pressure for cost savings, the number of complaints

(d)   Ways in which the organisational customer thinks the task can be simplified, such as convenience of access to the supplier, inertia and resistance to change

Webster and Wind's model of organisational buyer behaviour

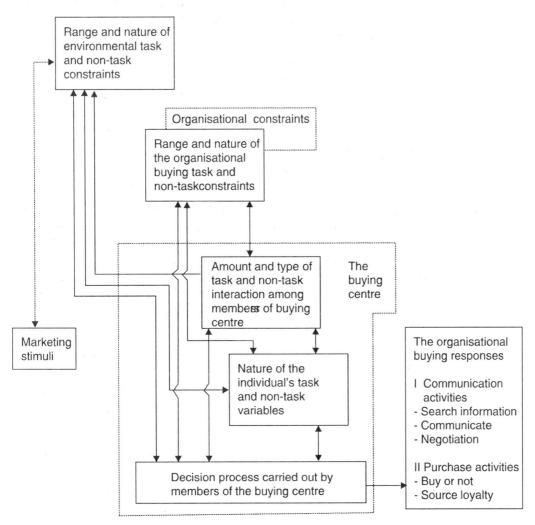

Source: adapted from Webster, F and Wind Y, *Organisational Buyer Behaviour*

Figure 4.4 Webster and Wind's model of organisation buyer behaviour

Webster and Wind together see organisational buyer behaviour as influenced by a number of sets of variables.

(a) The individual characteristics of the members of the buying centre, such as personality and preference, must be considered. These factors are similar to personal buying processes.

(b) The relationships between members of the buying centre are also important.

    (i) The user may have influence on the technical characteristics of the equipment (and hence the cost) and on reliability and performance criteria.

    (ii) The influencer is particularly useful where the purchase relies on technical knowledge. Unlike personal purchasing behaviour where opinions may be sought from colleagues, friends and family, competitive pressures and trade secret constraints may limit the sharing of information between companies. In this environment the salesperson can be a respected technical link with the buyer and so be able to influence the purchasing process. Trade journals and trade associations or professional bodies can often be a good source of influential information. Also, there is a tendency not to copy competitors but to seek one's own solution and thus demonstrate independence.

(iii) The buyer or decider. As already noted, decisions are made by individuals or groups of individuals. These individuals have personal idiosyncrasies, social pressures and organisational and environmental pressures. Thus each has a set of rational factors (task variables) and non-economic, subjective factors (non-task variables).

(iv) The gatekeeper who controls the flow of information about the purchaser may be senior or junior but is important because he or she influences the communication flow within the organisation.

(c) Organisational characteristics including the buying and organisational task, the size and structure of the organisation, the use of technology and so on. The relationships of the buyer within the organisation are particularly important. This post can be senior or junior and can involve power struggles with user departments. To retain or even increase organisational status, the buyer might use a variety of techniques designed to stress the buyer's role over that of financial or operational specialists.

(i) Role-orientated tactics involve keeping to the formal rules of the organisation where these rules work in favour of the buyer's intentions.

(ii) Role-evading tactics involve passive resistance to the rules where these rules do not work in favour of the buyer's intentions.

(iii) Personal-political tactics involve manipulating the relationship between informal and formal relationships in the buying process.

(iv) Educational tactics include using persuasive techniques.

(d) Environmental factors such as the physical, technological, economic and legal factors which affect general competitive conditions.

Activity 8

Try to position the following groups of people according to the Webster and Wind model, in other words, decide whether they are 'buyers', 'influencers' and so on.

(a) People who control the flow of purchasing information
(b) People who need the product to perform their work duties
(c) People who set specifications for the buying decision.

2.5 The decision making unit (DMU)

We can see that there are four main sets of variables influencing organisational buyer behaviour.

- Individual characteristics in the buying centre
- Group characteristics in the buying centre
- Organisational characteristics
- Environmental factors

NOTES

These four sets of variables interact in the decision process carried out by members of the buying centre. This is the decision making unit (DMU) of the buying organisation. In marketing terms the DMU is a vital target for the supplier's marketing initiatives. The size and structure of the DMU will vary between organisations, over time in the same organisation and for different types of purchase.

The marketing department of a supplier aiming at corporate clients therefore needs to be aware of the following.

- How buying decisions are made by the DMU
- How the DMU is constructed
- The identities of the most influential figures in the DMU

2.6 The decision process and the DMU

The diagram shows the decision process and the role of members of the DMU at each stage. Of course the process will vary according to the type of purchase being made.

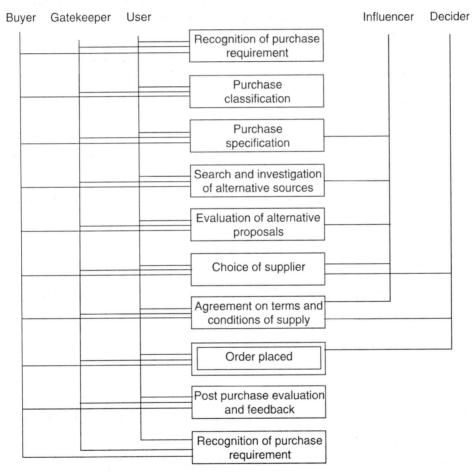

Figure 4.5 A decision process model of industrial purchase behaviour

The organisational buying process is complex and needs careful marketing action if the outcome is to be influenced favourably.

All buyers are affected by cultural factors which are often linked to nationality. This is a particularly important consideration when marketing goods internationally or to communities from different cultures.

3   NATIONAL DIFFERENCES AND SIMILARITIES

Most cultures are identified with a nation, although some regions have strongly independent cultural identities.

Cultural segmentation must be considered particularly carefully, therefore, in an international (or cross-cultural) context: the marketer needs to understand the beliefs, values, customs and rituals of the countries in which a product is being marketed in order to alter or reformulate the product to appeal to local needs and tastes, and reformulate the promotional message to be intelligible and attractive to other cultures.

(a)   Nestlé, the Swiss coffee maker, sells different strengths and styles of coffee in Europe to those sold in America.

(b)   Board games such as Monopoly are sold world-wide – with nationally-relevant street/area names, money and tokens.

(c)   Legal and regulatory provisions with regard to advertising vary from country to country: for example, the showing of cigarettes in advertisements, the use of comparative advertising, or the use of children in advertising.

(d)   Products sold abroad are positioned as exotic imports with the specific appeal of their country of origin (Australian lager, Italian pasta, French mineral water) – while in the domestic market they are sold on familiarity and cultural loyalty.

There are two ways of looking at cross-cultural marketing.

(a)   Localised marketing strategy stresses the diversity and uniqueness of consumers in different national cultures.

(b)   Global marketing strategy stresses the similarity and shared nature of consumers world-wide.

Activity 9

Try to identify the marketing problems arising from national differences in:

(a)   Language
(b)   Consumption patterns
(c)   Socio-economic factors
(d)   Marketing practices and conditions

A failure to understand cultural differences may thus cause problems with each of the four Ps.

(a)   The **product.** Nestlé coffee, Camay soap and a host of similar products are marketed internationally – with different names, flavours, aromas, and other characteristics. Coffee is preferred very strong, dark and in ground form in Continental Europe – but weaker, milder and instant in the USA. Colour is another interesting element in product and packaging: it means different things to different cultures. Blue is said to represent warmth in Holland, coldness in Sweden, purity in India and death in Iran! Product benefits also vary in appeal: Pepsodent apparently tried to sell their toothpaste using the slogan 'you'll wonder where the yellow went!' in south-east Asia – where chewing betel nuts is considered an elite habit (giving status-enhancing brown teeth).

(b)   **Promotion**. Customs, symbols and language do not always travel well. Apparently the Chevrolet Nova failed to sell in Latin America because in Spanish 'no va' means 'doesn't run'! 'Come alive with Pepsi' was translated as 'Pepsi brings your dead ancestors back to life' in one Far Eastern country! Advertising practices such as the extent and frequency of nudity used may vary widely from culture to culture, as do government regulations and voluntary guidelines on a number of issues.

(c)   **Price**. Large package sizes may not be marketable in countries where average income is low, because of the cash outlay required.

(d)   **Place**. Distribution tastes may vary. Supermarkets are very popular in some countries, while others prefer smaller stores for groceries and other foodstuffs. Newly-opening markets such as Eastern Europe exhibit poor distribution systems and very low salesperson effort and productivity – compared to Japan, say, which rates very highly.

3.1   Global perspectives

However, it should be remembered that culture is dynamic and adaptive: it changes as new values and behaviours are learned. Now that television and other forms of communication, and the speed of air travel, make the world more accessible to more people, cross-cultural exposure is increasing. So, too, is the global perspective encouraged by concerns for peace and the environment, which are global issues.

Consumers are more able to try out goods and customs from other national cultures – beyond those which already form subcultures within their own nation. They may experience different customs/products abroad and adopt them into their lifestyle when they return home – a process made easier by the fact that immigrants from the other countries bring those customs/products with them, so they can also be tried out (and/or subsequently adopted) at home. Apart from ethnic foodstores, which have become increasingly fashionable, there are previously unfamiliar products in UK supermarkets: Vegemite (yeast extract) from Australia, fromage frais from France, star fruit, papaya, plantain and other exotic fruits/vegetables from all over the world. There are sushi bars and Karaoke clubs from Japan. Meanwhile McDonalds hamburgers have invaded Red Square in Moscow and Coca-Cola is everywhere.

Consumers are also encouraged to become positively cosmopolitan and cross-cultural in their outlooks. International festivals of culture, foreign holidays, global environmental problems, the European Market completion in 1992 and the opening up of Eastern Europe have all helped to widen people's horizons, and make parochial, narrowly nationalistic viewpoints unfashionable. This is not an easy process: witness the UK's struggle with aspects of the European movement – giving up cultural emblems such as the pint, the mile, or the pound sterling.

Activity 10

In what ways is an increasingly cross-cultural outlook becoming evident in UK consumers?

Some marketers have argued that standardised marketing strategies are, therefore, becoming more and more feasible, as cultural assimilation makes markets more and more similar. There are world or global brands, which are manufactured, packaged and

BPP
PUBLISHING

Business Basics: Marketing

positioned in the same way in all the countries in which they are sold: the Marlboro (cigarettes) cowboy, the Coca Cola name and packaging and British Airways.

Given the case histories mentioned earlier, however, it is as well to be cautious about the feasibility of global marketing in general. Global manufacturing and promotion brings efficiencies and economies – where it works. (Hoover (UK) wanted to sell washing machines in Europe, but found that the number of different features wanted by consumers in different countries would have made the expansion plan simply not viable.)

Marketers should distinguish between:

- Global advertising/promotion/direct mail marketing
- Globally standardised products

They must understand the distinction between:

- Global strategy
- Global execution

Even Coca Cola, with a mainly global strategy, adds an element of local variation in execution. Campaigns show different people, settings and celebrities, according to local culture.

EXAMPLE

Pepsi experienced customer alienation when it attempted to mechanically import its global 'younger challenger to Coke' image into Russia. It lost ground to an obscure Swiss rival, Herschi, which used Russian sports stars and celebrities in its campaign.

In order to tailor a product and its advertising to a foreign or specific cultural market, the marketer must carry out appropriate research.

3.2 International marketing research

Monitoring is by far the most widespread activity in international marketing research. Studies have indicated that it accounts for about three quarters of all information received by international marketing managers. It involves passive information gathering in which the organisation or individual manager has identified a particular market on which information needs to be collected but which, as yet, does not warrant active measures. Managers thus 'keep their eyes open' for relevant information which is then collated and analysed.

Established international marketing companies are often engaged in continuous monitoring. They scan the business environment for changes which affect the products and markets of particular interest to them. In sophisticated companies it may form part of a wider marketing information system, in which information is classified and collated and then made available to managers across the organisation.

For companies with a wholly domestic orientation the position differs. Although a similar exercise may be carried out for the domestic market it is unlikely to extend internationally. A change occurs when a senior manager acquires information, often by chance, which suggests that there may be good marketing opportunities abroad. Such information may come from a very wide range of sources, such as friends, professional colleagues, reports of the success of a competitor or simply a general published analysis of the economy of a particular country.

If the information that has been acquired indicates the potential for a new market, the manager will proceed to the next stage, investigation. Otherwise he or she will return to scanning the business environment for general information, without any particular focus.

3.3 Social and cultural behaviour

Economic prosperity, in other words the ability to pay, accounts only partially for the demand for goods. The desire to acquire the goods is probably more significant. The importance we attach to the ownership of goods and use of services is determined by the learning process we acquire through cultural and social education. We learn how to be consumers by interacting with others and observing their reactions. Thus the comparison of the UK and French attitudes to food may explain why microwave cookers have had less acceptance in France than in the UK.

3.4 The development of attitudes and beliefs

Definition

> Attitudes are our general standpoint on things; the positions we have adopted with regard to particular issues, people and things.

We acquire our feelings about the worth of goods and services through a process of cultural and social development. This process establishes in our minds a set of values. In international marketing these differences in values may be quite marked, whereas in domestic markets they may be so subtle as to be unnoticeable. For the international marketer differences of attitude and belief may affect:

- Attitude towards ownership of an item
- Strength and direction of attitude
- Reason for desire/antipathy
- Perception of appropriate design/style
- Meaning of colours, symbols and words

Generally our value system is largely developed in childhood, when exposure to family influences, education and peers has an important formative influence on our values and attitudes. This exposure inculcates values derived from religious, class and cultural norms.

Such norms form part of an acceptable code of behaviour, and violation of this code is met by social sanctions to ensure correct behaviour is observed.

Definition

> Norms are the values or standards most frequently found in a given society or culture.

3.5   Motivation and cultural norms

In developed societies, or in those sectors of a developing society which are affluent, most basic, physiological and safety needs are met. The remaining needs are social needs, self-respect, respect from others, and 'self-actualisation'. Thus in affluent societies the needs are essentially social and so the value of goods is socially and culturally determined. In underdeveloped societies, however, the needs are more basic and physiologically determined. The implications are:

- Similar items may be purchased for different reasons
- In most societies the culture determines the attitude towards a product
- Marketers need to understand the cultural norms

3.6   Symbolism

Cultures develop symbols to represent ideas. Thus in Western cultures white is pure, but in Eastern cultures white is death. Logos too form a symbolism. The elephant symbolises bulk and durability in the West but in parts of Africa the value of the tusks may be its principal meaning. Colours, logos and other symbolic messages do not translate, but instead have a local meaning.

3.7   Language

Another problem that the international marketer faces is language. Literal translation often produces unfortunate consequences. Advertising literature is full of literal translation problems.

3.8   Taboos

We have already noted that each culture establishes its own norms. These apply to ways of conducting business and define excessive behaviour that is beyond what is socially acceptable. Excessive behaviours are taboo. Taboos extend to:

- Limiting what is acceptable behaviour in a situation
- Topics and subjects that are sensitive

Often these are derived from religious observance. Thus alcoholic drink, pork, unclad females, men doing housework and so on may all be taboo in certain cultures. What is acceptable in terms of behaviour, promotion or product in one country is not necessarily so in another. A recent example has been the novel The Satanic Verses by Salman Rushdie, which has been seen as harmless in most Christian cultures but has caused significant offence in Muslim societies.

3.9   Cultural convergence and divergence

For certain product groups, where social exposure is important, and to the social classes where status is also important, the acquisition and adoption of an 'international' lifestyle has led to international products such as Walkman, Coke, Boss etc. Two groups seem to be most affected.

- Young people, who have an above-average need for social acceptance
- International travellers, who are exposed to multicultural values

This convergence process has led to the idea of global products that have an appeal world-wide with little or no modification.

On the other hand, cultural groups which are isolated from exposure to external ideas, or which have strong religious or national affinity, tend to reject 'foreign' goods. The importer has at, least, to modify the offer to meet local needs.

According to innovation theory, the culturally convergent groups should become the models for other groups and so facilitate the introduction of new ideas. However the spread of fundamentalism can also be postulated by the same mechanism, and hence the processes of divergence and convergence may act concurrently. The implications for international marketers are:

- In any society there will be groups who will accept 'international' products

- For the remaining groups in that society, products will need modification to meet local needs

Activity 11

A firm has developed a drug which can cure Alzheimer's disease. What factors do you think would distinguish its export marketing efforts to a country in the EC from its export marketing efforts to a country in the Third World?

Chapter roundup

- Consumer behaviour is influenced by needs, motives, culture, socio-economic groups, family and other reference groups. Some insight into the behaviour of consumers is provided by models such as the Howard-Sheth model.

- Additional factors are at work in the case of organisational buyers. The Decision Making Unit (DMU) is an important concept. Some insight into the process of organisational buying is provided by models such as those of Wind and of Webster and Wind.

- In international marketing, the choice between a localised strategy and a global strategy can be the key to achieving sales success.

Quick quiz

1 For what reasons is customer loyalty important?

2 List as many as you can of the economic, social and psychological influences on the buying behaviour of a consumer.

3 A consumer's buying behaviour was described in this chapter as a sequence of five steps. List the five steps.

4 List as many as you can of the elements in the Howard-Sheth model.

5 Describe the differences between the buying process of an individual and that of an organisation.

6 In international marketing what specific problems may arise as a result of national differences in (a) language; (b) consumption patterns; and (c) market segmentation?

Answers to activities

1   The problem with the economist's view is that 'utility' has to be very widely defined to explain exactly why some purchases are made in preference to others. To give one example at random, its seems inconceivable that the Times would ever be published in a tabloid format, and yet it is hard to think of any logical reason why purchasers would object to it. Indeed if you have ever studied the behaviour of broadsheet readers on a crowded bus or train, you might think that they would positively welcome a more convenient format in their newspapers.

2   Your answer to this will depend on your own experience.

3   Obviously this one you can only answer yourself. In a 'typical' family, it might work as follows.

   (a)   Initiator – the father and the salesman

   (b)   Influencers – the mother, other family members, perhaps friends

   (c)(d) Decider and buyer – the father

   (e)   Users – both father and mother, and perhaps grown-up children too.

   Today, in an era when family structures are less rigid, your own answer may have differed considerably from the above.

4   (a)   If customers are satisfied with their experience of using the product or service then the next time a similar problem arises, they may short-circuit the decision process and buy the same product or use the same service. They become loyal customers.

   (b)   If a customer is dissatisfied, then not only will the same supplier not be used again but the customer may disseminate negative reports about the supplier and/or its products to others.

5   One example is the use of colouring agents, for example in frozen vegetables. The fact that such agents are entirely tasteless does not affect their value from a marketing point of view. On the same theme, people appear to prefer eggs with brown shells to those with white, and many farmers adjust their hen feed to produce the desired colour.

6   (a)   Most electrical appliances carry a guarantee.

   (b)   Cars – and even computers – can be 'test driven' at the showrooms.

   (c)   Sample packs of shampoos, perfumes, instant drinks etc are widely circulated.

   (d)   Most product packaging carries a sticker with the British Standards kitemark, or 'No animal testing' or 'Voted best ... of 20XX', or 'x million copies sold'.

7   The argument is that organisational buyers are more 'rational' in the sense that:

   (a)   they have more technical buying expertise and product knowledge than the consumer; and

   (b)   their purchasing decisions are dictated by organisational goals rather than by their own personal goals.

   While (a) is usually true, it is very doubtful whether (b) is. Buyers remain humans even if they are acting on behalf on an organisation.

8   (a)   Gatekeepers
    (b)   Users
    (c)   Influencers

9   *Language*

A promotional theme may not be intelligible – or properly translatable – whether in words or symbols.

Consumption patterns

One country may not use a product as much as another (affecting product viability), or may use it in very different ways (affecting product positioning).

Socio-economic factors

Consumers in one country may have different disposable incomes and/or decision-making roles from those in another.

Marketing practices and conditions

Differences in retail, distribution and communication systems, promotional regulation/legislation, trade restrictions etc may affect the potential for research, promotion and distribution in other countries.

10 Consumers in the UK are starting to learn languages, to drink wine as well as beer, to cook with garlic and herbs, to try other cuisines/music/ arts. Advertisements may be set in Italy and France: foreign or international 'style' is now recognised as acceptable and desirable, rather than alien.

11 You could write reams, but here are a few preliminary ideas.

Western countries

    (a)   Attitudes to elderly.

    (b)   Distribution: over the counter? Prescribed by doctors?

    (c)   Current health care of elderly.

    (d)   Demographic trends: is the age structure of the country becoming more heavily weighted towards older people?

    (e)   Drug testing and certification regime.

Third World country

    (a)   Is Alzheimer's seen as a major problem, compared to other medical conditions (eg diseases from poor sanitation)?

    (b)   Would the drug be affordable?

    (c)   Attitudes to elderly.

    (d)   Age structure of the country (fewer old people than in the West).

You will doubtless think of more.

Further question practice

Now try the following practice questions at the end of this text.

Multiple Choice Questions: 21–30

Exam Style Questions: 4–5

PUBLISHING

Chapter 5 :
STRATEGY AND PLANNING

Introduction

Strategy is a 'big' concept as you will no doubt learn in your later studies. For now be content with a simple definition: a strategy is a course of action to achieve a specific objective. We shall consider very briefly the link between an overall corporate strategy and the marketing strategy that is developed within that framework. Then we go on to look at the stages in strategic planning and strategy formulation, in particular SWOT analysis. Many of these topics are returned to later in this book.

In the remaining parts of this chapter we introduce a variety of techniques that are relevant to marketing strategy: segmentation is described in outline (there is more detail in the following chapter); then we look at product positioning. Finally we consider various aspects of marketing planning, notably forecasting and budgeting.

Your objectives

In this chapter you will learn about the following:

(a) Why an organisation needs to have a strategy

(b) The stages in strategic planning

(c) SWOT analysis and a variety of competitive strategies and growth strategies

(d) Segmentation and target markets

(e) Product positioning

(f) The stages of marketing planning, methods of sales forecasting and the elements of the marketing budget

1 MARKETING STRATEGY

Corporate strategic plans are intended to guide the overall development of an organisation. Marketing strategies will be developed within that framework. To be effective, these must be interlinked and interdependent with other functions of the organisation. The strategic component of marketing planning focuses on the direction which an organisation will take in relation to a specific market or set of markets in order to achieve a specified set of objectives. Marketing planning also requires an operational component which details specific tasks and activities to be undertaken in order to implement the desired strategy.

This approach ensures that marketing efforts are consistent with organisational goals, internally coherent and tailored to market needs and that the resources available within the organisation are systematically allocated.

1.1 Strategies

Strategies develop at several levels. Corporate strategy deals with the overall development of an organisation's business activities, while marketing strategy focuses on the organisation's activities in relation to its markets. Deliberate strategies are the result of planning. Emergent strategies are the outcome of activities and behaviour which develop unconsciously but which fall into some consistent pattern.

In practice, most strategies are part deliberate and part emergent.

Strategic marketing has three key components.

- The designation of specific, desired objectives
- Commitment of resources to these objectives
- Evaluation of a range of environmental influences

Note that the strategy does not just focus on organisational efficiency; it is more important that the organisation should be effective. Efficiency here relates to doing a task well, but effectiveness relates to doing the right task – having the right products in the right markets at the most appropriate times.

> **Activity 1**
>
> Do you understand the distinction between efficiency and effectiveness? Give an example to prove to yourself that you do.

An organisation can only be effective if it is aware of and responsive to its environment. Marketing is by definition 'strategic', since successful marketing of a product requires that the firm has the right type of product and is operating in the right markets.

Strategy also has a dynamic component. To be truly effective the organisation should not only be 'doing the right things now', it needs to be aware of and prepared to anticipate future changes to ensure that it will also be 'doing the right things in the future'. Planning and strategy enable managers to think through the possible range of future changes, and hence be better prepared to meet the changes that actually occur.

2 MARKETING PLANNING AND STRATEGY

2.1 Developing a marketing plan

A marketing plan should follow a logical structure.

(1) Historical and current analyses of the organisation and its market

(2) A statement of objectives

(3) The development of a strategy to approach that market, both in general terms and in terms of developing an appropriate marketing mix

(4) Finally, an outline of the appropriate methods for plan implementation

Implementation may appear at the end of any discussion of marketing plans. Arguably, the process of monitoring and controlling marketing activities is the most crucial factor in determining whether a plan is successful or not.

The main function of the plan is to offer management a coherent set of clearly defined guidelines, but at the same time it must remain flexible enough to adapt to changing conditions within the organisation or its markets. The stages in strategic planning are as follows.

Development of the organisation's mission statement
↓
Statement of objectives
↓
Situational analysis
↓
Strategy development
↓
Specific plans
↓
Implementation

2.2 Company mission statement

Definition

> The company mission statement is simply a statement of what an organisation is aiming to achieve through the conduct of its business; it can even be thought of as a statement of the organisation's reason for existence.

The purpose of the mission statement is to provide the organisation with focus and direction.

Factors influencing the development of the mission statement include the following.

- Corporate culture
- Organisational structure
- Product/market scope
- Customer needs
- Technology

This approach forces managers to think of the customer groups and the particular set of needs/wants which the firm wants to satisfy, and so is particularly relevant to marketing.

A mission statement can offer guidelines to management when considering how the business should develop and in which directions. With the benefits of a clear mission statement, future growth strategies can rely on what are regarded as distinctive competences and aim for synergies by dealing with similar customer groups, similar customer needs or similar service technologies.

Activity 2

Here is part of a proposed mission statement. How good do you think it is?

ROYAL MAIL: MISSION

As Royal Mail our mission is to be recognised as the best organisation in the world distributing text and packages. We shall achieve this by:

- excelling our Collection, Processing, Distribution and Delivery arrangements

- establishing a partnership with our customers to understand, agree and meet their changing requirements

- operating profitably by efficient services which our customers consider to be value for money

- creating a work environment which recognises and rewards the commitment of all employees to customer satisfaction

- recognising our responsibilities as part of the social, industrial and commercial life of the country

- being forward-looking and innovative.

2.3 Statement of objectives

Objectives enter into the planning process both at the corporate level and at the market level.

Definition

Corporate objectives define specific goals for the organisation as a whole and may be expressed in terms of profitability, returns on investment, growth of asset base, earnings per share and so on.

These factors will be reflected in the stated objectives for marketing, branch and other functional plans. They will not be identical to those specified at the corporate level and need to be translated into market-specific marketing objectives. These may involve targets for the size of the customer base, growth in the usage of certain facilities, gains in market share for a particular product type and so on, but all must conform to three criteria: they must be achievable, they must be consistent and they must be stated clearly and preferably quantitatively.

2.4 Situation analysis

Situation analysis requires a thorough study of the broad trends within the economy and society, as well as a detailed analysis of markets, consumers and competitors. Market segmentation is considered, and also an understanding of the organisation's internal environment and its particular strengths and weaknesses. Market research and external databases provide information on the external environment while an audit of the organisation's marketing activities provides information on the internal environment. A marketing information system may be used for processing and analysis, while SWOT analysis (see below) may be used to organise and present the results of such analysis.

2.5 Strategy development

Strategy development links corporate and market level plans. Most large organisations will have important resource allocation decisions to make. Financial and human resources must be allocated in a manner consistent with corporate objectives. This process is a key component of corporate strategy and indicates how specific markets or products are expected to develop, enabling the development of market level plans.

Market specific plans relate to particular markets or, in some cases, particular products, but are closely tied to the corporate plan through the statement of objectives and the resource allocation component. Situation analysis must supply further information on patterns of competition, consumer behaviour and market segmentation, as input to the development of marketing objectives and market specific strategies.

Since marketing mix variables are under the control of the marketing department, development is guided by the need to ensure that the product's features, image, perceived value and availability are appropriate to the market involved.

Marketing expenditure rests on resource allocation decisions at corporate level, but nevertheless a suggested budget is required.

2.6 Implementation

This requires an identification of the specific tasks, allocation of responsibility for those tasks and a system for monitoring their implementation. It may also include some elements of contingency planning. However well thought out the marketing plan may be, markets are dynamic. Planned activities may turn out to be inappropriate or ineffective and need a response – to modify the strategy as new information becomes available.

In developing a marketing strategy, the company is seeking to meet the specific needs of its consumers and to do so more effectively than its competitors. To do this, the company must be able to assess its position, relative to competitors and customers, accurately.

3 STRATEGY FORMULATION

3.1 SWOT analysis

This technique provides a method for organising information to identify strategic direction. The basic principle is that any statement about an organisation or its environment can be classified as a Strength, Weakness, Opportunity or Threat. An opportunity is simply any feature of the external environment which creates conditions which are advantageous to the firm in relation to a particular objective or set of objectives. By contrast, a threat is any environmental development which will present problems and may hinder the achievement of organisational objectives. What constitutes an opportunity to some firms will almost invariably constitute a threat to others.

A strength can be thought of as a particular skill or distinctive competence which the organisation possesses and which will aid it in achieving its stated objectives. A weakness is simply any aspect of the company which may hinder the achievement of specific objectives.

This information would typically be presented as a matrix of strengths, weaknesses, opportunities and threats. Effective SWOT analysis does not simply require a categorisation of information, it also requires some evaluation of the relative importance of the various factors. These features are only relevant if perceived to exist by consumers. Threats and opportunities are conditions presented by the external environment and they should be independent of the firm.

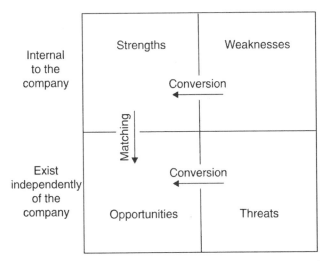

Figure 5.1 SWOT analysis

The two major strategic options from a SWOT analysis are as follows.

(a) Matching the strengths of the organisation to the opportunities presented by the market.

(b) Conversion of weaknesses into strengths in order to take advantage of some particular opportunity, or converting threats into opportunities which can then be matched by existing strengths.

It is also necessary to consider more specific aspects of strategies such as how best to compete, how to grow within the target markets. A number of analytical techniques can be used, not to offer definitive statements on the final form that a strategy should take, but rather to provide a framework for the organisation and analysis of ideas and information.

Activity 3

Can you carry out a SWOT analysis on yourself? Try it with a group of friends and compare the results.

NOTES

3.2 Competitive strategies

Management must identify the way in which it will compete with other organisations and what it perceives as the basis of its competitive advantage. The American strategist Michael Porter argues that the strategy adopted by a firm is essentially a method for creating and sustaining a profitable position in a particular market environment. Profit depends first on the nature of its strategy and second on the inherent profitability of the industry in which it operates. An organisation in a basically profitable industry can perform badly with an unsuitable strategy while an organisation in an unprofitable industry may perform well with a more suitable strategy.

The profitability of an industry depends on five key features.

- Bargaining power of suppliers
- Bargaining power of consumers
- Threat of entry
- Competition from substitutes
- Competition between firms

A competitive strategy requires the organisation to decide whether to compete across the entire market or only in certain segments (competitive scope) and whether to compete through low costs and prices or through offering a differentiated product range (competitive advantage). Four strategies are possible, according to Ennew, Watkins and Wright and these are as shown here.

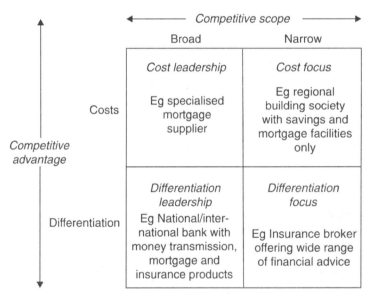

Figure 5.2 Competitive strategies

(a) **Cost leadership** attempts to control the market through being the low cost producer.

(b) **Differentiation** offers leadership or focus products which can be regarded as unique in areas which are highly valued by the consumer, creating customer loyalty which protects the firm from competition. The price premium must outweigh the costs of supplying the differentiated product for this strategy to be successful.

(c) **Focus/nicheing,** based on either costs or differentiation, aims to serve particularly attractive or suitable segments or niches.

An important feature of this approach is the need to avoid being 'stuck in the middle' – trying to be all things to all consumers. The firm trying to perform well on costs and on differentiation is likely to lose out to firms concentrating on either one strategy or the other.

3.3 Growth strategies

Ansoff's Product/Market matrix suggests that the growth strategy decision rests on whether to sell new or existing products in new or existing markets. This produces four possible options.

(a) **Market penetration**

This involves selling more of the existing products in existing markets. Possible options are persuading existing users to use more; persuading non-users to use; or attracting consumers from competitors. This is only a viable strategy where the market is not saturated.

(b) **Market development**

This entails expanding into new markets with existing products. These may be new markets geographically, new market segments or new uses for products.

(c) **Product development**

This approach requires the organisation to develop modified versions of its existing products which can appeal to existing markets. By tailoring the products more specifically to the needs of some existing consumers and some new consumers the organisation can strengthen its competitive position.

(d) **Diversification**

Diversification (new products, new markets) is a much more risky strategy because the organisation is moving into areas in which it has little or no experience. Instances of pure diversification are rare and use as a strategic option tends to be in cases when there are no other possible routes for growth available.

We will now look at how markets can be subdivided into groups of consumers with specific needs and how this is used in marketing planning.

4   MARKET SEGMENTATION: INTRODUCTION

Definition

> Market segmentation is the subdividing of a market into distinct subsets of customers, where any subset may conceivably be selected as a target market to be reached with a distinct marketing mix.   (Kotler)

Customers differ in various respects – according to age, sex, income, geographical area, buying attitudes, buying habits etc. Each of these differences can be used to segment a market.

NOTES

Steps in the analysis of segmentation

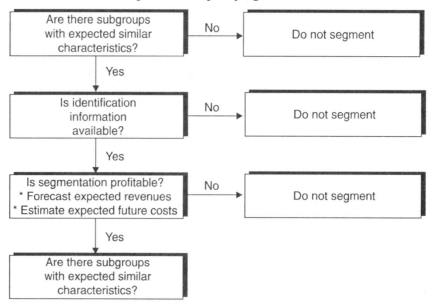

Figure 5.3 Steps in the analysis of segmentation

4.1 Market segmentation and marketing planning

Market segmentation is based on the recognition of the diverse needs of potential buyers. Different customer attitudes may be grouped into segments. A different marketing approach is needed for each market segment.

The important elements in any definition of market segmentation are as follows.

(a)   Each segment consists of people (or organisations) with common needs and preferences, who may react to 'market stimuli' in much the same way.

(b)   Each segment can become a target market with a unique marketing mix.

A total market may occasionally be homogeneous but this is rare. A segmentation approach to marketing succeeds when there are identifiable 'clusters' of consumer wants in the market.

Activity 4

Suggest how the market for umbrellas might be segmented.

4.2 The bases for segmentation

There are many different bases for segmentation; one basis will not be appropriate in every market, and sometimes two or more bases might be valid at the same time. One segmentation variable might be 'superior' to another in a hierarchy of variables.

Typical market segments are as follows.

- Geographical area
- End use (for example, different qualities of paper; work or leisure use)
- Age

- Sex
- Family size or family life cycle
- Income
- Occupation
- Education
- Religion or religious sect
- Race
- Nationality
- Social class
- Lifestyle. This can mean many things, as the table below illustrates.

Lifestyle dimensions			
Activities	**Interests**	**Opinions**	**Demographics**
Work	Family	Themselves	Age
Hobbies	Home	Social issues	Education
Social events	Job	Politics	Income
Vacation	Community	Business	Occupation
Entertainment	Recreation	Economics	Family size
Club membership	Fashion	Education	Dwelling
Community	Food	Products	Geography
Shopping	Media	Future	City size
Sports	Achievements	Culture	Stage in lifecycle

(Joseph Plummer, 'The concept and application of lifestyle segmentation', *Journal of Marketing*, January 1974)

- Buyer behaviour: the usage rate of the product by the buyer, whether purchase will be on impulse, customer loyalty, the sensitivity of the consumer to marketing mix factors (price, quality and sales promotion).

Segmentation may be based on the use or usefulness of the product. The market for various foods, for example, can be segmented into 'convenience foods', such as frozen chips and TV dinners, or 'wholesome foods' such as porridge or fresh vegetables.

Examples of segmentation can be seen in the toothpaste, magazine and sports facilities markets.

Segmentation of the toothpaste market						
Segment name	*Principal benefit sought*	*Demographic strengths*	*Special behavioural characteristics*	*Brands disproportion- ately favoured*	*Personality characteristics*	*Lifestyle characteristics*
The sensory segment	Flavour, product appearance	Children	Users of spearmint flavoured toothpaste	Colgate, Stripe	High self-involvement	Hedonistic
The sociables	Brightness of teeth	Teens, young people	Smokers	Macleans, Ultra Brite	High sociability	Active
The worriers	Decay prevention	Large families	Heavy users	Crest	High hypochon-driasis	Conservative
The independent segment	Price	Men	Heavy users	Brands on sale	High autonomy	Value-oriented

Magazines and periodicals

In this market the segmentation may be according to:

- Sex (Woman's Own)
- Social class (Country Life)
- Income (House & Garden)
- Occupation (Accountancy Age)
- Leisure interests (NME)
- Political ideology
- Age
- Lifestyle

Sporting facilities

Segmentation may be according to:

(i) Geographical area (rugby in Wales, skiing in parts of Scotland, sailing in coastal towns)

(ii) Population density (squash clubs in cities, riding in country areas)

(iii) Occupation (gymnasia for office workers)

(iv) Education (there may be a demand from ex-schoolboys for facilities for sports taught at certain schools, such as rowing)

(v) Family life cycle or age (parents may want facilities for their children, young single or married people may want facilities for themselves)

Segmentation in any particular market is a matter of 'intuition' or 'interpretation'. The examples in the previous paragraph merely suggest a few bases for segmentation in each case.

4.3 Segmentation of the industrial market

Segmentation can also be applied to an industrial market based on, for instance, the nature of the customer's business.

Components manufacturers specialise in the industries of the firms to which they supply components.

4.4 Target markets

Organisations are not usually able to sell with equal efficiency and success to an entire market: that is, to every market segment. The marketing management of a company may choose one of the following policy options.

(a) Undifferentiated marketing: this policy is to produce a single product and hope to get as many customers as possible to buy it; that is, ignore segmentation entirely.

(b) Concentrated marketing: the company attempts to produce the ideal product for a single segment of the market (for example, Rolls Royce cars, Mothercare mother and baby shops).

(c) Differentiated marketing: the company attempts to introduce several product versions, each aimed at a different market segment (for example, the manufacture of several different brands of washing powder).

The major disadvantage of concentrated marketing is reliance on a single segment of a single market. On the other hand, specialisation in a particular market segment can give a firm a profitable, although perhaps temporary, competitive edge over rival firms.

The major disadvantage of differentiated marketing is the additional cost of marketing and production (more product design and development costs, the loss of economies of scale in production and storage, additional promotion costs and administrative costs and so on). When the costs of further differentiation of the market exceed the benefits from further segmentation and target marketing, a firm is said to have 'over-differentiated'. Some firms have tried to overcome this problem by selling the same product to two market segments.

The choice of marketing strategy will depend on the following factors.

(a) How far can the product and/or the market be considered homogeneous? Mass marketing may be 'sufficient' if the market is largely homogeneous (for example, safety matches).

(b) Will the company's resources be overextended by differentiated marketing? Small firms may succeed better by concentrating on one segment only.

(c) Is the product sufficiently advanced in its 'life cycle' to have attracted a substantial total market? If not, segmentation and target marketing is unlikely to be profitable, because each segment would be too small in size.

The potential benefits of segmentation and target marketing are as follows.

(a) Product differentiation: a feature of a particular product might appeal to one segment of the market in such a way that the product is thought better than its rivals.

(b) The seller will be more aware of how product design and development may stimulate further demand in a particular area of the market.

(c) The resources of the business will be used more effectively, because the organisation should be more able to make products which the customer wants and will pay for.

Activity 5

See if you can draw up a chart similar to the toothpaste one on page 119 for a product that interests you (cars, newspapers, magazines or whatever).

We shall be exploring the topic of segmentation in a good deal more depth in the next chapter. Before that, we need to consider how a brand relates to other competing brands in the market.

5 POSITIONING PRODUCTS AND BRANDS

Brands can be positioned against competitive brands on product maps defined in terms of how buyers perceive key characteristics.

Yoram Wind identifies a comprehensive list of these characteristics.

(a) Positioning by specific product features, for example, price or specific product features

(b) Positioning by benefits, problems, solutions, or needs

NOTES

(c)   Positioning for specific usage occasions

(d)   Positioning for user category, for example, age, gender

(e)   Positioning against another product, for example, comparison with market leader

(f)   Product class dissociation, for example, organic food, lead-free petrol

(g)   Hybrid basis, for example, user and product features

Activity 6

Give an example for each of Yoram Wind's list of key characteristics.

A basic perceptual map plots brands in perceived price and perceived quality terms.

Figure 5.4 Perceptual map

Price and quality are important elements in the marketing mix, but they will not, in the customer's opinion, be considered independent variables. A 'high' price will usually be associated with high quality and equally low price with low quality. Thus, while everybody would like to buy a bargain brand, there is a problem to overcome. This is a question of belief: will customers accept that a high quality product can be offered at a low price?

Activity 7

Where would you place MFI in the quality/price map?

Public concern about the use of promotional pricing ('prices slashed') has led to the introduction of restrictions on the use of these techniques. Stores now have to provide evidence that the promotion is part of a genuine 'sale'.

5.1   Identifying a gap in the market

Market research can determine where customers think that competitive brands are located.

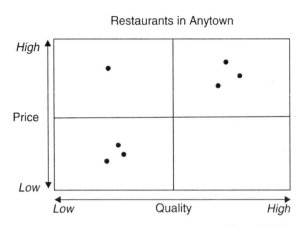

Figure 5.5 Restaurants in Anytown

In the hypothetical model above, there appears to be a gap in the market for a moderately priced reasonable quality eating place. This is shown between clusters in the high price/high quality and the low price/low quality segments.

Perceptual maps can also plot how customers perceive competitive brands performing on key product user benefits. Kotler's hypothetical examples consider the various products that serve the US breakfast market.

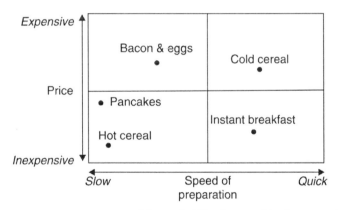

Figure 5.6 Product-positioning map: Breakfast market

Within the breakfast market, a producer might be interested in entering the instant breakfast market. It would then be advisable to plot the position of the various instant breakfast brands.

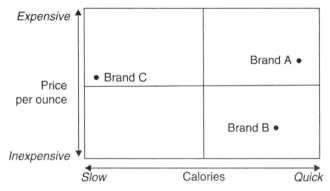

Figure 5.7 Brand-positioning map (Instant breakfast market)
(Kotler, Marketing Management)

The above analysis now shows an apparent gap for a modest priced slimmers' brand. Once again, it would be necessary to establish whether or not there is sufficient demand for such a product.

NOTES

5.2 Competitive positioning

Definition

> Competitive positioning concerns a general idea of what kind of offer to make to the target market in relation to competitors' offers. (Kotler)

Important considerations in competitive positioning are product quality against price, and Kotler identified a 3 × 3 matrix of nine different competitive positioning strategies.

Competitive positioning strategies

	High price	Medium price	Low price
High quality	Premium strategy	Penetration strategy	Superbargain strategy
Medium quality	Overpricing strategy	Average quality strategy	Bargain strategy
Low quality	Hit and run strategy	Shoddy goods strategy	Cheap goods strategy

Activity 8

Can you think of examples of some of these strategies?

5.3 Fragmented industries and market segmentation

The fragmentation of industries and proliferation of market segments tends to occur when the following conditions apply.

(a) There are low entry barriers and so new firms can enter the market relatively easily.

(b) There are few economies of scale or learning curve effects, and so it is difficult for big firms to establish a significant overall cost leadership.

(c) Transport and distribution costs are high, and so the industry fragments on a geographical basis.

(d) Customer needs vary widely.

(e) There are rapid product changes or style changes, which small firms might succeed in reacting to more quickly than large firms.

(f) There is a highly diverse product line, so that some firms are able to specialise in one part of the industry.

(g) There is scope for product differentiation, based on product design/quality differences or even brand images.

Having considered a product's best potential market and the place it should occupy in that market, the marketing manager must devise a detailed marketing plan.

6 THE MARKETING PLAN

The marketing plan in detail consists of several inter-related decisions.

(a)   Sales targets must be set for each product and each sales division (with sub-targets also set for sales regions, sales areas and individual salespeople). Sales targets may be referred to as sales quotas.

(b)   The total marketing budget must be set.

(c)   Given an overall marketing budget, resources (cash) must be allocated between:

   (i)   Salaries and other staff costs

   (ii)   Above the line expenditure (advertising)

   (iii) Below the line expenditure (sales promotion items, price reduction allowances etc)

(d)   The overall sales target set by top management will incorporate sales price decisions; but within the formulation of the marketing plan there is likely to be some room for manoeuvre and an element of choice in the pricing decision. In other words, top management will decide on a 'rough pricing zone' and a specific price within this zone will be fixed later within the marketing plan.

(e)   Expenditure on marketing will also be allocated to different products or services within the organisation's product or service range. Some products might justify additional marketing expenditure, whereas others, nearing the end of their life cycle, may lose a part of their previous allocation.

Market plan decisions (sales targets, total marketing expenditure budget, the marketing mix and the allocation of expenditure to products) are the main elements of marketing programming.

None of this can take place without detailed forecasts of future outcomes, particularly sales forecasts.

6.1   Sales forecasting

Sales forecasting is a key element in budgeting and in long-term strategic planning, both essential disciplines in running a business of any size. Without an accurate idea of a business's future sales it becomes difficult to make any meaningful plans for the short term, let alone the longer term.

Activity 9

How do you think a manager sets about making a sales forecast? To keep it simple, assume we are talking about a smallish company (say £5m turnover) with computerised accounting systems and a limited range of products.

Companies must be aware of factors both within and outside their control so they can plan effectively for the future. Sales figures do not simply depend on how well the sales force is performing or even how well the product fits customer requirements. In the long run performance will depend on many factors including the general economic climate, the level of technology and rate of technological change. Forecasting is a tool which, when used correctly, enables management to make informed decisions about the future.

There is a vast array of forecasting techniques that can be applied to sales forecasting but here we will only deal with a small number. Some forecasting methods are very basic, for instance using last month's sales figures to predict this month's. Others are very complex such as some econometric models. The use of computers has aided the development of forecasting techniques.

Managers should be aware of the different types of product that exist to serve a particular market before attempting to forecast demand. For example, a coffee producer must decide which forecast suits his objectives: a forecast for the total coffee market, the decaffeinated coffee market or the instant coffee market. The manager must also make a decision about the geographical area the forecast should cover. Companies can estimate sales at different levels of marketing effort and expenditure.

Assumptions will have to be made about the marketing environment: the external uncontrollable factors such as the economic, technological and political environment. Companies can attempt to make forecasts for these factors. Sales forecasting should not simply take into account competitor sales so market shares can be established. Government statistics in industry sectors can be used to evaluate past sales and base forecasts on future sales. Specialist research companies (such as Mintel) issue market reports that can be used to assess present positions.

Companies often arrive at sales forecasts in three stages:

- Environmental forecast
- Industry forecast
- Company sales forecast

There are three basic ways forecasts can be made.

(a)   By surveying the opinions of consumers, sales people or experts within the field. For example, an economist's opinion may be sought to give an assessment of future interest rate levels.

(b)   By looking at what people do if the product is made available. For example, a supermarket may make a new flavoured yoghurt available in a small number of stores and analyse the sales to test whether to distribute the yoghurt throughout its stores.

(c)   By looking at the past to evaluate what was purchased and when.

The method which is used to estimate sales will depend upon product characteristics. The product life cycle (PLC) (discussed in detail in later chapters) can be a useful tool in sales estimates. The shape and length of the PLC will depend upon the frequency of purchase. Companies should estimate first-time and replacement/repeat sales.

The diagram below shows some examples of forecasting requirements of a company, illustrating how many different forecasts are needed in addition to sales forecasts.

Chapter 5: Strategy and planning

NOTES

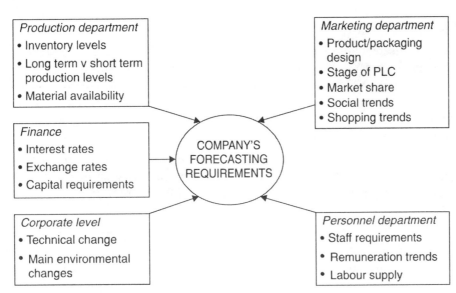

Figure 5.8 The variety of forecasts

Forecasts should take the following into account.

(a) **Accuracy**. Although this seems obvious the level of desired accuracy can differ. The longer the time span involved generally the less accuracy is possible.

(b) **Time period**. Short-term forecasts can be made to allow for the smooth production and delivery of products. Longer-term forecasts are usually used to help managers make strategic decisions.

(c) **Detail**. The level of detail required by a forecast will differ amongst functional departments. Production will want a very detailed assessment of the future demand for the product to enable them to make necessary adjustments.

6.2 Forecasting techniques

There are many different forecasting techniques available at different levels of complexity. Here we shall be evaluating the three broad categories of forecasting methods: time series, causal and qualitative techniques.

Time series forecasts

Historical (past) data is analysed and trends or patterns are projected into the future. This type of analysis is, of course, more useful in stable industries that have been in existence for some time. This means that data is available and is relatively reliable. In essence it is a short-term technique rather than a long-term one.

Statistical techniques are available that take into account seasonal variations, such as occur, for example, in the sales of fireworks. In the long term, fireworks may be used in more displays and entertainments throughout the year than the traditional Guy Fawkes night. Where the seasonal sales pattern is not expected to continue unchanged for the foreseeable future, in the longer term time series analysis may be less useful. Statistical methods that are used to make projections into the future include moving averages or weighted moving averages and exponential smoothing.

127

NOTES

Business Basics: Marketing

Causal models

Causal models use equations to explain the relationship between a dependent variable (the one being forecast) and a number of independent variables. Past data can be used in the model and with the use of computers complex models can be evaluated. Causal models are linked to probability so a forecast may be that there is a 95% chance that sales will achieve a certain target. They are useful for longer term forecasting as independent variables can be altered and their impact noted.

As an example of a causal model, demand for electricity may depend upon a number of independent variables such as the price of electricity, the price of alternative energies, electric appliances already in operation (so locked into supply) and past demand for electricity.

The mathematical technique of regression analysis is used to analyse causal models. Macroeconomic forecasting uses causal models to predict economic growth rates, for example. Demand for goods can also be forecast using causal models, and these can take into account many diverse aspects such as advertising and demand for complementary or substitute goods.

Qualitative forecasting

Qualitative forecasting techniques do not depend on historical data as the quantitative methods (time series and causal) do. Qualitative techniques are used either where quantitative data is unavailable or for long-term forecasts. They are used mainly in technological forecasting, corporate planning and monitoring changes in consumer tastes and culture. There are two types of qualitative forecasting: explorative and normative. Explorative techniques start with the current state of affairs and attempt to predict changes. Normative techniques start with a desired state of affairs in the future and work back to consider ways in which to get there. So, for example, qualitative techniques can attempt to forecast new product adoption, technological change and innovations.

6.3 The marketing budget

Top management must set an overall sales strategy and a series of sales objectives; only then should a more detailed marketing plan be prepared.

There are three types of annual budget planning for a marketing budget.

(a) **Top down planning**: the setting of goals for lower management by higher management.

(b) **Bottom up planning**: employees set their own goals and submit them to higher management for approval.

(c) **'Goals down – plans up planning'**: a mixture of the two styles; top management sets overall goals and employees formulate plans for achieving those goals. This is well suited to the formulation of sales budgets.

When budgeting for sales revenue and selling costs, variables are many and difficult to estimate. Setting budgets and budgetary control on the marketing side is different from the more 'mechanical' approach which can be adopted with other budgets.

A sales and marketing budget is necessary because:

(a) It is an element of the overall strategic plan of the business (the master budget) which brings together all the activities of the business

(b)   Where sales and other non-production costs are a large part of total costs, it is financially prudent to forecast, plan and control them

(c)   Since selling rests on uncertain conditions, good forecasts and plans become more important. If budgets are to be used for control, the more uncertain the budget estimates are, the more budgetary control is necessary

---

Activity 10

What would you expect to be the largest single item in the marketing budget of a small to medium sized company? What would you expect it to be in a large company?

6.4   Matching forecast demand with estimated available capacity

One of the problems in setting budgets is matching the forecast demand from customers with the estimated available capacity. There are three aspects to this problem.

(a)   It is difficult to make an accurate forecast of demand.

(b)   It is difficult to predict available capacity accurately too, given uncertainties about factors affecting production, operating conditions and performance.

(c)   There are often practical difficulties in matching demand with capacity (seasonability, variations in demand).

In order to match demand with capacity, management must be flexible and be prepared to take action.

(a)   To suppress demand if it exceeds capacity, by raising prices, for example

(b)   To stimulate demand if there is excess capacity, such as by advertising or price reductions

(c)   To reduce excess capacity by selling off surplus assets

(d)   To supplement production when there is undercapacity by subcontracting work to other organisations, and perhaps to take steps to increase capacity (by acquiring new premises, equipment and labour, or by negotiating for more overtime from existing employees)

6.5   The advertising budget decision

Setting an advertising budget is based on the theory of diminishing returns. For every extra £1 of advertising spent, the company should earn an extra £x of profit. Further expenditure on advertising is justified until the marginal return £x diminishes to the point where £x < £1.

Unfortunately, the marginal return from additional advertising cannot be measured easily in practice.

(a)   Advertising is only one aspect of the overall marketing mix

(b)   Advertising has some long-term effect, which goes beyond the limits of a measurable accounting period

(c)   Where the advertising budget is fixed as a percentage of sales, advertising costs tend to follow sales levels and not vice versa

Advertising budgets are often set by using rule of thumb methods or by taking competitor activity into consideration.

Recommended practice for fixing advertising cost budgets, however, would involve the use of:

(a) Empirical testing (for example, in a mail order business or in retail operations, since it may be possible to measure the effect of advertising on sales by direct observation)

(b) Mathematical models using data about media and consumer characteristics, desired market share and records of past results. Regression analysis can be conducted to find out the likely cost of advertising (through several media) to achieve a given target.

6.6 Control

Once the plan has been implemented, the task of management is to control the use of resources. This may involve:

(a) A comparison of actual sales against the budget

(b) A comparison of actual marketing costs against the budgeted expenditure levels and against actual sales

(c) Analysis of the profitability of individual products, and distribution outlets

(d) Strategic control, that is, checking whether the company's objectives, products and resources are being directed towards the correct markets

6.7 Allocation of costs

The allocation of direct selling costs to products, type of outlet and so on is fairly straightforward, but indirect costs such as administration overheads must be allocated on an arbitrary basis (such as to products by value of sales). This aspect of cost allocation should be carefully considered when deciding whether to eliminate an unprofitable expenditure from selling or distribution.

(a) The cost of distributing goods to a distant area may seem to be relatively unprofitable; but if, by not selling the goods in this area, there will be unused production capacity, the products which are produced and sold will have to bear a higher proportion of fixed costs which will still be incurred.

(b) The allocation of fixed selling costs to products may make a product seem unprofitable, but the product may still be making a contribution to those fixed costs.

6.8 Overviewing the marketing process: marketing audits

Top management is responsible for ensuring that the company is pursuing optimal policies with regard to its products, markets and distribution channels. Carrying out this responsibility is known as strategic control of marketing, and the means to apply strategic control is the marketing audit.

We considered the marketing audit in Chapter 2.

NOTES

Chapter roundup

- Use of strategic planning enables organisations to be effective, not just efficient. Information is gathered and used to develop a corporate plan, covering short-, medium- and long-term goals and acting as a framework within which specific functions such as marketing can develop their own plans.

- Techniques used in strategy formulation include SWOT analysis which enables an organisation to choose whether to match its strengths to available opportunities or to convert its weaknesses into strengths or its threats into opportunities. Competitive strategies involve deciding whether to compete across the whole market or only in certain segments and whether to compete through low costs/prices or by offering a differentiated product range. Possible growth strategies are market penetration or development, product development and diversification.

- Market segmentation should result in increased total sales and profits because products/services will be more likely to appeal to the target segments and pricing policy can be more sophisticated. There are many possible bases for segmentation. We look at these in more detail in the next chapter.

- Product/brand positioning may be determined in several ways, most commonly by highlighting specific product features, including price. Price and quality are very important in consumer perceptions of a product and analysis of existing products in a market can be used to identify gaps.

- The marketing plan should include sales targets and a total marketing budget analysed between above the line, below the line and other items.

- Sales forecasts form the basis of much of the activity of an organisation. Methods include using historical data, building causal models and qualitative forecasting.

- Budgeting is an essential financial discipline but a particularly tricky problem in marketing given the difficulty in determining both likely demand and likely cost of achieving a given sales target. The rules of thumb commonly used in setting promotional budgets (such as a percentage of budgeted or past sales or profit) are unsatisfactory because they are arbitrary.

Quick quiz

1. What is an emergent strategy?
2. Outline the stages in strategic planning.
3. What do the letters in SWOT analysis stand for?
4. Differentiate between market and product development.
5. List some typical market segments.
6. A bargain brand is perceived as low price, high quality. True or false?
7. What seven conditions tend to give rise to fragmentation of industries and proliferation of market segments?
8. What are the three stages by which forecasts are arrived at and what are the three basic ways of making forecasts?

PUBLISHING

9   Why is a sales and marketing budget necessary?

10   List the problems encountered in setting a sales budget.

Answers to activities

1   Efficiency relates to doing a given task well, making the best use of resources available to do it; effectiveness, however, means working out a way best calculated to achieve a given objective. For example if your objective is to get from London to Bristol quickly, and your resources are a bicycle, then careful route planning and staged rests will get you there as efficiently as possible; but a more effective approach might be to sell the bicycle and buy a rail ticket.

2   If you struggle with this try to put yourself in the position of a Post Office branch manager at Royal Mail. Does the statement give you clear guidelines on how you should be developing your branch?

4   The market for umbrellas might be segmented according to the sex of the consumer. Women might seem to prefer umbrellas of different size and weight. The men's market might further be subdivided into age (with some age groups buying few umbrellas and others buying many more) or occupation (for example, professional classes, commuters, golfers). Each subdivision of the market (each subsegment) will show increasingly common traits. Golfers, for example, appear to buy large multi-coloured umbrellas.

6   (a)   Positioning by specific product features. Most car advertisements stress the combination of product features available and may also stress what good value for money this represents.

     (b)   Positioning by benefits, problems, solutions, or needs. Pharmaceutical companies position their products to doctors by stressing effectiveness and side effects. Other examples include Crest, which positions its toothpaste as a cavity fighter, and DHL, which uses its world-wide network of offices as a basis for its positioning.

     (c)   Positioning for specific usage occasions. Johnson's Baby Shampoo is positioned as a product to use if you shampoo your hair every day, and Hennessy Cognac is for special occasions.

     (d)   Positioning for user category. Examples here include 7-Up's use of the Fido Dido character to target urban adolescents. Age has been used as a basis for positioning by Saga Holidays, by many breakfast cereal producers (compare the target markets for Kellogg's Rice Krispies and Special K) and by Affinity shampoo for women over 40.

     (e)   Positioning against another product. Although Avis never mentions Hertz explicitly in its advertising, its positioning as Number 2 in the rent-a-car market is an example of positioning against a leader.

     (f)   Product class dissociation. Lead-free petrol is positioned against leaded petrol.

     (g)   Hybrid basis. The Porsche positioning, for example, is based on the product benefits as well as on a certain type of user.

7   MFI would claim to be in the 'bargain' quadrant. Many potential customers think that they are at the lower end of the economy segment. MFI's practice of frequent sales and discounts has the effect of

overcoming at least some of the difficulties resulting from individuals using price as a surrogate for assessment of quality. Thus the price label shows the higher pre-discounted price and the low sale price. The assumption is that customers will use the pre-sale price to confirm promotional claims about quality.

8   Here are some possible choices. We have avoided naming names where we are likely to get sued for doing so, but you need not do so!

Premium strategy	Rolex	*Penetration strategy*	Lexus	*Bargain strategy*	Own brand champagne
Overpricing strategy	Computer games?	*Average quality strategy*	Anything	*Cheap goods strategy*	'Pick 'n' mix' chocolates
Hit and run strategy	Mobile phone call charges	*Shoddy goods strategy*	Some high street clothes shops		

9   In practice, the starting point is often the historical sales record, product by product. Trend analysis – which in this case may be less sophisticated than it sounds – might give a pointer to how sales are developing. Market information will help – the activities of competitors, the plans of intermediaries such as distributors and so on. Then internal plans must be taken into account: changes in the product mix, changes in the level of advertising, and so on.

In a larger company it all becomes more complicated.

10   There are no hard and fast rules about this. For a small to medium sized company the largest cost is likely to be the salaries of marketing staff. For a large company using expensive media like TV advertising costs may be the largest item.

Further question practice

Now try the following practice questions at the end of this text.

Multiple Choice Questions: 31–40

Exam Style Questions: 6–7

Chapter 6:

MARKETING RESEARCH AND MARKET SEGMENTATION

Introduction

Marketing research is defined as the investigation of factors related to the marketing activities of a company. Marketing decisions are made under conditions of uncertainty and risk. Marketing research aims to reduce risk by providing information about the factors involved and possible outcomes of particular actions.

'Market research' and 'marketing research' are often used interchangeably, however.

(a) Market research involves gathering information about the market for a particular product or service (typically, consumer attitudes, existing product usage and so on).

(b) Marketing research, according to the American Marketing Association is the systematic gathering, recording and analysing of data about problems relating to the marketing of goods and services.

It includes research on the effects of pricing, advertising and other marketing decision variables.

We introduced the concept of segmentation in the previous chapter. Now we go on to look in more detail at the various bases for market segmentation such as demographic segmentation and lifestyle segmentation.

Your objectives

In this chapter you will learn about the following.

(a) Market research, product research, price research, sales promotion research and distribution research

(b) A wide variety of procedures used in marketing research

(c) The requirements for and benefits of market segmentation

(d) Geographic, demographic and psychographic segmentation

(e) The value of marketing information systems

1 TYPES OF MARKETING RESEARCH

Marketing research may include the following specific types of research.

(a) **Market research**

- Analysis of the market potential for existing products
- Forecasting likely demand for new products
- Sales forecasting for all products
- Study of market trends
- Study of the characteristics of the market
- Analysis of market shares

(b) **Product research**

- Assessing customer acceptance of proposed new products
- Comparative studies between competitive products
- Studies into packaging and design
- Forecasting new uses for existing products
- Test marketing
- Research into the development of a product line (range)

(c) **Price research**

- Analysis of elasticities of demand;
- Analysis of costs and contribution or profit margins;
- Assessing the effect of changes in credit policy on demand;
- Analysing customer perceptions of price (and quality).

(d) **Sales promotion research**

- Motivation research for advertising and sales promotion effectiveness

- Analysing the effectiveness of advertising on sales demand

- Analysing the effectiveness of individual aspects of advertising such as copy and media used

- Research to establish where sales territories should be located

- Analysing the effectiveness of salespeople

- Analysing the effectiveness of other sales promotion methods

(e) **Distribution research**

- Investigating the best location and design of distribution centres

- The analysis of packaging for transportation and shelving

- Assessing dealer supply requirements

- Assessing dealer advertising requirements

- Assessing and comparing the cost of different methods of transportation and warehousing

The most important of these are product and market research, which we will now examine in more detail.

1.1 Product research

This aspect of marketing research attempts to make product research and development customer-oriented.

Definition

Product research is concerned with assessing and analysing the product itself, whether new, improved or already on the market, and customer reactions to it.

Activity 1

Where might the ideas for new products come from? Try to think of likely sources within and outside the firm.

New ideas are screened by specialists (market researchers, designers, research and development staff and so on) and rejected if they:

- Have a low profit potential or insufficient market potential
- Have a high cost and involve high risk
- Do not conform to company objectives
- Cannot be produced and distributed with the available resources

Ideas which survive the screening process will be product tested and possibly test marketed to indicate how well the product will sell if produced for a wider market.

Product research may examine:

- Product form and attributes in relation to consumer tastes and needs
- Competitive products and existing products in the company portfolio

Product research also includes

(a) the need to keep the product range of a company's goods under review as a way of reducing costs by eliminating unprofitable lines

(b) extending custom by diversification

(c) finding new segments by adapting products or their uses

(d) finding new uses for existing products, to extend a product range. Uses for plastics and nylon, for example, have been extended rapidly in the past as a result of effective research.

Activity 2

Without going into the detail of individual brands, can you think of some broad product areas where this kind of extension has been apparent in recent years?

Information about competitors' product ranges and their new or improved products is important if the company is to maintain a competitive edge.

1.2 Market research

Market research information can be collected directly (for example, from sample market results or questionnaires filled in by customers) or from secondary sources (internal, such as analyses of past sales, or external, such as the Nielsen Index, which gives summary information on sales by products and geographical areas).

The quantity and quality of information provided by market research has an associated cost and the trade-off between cost and accuracy is important, particularly because risk cannot be eliminated. Market research can help to reduce the risk in decision making but, usually, the more accurate the information, the higher the cost. Market research should always be cost effective.

1.3 Techniques of market research

Definition

> Market research comprises the assessment of environmental factors, outside the organisation's control, which will affect the demand for its products/services.

(a) An economic review (national economy, government policy, covering forecasts on investment, population, gross national product, and inflation).

(b) Specific market research (to obtain data about specific markets and forecasts concerning total market demand).

(c) Evaluation of total market demand for the firm's and similar products – including such factors as profitability and market potential.

As we saw in the previous chapter, sales forecasts attempt to predict how a product will sell when factors such as price and promotional activity are varied. Unlike the market forecast, a sales forecast concerns the firm's activity directly. It takes into account such aspects as sales to certain categories of customer, sales promotion activities, the extent of competition, product life cycle, performance of major products.

Sales forecasts are expressed in volume, value and profit, and in the case of national and international organisations regional forecasts are usually, by product.

Research into potential sales will involve an estimate of the part of the market which is within the possible reach of a product.

Market research needs to consider trends in economic, fiscal, political and social influences which may affect supply and demand. In addition, demand changes in market sectors, geographical areas or other changes which are cyclical or seasonal.

2 MARKETING RESEARCH PROCEDURE: SECONDARY DATA

Marketing research involves the following five stages.

(1) **Definition of the problem**. The marketing problem which management wishes to resolve must be properly defined. This usually involves careful consultation between managers and researchers to clarify the nature of the problem and decide what information it is appropriate and possible to collect.

(2) **Design of the research**. Once the research team knows what problem it must help to resolve, it will establish the type of data, the collection method to be used, the selection of a research agency (if appropriate) and, if a sample is to be taken, the design of the sample frame.

(3) **Collection of the data.**

 PUBLISHING

(4) **Analysis of the data.**

(5) **Presentation of a report** which should then lead to a management marketing decision.

The easiest and cheapest market research makes use of data already published by other researchers either inside or outside the organisation. This is called secondary data.

Definition

> Secondary data is data neither collected directly by the user nor specifically for the user, often under conditions that are not well known to the user
> (American Marketing Association)

The collection of secondary data for marketing research is sometimes known as desk research.

Desk research involves collecting data from internal and external sources.

(a) Records inside the firm, gathered by another department or section for its own purposes may be useful for the research task in hand. Internal data would include:

   (i) Production data about quantities produced, materials and labour resources used and so on

   (ii) Data about inventory

   (iii) Data about sales volumes, analysed by sales area, salesperson, quantity, price, profitability, distribution outlet, customer

   (iv) Data about marketing itself, such as promotion and brand data

   (v) All cost and management accounting data

   (vi) Financial management data relating to the capital structure of the firm, capital tied up in stocks and debtors and so on

(b) Published information from external sources includes:

   • Publications of market research agencies, such as the Nielsen Index
   • Government statistics
   • Publications of trade associations
   • Professional journals

Activity 3

What sort of internal data might be useful in a marketing research project?

Sources of secondary data for marketing vary according to the needs of the organisation.

The government is a major source of economic information and information about industry and population trends. Examples of UK government publications are:

(a)   The Annual Abstract of Statistics and its monthly equivalent, the Monthly Digest of Statistics, containing data about manufacturing output, housing, population etc

(b)   The Digest of UK Energy Statistics (published annually)

(c)   Housing and Construction Statistics (published quarterly)

(d)   Financial Statistics (monthly)

(e)   Economic Trends (monthly)

(f)   Census of Population

(g)   Census of Production (annual), which has been described as 'one of the most important sources of desk research for industrial marketers' and which provides data about production by firms in each industry in the UK

(h)   Department of Employment Gazette   (monthly) giving details of employment in the UK

(i)   British Business, published weekly by the Department of Trade and Industry, giving data on industrial and commercial trends at home and overseas

(j)   Business Monitors, giving detailed information about various industries

Non-government sources of information include:

(a)   The national press (broadsheets such as the Financial Times) and financial and professional magazines and journals

(b)   Companies and other organisations specialising in the provision of economic and financial data (such as the Financial Times Business Information Service, the Data Research Institute, Reuters and the Extel Group) and research organisations who analyse certain markets and publish and sell the results (such as Mintel, Euromonitor)

(c)   Directories and yearbooks

(d)   Professional institutions (such as Chartered Institute of Marketing, Industrial Marketing Research Association, British Institute of Management, Institute of Practitioners in Advertising)

(e)   Specialist libraries, such as the City Business Library in London, which collects published information from a wide variety of sources

(f)   Trade sources such as the Association of British Insurers (ABI) market share data on the life insurance industry; the Society of Motor Manufacturers and Trades (SMMT) data on the registration of new vehicles by brand. The trade press is also important.

We now look at the collection of primary data; that is, information researched within the target market and specifically related to the marketing problem we wish to address.

3   MARKETING RESEARCH PROCEDURE: PRIMARY DATA

The collection of primary data is sometimes known as field research. Techniques include:

- Experimentation   • Consumer panels
- Observation   • Trade audits, such as retail audits
- Sampling   • Pre-tests

Business Basics: Marketing

- Interviewing
- Questionnaires
- Post-tests
- Attitude scales and methods of analysis

Experimentation involves the systematic manipulation of a given variable in order to examine its effect on the performance of a subject or system. Measurements are taken before and after the variable is manipulated and comparisons are made with a suitably matched control case in order to make inferences about the effects of the variable. This may take place in a laboratory (for example, sensory testing of foods) or in the field (varying exposure to advertising in two matched TV regions).

Activity 4

Most people have seen this process – the collection of research data by physical observation – in action. Can you recall an example of it?

Observation may involve machines or fieldworkers. It may involve simply recording behaviour, or require the fieldworker to interpret behaviour, or even interact ('participant observation').

(a) Direct observation involves the examination, by an observer, of how people behave in particular situations (for example, customers' reactions to product displays and promotions).

(b) Recording devices can be used to monitor the responses of individuals:

　　(i) an eye camera is sometimes used to test response to advertisements;

　　(ii) a psychogalvanometer, which records changes in electrical resistance, and hence emotional reaction, is also used in advertising testing;

　　(iii) a tachistoscope exposes material for a brief moment and measures the visual impact or legibility of an advertisement.

3.1 Sampling

In marketing research for consumer goods, surveys of the large total number of consumers will necessarily involve the selection of an appropriate sample from the total population, for reasons of practicality and cost effectiveness. Surveying a total population is only feasible when the numbers are small, as in the case of industrial markets.

Samples must be representative of the populations from which they are chosen. Representativeness is a statistical concept, which rests on the theory of probability. Broadly, representativeness is achieved by seeking to ensure that samples are chosen at random, in a manner which gives all members of a population an equal chance of being chosen and in numbers sufficient to minimise the influence of small numbers of individuals from one section of the population on the data which is gathered.

A sample frame is constructed to include all the members of a population (for example, 'real ale' drinkers, car drivers). Population here does not mean 'everyone in the electoral roll' or 'everyone living in town Y'.

A complete sampling frame is difficult to obtain in practice because data is often inaccurate, but in any case a comprehensive sampling frame is not justified if the benefits from greater confidence in the accuracy of sample estimates are less than the cost of obtaining or maintaining the sampling frame.

Activity 5

Suppose you are developing a new product: a piece of computer software designed to simplify the completion of an income tax return. You wish to assess demand for the product by sampling potential users. How would you go about obtaining a sampling frame?

Various techniques of sampling (methods of sample design) have been developed so that samples which are 'nearly' random ('quasi-random') can be obtained.

Random sampling

Definition

> A random sample is one selected in such a way that every member of the population has an equal chance of being included.

The use of random number tables, or computer generated random numbers, seeks to eliminate conscious or unconscious bias.

Non-random sampling

In many situation it is either not possible or not desirable to use a random sample. The main methods of non-random sampling are:

- Systematic sampling
- Stratified sampling
- Multistage sampling
- Quota sampling
- Cluster sampling

Some of these methods try to approximate the random sampling technique, and are 'quasi-random' sampling methods.

Systematic sampling involves selecting every nth item after a random start. For example, if it was decided to select a sample of 20 from a population of 800, then every 40th (800 ÷ 20) item after a random start in the first 40 should be selected. If (say) 23 was chosen, then the sample would include the following items.

23rd, 63rd, 103rd, 143rd 783rd

The gap of 40 is known as the sampling interval.

Stratified sampling divides the population into strata, which may conform to a consumer characteristics or a market segment.

For example, a manufacturer of machine equipment may know that 40% of its sales come from one industry A, 30% from another industry B, 10% from industry C and so on. A stratified sample would aim to obtain 40% of its respondents from industry A, 30% from group B, and 10% from C. If all potential customers in each industry are known, the sample within each group could then be selected by random sampling methods using a sampling frame.

Multistage sampling divides the country into a number of areas and a small sample of these is selected at random. Each of the areas selected is subdivided into smaller units and again, a small number of these is selected at random. This process is repeated as many times as necessary and, finally, a random sample of the relevant people living in each of the smallest units is made. A fair approximation to a random sample can be obtained.

In quota sampling, investigators are told to interview certain numbers of people in different categories.

- Age groups (16–25; 26–35 and so on)
- Gender groups (male; female)
- Product user groups (light users; medium users; heavy users; non-users)

These are called 'quota controls'. Out of a quota of, say, 50, an interviewer may be required to find at least 20 men and at least 20 women. Ten may be either. The same interviewer may be asked to find ten aged 16–25, ten aged 26–35, ten over 35 and 20 who may be any age. This gives the interviewer greater flexibility and it is easy to administer, although there is still some risk of bias.

Using cluster sampling, investigators are told to examine every item in the small areas which fit the required definition. Cluster sampling has the advantage of low cost and ease of administration in the same way as multistage sampling, but suffers from a risk of unrepresentativeness because of the restricted group chosen.

Potential faults in a sampling exercise

There are several faults or weaknesses which might occur in the design or collection of sample data.

(a) Bias: unless random sampling is used, there will be a likelihood that some 'units' (individuals or households) will have a poor or even zero chance of being selected. Where this occurs, samples are said to be biased.

A biased sample may occur when:

(i) The sampling frame is out of date, and consequently excludes a number of individuals or 'units' new to the population

(ii) Some individuals selected for the sample decline to respond

(b) Insufficient data: the sample may be too small to be reliable as a source of information about an entire population.

(c) Unrepresentative data: data collected might be unrepresentative of normal conditions or might be affected by the process of being collected. This is called the 'Hawthorne Effect' after a study in the 1920s in which the workers involved performed better than usual simply because they were being studied.

(d) Omission of an important factor: data might be incomplete because an important item has been omitted in the design of the 'questions'.

(e) Carelessness: data might be provided without due care and attention. An investigator might also be careless in the way he or she gathers data.

(f) Confusion between 'cause' and 'correlation': it may be tempting to assume that if two variables appear to be related, one variable is the cause of the other. Variables may be associated but it is not necessarily true that one causes the other. For example, in a period of hot weather both sales of swimwear and ice creams are likely to rise (a positive correlation). However, one is not causing the other; they are both 'caused' by the hot weather.

(g) Where questions call for something more than simple 'one word' replies, there may be difficulty in interpreting the results correctly. This is especially true of 'depth interviews' which try to determine the reasons for human behaviour (motivation research).

3.2 Questionnaires

Questionnaires may be administered by personal interview, telephone or post.

Postal surveys tend to attract a relatively low response rate and unrepresentative respondents. Unsolicited questionnaires often obtain only a 2% – 3% return. Great care should be taken when extrapolating from such results. Follow up letters may improve responses. These are also better in specialist populations (such as enthusiasts for a particular product line) and when inducements are offered.

Activity 6

Think of some simple techniques which might improve the response rate to a postal survey.

Questionnaire design

There are two main considerations in designing questionnaires.

(a) Questions should generate valid and reliable information on the matter being surveyed. Respondents must therefore find the questions comprehensible. Questions that are likely to produce biased answers should also be avoided.

(b) The questionnaire should be designed with the subsequent data analysis in mind.

The following guidelines should therefore be adopted.

(a) Leading questions should be avoided.

(b) Questions should be short and unambiguous wherever possible.

(c) Questions should fall in a logical sequence.

(d) The working language of the target group should be used.

(e) Funnelling, a technique of moving from general to restricted questions more directly related to the research objectives, can be applied. This technique is sometimes reversed to check limited responses.

(f) Personal questions on potentially sensitive issues such as sex, politics, religion and personal habits should only be asked in exceptional circumstances. Before attempting such questions interviewers need to establish goodwill.

Pilot testing is essential to questionnaire design. It involves testing a proposed questionnaire to avoid confusing, ambiguous, silly or unnecessary questions. Pilot testing also permits the methods of analysis to be given a trial run.

Classification of respondents is important. This is used to analyse responses to find if there are variations between attitudes and behaviour of different types of people. These questions are usually asked at the end of an interview, since some (such as age) may be sensitive.

Questionnaires can be administered by the following means.

(a)   Telephone interviews: these offer a speedy response and can cover a wide geographical area fairly cheaply. The drawback is that interviews must be fairly short and cannot use visual methods.

(b)   Personal interviews: the best, but slowest and most expensive method.

(c)   Replies by mail: these are fairly cheap and avoid interviewer interference, but there is no control over the completion of the questionnaire. Low response (say 2–3%) might make the sample data unrepresentative.

(d)   Self-completion, perhaps at the place of purchase. The disadvantage of this form of survey is that respondents may not understand questions properly (as with mail surveys). The questionnaire will also need to be short to optimise completion.

3.3   Consumer panels

Definition

> Consumer panels consist of a representative cross-section of consumers who have agreed to give information about their attitudes or buying habits (through personal visits or mail questionnaires or data transferred from a home recording computer by modem) at regular intervals of time.

Consumer panels with personal visits are called home audit panels and panels which send data by post or by computer are called diary panels. Panels might be established for either the long term or the short term.

Consumer panels provide continuous information over time from willing guinea pigs, but recruitment and representativeness are big problems.

Willing participants may be atypical and probably represent only a limited section of the population in question.

3.4   Trade audits or retail audits

Trade audits are carried out among panels of wholesalers and retailers, and the term 'retail audits' refers to panels of retailers only. A research firm sends auditors to selected outlets at regular intervals to count stock and deliveries, thus enabling an estimate of throughput to be made. This details:

(a)   Retail sales for selected products and brands, sales by different type of retail outlet, market shares and brand shares

(b)   Retail stocks of products and brands (enabling a firm subscribing to the audit to compare stocks of its own goods with those of competitors)

(c)   Selling prices in retail outlets, including information about discounts

---

Activity 7

How can the data from a retail audit be of any value to a manufacturer who is not making retail sales?

A well-known example of a retail audit is the Inventory Audit of Retail Sales, also called the Nielsen Index (after its originator) which has operated since 1939. This monitors sales and stock levels for three product groups: food, drugs and pharmaceuticals. The Nielsen Food Index audits about 800 grocers bi-monthly and reports on each brand, size, flavour etc specified by the client.

  (a)   Consumer sales in units and by value

  (b)   Retailer purchases in units

  (c)   The source of delivery (co-operatives, multiple stores depot, independent wholesalers)

  (d)   Retailers' stocks and stock cover (in days/weeks)

  (e)   Prices

  (f)   Details of out of stock items

  (g)   Press, magazine and TV expenditure

The report is subdivided into shop types (all grocers, co-operatives, multiples, major multiples and independents) and television regions.

3.5   Pre-testing and post-testing

Marketing research may be carried out before, during and after marketing decisions are implemented. Not all areas of marketing can be investigated easily. While the effects of sales promotions (coupons, 'three for the price of two' and the like) are directly measurable in terms of sales, the effectiveness of advertising often needs to be inferred and is difficult to distinguish from other factors.

Other powerful influences in the market place, such as price cuts and sales promotions by competitors, can mask the true effect. Much research therefore focuses on the effectiveness of the campaign in communicating with its target audience.

Measurement of the communication effect is more reliable than attempts to measure the sales effect attributable to a particular advertising campaign.

Pre-testing

  (a)   Motivational research is carried out to pre-test advertising copy. Subjects are invited to watch a film show which includes new TV advertising, and a measure of the shift in their brand awareness is taken after the show. Copy research might involve showing members of the public a number of press advertisements and then asking questions about them (in order to measure the impact of different slogans or headlines).

  (b)   Laboratory tests, recording the physiological reactions of people watching advertisements (for example, heart beat, blood pressure, dilation of the pupil of the eye, perspiration), measure the arousal or attention-drawing power of an advertisement.

BPP
PUBLISHING

(c)   Ratings tests involve asking a panel of target consumers to look at alternative advertisements and to give them ratings (marks out of ten) for attention-drawing power, clarity, emotional appeal and stimulus to buy.

In 1979, when Ford launched the Fiesta their advertising agency, Ogilvy, Benson, Mather, abandoned their first creative idea after motivational research. The proposed copy for the advertisement focused on the theme of Ford's 'new baby'. An expectant father was seen pacing up and down outside his garage. Suddenly, from inside the garage came the sounds of a new born baby crying. The garage door was opened to reveal a proud wife with the new Fiesta. Women reacted very unfavourably to the advertisement which was shown in its pre-production animated form (drawings with soundtrack). They expressed uncomfortable feelings and anxiety at the thought of a baby being locked up in a garage. The advertisement was reformulated to a high technology theme.

Test marketing aims to obtain information about how consumers react to the product – will they buy it, how frequently, and so on? Total market demand for the product can then be estimated.

Definition

> A test market involves testing a new consumer product in selected areas which are thought to be 'representative' of the total market.

This avoids the costs of a full-scale launch while permitting the collection of market data. The firm will distribute the product through the same types of sales outlets it plans to use in the full market launch, and use the promotion plans it intends to use in the full market. This enables the company to 'test the water' before launching the product nationally. It helps in making sales forecasts and can also be used to identify flaws in either the product or the promotional plans.

Other forms of product testing include the following.

(a)   Simulated store technique (or laboratory test markets) involves a group of shoppers watching a selection of advertisements for a number of products, including an advertisement for the new product. They are then given some money and invited to spend it in a supermarket or shopping area. Their purchases are recorded and they are asked to explain their purchase decisions (and non-purchase decisions). Some weeks later they are contacted again and asked about their product attitudes and repurchase intentions. These tests provide a quick, simple way to assess advertising effectiveness and forecast sales volumes.

(b)   Controlled test marketing. A panel of stores carries the new product for a given length of time. Shelf locations, point-of-sale displays and pricing are varied; the sales results are then monitored. This test (also known as 'minimarket testing') helps to provide an assessment of 'in-store' factors in achieving sales as well as to forecast sales volumes.

Post-testing

Post-testing concentrates on the communication effect of advertisements. It uses:

(a)   Recall tests, which ask the interviewee to remember, unaided, advertisements which have been seen before the interview

(b) Recognition tests, which involve giving the interviewee some reminder of an advertisement, and testing his/her recognition of it

EPOS

The recording and use of electronic point of sale (EPOS) data has become widespread and offers a real opportunity to measure directly the effect of, say, local radio advertising on the immediate sales of a brand in the media's catchment area. The use of such disaggregated tactical data (that is, data that isolates particular factors) overcomes the problems of external effects which distort aggregated sales figures.

EPOS enables major retailers, such as the supermarkets, to measure directly the performance of competitive brands. Previously, this information had to be inferred from the use of consumer purchasing audits conducted by organisations like Audits of Great Britain (AGB).

The tracking of sales in this way increasingly allows managers to carry out monitoring and analysis of market data using decision support systems.

3.6 Recording data about attitudes

Attitudes are measured by means of attitude scales, and there are two common types used in marketing research.

(a) Likert scales consist of statements, about product qualities, consumer attitudes or behaviour and so on. Respondents are asked to state the level of agreement or disagreement which they have towards the statement. Responses are selected from a 5, 7, 9 or 11 point scale marking these levels (such as from 'very strongly agree' to 'very strongly disagree').

(b) Semantic differential scales consist of bipolar adjectives (strong-weak, good-bad, masculine-feminine) with intervening gradations. Respondents are typically asked to rate or place a product on these scales.

3.7 Evaluating data

The evaluation of data collected in a survey will be carried out using statistical techniques. Some forms of analysis are as follows.

(a) Multiple regression analysis. This might be used, for example, to analyse the effect on sales of changes in a variety of other variables such as price and advertising.

(b) Discriminant analysis. This might be used when the researcher wants to know what consumer traits (for example, socio-economic groupings, lifestyle, age and sex) are associated with frequent or infrequent purchase of a particular product or brand.

(c) Tests of statistical significance, for example chi-squared tests and calculation of standard errors.

3.8 The reliability of sample data

A sample is intended to provide a measure of the attitudes or behaviour of a population as a whole. This is usually checked by making statistical tests of significance. Computer packages for statistical analysis will often carry out tests for the significance of data variation automatically.

Sampling can be used to identify consumer attitudes and behaviour, but also to identify potential market segments.

3.9 The value of research information

Information is only worth having if the benefits derived from it are worth more than the costs of its collection. The greater the accuracy of information provided, the more it will cost. At high levels of accuracy the high level of the marginal costs of collection will probably exceed the marginal benefits of the extra accuracy obtained.

It is also worth noting that it is only worth paying for market research that provides additional information. Marketing research that merely confirms information that is already widely known has little real value.

3.10 Interpretation of results

Interpretation of results takes great care. There is some controversy as to how much interpretation market researchers should offer clients. One school of thought suggests presenting the facts only, leaving the client to draw conclusions. A contrasting approach is for the researcher to interpret results and suggest conclusions or interpretations based on evidence in the findings. The guiding principle should be the brief given to the researcher at the outset of the project.

In the last chapter we considered market segmentation in relation to marketing strategy and planning. We now need to look in much more detail at how and why markets are segmented.

4 MARKET SEGMENTATION

Market segmentation is an attempt to analyse markets in terms of different customer characteristics and variations in taste, usage and so on. An homogenous mass market is sub-divided into subsets of customers. Within each subset, customers have similar needs which are distinct from those in other subsets.

By using different marketing approaches for each segment, it should be possible to increase profit contribution for each segment. The marketing approach used for each segment should reflect the particular needs of customers and potential customers in that segment. It is akin to using a rifle (to aim at specific targets) rather than a shotgun (to aim at all targets at the same time).

4.1 Requirements for effective market segmentation

Clearly there are many possible characteristics of buyers which could be used as a basis for segmenting markets. There are criteria that can be used to identify the most effective characteristics for use in market segmentation decisions.

(a) **Measurability**

This is the degree to which information exists or is obtainable cost effectively in respect of the particular buyer characteristic. Bookshops may be able to obtain information on sales relatively easily, but it is more difficult for them to obtain information about the personality traits of buyers.

(b) **Accessibility**

This is the degree to which the organisation can focus effectively on the chosen segments using marketing methods. Educational establishments in a bookshop's area can be identified easily and approached using direct mail or telemarketing, while individuals with income over £30,000 per annum in the same area might be more difficult to isolate effectively.

(c)   **Substantiality**

This is the degree to which the segments are large enough to be worth considering as separate markets. Mounting marketing campaigns is expensive, and so a minimum size for a segment is based on likely profitability. For example, whilst a large number of people in social group DE aged over 65 could be identified, their potential profitability for a bookshop is likely to be less in the long term than a smaller number of 17–18 year old students.

4.2   Benefits of market segmentation

Apart from improved contribution to profits, other benefits from successful market segmentation include the following.

(a)   The organisation may be able to identify new marketing opportunities, because it will have a better understanding of customer needs in each segment, with the possibility of spotting further sub groups.

(b)   Specialists can be used for each of the organisation's major segments. For example, small business counsellors can be employed by banks to deal effectively with small firms and a computer consultancy can have specialist sales staff for, say, shops, manufacturers, service industries and local authorities. This builds competencies and establishes effective marketing systems.

(c)   The total marketing budget can be allocated proportionately to each segment and the likely return from each segment. This optimises return on investment.

(d)   The organisation can make fine adjustments to the product and service offerings and to the marketing appeals used for each segment. This again promotes efficient use of resources.

(e)   The organisation can try to dominate particular segments, thus gaining competitive advantage. Advantages accrued function synergistically to promote improved competitive ability; in other words, the outcome is more than the sum of its parts.

(f)   The product range can more closely reflect differences in customer needs. All modern marketing relies on responsiveness to the consumer. When this is improved, benefits flow.

4.3   Bases for market segmentation

A number of bases are possible and these are discussed in the following paragraphs.

Geographic segmentation

Here, the basis for segmentation is location. A national chain of supermarkets will use geographic segmentation because it interacts closely with the chain's outlet strategy. Each branch or group of retail outlets could be given mutually exclusive areas to service. The supermarket chain can then make more effective use of target marketing to cover the market available. The obvious advantage to customers is convenience of access, which is a primary motivation to retailers when considering ways of segmenting the grocery shopping market. This customer benefit needs to be considered against the cost of provision of retail branches. Research has shown that one of the major reasons why customers choose particular stores in which to shop is convenience of access.

Demographic segmentation

Here the market is divided on the basis of age, gender, socio-economic group, housing, family characteristics or family life cycle stage. These factors may be used in combination.

Activity 8

Before reading on, what do you think is meant by 'the decline of the traditional family', supposedly now a strong feature of UK society?

Segmentation by age is the basis of the attempt by the High Street banks to attract 18 year olds as customers, especially new students in the higher education sector. Customers are unlikely to switch accounts between competing suppliers, so banks expect long-term relationships (and profit) to result from success in this target marketing effort, in a highly competitive market.

Products targeted by gender include cosmetics, clothing, alcohol, cars and even financial services.

The JICNARS scale is used by the UK market research industry to provide standardised social groupings. These are based entirely on the occupation of the head of the household.

Socio-economic groups in the UK		
Social grade	*Description of occupations*	*Example*
A	Higher managerial and professional	Company director
B	Lower managerial and supervisory	Middle manager
C1	Non-manual	Bank clerk
C2	Skilled manual	Electrician
D	Semi-skilled and unskilled manual	Labourer
E	Those receiving no income from employment/casual workers	Unemployed

Other scales (such as the Registrar General's Classification, and the Hall-Jones Scale) are used elsewhere. Classification is very commonly used in marketing and market research in the UK, yet it is simplistic to make easy assumptions about the implications of classification for consumption. For example, in terms of disposable income (the take-home pay of workers) C2 members often have more money than do C1, which obviously affects buying capability. Also there is class mobility in that individuals and their families can move between groups, although their underlying influences may remain as they were or change only slowly.

Socio-economic groups are a useful way of segmenting markets for the following reasons.

(a) With some exceptions we can make many reliable inferences about the relationship between occupation and income

(b) They can be used to infer differences in purchase and consumption patterns even where the total disposable income between two groups may be similar

(c) The categories are stable and enduring, and can be compared across time

(d)   Each group tends to have identifiable attitudinal and behavioural patterns. For instance, ABC1 groups tend to be more 'future orientated' than do C2DE groups which are more 'present orientated'. Such attitudes are clearly highly significant for the marketing of endowment policies or private education, for example

Because of criticisms of the JICNARS classification, more sophisticated measures of socio-economic and group membership have been devised. Housing type and ownership are particularly important methods of segmentation for many types of good. The use of this method is made much easier by the major categorisation scheme for all housing types in the UK, known as ACORN (A Categorisation Of Residential Neighbourhoods), which enables precise target marketing based on housing type to be conducted by suppliers. It is based on the Census data gathered by the government every ten years which records details of residential households and their occupants, and also other data collected by HM Statistical Service on employment, consumption and so on.

ACORN data provides for a much higher level of segmentation, linking the type of housing and implied economic status with geographic location (geodemographics). The 1995 ACORN geodemographic profile of the UK, based on the 1991 Census, is given below followed by a discussion of life-style dimensions.

A classification of residential neighbourhoods (ACORN) UK 1995

(a)	Geo-demographic dimensions	% of population
A	*Thriving (19.7% of population)*	
A1	*Wealthy achievers, Suburban areas (15.9%)*	
1.1	Wealthy suburbs, large detached houses	2.5
1.2	Villages with wealthy commuters	3.2
1.3	Mature affluent home owning areas	2.7
1.4	Affluent suburbs, older families	3.7
1.5	Mature, well-off suburbs	3.0
A2	*Affluent greys, rural communities (2.3%)*	
2.6	Agricultural villages, home based workers	1.6
2.7	Holiday retreats, older people, home based workers	0.7
A3	*Prosperous pensioners, retirement areas (2.4%)*	
3.8	Home owning areas, well-off older residents	1.4
3.9	Private flats, elderly people	0.9
B	*Expanding (11.6% of population)*	
B4	*Affluent executives, family areas (3.8%)*	
4.10	Affluent working families with mortgages	2.1
4.11	Affluent working couples with mortgages, new homes	1.3
4.12	Transient workforces, living at their place of work	0.4
B5	*Well-off workers, family areas (7.8%)*	
5.13	Home owning family areas	2.6
5.14	Home owning family areas, older children	3.0
5.15	Families with mortgages, younger children	2.2
C	*Rising (7.8% of population)*	
C6	*Affluent urbanites, town and city areas (2.3%)*	
6.16	Well-off town and city areas	1.1
6.17	Flats and mortgages, singles and young working couples	0.7
6.18	Furnished flats and bedsits, younger single people	0.4

NOTES

		% of population
C7	*Prosperous professionals, metropolitan areas (2.1%)*	
7.19	Apartments, young professional singles and couples	1.1
7.20	Certified multi-ethnic areas	1.0
C8	*Better-off executives, inner city areas (3.4%)*	
8.21	Prosperous enclaves, highly qualified executives	0.7
8.22	Academic centres, students and young professionals	0.7
8.23	Affluent city centre areas, tenements and flats	0.4
8.24	Partially gentrified multi-ethnic areas	0.7
8.25	Converted flats and bedsits, single people	0.9
D	***Settling (24.1% of population)***	
D9	*Comfortable middle agers, mature home owning areas (13.4%)*	
9.26	Mature established home owning areas	3.3
9.27	Rural areas, mixed occupations	3.4
9.28	Established home owning areas	4.0
9.29	Home owning areas, council tenants, retired people	2.6
D10	*Skilled workers, home owning areas (10.7%)*	
10.30	Established home owning areas, skilled workers	4.5
10.31	Home owners in older properties, younger workers	3.1
10.32	Home owning areas with skilled workers	3.1
E	***Aspiring (13.7% of population)***	
E11	*New home owners, mature communities (9.7%)*	
11.33	Council areas, some new home owners	3.8
11.34	Mature home owning areas, skilled workers	3.1
11.35	Furnished flats and bedsits, younger single people	0.4
E12	*White collar workers, better-off multi-ethnic areas (4.0%)*	
12.36	Home owning multi-ethnic areas, young families	1.1
12.37	Multi occupied town centres, mixed occupations	1.8
12.38	Multi-ethnic areas, white collar workers	1.1
F	***Striving (22.7% of population)***	
F13	*Older people, less prosperous areas (3.6%)*	
13.39	Home owners, small council flats, single pensioners	1.9
13.40	Council areas, older people, health problems	1.7
F14	*Council estate residents, better-off homes (11.5%)*	
14.41	Better-off council areas, new home owners	2.4
14.42	Council areas, young families, some new home owners	3.0
14.43	Council areas, young families, many lone parents	1.6
14.44	Multi-occupied terraces, multi-ethnic areas	0.9
14.45	Low rise council housing, less well-off families	1.8
14.46	Council areas, residents with health problems	
F15	*Council estate residents, high unemployment (2.7%)*	
15.47	Estates with high unemployment	1.1
15.48	Council flats, elderly people, health problems	0.7
15.49	Council flats, very high unemployment, singles	0.9
F16	*Council estate residents, greatest hardship (2.8%)*	
16.50	Council areas, high unemployment lone parents	1.9
16.51	Council flats, greatest hardship, many lone parents	0.9

	% of population
F17 People in multi-ethnic, low-income areas (2.1%)	
17.52 Multi-ethnic, large families, overcrowding	0.6
17.53 Multi-ethnic, severe unemployment, lone parents	1.0
17.54 Multi-ethnic, high unemployment, overcrowding	0.5
Rounding	0.5

This system introduces house type into the classification and every UK household has been classified in ACORN groups. Other work has cross-referenced ACORN with postcodes for every address in the UK making specific identification of customer types more flexible.

Another method of segmentation is based on the family type: the size and constitution of the family unit. There have been changes in the characteristics of the family unit in the last few decades. These household structural changes have been accompanied by other important social trends:

(a)   Later marriage and delayed childbearing

(b)   House price rises have meant that newly formed households contain partners who both work

(c)   The 'enterprise economy' has encouraged a greater interest in career development

(d)   Greater financial independence for women caused by recent economic and social changes

(e)   An increased number of 'single person of pensionable age' households

The implication for marketing is that new niche markets are likely to grow whilst traditional markets may be declining. Products aimed at single pensioners living alone, such as alarms to use in case of accidents, are developed and marketed. TV and radio shows aimed at young housewives will have smaller potential audiences than thirty years ago. The use of customer databases to direct more specific target marketing may be one solution, as may product proliferation. Advertising has begun to make explicit references to divorce and separated families. This has come to be an acceptable subject for certain advertising.

Definition

> The family life cycle (FLC) is a summary demographic variable; that is, it combines the effects of age, marital status, career status (income) and the presence or absence of children.

The FLC is used to identify the various stages through which households progress. The table on page 158 shows features of the family at various stages of its life cycle. It is clear that particular products and services can be target-marketed at specific stages in the life cycle of families. We outlined some criticisms of the family life cycle model in Chapter 2 in the context of the modern marketing environment.

Business Basics: Marketing

Activity 9

Advertisers make much use of the family life cycle concept and current sociological trends.

'In 1984, a year into the Oxo family soap opera, Mum began her bid for freedom by leaving Dad to cook a weekend lunch while she goes off on a shopping jaunt. ... Three years later, Mum, like most women, has a job; like most mums the job she has is part-time and she still carries the main domestic responsibilities. ... By 1990 Mum is venturing even further afield to a Friday night keep-fit class. ... In 1989 (when vegetable Oxo was launched) the TV soap has a vegetarian friend of son Nick coming over to lunch and daughter Alison finding his veggie pal madly attractive. ... In 1990 Nick invites his girlfriend back for a meal while Mum and Dad are out. Their eyes meet seductively over the gravy boat. ... Two years later Nick has stayed the night at his girlfriend's flat – they appear to spend their time preparing a risotto together. ... A recent development was the appearance of a wok. How many viewers would have known what one was ten years ago?'

Financial Times, October 1993

A later Oxo ad has Mum getting weepy as she hits the 'empty nest' stage and then finally, moving away from the house as the series ends.

Can you think of other examples of advertisements that use (or abuse) these basic ideas?

Demographic segmentation methods are powerful tools to specify target market segments. They are even more effective when each of the bases is used in combination with other factors, since it is clear that bases for demographic segmentation are interdependent. Age and family life cycle stage are strongly linked, as are housing type and socio-economic classification. By using bases in combination, target markets can be very precisely defined.

Psychographic segmentation

Definition

> Psychographics or lifestyle segmentation seeks to classify people according to their values, opinions, personality, characteristics and interests.

In today's competitive world where innovation is the key to improved organisational performance, lifestyle segmentation deals with the person as opposed to the product and attempts to discover the particular lifestyle patterns of customers. This offers a richer insight into their preferences for various products and services. Lifestyle refers to 'distinctive ways of living adopted by particular communities or subsections of society'. Lifestyle involves combining a number of behavioural factors, such as motivation, personality and culture. Effective use in marketing depends on accurate description, and the numbers of people following a particular lifestyle must be quantified. Then marketers can assign and target products and promotion at particular target lifestyle groups. Lifestyle is a controversial issue and a full analysis of the arguments is beyond the scope of this text. Its implications for marketing, and the problems of definition involved, can perhaps best be illustrated by some examples.

Database marketing, which is becoming much more important in identifying and targeting market segments for direct selling, relies heavily on the theories underlying psychographic segmentation.

One simple example generalises lifestyle in terms of four categories, as follows.

(a) Upwardly mobile, ambitious: these individuals seek a better and more affluent lifestyle, principally through better paid and more interesting work, and a higher material standard of living. A customer with such a lifestyle will be prepared to try new products.

(b) Traditional and sociable: here, compliance and conformity to group norms bring social approval and reassurance to the individual. Purchasing patterns will therefore be 'conformist'.

(c) Security and status seeking: this group stresses 'safety' and 'ego-defensive' needs. This lifestyle links status, income and security. It encourages the purchase of strong and well known products and brands, and emphasises those products and services which confer status and make life as secure and predictable as possible. These would include insurance, membership of the AA or RAC etc. Products that are well established and familiar inspire more confidence than new products, which will be resisted.

(d) Hedonistic preference: this lifestyle places emphasis on 'enjoying life now' and the immediate satisfaction of wants and needs. Little thought is given to the future.

Two more complex lifestyle analyses are shown in the table on page 157. These analyses are based on empirical attitude research, and the agencies that have constructed them use them to advise their clients on how best to design and position existing and new products at target segments made up of people who have similar lifestyle patterns.

It is possible to gain further insights into lifestyle behaviour by cross-referring demographic variables to the observed behaviour of specific lifestyle types. For example, tables are available showing the percentage of men aged, say, 35 to 44, who have recently travelled by air, visited a pub and listened to Jazz FM.

Clearly, the power of data handling and analysis provided by computer systems will only increase the value and use of the psychographic method of segmentation.

Geodemographic segmentation

Geodemographics is a segmentation technique which was introduced in the early 1980s, but came into its own in the late 1980s and early 1990s. Basically, it classifies people according to where they live. It rests on a similar idea to the ACORN scheme – that households within a particular neighbourhood exhibit similar purchasing behaviour, outlook and so on.

The central themes of geodemographics were outlined by one leading market research expert as:

... that two people who live in the same neighbourhood, such as a Census Enumeration District, are more likely to have similar characteristics than are two people chosen at random. The second is that neighbourhoods can be categorised in terms of the characteristics of the population which they contain, and that two neighbourhoods can be placed in the same category, that is they can contain similar types of people, even though they are widely separated.

Geodemographics is thus able to target customers in particular areas who exhibit similar behaviour patterns. This system allows organisations to profile the users or potential users of a product or service and then proceed to target customers who match these profiles. This of course should increase the profitability and take-up of the offered product/service.

Modern techniques also allow for data to be combined and projected so that knowledge about neighbourhood and age will also permit projections about attitudes and behaviour with strong statistical reliability. One such system can make useful inferences about consumers based only on their first names.

Segmenting the green market

Profiles of green consumers show that the force of green concern varies according to product class, prevailing market conditions, attitudes and beliefs about the product in question. Many consumers have not resolved the complex, confusing and often contradictory messages which are being sent out by various interest groups in this area. Broadly, females are more environmentally-aware than males, and families with children (particularly young children) are more likely to be concerned about making green consumption choices. The evidence also shows that consumers are becoming both more aware and more sophisticated in their approach to green issues.

Marketing Diagnostics has developed a typology of green consumers which identifies four main groups.

(a) Green activists (5–15% of the population) are members/supporters of environmental organisations.

(b) Green thinkers (30% includes activists) seek out green products and services, and look for new ways to care for the environment.

(c) Green consumer base (45–60%) is anyone who has changed their behaviour in response to green concerns.

(d) Generally concerned (90%) claim to be concerned about green issues.

A behaviourally-based psychographic typology by Ogilvy and Mather involves a range of factors. Four categories of consumers are identified in terms of tendencies and characteristics.

(a) Activists (16%)

- Aware of the issues
- Likely to buy green products
- Concerned for their children
- Optimistic about technological change
- People oriented
- Home owners with children
- Conservative voters
- Likely to be upmarket consumers

(b) Realists (34%)

- The youngest group – those with young children
- Worried about the environment
- Consider profit and environmental protection as conflicting
- Are pessimistic about a solution
- Are sceptical about a 'green bandwagon'
- Vote Labour

McCann-Erikson Men	McCann-Erikson Women	Taylor Nelson
Avant Guardians. Concerned with change and well-being of others, rather than possessions. Well educated, prone to self righteousness.	*Avant Guardians.* 'Liberal left' opinions, trendy attitudes. But out-going, active, sociable.	*Self-explorers.* Motivated by self-expression and self-realisation. Less materialistic than other groups, and showing high tolerance levels.
Pontifactors. Strongly held, traditional opinions. Very British, and concerned about keeping others on the right path.	*Lady Righteous.* Traditional, 'right-minded' opinions. Happy, complacent, with strong family Orientation.	*Social resisters.* The caring group, concerned with fairness and social values, but of ten appearing intolerant and moralistic.
Chameleons. Want to be contemporary to win approval Act like barometers of social change, but copiers not leaders.	*Hopeful seekers.* Need to be liked, want to do 'right'. Like new things, want to be trendy.	*Experimentalists.* Highly individualistic, motivated by fast-moving enjoyment. They are materialistic, pro-technology but anti-traditional authority.
Self-admirers. At the young end of the spectrum. Intolerant of others and strongly motivated by success. Concerned about self-image.	*Lively ladies.* Younger than above, sensual, materialistic, ambitious and competitive.	*Conspicuous consumers.* They are materialistic and pushy, motivated by acquisition, competition, and getting ahead. Pro-authority, law and order
Self-exploiters. The 'doers' and 'self-starters', competitive but always under pressure and often pessimistic. Possessions are important.	*New unromantics.* Generally young and single, adopting a hard-headed and unsentimental approach to life. Independent, self-centered.	*Belongers.* What they seek is a quiet, undisturbed family life. They are conservative, conventional rules followers.
Token triers. Always willing to try new things to 'improve their luck', but apparently on a permanent try-and-fail cycle. Includes an above average proportion of unemployed.	*Lack-a-daisy.* Unassertive and easy-going. Try to cope but often fail. Not very interested in the new.	*Survivors.* Strongly class-conscious and community spirited their motivation is to 'get by'.
Sleepwalkers. Contented under-achievers. Do not care about most things, and actively opt out. Traditional macho views.	*Blinkered.* Negative, do not want to be disturbed. Uninterested in conventional success – in fact, few interests except TV and radio.	*Aimless.* Comprises two groups, (a) the young unemployed, who are often anti-authority, and (b) the old, whose motivation is day-to-day existence.
Passive endurers. Biased towards the elderly, they are often economically and socially disenfranchised. Expect little of life, and give little.	*Down-trodden.* This group is shy, introverted, but put upon. Would like to do better. Often unhappy and pressurised in personal relationships.	

	I	II	III	IV	V	VI	VII	VIII	IX
	Bachelor Stage	Newly married couples	Full nest I	Full nest II	Full nest III	Empty nest I	Empty nest II	Solitary survivor in labour force	Solitary survivor(s) retired
	Young single people not living at home	Young, no children	Youngest child under six	Youngest child six or over	Older married couples with dependent children	Older married couples, no children living with them, head of family still in labour force	Older married couples, no children living at home, head of family retired		
	Few financial burdens.	Better off financially than they will be in the near future.	Home purchasing at peak.	Financial position better.	Financial position still better.	Home ownership at peak.	Significant cut in income.	Income still adequate but likely to sell family home and purchase smaller accommodation.	Significant cut in income.
	Fashion / opinion leader led.	High levels of purchase of homes and consumer durable goods.	Liquid assets / savings low.	Some wives return to work.	More wives work.	More satisfied with financial position and money saved.	Keep home.	Concern with level of savings and pension.	Additional medical requirements. Special need for attention, affection and security.
	Recreation orientated.	Buy cars, fridges, cookers, life assurance, durable furniture, holidays.	Dissatisfied with financial position and amount of money saved.	Child dominated household.	School and examination dominated household.	Interested in travel, recreation, self-education.	Buy medical appliances or medical care products which aid health, sleep and digestion.	Some expenditure on hobbies and pastimes.	May seek sheltered accommodation.
	Buy basic kitchen equipment, basic furniture, cars, equipment for the mating game, holidays.	Establish patterns of personal financial management and control.	Reliance on credit finance, credit cards, overdrafts etc.	Buy necessities foods, cleaning material, clothes, bicycles, sports gear, music lessons, pianos, holidays etc.	Some children get first jobs; others in further / higher education.	Make financial gifts and contributions.	Assist children. Concern with level of savings and pension. Some expenditure on hobbies and pastimes.	Worries about security and dependence.	Possible dependence on others for personal financial management and control.
	Experiment with the patterns of personal financial management and control.		Child dominated household.		Expenditure to support children's further / higher education.	Children gain qualifications: move to Stage 1.			
			Buy necessities washers, dryers, baby food and clothes, vitamins, toys, books etc.		Buy new, more tasteful furniture, non-necessary appliance, boats etc holidays.	Buy luxuries, home improvements eg fitted kitchens etc.			

(c)   Complacents (28%)

- Upmarket consumers with older children;
- Are optimistic – about mankind, business and government;
- See this as someone else's problem;
- Are not very conscious of green issues;
- Are right wing politically.

(d)   Alienated (22%)

- Less well educated, downmarket consumers
- Young families/senior citizens
- Unaware of green issues
- See greenness as a fashion or a fad
- Are pessimistic about a solution
- Are left wing politically

Activity 10

C2 met C1 and fell in love. They moved to FLCII and lived in a C11. He was a belonger and she was lady righteous: it would not be long before they reached stage III of the FLC!

What are we talking about?

Marketing segmentation research will yield a great deal of information which must be collated, analysed and put to use. There will need to be an efficient system in place to handle all the data.

5   MARKETING INFORMATION SYSTEMS

Marketing information systems (MKIS) represent a systematic attempt to supply continuous, useful, usable marketing information within an organisation to decision makers, often in the form of a database.

The design of an MKIS should start with the information needs of decision-makers rather than with technical considerations of the database. It has three components which need to be planned.

(a)   **System inputs**

The sources of information which can form an input to an MKIS are, in principle, the same as those discussed above, that is, internal and external (secondary) sources and primary research. The starting point is very likely to be existing customer account records. These sources can be used to identify the types of service which each type of customer is buying along with trend data. These records can be amended as necessary over time and can be augmented by specific market research projects so as to provide a complete picture.

(b)   **Data manipulation**

Once collected, the data needs to be manipulated into a suitable form for use by decision makers. Again, the principles of this manipulation are those noted in the earlier part of this chapter: the mass of information needs to be summarised so that trends and major features can be identified.

(c) **System outputs**

Once manipulated into a form in which the information can be used by decision makers, outputs from the system (inferences the organisation can act on) can be determined. The information obtained can be applied to the whole range of marketing decisions.

Activity 11

'The power of databases can be illustrated by the experience of Felix petfood in the Netherlands ... the names of 100,000 cats have been collected: they get their own junk mail, with details of offers and information on new developments.

When Felix, known mainly for its dry packet catfood, introduced a new wet canned product, club members were mailed and offered trial vouchers. Rather than a gradual build up of sales ... the product was moving off the shelves from day one. Now Felix has introduced a variation on the usual "member-get-member" scheme, where databases are expanded by existing members giving names of others who may be interested. A "cat-get-cat" scheme is resulting in cats recommending their friends for membership of the Felix club.' (Financial Times)

How well do you think Felix understands its customers?

5.1 Databases

It should be clear from the above discussion of segmentation methods that for large scale use of the more sophisticated methods to be effective, computerised systems have to be adopted. These systems can often be used by organisations which actually hold detailed data on customers, such as banks, building societies and insurance companies. The systems are based on the array of data held about each customer in a relational database. In other words, a sub sample of customers could be formed by the use of any one specifying variable (or combination of variables). For example, all customers aged 18–24 could be identified for the development of long-term relations, as discussed above, as could all customers aged 25–34 with incomes over £20,000 pa and who live in ACORN type B6 housing.

This data has become more important as POS (point of sale) information is routinely gathered, and personal computer systems have become cheaper, more widely available and more 'user-friendly'.

Databases can provide valuable information to strategic planners and marketing management.

(a) Computer databases make it easier to collect and store more **data/information**.

(b) Computer software allows the data to be **extracted** from the file and **processed** to provide whatever information management needs.

(c) Developments in information technology allow businesses to have access to the databases of **external organisations**. Reuters, for example, provides an on-line information system about money market interest rates and foreign exchange rates to firms involved in money market and foreign exchange dealings, and to the treasury departments of a large number of companies.

PUBLISHING

(d) The growing adoption of technology at **point of sale** provides a potentially invaluable source of data to both retailer and manufacturer.

Other benefits of database systems might include:

(a) Increased **sales and/or market share** (due to enhanced lead follow-up, cross-selling, customer contact)

(b) Increased **customer retention** (through better targeting)

(c) Better use of **resources** (targeting, less duplication of information handling)

(d) Better **decision-making** (from quality management information)

EXAMPLE

CACI is a company which provides market analysis, information systems and other data products to clients. It advertises itself as "the winning combination of marketing and technology".

As an illustration of the information available to the marketing manager through today's technology, here is an overview of some of their products.

Paycheck: this provides income data for all 1.6 million individual post codes across the UK. This enables companies to see how mean income distribution varies from area to area.

People UK: this is a mix of geodemographics, life stage and lifestyle data. It is person rather than household specific and is designed for those companies requiring highly targeted campaigns.

InSite: this is a geographic information system (GIS). It is designed to assist with local market planning, customers and product segmentation, direct marketing and service distribution.

Acorn: this stands for A Classification of Residential Neighbourhoods, and has been used to profile residential neighbourhoods by post code since 1976. ACORN classifies people in any trading area or on any customer database into 54 types.

Lifestyles UK: this database offers over 300 lifestyle selections on 44 million consumers in the UK. It helps with cross selling and customer retention strategies.

Monica: this can help a company to identify the age of people on its database by giving the likely age profile of their first names. It uses a combination of census data and real birth registrations.

Database maintenance

If the customer database is linked to **on-line transaction processing** (for example, via EPOS), purchase data will automatically be updated with each new transaction. However, a typical contacts database will have to be regularly and systematically maintained.

(a) Contacts who become customers should be transferred to the customer database and deleted from the contacts database in order to avoid duplicated mailings.

(b) Any up-dated or altered information should be entered in the database: changes of address or customer status and so on.

(c)   Additional information obtained from contacts should be added to the relevant records.

(d)   New names and records should periodically be added to the database, and names which have received no response after a certain period of time or number of contacts, deleted.

(e)   'Undeliverable' items are returned to the sender, often marked with reason for non-delivery: no longer at this address, not known at this address and so on. If the mailing list has been bought or rented, any undeliverables should be returned to the owner or broker so they can update their database. If the mailing was based on an in-house list, addresses and names should be checked (common errors include misspelt names, missing lines of the address, wrong company name and so on) and if no error can be readily identified, the record should be erased.

(f)   Requests from customers or members of the public to have their details erased from the database should be honoured.

(g)   New fields can be added to the database design as new types of information become available.

Identifying buying trends

By tracking purchases per customer (or customer group) you may be able to identify:

(a)   **Loyal repeat customers** (who cost less to retain than new customers cost to find and attract, and who therefore need to be retained

(b)   **'Backsliding'** or lost customers, who have reduced or ceased the frequency or volume of their purchases (These may be a useful diagnostic sample for market research into declining sales or failing customer care.)

(c)   **Seasonal** or local purchase patterns (heavier consumption of soup in England in winter, for example)

(d)   **Demographic purchase patterns**. These may be quite unexpected. Grey Advertising carried out studies in the US in 1987 which showed that many consumers behave inconsistently to the patterns assumed for their socio-economic groups. Lower income consumers buy top-of-the-range products, which they value and save for. Prestige and luxury goods, which marketers promote largely to affluent white-collar consumers, are also purchased by students, secretaries and young families, which have been dubbed 'Ultra Consumers' because they transcend demographic clusters.

(e)   Purchase patterns in response to **promotional campaigns** (Increased sales volume or frequency following promotions is an important measurement of their effectiveness.)

Identifying marketing opportunities

More detailed information (where available) on customer likes and dislikes, complaints, feedback and lifestyle values may offer useful information for:

(a)   **Product** improvement

(b)   **Customer care** and quality programmes

(c)   New **product development,** and

(d)   **Decision-making** across the marketing mix: on prices, product specifications, distribution channels, promotional messages and so on

Simple data fields such as 'contact type' will help to evaluate how contact is made with customers, of what types and in what numbers. Business leads may be generated most often by trade conferences and exhibitions, light users by promotional competitions and incentives, and loyal customers by personal contact through representatives.

Customers can be investigated using any data field included in the database: How many are on e-mail or the Internet? How many have spouses or children? Essentially, these parameters allow the marketer to **segment** the customer base for marketing purposes.

EXAMPLE

Hallmark salespeople in the US have laptop computers which allow them to analyse the mix of greeting cards sold at individual stores, in order to create a merchandising package tailored to capitalise on the strengths of each store customer.

Compaq Computers has a similar program, with sales people linked by computer to the headquarters' databases providing information on every product and every client. In the first two years of the programme, it reduced its sales force by a third - and doubled its sales volume.

Using database information

The following is a summary of the main ways in which database information can be used.

(a)   Direct mail used to:

- Maintain customer contact between (or instead of) sales calls
- Generate leads and 'warmed' prospects for sales calls
- Promote and/or sell products and services direct to customers
- Distribute product or service information

(b)   Transaction processing. Databases can be linked to programmes which generate order confirmations, despatch notes, invoices, statements and receipts.

(c)   Marketing research and planning. The database can be used to send out market surveys, and may itself be investigated to show purchasing patterns and trends.

(d)   Contacts planning. The database can indicate what customers need to be contacted or given incentives to maintain their level of purchase and commitment. A separate database may similarly be used to track planned and on-going contacts at conferences and trade shows and invitation lists to marketing events.

(e)   Product development and improvement. Product purchases can be tracked through the product life cycle, and weaknesses and opportunities identified from records of customer feedback, complaints and warranty/guarantee claims.

On-line databases

Most external databases are on-line databases, which are very large computer files of information, supplied by **database providers** and managed by '**host**' companies whose business revenue is generated through charges made to **users**. Access to such databases is

BPP
PUBLISHING

open to anyone prepared to pay, and who is equipped with a PC plus a modem (to provide a phone link to the database) and communication software. These days there are an increasing number of companies offering free internet access. Most databases can be accessed around the clock.

Providers of **database information** include the following.

- Directory publishers such as Kompass
- Market research publishers such as Mintel, Keynote and Front & Sullivan
- Producers of statistical data, including the UK government and Eurostat
- Reuters Business Briefing
- FT Profile

There is an enormous breadth of data available through on-line databases. Comprehensive sources of detailed information include the *On Line Business Sourcebook* from Headland Press and two directories published by ASLIB, *On Line Business and Company Databases* by Helen Parkinson and *On Line Management and Marketing Databases* by Nick Parker. Other possible sources include the following.

(a) Statistics, articles and news from the general and trade press

(b) Market research reports

(c) Key statistical data from the Central Statistical Office (for the UK), CENDATA (for the USA) and Eurostat (for the EU)

(d) Material from the foreign press and major trade journals

(e) Data from some of the providers of continuous market research such as BMRB's TGI (Target Group Index)

(f) Company information produced by organisations such as Kompass, Dunn & Bradstreet, Infocheck and Extel

5.2 Direct mailing

Such database systems allow highly specific target marketing. The most obvious marketing use is by direct mail methods, the particular advantage of which is the capability for exact monitoring of results using the computer system. The costs of each mailshot can be related to the increase in business which results and the types of customers who buy can be used to refine the target marketing further.

NOTES

Chapter roundup

- Marketing research has been a growing source of organisation expenditure in recent years. Very few organisations can afford a large full-time staff of marketing research workers. It is quite probable, therefore, that the organisation will have a small full-time marketing research department, and that it will use the services of external marketing research consultants for specific projects. In addition to specialist market research agencies, there are market research departments in many of the large UK advertising agencies.

- An external agency can supply expertise in marketing research not available in-house and can bring together its general knowledge of a particular market for all clients or subscribers.

- Marketing research enables companies to gain information on the market and marketing mix variables and therefore to make decisions in the light of this information.

- Market segmentation is an attempt to take into account different customer characteristics and variations in taste, usage and so on. Geographic segmentation depends on location; demographic segmentation focuses on age, gender, housing and so on; psychographic segmentation considers lifestyle, values, opinions and so on.

- The organisation must collate, analyse and put to use the marketing data gathered through its marketing research activities. Databases can provide valuable information on to strategic planners and marketing management.

Quick quiz

1. Differentiate between market research and marketing research.
2. What is involved in (i) price research and (ii) distribution research?
3. What is a market forecast?
4. Secondary data is collected directly by the user. True or false?
5. What is field research?
6. What is a diary panel?
7. What details are provided by trade and retail panels?
8. What is pre-testing?
9. What are the benefits of market segmentation?
10. What is the JICNARS scale and what is ACORN?
11. Describe one set of life-style categories.
12. What sort of information might be held in a customer database?

Answers to activities

1. The possibilities are endless, but you might have thought of research and development personnel; marketing and sales personnel; competitors; customers; ideas springing from new scientific or technological discoveries.

PUBLISHING

NOTES

2   Again, there are many possibilities. You might have thought of the vast expansion in the range of uses for man-made materials such as plastics or nylon. Or you might cite the proliferation of computer hardware: whereas twenty years ago computer usage was confined to the mainframe installations in large companies, nowadays even very small organisations have a PC or two to streamline their operations.

3   Internal data would include:

(a)   production data about quantities produced, materials and labour resources used etc;

(b)   data about inventory;

(c)   data about sales volumes, analysed by sales area, salesperson, quantity, price, profitability, distribution outlet, customer etc;

(d)   data about marketing itself, such as promotion and brand data;

(e)   all cost and management accounting data;

(f)   financial management data relating to the capital structure of the firm, capital tied up in stocks and debtors and so on.

4   It is common to see researchers logging details of traffic passing along a particular road at certain times of day. This enables local authorities to improve services (by introducing traffic lights, constructing roundabouts or whatever). Users of public transport will often see researchers counting the number of passengers passing through, say, a railway station at a particular time, again with a view to assessing and possibly improving service levels.

5   Potential users might conceivably include individuals daunted by their own tax returns, but a sampling frame for all such individuals would be almost impossible to obtain. It would be better to reflect that most people with complicated tax affairs use the services of an accountant. Targeting firms of accountants is much easier: they are all registered with a professional body, and the membership lists of these bodies provide a convenient sampling frame.

Another group to target would be people who have retired in, say, the last two years, who no longer have an employer to take care of the Inland Revenue's hunger for information about their finances, and often find their new status confusing.

6   Measures could include sending to named individuals and taking care that information such as job titles is up to date. (This can be difficult if the sample is being drawn from a trade directory. It takes up to one year to update such directories, and the current year's edition will be on average six months old when reference is made.) It also helps to send a covering letter and to stress confidentiality and anonymity for the respondent. Finally, the inclusion of a stamped and addressed envelope for the reply helps, particularly if a stamp rather than a prepaid envelope is used: there is a sort of moral pressure here!

7   Because they provide continuous monitoring of retail activity, retail audits may be of value to such a firm for the following reasons.

(a)   Problems in retail sales provide an early warning of problems the manufacturer may soon have to expect in ex-factory sales.

(b)   They indicate long-term trends in the market place, thus providing helpful information for strategic marketing planning.

(c)   In the shorter term, they may indicate the need for changes in pricing policy, sales promotion or advertising, distribution policy, package design or product design.

8   Couples with dependent children formed the majority of households as recently as the 1970s. By the early 1990s they constituted less than 40%, and it is increasingly likely that such couples will now not be married. There is a growing proportion of people living alone. Single people account for more than a quarter of all households – a threefold increase during the past 30 years. The ageing of the population will fuel a continuing increase in this statistic. Lone-parent families have quadrupled since the 1960s and now amount to 21% of families. Marriages have declined by nearly 16% during the past 20 years while divorces have nearly doubled.

9   There are plenty of examples to choose from. Ads for numerous products have been targeted at those just entering the empty nest stage.

11   Felix understands its customers very well – the point being that the customer is the cat lover, and cat lovers in general are unusually appreciative of others who take an interest in their cats. This is an amusing and appealing example to reinforce both the potential for imaginative use of computers in marketing and the point that the consumer and the customer for many products and services are not the same person.

Further question practice

Now try the following practice questions at the end of this text.

Multiple Choice Questions: 41–50

Exam Style Question: 8

BPP
PUBLISHING

Chapter 7 :
PRODUCTS AND SERVICES

Introduction

We could consider the four Ps in any order (depending on the type of business), but we start with the Product. This chapter begins by considering the different types of product that are made and gives an overview of possible ways of sending products out into markets.

The product life cycle concept is useful for monitoring the progress of a product. We describe and criticise it in depth here and return to it in the final chapter once we have considered the other Ps of the marketing mix.

Product portfolio planning looks at product ranges and how they can be managed. Important for allocating resources are product-market matrices such as the BCG matrix.

Innovation is vital: organisations must generate new products in order to survive in the long term. We look at where ideas come from, how new products are developed and tested, and how they gain a hold on the market.

Service industries make up a sizeable proportion of developed economies like the UK. We shall be describing the unique features of services and their impact on marketing, and discussing some more Ps that are particularly appropriate for service marketing. The concept of relationship marketing is also discussed.

Finally, brands are briefly introduced (there is more on branding in the chapter on Promotion) and the use that is made of packaging is described.

Your objectives

In this chapter you will learn about the following.

   (a)   What types of product there are and how they may be classified

   (b)   The validity of the product life cycle concept

   (c)   How a business manages its range or portfolio of products

   (d)   The importance of new products and how new products are developed

   (e)   The definition of a service and the marketing of services

   (f)   The concept of relationship marketing

   (g)   The functions and qualities of packaging

1 THE PRODUCT

Those unfamiliar with marketing probably think of a 'product' as a physical object. However, in marketing the term must be understood in a broader sense. A product is something that satisfies a set of wants that customers have. When you buy a set of wine glasses, for example, you are buying them because you want to drink wine and you prefer not to do so straight from the bottle. You may also want to impress your dinner guests with your taste, and choose to do so by possessing a particularly fine set of wine glasses.

A product may be said to satisfy needs by possessing the following attributes.

(a) Tangible attributes

- Availability and delivery
- Performance
- Price
- Design

(b) Intangible attributes

- Image
- Perceived value

These features are interlinked. A product has a tangible price, for example you hand over your hard earned money, but for your money you obtain the value that you perceive the product to have. You may get satisfaction from paying a very high price for your wine glasses, because this says something about your status in life: the glasses become part of your self-image.

1.1 Product classification: consumer goods

You have probably often heard the term consumer goods. It is used to distinguish goods that are sold directly to the person who will ultimately use them from goods that are sold to people who will use them to make other products. The latter are known as industrial goods.

Consumer goods may be classified as follows.

(a) **Convenience goods**. The weekly groceries are a typical example. There is a further distinction between staple goods like bread and potatoes, and impulse buys, like the unplanned bar of chocolate that you find at the supermarket checkout. For marketing purposes, brand awareness is extremely important in this sector. Advertising tries to make sure that when people put 'beans' on their list they have in mind Heinz beans.

(b) **Shopping goods**. These are the more durable items that you buy, like furniture or washing machines. This sort of purchase is usually only made after a good deal of advance planning and shopping around.

(c) **Speciality goods**. These are items like jewellery or the more expensive items of clothing.

(d) **Unsought goods**. These are goods that you did not realise you needed! Typical examples would be the sort of items that are found in catalogues that arrive in the post.

Business Basics: Marketing

Activity 1

Think of three products that you have bought recently, one low-priced, one medium priced, and one expensive item. Identify the product attributes that made you buy each of these items and categorise them according to the classifications shown above.

1.2 Industrial goods

These may be classified as follows.

(a) Installations, for example, major items of plant and machinery such as a factory assembly line.

(b) Accessories, such as PCs.

(c) Raw materials: plastic, metal, wood, foodstuffs, chemicals and so on.

(d) Components, for example, the Lucas headlights in Ford cars or the Intel microchip in most PCs.

(e) Supplies: office stationery, cleaning materials and the like.

1.3 Products and services

There are very few pure products or services. Most products have some service attributes and many services are in some way attached to products. However, we shall consider some of the features that characterise service marketing at the end of this chapter.

1.4 Product/market decisions

In order to grow, an organisation can use particular combinations of product and market decisions. Ansoff expressed these options as follows.

	Existing Products	New Products
Existing Markets	Market Penetration	Product Development
New Markets	Market Development	Diversification

Market penetration involves trying to increase the market share for existing products in existing markets. This aim could be achieved by tailoring products more closely to the needs of target groups of customers within the existing market. The danger to be borne in mind with this strategy is of putting all the organisation's eggs in one basket.

Product development involves developing new products for the existing market. Using existing knowledge of customers and the existing distribution network it may be possible to extend the product range and increase sales. A danger is cannibalisation: that is, sales of new products may be achieved at the expense of existing products. Nevertheless, such a strategy may work if the new products make a greater contribution per unit to profit or if there is a danger that, without the new product, customers would switch from the existing product anyway, but to competitors' products.

Market development involves marketing existing products into new markets. Clearly, there is a need for market research to ensure a thorough understanding of the needs of the new market.

Diversification is the highest risk and involves new markets with new products. Not only is there a need to understand the new market but also intensive product development work is likely to be necessary.

PUBLISHING

170

Activity 2

Try to think of at least one example of each of these strategies that you have observed in practice.

Having looked at the different classes of products, we now consider the stages any given product may go through over a period of time. Like a family, it is claimed that the product also has a 'life cycle'.

2 THE PRODUCT LIFE CYCLE

The product life cycle concept has an almost 'biological' basis. It asserts that products are born (or introduced), grow to reach maturity and then enter old age and decline.

Despite criticisms, the product life cycle has proved to be a useful control device for monitoring the progress of new products after introduction. As Professor Robin Wensley of Warwick University puts it:

The value of the product life cycle depends on its use, ie it has greater value as one goes down the scale from a predictive or forecasting tool, through a planning tool to a control tool.

The profitability and sales position of a product can be expected to change over time. The 'product life cycle' is an attempt to recognise distinct stages in a product's sales history. Here is the classic representation of the product life cycle.

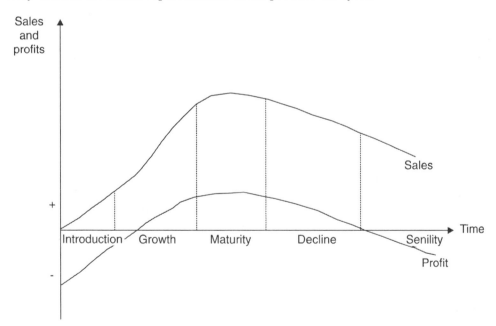

Figure 7.1 The classic representation of the product life cycle

(a) **Introduction.** A new product takes time to find acceptance by would-be purchasers and there is a slow growth in sales. Only a few firms sell the product; unit costs are high because of low output; there may be early teething troubles with production technology and prices may be high to cover production costs and sales promotion expenditure as much as possible. For example, pocket calculators, video cassette recorders and mobile telephones were all very expensive when launched. The product, for the time being, is a loss maker.

(b) **Growth**. If the new product gains market acceptance, sales will eventually rise more sharply and the product will start to make profits. New customers buy the product and as production rises, unit costs fall. Since demand is strong, prices tend to remain fairly static for a time. However, the prospect of cheap mass production and a strong market will attract competitors so that the number of producers is increasing. With the increase of competition, manufacturers must spend a lot of money on product improvement, sales promotion and distribution to obtain a dominant or strong position in the market.

(c) **Maturity**. The rate of sales growth slows down and the product reaches a period of maturity which is probably the longest period of a successful product's life. Most products on the market will be at the mature stage of their life. Eventually sales will begin to decline so that there is overcapacity of production in the industry. Severe competition occurs, profits fall and some producers leave the market. The remaining producers seek means of prolonging the product life by modifying it and searching for new market segments.

(d) **Decline**. Most products reach a stage of decline which may be slow or fast. Many producers are reluctant to leave the market, although some inevitably do because of falling profits. If a product remains on the market too long, it will become unprofitable and the decline stage in its life cycle then gives way to a 'senility' stage.

EXAMPLE: PLC AND FABRIC DETERGENT

Fabric washing detergents is a mature market, dominated in the UK by Lever Brothers and Procter & Gamble, whose strongest brands respectively are Persil and Ariel.

The introduction of Persil tablets by Lever Brothers came in response to consumers' wishes for a more convenient washing product, and has sliced Ariel's share of the concentrated powder market to 2.5% from 7.5%. Persil phased out their own concentrated powder at the launch of the tablets, the concentrated powder sector having been in decline for many years.

Being the first to market meant that Persil tablets gained a lot of buyers who had not bought Persil before, and sales quickly grew to £6.6m per month. Persil has re-established itself at the same time as an innovative and youthful brand.

Adapted from: Marketing Business, September 2000

Activity 3

Can you think of any products that have disappeared in your lifetime or are currently in decline?

2.1 Buyers at different PLC stages

The introductory stage represents the highest risk in terms of purchasing a new, as yet untested product. Buyers reflect this: they typically consist of the relatively wealthy, to whom the risk of a loss is relatively small, and the young, who are more likely to make risky purchases.

In the growth and mature stages the mass market needs to be attracted. By the time decline sets in the product is well tested with all its faults 'ironed' out. At this stage, the most risk-averse buyers, termed laggards, will start to buy the product. These people are the mirror image of those who participated in the introductory stage, being the poorer and older sections of the community.

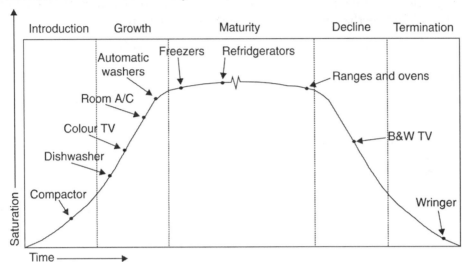

Figure 7.2 Comparing products at different PLC stages

The above display of products at various stages through the PLC is taken from the USA in the late 1960s and early 1970s.

2.2 How life cycles are assessed

It is plausible to suggest that products have a life cycle, but it is not so easy to sort out how far through its life a product is, and what its expected future life might be. To identify these stages, the following should be carried out.

(a) There ought to be a regular review of existing products, as a part of marketing management responsibilities.

(b) Information should be obtained about the likely future of each product.

- An analysis of past trends
- The history of other products
- Market research
- If possible, an analysis of competitors

The future of each product should be estimated in terms of both sales revenue and profits.

(c) Estimates of future life and profitability should be discussed with any experts available to give advice, for example R & D staff about product life, management accountants about costs and marketing and sales staff about prices and demand.

Once the assessments have been made, decisions must be taken about what to do with each product.

(a) To continue selling the product, with no foreseeable intention of stopping production

(b) To initiate action to prolong a product's life, perhaps by advertising more; by trying to cut costs or raise prices; by improving distribution, or packaging or sales promotion methods; or by putting in more direct selling effort

(c) To plan to stop producing the product and either to replace it with new ones in the same line or to diversify into new product-market areas.

Costs might be cut by improving the productivity of the workforce, or by redesigning the product slightly, perhaps as a result of a value analysis study.

Activity 4

Where do you consider the following products or services to be in their product life cycle?

(a) Mobile telephones
(b) Baked beans
(c) Satellite television
(d) Cigarettes
(e) Carbon paper
(f) Mortgages
(g) Writing implements
(h) Car alarms
(i) Organically grown fruit and vegetables

2.3 Criticisms of the practical value of the PLC

(a) Stages cannot easily be defined.

Activity 5

How can managers recognise where a particular product is in its life cycle? In practice, they can't, with any degree of certainty. But how might they begin to attack the problem?

(b) The traditional S-shaped curve of a product life cycle (shown on page 175) does not always occur in practice. Some products have no maturity phase, and go straight from growth to decline. Others have a second growth period after an initial decline. Some have virtually no introductory period and go straight into a rapid growth phase.

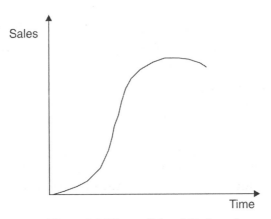

Figure 7.3 The traditional S-shaped curve of the product life cycle

(c)   Strategic decisions can change a product's life cycle: for example, by repositioning a product in the market, its life can be extended. If strategic planners 'decide' what a product's life is going to be, opportunities to extend the life cycle might be ignored. The impact of mix decisions is discussed in a later chapter.

(d)   Competition varies in different industries, and the strategic implications of the product life cycle will vary according to the nature of the competition. The 'traditional' life cycle presupposes increasing competition and falling prices during the growth phase of the market and also the gradual elimination of competitors in the decline phase. Strategic planning may well not be based on these presuppositions. This pattern of events is not always found in financial markets, where there is a tendency for competitors to follow-my-leader very quickly. Competition may build up well ahead of demand. The rapid development of various banking services is an example of this: for example, with bank cash dispenser cards, when one bank developed the product all the other major banks followed immediately.

2.4   The PLC and the marketing mix

In the later chapter on the marketing mix, we consider how the PLC influences decisions on product, distribution, price and promotion.

Activity 6

There must be many products that have been around for as long as you can remember. Companies like Cadbury's have argued that they spend so much on brand maintenance that they should be able to show a value for their brands as an asset in their accounts (though accountants find this hard to swallow).

Think of some examples of products that go on and on from your own experience and try to identify what it is about them that makes them so enduring.

NOTES

> **Activity 7**
>
> The Marketing and Advertising column in the Financial Times described baking soda toothpaste as a quintessential 'now' product. Given that Americans have been using baking soda to clean their teeth for more than a century, why is this so?

Most manufacturing companies, and many service companies, will market more than one product. They will have a 'portfolio' of different products which all need a proportion of the marketing budget and therefore cannot be treated in isolation.

3 PRODUCT PORTFOLIO PLANNING

Product mix	Characteristics of company's product line
Width	Number of product lines
Depth	Average number of items per product line
Consistency	Closeness of relationships in product range, for example, end users, production, distribution

Definition

> A company's product mix (or product assortment or portfolio) is all the product lines and items that the company offers for sale.

(a) Width is the number of product lines that the company carries.

(b) Depth is calculated by dividing the total number of items carried by the number of product lines.

(c) Consistency is the closeness of items in the range in terms of marketing or production characteristics.

The product mix can be extended in a number of ways.

(a) By introducing variations in models or style

(b) By changing the quality of products offered at different price levels

(c) By developing associated items, for example, a paint manufacturer introducing paint brushes

(d) By developing new products that have little technical or marketing relationships to the existing range

Managing the product portfolio involves more than the simple extension or reduction of a company's product range. It also raises broad issues such as what role should a product play in the portfolio, how should resources be allocated between products and what should be expected from each product. Maintaining balance between well established and new products, between cash-generating and cash-using products and between growing and declining products is very important. Managing the product portfolio is thus a key component of marketing. If products are not suitable for the market or not profitable, then corporate objectives will be jeopardised and the marketing function will fall short of its stated goals. Equally, if potentially profitable products are ignored or not given sufficient support then crucial marketing opportunities will be lost.

It follows that there are benefits to be gained from using a systematic approach to the management of the product range. Marketing is not an exact science and there is no definitive approach or technique which can determine which products should remain, which should be pruned and how resources should be shared across the current product range. There are, however, techniques which can aid decision making. Ultimately the burden of the decision is a management responsibility and requires judgement, but analytical tools such as product-market matrices and the product life cycle can illuminate the decision process and help to evaluate the product range.

3.1 Product-market matrices

The product-market matrix is a simple technique used to classify a product or even a business according to the features of the market and the features of the product. It is often used at the level of corporate strategy to determine the relative positions of businesses and then select strategies for resource allocation between them. For example, a bank might apply such a technique to evaluate the relative position and profitability of its corporate division and its personal division, its international division, its merchant banking division and so on. The same techniques are equally valuable when considering products and the management of the product portfolio. The two most widely used approaches are the Boston Consulting Group (BCG) growth-share matrix and the General Electric (GE) Business Screen.

The BCG matrix

The BCG matrix, illustrated below, classifies products (or businesses) on the basis of their market share relative to that of their competitors and according to the rate of growth in the market as a whole. The split on the horizontal axis is based on a market share identical to that of the firm's nearest competitor, while the precise location of the split on the vertical axis will depend on the rate of growth in the market. Products are positioned in the matrix as circles with a diameter proportional to their sales revenue. The underlying assumption in the growth-share matrix is that a larger market share will enable the business to benefit from economies of scale, lower per-unit costs and thus higher margins.

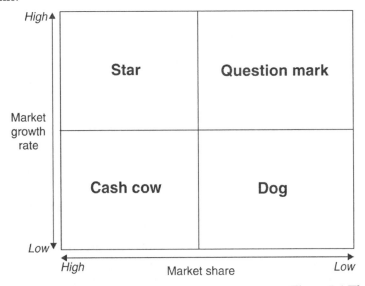

Figure 7.4 The BCG matrix

On the basis of this classification, each product or 'strategic business unit' will then fall into one of four broad categories.

(1) **Problem Child** (or question mark): a product having a small market share but in a high growth industry. The generic product is clearly popular, but customer support for the company brand is limited. A small market share implies that competitors are in a strong position and that if the product is to be successful it will require substantial funds and a new marketing mix. If the market looks good and the product is viable, then the company should consider a build strategy to increase market share. This would essentially involve increasing the resources available for that product to permit more active marketing. If the future looks less promising then the company should consider the possibility of withdrawing the product. What strategy is decided will depend on the strength of competitors, availability of funding and so on.

(2) **The Star**: this is a product with a high market share in a high growth industry. By implication, the star has potential for generating significant earnings currently and in the future. At this stage it may still require substantial marketing expenditures to 'maintain' this position, but this would probably be regarded as a good investment for the future.

(3) **The Cash Cow**: a product having a high market share but in a mature slow growth market. Typically, a well established product with a high degree of consumer loyalty. Product development costs are typically low and the marketing campaign is well established. The cash cow will normally make a substantial contribution to overall profitability. The appropriate strategy will vary according to the precise position of the cash cow. If market growth is reasonably strong then a 'holding' strategy will be appropriate, but if growth and/or share are weakening, then a harvesting strategy may be more sensible: cut back on marketing expenditure and maximise short-term cash flow.

(4) **The Dog**: a product characterised by low market share and low growth. Again, typically a well established product, but one which is apparently losing consumer support and may have cost disadvantages. The usual strategy would be to consider divestment unless cash flow position is strong, in which case the product would be harvested in the short term prior to deletion from the product range.

Implicit in the matrix is the notion that markets are dynamic. The typical new product is likely to appear in the 'problem child' category to begin with; if it looks promising and with effective marketing it might be expected to become a 'star', then, as markets mature, a 'cash cow' and finally a 'dog'. The suggestion that most products will move through these stages does not weaken the role played by marketing. On the contrary, it strengthens it, since poor marketing may mean that a product moves from being a problem child to a dog without making any substantial contribution to the profitability. Equally, of course, good marketing may enable the firm to prolong the 'star' and 'cash cow' phases, thus maximising cash flow from the product.

The matrix also places great emphasis on the strategic significance of growth, and behind this is the strong reliance on the life cycle concept.

The framework provided by the matrix can offer guidance in terms of developing appropriate strategies for products and in maintaining a balanced product portfolio, ensuring that there are enough cash-generating products to match the cash-using products.

Activity 8

If products are going to develop through these stages anyway, then what is the purpose of spending money on marketing?

However, there are a number of criticisms.

(a) The BCG matrix oversimplifies product analysis. It concentrates only on two dimensions of product markets, size and market share, and therefore may encourage marketing management to pay too little attention to other market features.

(b) It is not always clear what is meant by the terms 'relative market share' and 'rate of market growth'. Not all companies or products will be designed for market leadership, in which case describing performance in terms of relative market share may be of limited relevance. Many firms undertaking this approach have found that all their products were technically 'dogs' and yet were still very profitable, so saw no need to divest. Firms following a nicheing strategy will commonly find their markets are (intentionally) small.

(c) The matrix assumes a relationship between profitability and market share. There is empirical evidence for this in many but not all industries. It tends not to be true where there is demand for more customised products. Some commentators, such as Tom Peters, have argued that the latter is a very strong trend in modern markets.

(d) The basic approach may oversimplify the nature of products in large diversified firms with many divisions. In these cases, each division may contain products which fit into several of the categories.

Despite these criticisms, the BCG matrix can offer guidance in achieving a balanced portfolio. However, given the difficulty of generalising such an approach to deal with all product and market situations, its recommendations should be interpreted with care.

3.2 The General Electric Business Screen

The basic approach of the GE Business Screen is similar to that of the BCG matrix. Because the BCG matrix is criticised for using a highly restrictive classification system, the GE Business Screen avoids this by including a broader range of company and market factors in assessing the position of a particular product or product group. A typical example of the GE matrix is provided below. This matrix classifies products (or businesses) according to industry attractiveness and company strengths. There is no single factor which can be used to measure industry attractiveness or company (product) strength; instead, the approach considers a variety of factors which contribute to both these variables. It sectionalises the matrix into high, medium and low categories. Typical examples of the factors which determine industry attractiveness and company strength are the following.

(a) Industry attractiveness: market size, market growth, competitive climate, stability of demand, ease of market entry, industry capacity, levels of investment, nature of regulation, profitability.

(b) Company strengths: relative market share, company image, production capacity, production costs, financial strengths, product quality, distribution systems, control over prices/margins, benefits of patent protection.

NOTES

Although the GE Business Screen uses a broader range of factors than the BCG matrix to classify products, it is a highly subjective assessment. Products are positioned on the grid with circles representing market size and segments representing market shares. The strategy for an individual product is then suggested on the basis of that position. It is interesting to note the apparent similarity in recommendations between the BCG matrix and the GE matrix; the basic difference arises from the method of classification.

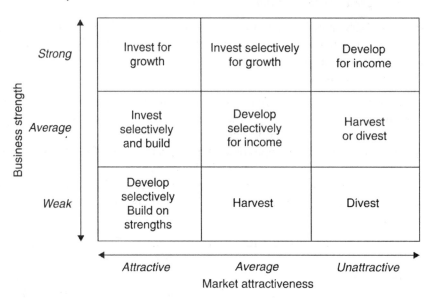

Figure 7.5 The GE Business Screen

The broader approach of the GE matrix emphasises the attempt to match distinctive competences within the company to conditions within the market place. Difficulties associated with measurement and classification mean that again the results of such an exercise must be interpreted with great care and not seen as a prescription for strategic decisions.

As a result of analysing the product portfolio using one or more of the methods described above, the firm may decide that it is necessary or desirable to develop and launch new products.

4 NEW PRODUCT DEVELOPMENT

Innovation is the life blood of a successful organisation and the management of innovation is central to this success. New products may be developed as a result of a technical breakthrough, or as a consequence of changes in society; or simply to copy and capitalise on the success of existing products. Management can adopt a proactive approach to product development by establishing research and development departments to look into ideas for new products, although such ideas do not have to come through this formal departmentalised system. Management, sales people, customers and competitors can all generate new product ideas. One of the tasks of marketing management is to 'tap' these ideas and select some for further development. Later in this chapter new product development will be discussed in more detail.

What is a new product?

- One that opens up an entirely new market
- One that replaces an existing product
- One that broadens significantly the market for an existing product

EXAMPLE: INNOVATION AT MARS

Innovation can come in small sizes ...

Despite success in the UK market with its chocolate bars, Mars was outclassed by Quality Street (Nestlé) and Roses (Cadbury) when it came to the 'selections' category.

Identifying a gap in this market for familiar flavours and transparent packaging, the 'Celebrations' offer of miniature Mars Bars, Snickers, Bounty, Maltesers and Galaxy was a huge success. Mars now leads in selection products, from a standing start. The idea was first put forward in 1994, but Mars spent a lot of time getting key points exactly right, from flavours to consumer safety issues. This time and effort has paid off.

An old product can be new if:

- It is introduced to a new market
- It is packaged in a different way
- A different marketing approach is used
- A mix variable is changed

The last three will not necessarily convert an 'old' product into a 'new' one; this will depend on what is done and how.

Any new product must be perceived in terms of customer needs and wants.

Activity 9

Can you think of examples of new products and 'new' old products to fit into each of the above categories?

There are several degrees of newness.

(a) The unquestionably new product, such as the electronic pocket calculator. Marks of such a new product are technical innovation – high price – performance problems – patchy distribution.

(b) The partially new product, such as the cassette tape recorder. The mark of such a product is that it performs better than the old one did.

(c) Major product change, such as the transistor radio. The mark of such a product is seen in radical technological change altering the accepted concept of the order of things.

(d) Minor product change, such as styling changes. The marks of such a product are extras which give a boost to a product.

Sources for new products include the following.

(a) Licensing.

(b) Acquisition (buy the organisation making it).

(c) Internal product development (your own Research and Development team).

(d) Customers (listen to and observe them, analyse and research – this is how the Walkman developed).

(e) External inventors (Kodak and IBM rejected Xerox).

(f)   Competition (Kodak instant cameras, following the Polaroid concept of the 'hand' camera).

(g)   Patent agents.

(h)   Academic institutions (for example, the pharmaceutical industry funds higher education department research).

4.1   Screening new product ideas

The mortality rate of new products is very high.

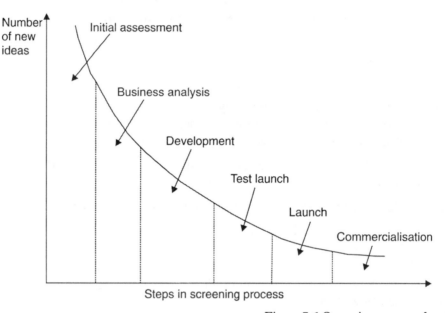

Figure 7.6 Screening new product ideas

To reduce the risk of failure new product ideas should always be screened. There is some evidence that the product screening process is becoming more effective. A study by Booz, Allen and Hamilton in 1968 concluded that it took fifty-eight ideas to yield one successful product that achieved commercial success. Their repeat study in 1981 showed a dramatic improvement: 700 companies in the USA found that on average only seven ideas were needed for every successful product.

4.2   New product development plan

New products should only be taken to advanced development if there is evidence of:

- Adequate demand
- Compatibility with existing marketing ability
- Compatibility with existing production ability

4.3   Initial concept testing

At a preliminary stage the concept for the new product should be tested on potential customers to obtain their reactions. It is common to use the company staff as guinea pigs for a new product idea although their reaction is unlikely to be typical. It is difficult to get sensible reactions from customers. Consider the following examples.

(a)   New designs for wallpaper. When innovative new designs are tested on potential customers it is often found that they are conditioned by traditional designs and are dismissive of new design ideas.

(b) New ideas for chocolate confectionery have the opposite problem. Potential customers typically say they like the new concept (because everyone likes chocolate bars) but when the new product is launched it is not successful because people continue to buy old favourites.

Nevertheless, concept testing may also permit useful refinements to be made to the product, if it is not totally rejected.

4.4 Product testing

A working prototype of the product, which can be tried by customers, is constructed. This stage is also very useful for making preliminary explorations of production costs and practical problems. We need to have some idea of whether the product could be produced in sufficient quantities at the right price if it were launched. The form that the product test takes will depend very much on the type of product concerned. To get realistic responses the test should replicate reality as closely as possible.

(a) If the product is used in the home, a sample of respondents should be given the product to use at home

(b) If the product is chosen from among competitors in a retail outlet (as with chocolate bars) then the product test needs to rate response against competitive products

(c) If inherent product quality is an important attribute of the product then a 'blind' test could be used in which customers are not told who is producing the new product

(d) An industrial product could be used for a trial period by a customer in a realistic setting

4.5 Quality policy

Quality is an important policy consideration as we saw in Chapter 3. Different market segments will require products of different price and quality. When a market is dominated by established brand names, one entry strategy is to tap potential demand for a (cheaper) lower quality 'me-too' item.

Customers often judge the quality of an article by its price. Quality policy may well involve fixing a price and then manufacturing a product to the best quality standard that can be achieved within these constraints, rather than making a product of a certain quality and then deciding what its price should be.

Quality should also be determined by the expected physical, technological and social life of the product for the following reasons.

(a) There is no value in making one part of a product good enough to have a physical life of five years, when the rest of the product will wear out and be irreplaceable within two years (unless the part with the longer life has an emotional or symbolic appeal to customers; for example, a leather covering may be preferred to plastic).

(b) If technological advances are likely to make a product obsolescent within a certain number of years, it is wasteful and uneconomic to produce an article which will last for a longer time.

(c) If fashion determines the life of a product, the quality required need only be sufficient to cover the period of demand; the quality of fashion clothes, for example, is usually governed by their fashion life. Fashion items are only

NOTES

intended to be worn a relatively small number of times, while non-fashion items are more durable.

Quality policy must be carefully integrated with sales promotion. If a product is branded and advertised as having a certain quality but customers find this is not true, the product will fail. The quality of a product (involving its design, production standards, quality control and after-sales service) must be established and maintained before a promotion campaign can use it as a selling feature.

4.6   Test marketing

The purpose of test marketing is to obtain information about how consumers react to the product in selected areas thought to be 'representative' of the total market. This avoids a blind commitment to the costs of a full scale launch while permitting the collection of market data. The firm will use the sales outlets it plans to use in the full market launch, and the same advertising and promotion plans it will use in the full market. This can be expensive, but it enables the company to 'test the water' before launching the product nationally. It helps to forecast sales, and can also be used to identify flaws in the product or promotional plans which can be dealt with before the national launch.

In short, then, the stages of new product development are as follows.

CONCEPTION OF IDEAS

↓

SCREENING OF IDEAS

↓

ANALYSE (IN BUSINESS SENSE)

↓

TESTING – Concept and Use

↓

PRODUCT DEVELOPMENT

↓

DECIDING MARKETING MIX ISSUES

↓

MARKET TESTING

↓

PRODUCT LAUNCH

4.7   The diffusion of innovation

The 'diffusion' of the new product refers to the spread of information about the product in the market place. Adoption is the process by which consumers incorporate the product into their buying patterns. The diffusion process is assumed to follow a similar shape to the PLC curve. Adoption is also thought usually to follow a 'normal' bell shaped curve. The classification of adopters devised by Everett Rogers is shown below.

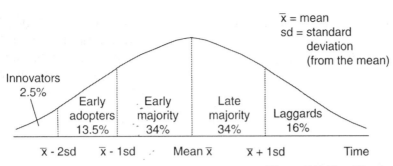

Figure 7.7 Classification of adopters

Early adopters and innovators are thought to operate as 'opinion leaders' and are therefore targeted by companies in order to influence the adoption of a product by their friends.

The main problem with this model is that the categories appear to add up to 100% of the target market. This does not reflect marketers' experience. Some potential consumers do not adopt/purchase at all. It has consequently been suggested that an additional category is needed: non-adopters, or non-consumers.

Activity 10

How does word of a new product circulate to the 'innovators'?

Some researchers prefer a two or three category scheme, comparing innovators/early triers with later triers and/or non-triers. This enables them to identify the general characteristics of the important innovator/early trier segments, which has practical significance for marketing.

Service industries have proliferated over the last 30 years; they rival manufacturing industries in their economic importance. The marketing of services shares some features with the marketing of goods but also has special characteristics of its own.

5 SERVICE MARKETING

5.1 The rise of the service economy

There are a number of reasons why services are more important today than they were in the past. These include the following.

(a) The growth of service sectors in advanced industrial societies

In terms of employment, more people now work in the service sector than in all other sectors of the economy. In terms of output, the major contributor to national output are the public and private service sectors. 'Invisible' service earnings from abroad are of increasing significance for Britain's balance of trade.

(b) Service-providing organisations are increasingly market oriented (for example, 'internal markets', 'market testing' and so on)

The extension of the service sector and the application of 'market principles' across what were previously publicly owned utilities has made a large number of service providers much more marketing conscious.

BPP PUBLISHING

The service sector in Britain extends across public provision in the legal, medical, educational, military, employment, credit, communications, transportation, leisure and information fields. In the past the public sector was not-for-profit but an increasing number of these services now have a profit element. The private sector embraces not-for-profit areas such as arts, charities, religious and educational organisations but also, of course, profit making business and professional services involved in travel, finance, insurance, management, the law, building, commerce, entertainment and so on.

5.2   Services: some definitions

Definitions

> ... those separately identifiable but intangible activities that provide want-satisfaction, and that are not, of necessity, tied to, or inextricable from, the sale of a product or another service. To produce a service may or may not require the use of tangible goods or assets. However, where such use is required, there is no transfer of title (permanent ownership) to these tangible goods.
> (Donald Cowell, The Marketing of Services)
>
> ... any activity of benefit that one party can offer to another that is essentially intangible and does not result in the ownership of anything. Its production may or may not be tied to a physical product.   (P Kotler, Social Marketing)

5.3   Goods and services: the differences

Services marketing differs from the marketing of other goods in a number of crucial ways. The marketing of services faces a number of distinct problems and so the approach adopted must be varied, and appropriate marketing practices must be developed. While there is a wide variety within service types and situations and many service organisations are highly market oriented (for instance, in retailing, transport hire, cleaning and hotel groups), there are still many which remain relatively unaffected by marketing ideas and practices, or which have only just begun to adopt them (for example, legal and financial services). Marketing ideas are likely to become much more important as competition within the service sector intensifies.

Characteristics of services which make them distinctive from the marketing of goods have been proposed. There are five major differences.

- Intangibility
- Inseparability
- Heterogeneity
- Perishability
- Ownership

We shall consider each of these in detail.

5.4   Intangibility

'Intangibility' refers to the lack of substance which is involved with service delivery. Unlike a good, there is no substantial material or physical aspect to a service: no taste, feel, visible presence and so on. Clearly this creates difficulties and can inhibit the propensity to consume a service, since customers are not sure what they have.

Ultimately the customer may have no prior experience of a service in which he or she is interested, nor any conception of how it would satisfy the requirements of the purchase context for which it was intended.

(Morden, *The Marketing of Services*)

In fact it would be incorrect to make this a 'black or white' phenomenon. Shostack has suggested viewing insubstantiality, not as an 'either/or' issue, but rather as a continuum.

Shostack has also proposed that marketing entities are combinations of elements which are tangible or intangible. She uses the metaphor of a molecule to represent the 'total market entity'; a molecule (product) is created not only by various atoms (goods or services), but also by the way the atoms (goods and services) are connected (interrelationships) and the relevant dominance of those goods and services, both tangible and intangible. A product then comes to be conceived as a 'gestalt', or blend of various elements which is constituted by combining material entities (the aeroplane we are flying in, the airport lounge and so on) with various sorts of processes (the courtesy of the airline staff, the frequency of services and so on).

For each service the number, complexity and balance of the various elements involved will vary a great deal. What is experienced at the end of the process when the service is delivered remains insubstantial. Although many parts of the process (the machines, buildings and staff of an airline, for instance) are very substantial, the actual service itself cannot be owned, only experienced.

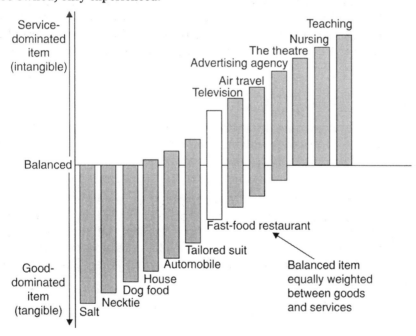

Figure 7.8 The service continuum

Marketers and consumers need to try to overcome this problem and typically seek to do so in a number of different ways, and for different reasons. The consumer needs information to avoid making a mistake, to obtain some grounds for forming a judgement and to cut down risk. The marketer wishes to make the choice of the product 'safer' and make the consumer feel more comfortable about paying for something they do not then own and which has no physical form.

This may be countered by:

• The consumer seeking opinions from other consumers

• The marketer offering the consumer something tangible to represent the service

NOTES

Intangibility, once again, is a matter of degree varying between:

(a) Intangibles involved in making a tangible product available

(b) Intangibles adding value to a tangible product (house decorating, hairdressing, vehicle or plant maintenance and so on)

(c) Complete intangibility (entertainment or leisure services)

Marketing implications

Dealing with the problems discussed above may involve the following strategies.

(a) Increasing the level of tangibility. When dealing with the customer, staff can use physical or conceptual representations/illustrations to make the customer feel more confident about what the service is delivering.

(b) Focusing the attention of the customer on the principal benefits of consumption. This could take the form of communicating the benefits of purchasing the service so that the customer visualises its appropriateness to the principal benefit sought. Promotion and sales material could provide images or records of previous customers' experience.

(c) Differentiating the service and reputation-building: enhancing perceptions of customer service and customer value by offering excellence in the delivery of the service and promoting values of quality, service reliability and value for money. These must be attached as values to brands, which must then be managed to secure and enhance their market position.

Activity 11

Insurance is perhaps the least tangible of all the purchases that people commonly make. Insurance adverts create fears and then try to sell peace of mind.

Life assurance company Allied Dunbar's Dennis Potter/Nat King Cole style advertisements were part of a £75m campaign to move the company ahead. Part of the research for the campaign aimed to discover how the company was seen by employees and consumers. The message that came back was that the company was both crusading and manipulative, simultaneously caring and aggressive. The next step was to establish what Allied Dunbar's brand or reputation ought to be.

What do you think was the response of consumers?

5.5 Inseparability

Services often cannot be separated from the provider. The creation or performance of a service often occurs at the same instant a full or partial consumption of it occurs. Goods in the vast majority of cases have to be produced, then sold, then consumed, in that order. Services are only a promise at the time they are sold: most services are sold and then they are produced and consumed simultaneously. Think of having dental treatment or a journey. Neither exists until they are actually being experienced/consumed by the person who has bought them.

Creation of many services coincides with consumption. Services may have to be, at the same time:

- Made available
- Sold
- Produced
- Consumed

Marketing implications

Provision of the service may not be separable from the person or personality of the seller. Consequently increasing importance is attached to the need to instil values of quality and reliability and to generate a customer service ethic in the personnel employed within an organisation, which is expressed in the service provision. High quality people with high quality training are needed to create standards of excellence and a true customer orientation.

5.6 Heterogeneity

Many services face the problem of maintaining consistency in the standard of output. Variability of quality of delivery of a service is inevitable because of the number of factors involved. This may create problems of operation management, for example, it may be difficult or impossible to attain precise standardisation of the service offered. The quality of the service may depend heavily on who it is that delivers the service, or exactly when it takes place. Booking a holiday using standard procedures may well be quite different on a quiet winter afternoon and on a hectic spring weekend, and may well vary according to the person dealing with your case.

It may also be impossible to obtain influence or control over perceptions of what is good or bad customer service. From the customer's perspective it is very difficult to obtain an idea of the quality of service in advance of purchase/consumption. This points up the need to constantly monitor customer reactions. A common way of applying a system to deliver a service is to franchise it to operators. The widespread location of numerous franchises ensures that customers have local, fast access to the service and direct contact with the immediate service provider. The problem remains, however, and almost the only way to address it is by constant monitoring and response to problems.

Marketing implications

In terms of marketing policy, the problem of heterogeneity (variability) of service illustrates the need to maintain an attitude and an organisational culture which emphasises the following.

- Consistency of quality control
- Consistency of customer service
- Effective staff selection, training and motivation

Note also the importance of:

(a) Clear and objective quality measures

(b) Standardising as much as possible within the service

(c) Assuming the Pareto principle (80% of the difficulties arise from 20% of events surrounding the provision of the service). Therefore identify and respond most rapidly to these potential 'troublespots'

5.7 Perishability

Services cannot be stored, of course. They are innately perishable. Seats on a bus or the services of a chiropodist consist in their availability for periods of time, and if they are not occupied, the service they offer cannot be used 'later'.

This presents specific marketing problems. Meeting customer needs in these operations depends on staff being available as and when they are needed. This must be balanced against the need to minimise unnecessary expenditure on staff wages. Anticipating and responding to levels of demand is, therefore, a key planning priority.

Risks

- Inadequate level of demand accompanied by substantial costs
- Excess demand resulting in lost custom through inadequate service provision

Marketing implications

Policies must seek to smooth the supply/demand relationship by:

- Price variations which encourage off-peak demand
- Promotions to stimulate off-peak demand

5.8 Ownership

One fundamental difference between a service and a consumer good is that the service does not result in the transfer of property. The purchase of a service only confers on the customer access to or a right to use a facility (access to or the hire of particular items), not ownership. Often there are tight constraints on the length of time involved in such usage, as in the case of a cinema visit. In the case of purchasing a product, such as a video, there is transfer of title and control over the use of an item. This may well lessen the perceived customer value of a service and consequently make for unfavourable comparisons with tangible alternatives. The customer may prefer to wait for the video release and purchase it, rather than going to the cinema to see the film.

Marketing implications

The marketer must overcome the customer's reluctance to purchase the service.

(a) Promote the advantages of non-ownership. This can be done by emphasising, in promotion, the benefits of paid-for maintenance, and periodic upgrading of the product. Radio Rentals have used this as a major selling proposition with great success.

(b) Make available a tangible symbol or representation of ownership (certificate, membership of professional association). This can come to embody the benefits enjoyed.

(c) Increasing the chances or opportunity of ownership, for example, time-shares or shares in the organisation for regular customers.

(d) Promoting advantages specific to the service: widescreen viewing in the cinema, the actual presence of 'star' actors in the theatre.

The issue of how to deal with these problems has occupied many different writers. Some have claimed that the marketing mix is critical. Research into the ways in which service quality is evaluated shows that the dimensions of service evaluation are distinctive and quite different criteria are given emphasis when customers are making a judgement.

Aspects of quality and customer care are demonstrated in the following table.

Dimension	Definition	Examples of specific questions raise by stock brokerage customers
Tangibles	Appearance of physical facilities, equipment, personnel and communication materials	Is my stockbroker dressed appropriately?
Reliability	Ability to perform the promised service dependably and accurately	Does the stockbroker follow exact instructions to buy or sell?
Responsive-ness	Willingness to help customers and provide prompt service	Is my stockbroker willing to answer my questions?
Competence	Possession of the required skills and knowledge to perform the service	Does my brokerage firm have the research capabilities to track market developments accurately?
Courtesy	Politeness, respect, consideration and friendliness of contact personnel	Is my broker readily available and polite when I ask questions?
Credibility	Trustworthiness, believability and honesty of the service provider	Does my broker avoid pressuring me to buy?
Security	Freedom from danger, risk or doubt	Does my brokerage firm know where my stock certificate is?
Access	Approachability and ease of contact	Is it easy to get through to my broker over the telephone?
Communi-cation	Keeping customers informed in language they can understand, and listening to them	Does my broker avoid using technical jargon?
Understand-ing the customer	Making the effort to know customers and their needs	Does my broker try to determine what my specific financial objectives are?

(Zeithaml, Parasuraman and Berry, *Delivering Quality Service*, 1990)

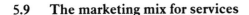

Activity 12

Apply the dimensions above to two similar services that you use frequently, such as two different supermarkets, two types of public transport or the like. Devise appropriate questions and see how your chosen services measure up against each other.

5.9 The marketing mix for services

As always, each firm has its own unique formula of people, processes and problems to deal with and, in that sense, arriving at a marketing mix for services is little different from the process involved for goods.

It has, however, been pointed out that in the marketing of services, the four Ps do not adequately describe the mix elements. It has been suggested that an extra three, and perhaps four, Ps should be added to the mix for services.

- Personal selling
- Place of availability (operations management)
- People and customer service
- Physical evidence

Personal selling

Personal selling is more important here because it is harder to sell services than products, for reasons outlined above. Because of greater perceived risk involved and greater uncertainty about quality and reliability, the reputation of the supplier may be of greater importance, and the customer has greater reliance on the honesty, sincerity and so on of the individual salesperson. When consumers seek reassurance, personal contact with a competent, effective representative may provide the necessary confidence. If the salesperson is badly trained and inefficient, greater contact with him or her may potentially generate even more anxiety about the quality of the service. This underlines the need to reduce customer uncertainty and to develop standard procedures to minimise customer anxiety ('closing techniques').

Place of availability

Place of availability is really covered by the distribution system, but of course there are special problems for services in the area of operations management. The place of availability and the frequency of availability are key service variables, while planning capacity utilisation and optimising levels of productivity for the assets to be used are essential for efficient and profitable operation.

To the efficient organisation, the level and quality of service which are available to the customer are especially sensitive, especially the processes by which services are delivered. Problems with regulating the supply make this a key factor in competitive advantage – a company which gets it right is likely to be clearly differentiated from competitors.

(a) Capacity utilisation, matching demand periods to staff availability to avoid unprofitable overprovision and problematic understaffing

(b) Managing customer contact, to avoid crowding and customer disruption, meet needs as they arise and increase employee control over interactions

(c) Establishing objectives within the not-for-profit sector, for example, standards for teachers or medical staff

For marketing service managers, the 'quality control' and 'engineering' of the interactions which take place between customers are key strategic issues. Customers are often, in the course of service delivery, interacting with other customers to gather information and form views about the nature and quality of the service which they are contemplating buying. Minimising exposure to negative feedback and promoting the dissemination of positive images and messages about the value of the service and the quality of customer response to it, are important objectives here.

People

The personnel of the service deliverer are uniquely important in the service marketing process. In the case of some services, the physical presence of people actually performing the service is a vital aspect of customer satisfaction: think of clerks in a bank (for customers who are not yet converts to Internet banking!), or personnel in catering establishments. The staff involved are performing or producing a service, selling the service and also liaising with the customer to promote the service, gather information and respond to customer needs.

Thus, another key strategic issue for the service marketing mix is the way in which personnel are involved in implementing the marketing concept. Measures need to be established which will institute a customer orientation throughout the organisation.

Customers who lack security and confidence in an intangible service will tend to use cues from the demeanour and behaviour of staff to establish a view about the image and efficiency of the organisation. The higher the level of customer contact involved in the delivery of a service, the more crucial is the staff role in generating customer service and adding value. In many cases the delivery of the service and the physical presence of personnel involved are completely inseparable, as in a restaurant or hairdresser's; technical competence and skill in handling people are of equal importance in effective delivery of a service since, as we have already noted, quality is in the eye of the (consuming) beholder.

All levels of staff must be involved in customer service; to achieve this end, it is vital for senior management to promote values of customer service constantly, to create and build a culture of customer service within the company. This means concrete policies and continuous development.

- Policies of selection
- Programmes of training
- Standard, consistent operational practices ('McDonaldisation')
- Standardised operational rules
- Effective motivational programmes
- Managerial appointments
- The attractiveness and appropriateness of the service offer
- Effective policies of staff reward and remuneration

Physical evidence

Physical evidence, as we have already seen, is an important remedy for the intangibility of the product. This may be associated with the service itself, providing cues as to its nature (for example, reports of previous work, or credit cards which represent the service available to customers), building up an association with a particular event, person or object, or building up an identification with a specific individual (a 'listening' bank manager).

Alternatively, the physical evidence may be incorporated into the design and specification of the service environment involving the building, location or atmosphere.

(a) Convey the nature of the service involved

(b) Transmit messages and information

(c) Imply aesthetic qualities, moral values or other socio-cultural aspects of a corporate image

(d) Reinforce an existing image

(e) Reassure

(f) Engender an emotional reaction in the customer, through sensory and symbolic blends

NOTES

Activity 13

A national charity want to send out a mailshot to attract donations. Describe in detail what you would suggest that receivers should find in the envelope (or if you prefer, create the contents of such a mailshot for a charity of your choice).

We will look at how the product is presented to the consumer (its branding and packaging) later in the chapter. These concepts apply to both goods and services.

6 RELATIONSHIP MARKETING

6.1 Background

Before the evolution of mass markets, the natural approach to marketing was through building a relationship with individual customers. The traditional corner shop in the UK, now driven almost to extinction by the power of the big supermarkets, provides an example of a business based on understanding individual customer needs. A good relationship with the customer was essential for repeat business.

During the twentieth century, mass media (television, newspapers, radio) created mass marketing and mass consumption, aided by production efficiencies. Products became nationally recognisable via distribution and advertising. Technology impacted dramatically on transportation, travel and communications, helping to create a global market. The emphasis on individual customer service became, to an extent, diluted.

This situation is now changing. For example, long-standardised products such as Coca Cola now have different variants (Diet, Cherry) to appeal to different customer segments. Now that there are more products to promote, companies need to target the market more carefully.

Relationship marketing can be seen as the successor to mass marketing, and is the process by which information about the customer is consistently applied by the company when developing and delivering products and services. Developments are communicated to the customer, for example via specially targeted promotions and product launches, in order to build a 'partnership' with him and encourage a long term relationship by paying attention to his specific needs.

6.2 Relationship marketing in practice

The rewards from effective relationship marketing are potentially impressive (and are linked to the whole exercise of customer retention).

(a) One credit card company calculated that a 5% increase in customer retention would create a 125% increase in profits.

(b) American Express believes that by extending customer lifecycles by five years, it could treble its profits per customer.

(c) According to Coca-Cola, a 10% increase in retailer retention should translate to a 20% increase in sales.

To work, relationship marketing has to operate in three ways.

(a) Borrow the idea of customer/supplier partnerships from industry: by sharing information and supporting each other's shared objectives, marketers and their customers can create real mutual benefit.

PUBLISHING

(b)   Recreate the personal feel that characterised the old-fashioned corner shop or Edwardian department store: make customers feel valued as individuals, and (using modern IT systems) convince them that their individual needs are being recognised and catered for.

(c)   Continually deepen and improve the relationship by making sure that everything which impinges on the customer's experience of the brand delights them.

The value of relationship marketing for the marketer lies in the fact that customers, consumers, retailers, distributors and agents may be spread all over the world, but they will still look for the familiar features when deciding whether or not to do business: product or service performance, enhancements and reliability of supply. If these business partners are looked after, market share will be of better quality because a greater proportion of sales will be derived from repeat business. Relationship marketing in this way provides an alternative to the traditional marketing mix.

6.3   Customer relationship management (CRM)

The magazine *Business Age* says in its February 2000 issue: "CRM will soon be as common a sound to the human ear as any other modern-day computer acronym". Purchasing, distribution, marketing and other activities are all inextricably linked to CRM, as is the Internet. CRM can be built into e-commerce, websites and email, and there is a whole new CRM software industry.

The whole point of CRM is not a new one: "Keeping the customer satisfied". The call centre is at the heart of its development. Data warehousing and data mining techniques are important, but the key for any company interested in CRM is to deliver the right message and offers to the right customers. Customers can be put off by a deluge of direct mail and hand sell. CRM should aim to target and communicate the following.

- Inform pre-sales prospects of the benefits of a relationship
- Sell more and new products to existing customers
- Retain existing customers

A CRM system is integrated and covers the entire sales and marketing process, and brings together a number of marketing and customer facing systems within one strategy or homogeneous software application.

EXAMPLE

From *Computer Business Review*, March 1999:

Customer relationship management (CRM) software is an industry in its own right. California-based Siebel Systems is market leader and its chief executive, Tom Siebel, says: 'I think now we have entered an era where the most precious resource is being recognised as the customer relationship. 'A customer in Paris, London or New York ordering on the Internet or by telephone does not care where the supplier is based, he just wants good service and quick delivery. 'There is a huge feeling, even in formerly not-so-service-oriented economies, that companies need to reach, serve and embrace customers. And the game they are playing is absolutely economic survival'.

Another CRM company boss says 'Think of any industry - telecoms, high tech, consumer packaged goods, financial services. There is no time for building relationships ... a system has to be implemented immediately. Loyalty and retention equal revenue ... [and] ... it is the level of service that will keep customers coming back'.

In many industries, mass globalisation has diluted the significance of product features and functionality. Customers are clamouring for a more personalised service, and companies have to satisfy highly individualised markets - ultimately a target market of one customer. Companies like One 2 One, BAT and the Prudential are all using CRM software to build databases and customer information profiles.

6.4 Importance of relationships: the cost of lost customers

If a company loses customers unnecessarily, it sacrifices a potential lifetime of profits. This is known as **lifetime customer value**.

Unless an industry is characterised by one-off sales, it is likely that customers will go through a **life cycle** of acquisition, development, maturity and decline. Each of these stages will carry a different level of revenue and profitability.

Existing, loyal customers are valuable because:

- They do not have to be **acquired**

- They buy a **broader range** of products

- They **cost less to service** as they are familiar with the company's ways of doing business

- They become **less sensitive to price** over time

- They can recommend by **word of mouth**

The justification for relationship marketing comes from this need to retain customers. There are five different levels of **customer relationship**.

(a) **Basic**. The salesperson sells the product without any further contact with the customer.

(b) **Reactive**. The customer is encouraged to call the salesperson if there are any problems.

(c) **Accountable**. The salesperson phones the customer to see if there are any problems and to elicit ideas for product improvements.

(d) **Proactive**. The salesperson contacts the customer on a regular basis.

(e) **Partnership**. The salesperson and customer work together, to ensure that all aspects of the deal suit the needs of both parties.

Broadly speaking, the greater the number of customers and the smaller the profit per unit sold, the greater the likelihood that the type of marketing will be **basic**. At the other extreme, where a firm has few customers, but where profits are high, the **partnership** approach is most likely.

EXAMPLE

Some firms convert a basic approach into relationship marketing. Many car dealerships, for example, seek to generate additional profits by servicing the cars they sell, and by keeping in touch with their customers so that they can earn repeat business.

Building up customer relationships requires a change of focus from the transaction-based approach to the relationship approach. The contrast is shown in the table below.

TRANSACTION MARKETING (mainly one-way communication)	RELATIONSHIP MARKETING (mainly two-way communication)
• Focus on single sale	• Focus on customer retention
• Orientation on product features	• Orientation on product benefits
• Short time scale	• Long time-scale
• Little customer service	• High customer service
• Limited customer commitment	• High customer commitment
• Moderate customer contact	• High customer contact
• Quality is the concern of production	• Quality is the concern of all

The process of retaining customers for a lifetime is an important one. Instead of one-way communication aimed solely at gaining a sale it is necessary to develop an effective two-way communication process to turn a **prospect into a lifetime advocate**. This is shown in the following ladder of customer loyalty.

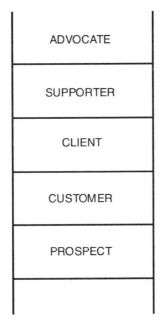

Figure 7.9 Ladder of customer loyalty

The purpose of relationship marketing is to establish, maintain and enhance relationships with customers and other parties so that the objectives of both parties involved are met.

(a) Because **service and industrial companies** have direct, regular and often multiple contacts with their customers (for example the regular hotel guest who interacts with reception), the importance of 'part-time' marketers is increased. Customer contact with all employees is vital.

(b) **Trust and keeping promises**. To have an ongoing relationship, both parties need to trust each other and keep the promises they make. Marketing moves from one-off exchanges towards co-operative relationships built on financial, social and structural benefits.

(c) **Network of exchange partners**. Customer relationships are important but so too are the relationships which organisations have with other parties such as suppliers, distributors, professional bodies, banks, trade associations etc.

Loyalty schemes

Loyalty cards are designed to reward customers for repeat purchase. They:

- Collect information about customer purchasing habits
- Reward customers for repeat purchase, to encourage sales volumes.

Loyalty schemes vary in the benefit they offer. Recent UK research indicates that owners of 'loyalty' cards spend more, but they are not necessarily loyal. Furthermore, most customers still shop around and have one or more loyalty cards.

Recently there has been a backlash against relationship marketing, especially as applied to the consumer sector. Not all customers want such a relationship, and resent the potential for intrusion. Furthermore, many firms practise relationship marketing purely as an **information gathering** exercise. Does the customer benefit from such a relationship?

According to CIM research, 30% of customers are not interested in developing relationships with companies. Only 8% of respondents think that customer relationship management holds any benefits for consumers, and of those who are interested in building a relationship, half want it to be focused upon saving money and are not interested in new products and services.

EXAMPLE

In the UK, Safeway abolished its expensive loyalty card scheme, ABC, in early 2000 to concentrate on its promotion of instore offers. Other supermarkets such as Tesco and Sainsbury have not (yet) followed suit.

To summarise, these are the distinguishing characteristics of relationship marketing.

- A focus on **customer retention** rather than attraction
- The development of an **on-going relationship** as opposed to a one-off transaction
- A **long time scale** rather than short time scale
- Direct and **regular customer contact** rather than impersonal sales
- **Multiple employee/customer contacts**
- **Quality and customer satisfaction** being the concern of all employees
- Emphasis on **key account relationship management**
- Importance of **trust** and keeping promises
- **Multiple exchanges** with a number of parties

EXAMPLE: CUSTOMER FOCUS AT CENTRICA

Centrica encompasses the British Gas, Goldfish and Automobile Association brands. Its director of marketing, Simon Waugh, says that marketing is about the entire customer proposition, by which he means: "How does the customer experience the product? How does it feel, literally, at the point of being used or experienced? The problem is that in most service sectors marketers don't spend enough time understanding what that experience is like." Waugh believes that marketers should build up better relationships with front line people, and thereby get a lot more information about customer contact and the customer's experience.

For the past year, Waugh has been overseeing the trial of a customer service 'laboratory' to test the value of different approaches to service delivery in terms of customer satisfaction, productivity, costs and income.

Adapted from Marketing Business, September 2000

---

7 BRANDS AND PACKAGING

A manufacturer might produce goods under his or her own brand name and at the same time (or perhaps exclusively) supply large retailers with goods under their own brand name, 'own label' brands or dealer brands. The major examples are the own brands of supermarkets and major chain stores (for example, Tesco, Sainsbury, St Michael for Marks & Spencer). The advantages of dealer brands to a manufacturer are as follows.

(a) A high level of sales may be necessary to cover fixed costs of production; supplying dealer branded goods to a large retail organisation may be a necessary way of achieving a profitable sales level. New market segments can be covered profitably at less risk and outlay to the producer.

(b) Large retailers with a high sales turnover and considerable control over the retail trade may insist on having their own brand, and supplying dealer branded goods may be essential to retain their business.

(c) It may be a well established and common practice in the industry.

(d) A manufacturer may wish to concentrate on production only, leaving the problem of design, quality and distribution to a multiple retailer.

The attraction of dealer brands to dealers

(a) The use of a brand helps to create customer loyalty to the store

(b) The buying in price is lower and cost of sales promotion (if any) negligible; therefore the price of dealer branded goods to customers can be lower (price consciousness is a notable feature of dealer brands)

(c) 'Me-too' products may benefit from the generic promotion effect of the market leader's success, but enjoy a price advantage.

Brands are discussed in more detail in Chapter 9.

7.1 Packaging

Packaging has five functions:

(a) Protection of contents

(b) Distribution, helping to transfer products from the manufacturer to the customer

(c) Selling, as the design and labelling serve promotional objectives of providing information and conveying an image (the uniforms of staff in a fast food chain, car hire company, airline or other service provider are an example of this in the service sector)

(d) User convenience, as an aid to storage and carrying, such as aerosol cans and handy packs

(e) To conform to government regulations (for example, by providing a list of ingredients and contents by weight, as in food packaging)

Remember that goods are usually packaged in more than one layer. Consumer goods might be packaged for sale to individual customers, but delivered to resellers in cartons or some similar bulk package.

7.2 The qualities required of a pack

The qualities required of a pack are as follows.

(a) The range of size and variety should be minimised in order to keep down purchasing, production and distribution costs, but it should succeed in making the product attractive and distinctive to the target consumer.

(b) In industries where distribution is a large part of total costs, packaging is an important issue.

(i) Packs should protect, preserve and convey the product to its destination in the desired condition.

(ii) They should use vehicle space cost effectively.

(iii) They should fit into the practices of mechanised handling and storage systems.

(iv) They should be space efficient, but also attractive display items.

(v) They should convey product information to shoppers effectively.

(vi) They should preserve the products' condition.

(c) Packaging is an important aid to selling. Where a product itself cannot be differentiated by design, its pack can be distinctively designed. This is crucial where there are no real product differences between rival brands, or in the case of commodities such as flour, which are basic goods.

(i) A pack should help to promote the advertising/brand image. For example, a logo should be clearly identifiable on the package, to exploit customer brand loyalty to a particular range of products.

(ii) Shape, colour and size should relate to customer motivation (for 'value' or 'quantity').

(iii) It should be the appropriate size for the expected user of the product (for example, family size packets of food).

(iv)   Some may be designed to promote impulse buying (for example, new fast moving consumer good (FMCG) products such as snack foods and so on).

(v)   A convenience pack (tubes, aerosols) should be provided where this is an important attribute.

(vi)   Packaging should maintain product quality standards.

(vii)   It should attract attention of potential customers, where appropriate.

While some of the above points will relate only to actual goods, many can be applied to services if one considers aspects such as staff uniforms, the design of premises and vehicles or of tableware in a restaurant.

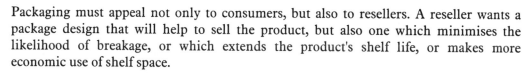

Activity 14

The list above does not by any means exhaust the uses to which packs are put by producers. Try to think of some more.

Packaging must appeal not only to consumers, but also to resellers. A reseller wants a package design that will help to sell the product, but also one which minimises the likelihood of breakage, or which extends the product's shelf life, or makes more economic use of shelf space.

The packaging of industrial goods is primarily a matter of maintaining good condition to the point of use. In itself this is a selling aid in future dealings with the customer. Large, expensive and/or fragile pieces of equipment must be well packaged.

EXAMPLE: PACKAGING AS A SELLING POINT

In the mid-1960s, Heinz held a 95% share of the baby foods market in the UK, selling their food in tins. Gerber then entered the market and secured a wide distribution network, but needed a unique selling point (USP) for consumers. The USP they decided upon was glass jars instead of tins, in the belief that mothers would consider them to be more hygienic. This campaign was successful and Gerber gained a 10% share of the baby foods market (even though Heinz countered with their own range of foods in glass jars).

Chapter roundup

- A product is something that satisfies a set of wants that customers have. Products can be classified as consumer goods or services or industrial goods or services. Strategies for sending products out into markets are market penetration, product development, market development and diversification.

- The product life cycle (introduction, growth, maturity, decline) can be demonstrated best by reference to the standard diagram, showing the PLC 'curve'. Remember that the PLC can be criticised both as a theory and as a practical tool. The implications of the PLC are important for a proper understanding of how an organisation's strategy develops over time.

- All businesses have limited resources so it is important to identify which products in a product range need special support at different times. Remember the different terms used in product portfolio planning when classifying products: Problem child, Star, Cash Cow, Dog.

- New products must be perceived in terms of customer needs and wants and so marketing plays a key role in new product development. Remember the different types of testing that must be carried out and the relevance of ideas about the diffusion of innovation.

- Services are characterised by intangibility, inseparability, heterogeneity, perishability and ownership, each characteristic having its own marketing implications. Four extra Ps may need to be added to the marketing mix: personal selling, special 'place' problems, people, and physical evidence.

- Relationship marketing focuses on the individual customer and seeks to foster a relationship that will engender increased levels of retention. Customer relationship management is emerging as a key discipline in its own right.

- Packaging serves a variety of functions and the qualities required of it in different contexts need to be given full consideration.

Quick quiz

1   How can consumer goods be classified?

2   What is Ansoff's product/market matrix?

3   Describe the stages in the product life cycle.

4   Describe and explain the major criticisms of the PLC.

5   A cash cow is a product with a high market share in a growth market. True or false?

6   Using the GE Business Screen, what should be done with a strong product in an unattractive market?

7   List sources of new products.

8   What quality issues should be borne in mind when developing a new product?

9   What is the meaning of the 'inseparability' and 'heterogeneity' of a service and what are the marketing implications?

10   Why are people so important in service marketing?

11   What qualities are required of a pack?

Answers to activities

2   You are observing an example of market development at this very moment! BPP Publishing is already the market leading producer of books for students of professional bodies. Business Basics is a product range for the university and college market.

3   Some ideas to start you off are manual typewriters and vinyl records. Also, almost anything subject to fads or fashions.

4   You could perhaps pin down some of these items, but most are open to discussion, especially if you take an international perspective. For many you may consider that the PLC is not valid, and you will not be alone: see the following paragraphs in the main body of the chapter.

5   For one thing, they can look at the product's sales history. They can also attempt to extrapolate past sales into forecasts of future sales. Finally, their experience of earlier products may provide indications relevant to later products.

7   It is no doubt part of the trend for health consciousness, appearance, and back to basics values. As the FT article says, 'Disciples argue that baking soda acts as a mild abrasive on teeth, cuts down on plaque acid and generally deodorises the mouth', though it is not proven to be more effective than other kinds of toothpaste. Some of the advertising claims that two out of three dentists and hygienists recommend brushing with baking soda (though this may be because it is regarded as the least harmful of teeth whitening products, rather than for any particular positive virtues). It is also claimed that 'dentists recognise that when consumers enjoy the taste of a toothpaste they brush their teeth more', again not proven. Nevertheless in the US baking soda products now have about 15% of the market and the segment has grown by 65% since the late 1980s: 'a triumph of clever marketing'.

8   This argument has been suggested as one that weakens the case in favour of marketing. But looked at another way, it is the reverse of that. Poor marketing may mean that a product moves from being a problem child to being a dog without making much contribution to profits in the meantime. Equally, good marketing may prolong the 'star' and 'cash cow' phases.

9   You should try to think of your own examples, but these suggestions may help.

     New product
     Entirely new market   Multimedia products, WAP phones
     Replacing an existing product Washing powder tablets
     Broadening the market   Cable for satellite TV and telephones

     'New' old product
     In a new market   Covers or remixes of old songs
     New packaging   'Celebrations' chocolates

New marketing	Kellogg's Corn Flakes (as 'anytime' food)

10 Communication is usually in social or work settings by word of mouth.

11 Consumers wanted to know that the company was large, successful and financially secure; they wanted to be treated as individuals and have individually tailored solutions to their financial needs throughout their life; and they wanted to find the company caring, honest, knowledgeable and experienced. They also wanted unpleasant and difficult issues confronted when investments, life assurance and pensions were discussed, and to have a clear idea what provision was being made for which eventualities.

Watch out for life assurance marketing to see how companies try to meet these needs.

13 You may well have received such a mailshot yourself. One received from the National Society for the Prevention of Cruelty to Children (NSPCC) contained five items in an envelope printed with a black and white photo of a sad and bedraggled-looking little girl. The five items were as follows, in no particular order.

(a) An A3 sheet folded to make a four A4 page letter printed in two colours and with more black and white photos of neglected children on paper with a recycled feel. The letter tells the story of Ellie, the child shown on the envelope, in highly emotive language, asks for £15 and describes what good can be done with that money by the NSPCC.

(b) An A5 size donation form printed on both sides. You can tick a box saying '£15' or fill in your own amount. You can give your credit card details. You can opt not to receive further mailings. On the other side, Ellie's story and NSPCC action is described again in a sort of brief 'photo-story'.

(c) An envelope addressed to the Director of the NSPCC at a FREEPOST address (but suggesting that if you use a stamp it will save the NSPCC the postage).

(d) A 'Thank You' card with a picture of Ellie smiling on the front, a further plea from the Director of the NSPCC, and a thank you message in a 'hand-written' typeface.

(e) A car sticker saying 'Support the NSPCC'.

14 Two possibilities are:

(a) as a vehicle for carrying sales promotions (eg collecting labels to earn a prize);

(b) as a toy (breakfast cereal packets sometimes have designs that you can fold up to make a model. For example at the time when Jurassic Park was all the rage Kellogg's Corn Flakes carried a dinosaur feature. Once you had finished eating the cornflakes you could fold the packet to make a model pteranodon, euplocephalus and so on).

BPP
PUBLISHING

Further question practice

Now try the following practice questions at the end of this text.

Multiple Choice Questions: 51–60

Exam Style Question: 9

Chapter 8 :
PRICE

Introduction

All profit organisations and many non-profit organisations face the task of setting a price on their products or services. Price can go by many names: fares, tuitions, rent, assessments and so on. Historically, price was the single most important decision made by the sales department, but the importance of the interrelated elements of the marketing mix has been realised in modern approaches. Price, whilst important, is not necessarily the predominant factor nowadays. Marketing managers may now respond to competition by trying to interpret consumer wants and needs more precisely and to satisfy them by modifying existing products or introducing new products to the range. The typical reaction in production-oriented times was to cut prices in order to sell the firm's product.

It is sometimes suggested that marketing aims to make price relatively unimportant to the consumers' decision making process. There is certainly some truth in this view. The other elements of the marketing mix are ultimately concerned with adding value to the product and tailoring it to the consumers' needs, to ensure that the choice between two products is not simply based on their different prices. This underestimates the role of pricing within the marketing mix.

Your objectives

In this chapter you will learn about the following.

(a) The importance of price

(b) How prices are determined

(c) Factors influence pricing policies

(d) A variety of price-setting strategies

1 THE IMPORTANCE OF PRICE

Definition

> Price can be defined as a measure of the value exchanged by the buyer for the value offered by the seller.

It might be expected, therefore, that the price would reflect the costs to the seller of producing the product and the benefit to the buyer of consuming it. Unlike the other marketing mix elements, pricing decisions affect profits through their impact on revenues rather than costs. Pricing is of course the only element of the mix which generates revenue rather than creating costs. It also has an important role as a competitive tool to differentiate a product and an organisation and thereby exploit market opportunities. Pricing must also be consistent with other elements of the marketing mix since it contributes to the overall image created for the product. No organisation can hope to offer an exclusive high quality product to the market with a low price – the price must be consistent with the overall product offer.

Activity 1

In what circumstances would you expect price to be the main factor influencing a consumer's choice?

Although pricing fulfils a number of roles, in overall terms price is set to produce the level of sales necessary to meet the objectives of the business strategy. Pricing must be systematic and at the same time take into account the internal needs and the external constraints of the organisation. Two broad categories of objectives may be specified for pricing decisions. These are different but not mutually exclusive.

(a) Maximising profits is concerned with maximising the returns on assets or investments. This may be realised even with a comparatively small market share depending on the patterns of cost and demand.

(b) Maintaining or increasing market share involves increasing or maintaining the customer base which may require a different, more competitive approach to pricing, while the company with the largest market share may not necessarily earn the best profits.

Either approach may be used in specifying pricing objectives. They may appear in some combination, based on a specified rate of return and a specified market share. It is important that stated objectives are consistent with overall corporate objectives and corporate strategies.

We will now look at the theoretical framework for determining prices and then at the way theory is applied in practical marketing strategies.

BPP PUBLISHING

2 METHODS OF PRICE DETERMINATION

2.1 Price setting in theory

In classical economic theory, price is the major determinant of demand. The equilibrium market price is the price at which supply and demand balance each other. More recently, emphasis has been placed on the importance of non-profit factors in demand. Thus the significance of product quality, promotion, personal selling and distribution and, in overall terms, branding, has grown. A competitor may easily copy a price cut, at least in the short term, but it is much more difficult to duplicate a successful brand image based on a unique selling proposition (USP). Successful branding can allow premium pricing.

Economic theory can only determine the optimal price structure under the two extreme market conditions.

(a) **Perfect competition**: many buyers, many sellers all dealing in an identical product. Neither producer nor user has any market power and both must accept the prevailing market price.

(b) **Monopoly**: one seller who dominates many buyers. The monopolist can use his market power to set a profit maximising price.

However, in practice most of British industry can be described as an oligopoly: relatively small numbers of competitive companies dominate the market. Whilst each large firm has the ability to influence market prices, the unpredictable reaction from the other giants makes the final industry price indeterminate. Economists in the field of oligopoly pricing think that price competition is dangerous, given that there are no clear market forces to support a given price level in this situation.

Activity 2

When Sir Freddie Laker introduced his cut price Skytrain service on the transatlantic air routes he challenged the legally protected cartel of IATA (the International Air Traffic Association). IATA fixed air fares on many international routes. The fares were typically priced at a relatively high level that allowed the least efficient, marginal carrier to remain in business. IATA has international blessing as its rules allow every small (and therefore high cost) national airline carrier to remain in business. As having an airline is a mark of national prestige this approach is much favoured in the United Nations.

Initially, British Airways, TWA and Pan Am ignored Laker. But when the service started picking up significant market share, the major airlines reacted by introducing their own cut-price transatlantic fares.

What do you think happened next? Try to think of another industry in which 'price wars' periodically take place.

It is difficult to identify market power precisely in economic theory terms. Many small producers enjoy some market power by producing distinctly different products and they enjoy a degree of local monopoly.

Whilst economic theory gives an insight into price decisions, it may be of little practical help.

However, the concept of price elasticity is important. Price elasticity is measured as:

$$\frac{\% \text{ change in sales demand}}{\% \text{ change in sales price}}$$

(a) When elasticity is greater than 1 (elastic), a change in price will lead to a change in total revenue

    (i) If the price is lowered, total sales revenue will rise, because of the large increase in demand

    (ii) If the price is raised, total sales revenue will fall, because of the large fall in demand

(b) When elasticity is less than 1 (inelastic)

    (i) If the price is lowered, total sales revenue will fall, because the increase in sales volume will be too small to compensate for the price reductions

    (ii) If the price is raised, total sales revenue will go up because the drop in sales quantities will be very small

Marketing management needs to be able to estimate the likely effects of price changes on total revenue and profits.

Price elasticity of demand gives precision to the question of whether the firm's price is too high or too low. From the point of view of maximising revenue, price is too high if demand is elastic and too low if demand is inelastic. Whether this is also true for maximising profits depends on the behaviour of costs.

(Kotler)

In some cases, however, other factors may influence price elasticity, so that previous responses to price changes no longer produce the same consumer responses. Products do not stay the same forever.

Activity 3

What are the limitations of price elasticity as a factor in determining prices?

2.2 Price setting in practice

There are three influences on price setting: costs, competition and demand.

Costs

In practice, cost is the most important influence on price. Many firms base price on simple cost-plus rules: in other words, costs are estimated and then a profit margin is added in order to set the price. Cost-based pricing is, in the main, an accountant's method.

There are two types of cost-based pricing: full cost pricing and cost-plus pricing.

Full cost pricing takes account of the full average cost of production of a good, including an allocation for overheads. A conventional profit margin is then added to determine the selling price. This method is often used for non-routine jobs which are difficult to cost in advance, such as the work of solicitors and accountants where the price is often determined after the work has been performed.

Although the full cost pricing method is basically straightforward in principle, the allocation or apportionment of overheads between brands in a multibrand company can be difficult, especially when related products or by-products are involved.

Superficially, it would appear that demand factors are ignored in this analysis; in practice, however, especially in the longer term, demand can be reflected through the level of the profit margin which is added (the margin is not going to be high if demand is being squeezed). The profit margin is also likely to reflect the level of actual or potential competition from firms already in the industry or capable of entering it.

Using **cost-plus pricing** only the more easily measurable direct cost components such as labour and raw material inputs are calculated in the unit cost, whilst an additional margin incorporates an overhead charge and a residual profit element. This method is used where overhead allocation to unit costs is too complex or too time consuming to be worthwhile.

A common example occurs with the use of **mark up pricing**. This is used by retailers and involves a fixed margin being added to the buying-in price of goods for resale. This fixed margin tends to be conventional within product classes. In the UK, for example, fast moving items such as cigarettes carry a low 5–8% margin (also because of tax factors), fast moving but perishable items such as newspapers carry a 25% margin, while slow moving items which involve retailers in high stockholding costs such as furniture or books carry 33%, 50% or even higher mark up margins.

While the percentage margin may vary to reflect changes in demand or competition, the cost basis for calculations may be actual costs, expected costs or standard costs. If all the firms in the industry use the same pricing basis, prices will reflect efficiency; the most efficient firm will charge the lowest prices.

Activity 4

Cost-based pricing is quite common in practice, even though it is not necessarily a profit maximising policy. What do you think are the reasons for its popularity?

The problems with cost-plus pricing arise out of difficulties in defining direct costs and allocating overheads, and with over- or under-estimation of attainable production levels (particularly where standard costs are used). In addition, price adjustments may cause high administrative costs because of the cost-based price-setting process used.

However, because the cost-plus approach leads to price stability, with price changing only to reflect cost changes, it can lead to a marketing strategy which is reactive rather than proactive.

In addition, there is very limited consideration of demand in cost-based pricing strategies. From a marketing perspective, cost-based pricing may lead to missed opportunities as little or no account is taken, particularly in the short run, of the price consumers are willing to pay for the brand, which may actually be higher than the cost-based price.

But the approach does provide a comprehensible, practical and popular solution to the pricing problem, whereas the traditional imperfect competition model in economic theory is of limited practical value for a number of reasons:

(a)   It assumes that the demand curve can be identified with certainty

(b) It ignores the market research costs associated with acquiring knowledge of demand

(c) It assumes the firm has no productive constraint which could mean that the equilibrium point between supply and demand cannot be reached

(d) It is a static analysis (concerned with only one point in time)

Particular problems may be caused by the use of cost-based pricing for a new brand as initial low production levels in the introduction stage may lead to a very high average unit cost and consequently a high price. A longer term perspective may thus be necessary, accepting short-term losses until full production levels are attained. Finally, if the firm is using a product line promotion strategy then there is likely to be added complexity in the pricing process.

Activity 5

The Times carried the following advertisement.

FROM PLASTIC
TO PLATINUM

WORLDWIDE INDIVIDUALLY
NUMBERED LIMITED EDITION
OF 12,999
£1,000 INC VAT

Most exclusive Swatch ever produced.

- 950 Platinum case and crown.
- Stainless steel presentation case with acrylic glass inlay.
- Interchangeable royal blue leather and padded plastic straps.
- Limited availability in the UK.

Suggest how Swatch might have chosen the price of £1,000.

Competition-based pricing

Prices may be set on the basis of what competitors are charging rather than on the basis of cost or demand. A theoretical justification of the phenomenon was presented by Sweezy as the kinked demand curve theory. This is shown below.

PUBLISHING

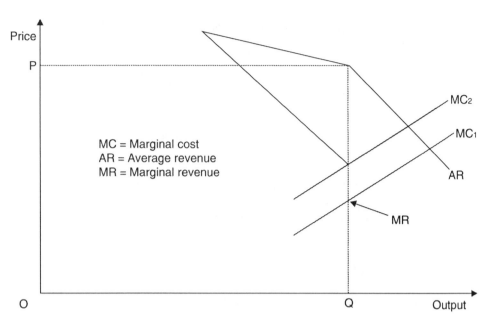

Figure 8.1 The kinked demand curve

It is suggested that price remains at OP even if marginal costs increase from MC1 to MC2. The argument is that firms assume that competitors will all follow a price decrease but that none will follow a price increase. Thus they assume that demand is elastic for a price rise, but is inelastic for a price fall. In each case a price change would reduce sales revenue. But note that this approach does not explain how the price is arrived at in the first place!

In reality, the kinked demand curve theory would produce going rate pricing in which some form of average level of price becomes the norm, perhaps, in the case of a high level of branding in the market, including standard price differentials between brands.

In some market structures price competition may be avoided by tacit agreement leading to concentration on non-price competition; the markets for cigarettes and petrol are examples of this. Price-setting here is influenced by the need to avoid retaliatory responses by competitors resulting in a breakdown of the tacit agreement and so to price competition. Price changes based on real cost changes are led in many instances by a 'representative' firm in the industry and followed by other firms.

Activity 6

There is at least one service industry in which this practice is the norm and which is regularly reported in the headlines. Can you think of it?

From time to time tacit agreements break down leading to a period of price competition. This may then be followed by a resumption of the tacit agreement. Often such actions are the result of external factors at work on the industry. Industry-level agreements do not necessarily preclude short-term price competition for specific brands, especially where sales promotion devices, such as special offers, are used (these are discussed later in this book).

Competitive bidding is a special case of competition-based pricing. Many supply contracts, especially concerning local and national government purchases, involve would-be suppliers submitting a sealed bid tender. In this case, the firm's submitted price needs to take account of expected competitor bid prices. Often the firms involved will not even know the identity of their rivals but successful past bids are often published by purchasers and, if this is so, it is possible to use this data to formulate a current bid price.

If the firm has the particular problem of bidding for a number of contracts before the result of any one bid is known, the production (or supply) capacity may be important. The firm needs to win only some contracts: not too few nor too many.

If past bid data is not published, then there is very little data on which to base bid price setting. The firm may have to rely on trade gossip, on conjecture or on an estimate of likely competitors' cost and profit requirements in price-setting.

If the contract is not awarded purely on price (that is, if the lowest bid is not automatically accepted) the problem is more acute. In the case of the supply of branded goods, the relative value of each brand must be considered on a 'value for money' basis by the purchaser. The bidder may have to rely on subjective 'feel of the market' analysis in arriving at bid prices. There are, of course, numerous instances where cases of actual and attempted bribery of officials have been uncovered as firms employ underhand means in the attempt to win contracts.

Demand

A firm may base pricing strategy on the intensity of demand rather than on cost or competition. The latter both remain influences or constraints on its freedom to set price, however.

A strong demand may lead to a high price and a weak demand to a low price: much depends on the ability of the firm to segment the market price in terms of elasticity.

In practice, measuring price elasticity and hence implementing differential pricing can be very difficult. There are a number of bases on which discriminating prices can be set.

(a) **By market segment**

A cross-channel ferry company would market its services at different prices in England, Belgium and France, for example. Services such as cinemas and hairdressers are often available at lower prices to old age pensioners and/or juveniles.

(b) **By product version**

Many car models have 'add on' extras which enable one brand to appeal to a wider cross-section of customers. Final price need not reflect the cost price of the add on extras directly: usually the top of the range model carries a price much in excess of the cost of provision of the extras, as a prestige appeal.

(c) **By place**

Theatre seats are usually sold according to their location so that patrons pay different prices for the same performance according to the seat type they occupy.

(d) **By time**

Perhaps the most popular type of price discrimination. Hotel prices vary according to season, telephone and electricity charges vary through the day. These are all attempts to increase sales revenue by covering variable but not necessarily average cost of provision. Lower prices at 'unpopular' times help to increase demand at these times and possibly reduce or avoid 'over demand' at other times.

> **Activity 7**
>
> Think of another common example in which price discrimination is practised based on the time at which services are consumed.

In each of these cases, some customers pay more than others for essentially the same product or service, reflecting different intensities of demand. There is an ethical dimension to this practice and firms need to consider their objectives carefully before using this approach. For instance, by taking advantage of a short-term shortage of a product and increasing price, a firm may harm long-term profit prospects because customers resent what they interpret as exploitation. This is particularly the case as consumerism develops (refer back to Chapter 3), since vociferous groups of consumers can create damaging publicity for the product supplier in the short and/or longer term.

Price discrimination can only be effective if a number of conditions hold.

(a) The market must be segmentable in price terms, and different sectors must show different intensities of demand. Each of the sectors must be identifiable, distinct and separate from the others and be accessible to the firm's marketing communications.

(b) There must be little or no chance of a black market developing so that those in the lower priced segment can resell to those in the higher priced segment.

(c) There must be little chance that competitors can and will undercut the firm's prices in the higher priced (and/or most profitable) market segments.

(d) The cost of segmenting and administering the arrangements should not exceed the extra revenue derived from the price discrimination strategy.

The firm could use a market test to estimate the effect on demand of a price change. This would involve a change of price in one region and a comparison of demand for the brand with past sales in that region and with sales in similar regions at the old prices. This is a high risk strategy: special circumstances (confounding factors such as a competitor's advertising campaign) may affect the test area and could affect the results. Also customers may switch from the test brand if a price rise is being considered and become loyal to a competitive brand; they may not switch back even if the price is subsequently lowered.

Alternately, a direct attitude survey may be used with respondents. Pricing research is notoriously difficult, especially if respondents try to appear rational to the interviewer or do not wish to offend him or her. Usually there is a lack of realism in such research; the respondent is not in an actual 'choice' situation faced with having to pay out hard earned income and therefore may give a hypothetical answer which is not going to be translated into actual purchasing behaviour. Nevertheless, pricing research is increasingly common as firms struggle to assess the perceived value customers attribute to a brand before making pricing decisions.

Having assessed the theoretical and practical aspects of determining its prices, the firm must formulate and apply a pricing policy for its brands.

3 PRICING POLICY

Price sensitivity will vary among purchasers. Those who can pass on the cost of purchases will be least sensitive and will respond more to other elements of the marketing mix.

(a) Provided that it fits the corporate budget, the business traveller will be more concerned about the level of service and quality of food in looking for an hotel than price. In contrast, a family on holiday are likely to be very price sensitive when choosing an overnight stay.

(b) In petrol retailing, the largest take up of trading stamps and other promotional offerings has been from the company representative, obtaining perks whilst charging relatively expensive petrol to the company.

(c) In industrial marketing the purchasing manager is likely to be more price sensitive than the engineer who might be the actual user of new equipment that is being sourced. The engineer and purchasing manager are using different criteria in making the choice. The engineer places product characteristics as first priority, the purchasing manager is more price oriented.

3.1 Finding out about price sensitivity

Research on price sensitivity of customers has shown the following.

(a) Customers have a good concept of a 'just price' – an intuitive feeling about the right price to pay

(b) Unless a regular purchase is involved, customers search for price information before buying, becoming price aware when wanting to buy but forgetting soon afterwards

(c) Customers will buy at what they consider to be a bargain price without full regard for need and actual price

(d) For consumer durables the down payment and instalment price may be more important than total price

(e) In times of rising prices the price image tends to lag behind the current price, which indicates a resentment of the price increase. It is thus very important to relate customers' image of price to the actual price as this image will determine reactions to a price change. For instance, Bell Telephones in the US were concerned about the lack of sales of extension telephones. When, as part of a market research survey, customers were asked to name the actual price of an extension telephone, most overestimated it. By keeping the existing price but running an advertising campaign featuring it, Bell were able to increase sales as customers became aware of the lower-than-anticipated price.

Activity 8

You ask a friend to empty his wallet of receipts and lay them on the table. You find receipts from different shops for the following.

(a)	A pint of milk	£0.47
(b)	A man's suit	£199.99
(c)	A bottle of wine	£7.50
(d)	A book of 10 first class stamps	£2.70

In each case the price tells you something about one or more of the following:

(a) The product purchased
(b) The place where it was purchased
(c) The circumstances in which it was purchased
(d) The purpose for which it was purchased
(e) The person making the purchase

Explain each of the purchases in these terms. Does your interpretation of the price say anything about you?

3.2 Finding out about price perception

Price perception is important in the ways customers react to prices. The economist's downward sloping demand curve may not in fact hold, at least in the short term. For example, customers may react to a price increase by buying more because:

- They expect further price increases to follow (they are 'stocking up')
- They assume the quality has increased
- The brand takes on a 'snob appeal' because of the high price

Several factors complicate the pricing decisions which an organisation has to make.

3.3 Intermediaries' objectives

If an organisation distributes products or services to the market through independent intermediaries, the objectives of these intermediaries have an effect on the pricing decision. Such intermediaries are likely to deal with a range of suppliers and their aims concern their own profits rather than those of suppliers. Also, the intermediary will take into account the needs of its customers. Thus conflict over price can arise between suppliers and intermediaries which may be difficult to resolve.

Many industries have traditional margins for intermediaries; to deviate from these might well cause problems for suppliers. In some industries, notably grocery retailing (as we have seen), the power of intermediaries allows them to dictate terms to suppliers. The relationship between intermediaries and suppliers is therefore complex, and price and the price discount structure is an important element.

Activity 9

Are you familiar with the relationship between Marks & Spencer and its suppliers? If not, try to find out about it and analyse its effects in the light of the discussion above.

BPP
PUBLISHING

3.4 Competitors' actions and reactions

In setting prices, an organisation sends out signals to its rivals. These rivals are likely to react in some way. In some industries (such as petrol retailing) pricing moves in unison; in others, price changes by one supplier may initiate a price war, with each supplier undercutting the others.

3.5 Suppliers

If an organisation's suppliers notice that the prices for that organisation's products are rising, they may seek a rise in the price for their supplies to the organisation, arguing that it is now more able to pay a higher price. This argument is especially likely to be used by the trade unions in the organisation when negotiating the 'price' for the supply for labour.

3.6 Inflation

The organisation's prices may need to change in order to reflect increases in the prices of supplies, labour, rent and so on, caused by inflation. Such changes may be needed to keep relative (real) prices unchanged (this is the process of prices being adjusted for the rate of inflation).

3.7 Quality connotations

In the absence of other information, customers tend to judge quality by price. Thus a price change may send signals to customers concerning the quality of the product. A rise may be taken to indicate improvements, a reduction may signal reduced quality, for example through the use of inferior components or a poorer quality of raw material. Thus any change in price needs to take such factors into account.

3.8 New product pricing

Most pricing decisions for existing products relate to price changes. Such changes have a reference point (the existing price) from which to move. When a new product is introduced for the first time there may be no such reference points; pricing decisions are most difficult to make in such circumstances. It may be possible to seek alternative reference points, such as the price in another market where the new product has already been launched, or the price set by a competitor.

3.9 Income effects

In times of rising incomes, price may become a less important marketing variable than, for instance, product quality or convenience of access (distribution). When income levels are falling and/or unemployment levels rising, price will become a much more important marketing variable. In the recession of the early 1990s, the major grocery multiples such as Tesco, Sainsbury, Safeway and Waitrose, who steadily moved up-market in the 1980s with great success leaving the 'pile it high, sell it cheap' philosophy behind, suddenly found bargain stores such as 'Foodgiant' and 'Netto' a more serious threat.

3.10 Multiple products

Most organisations market not just one product but a range of products. These products are commonly interrelated, perhaps being complements or substitutes. The management of the pricing function is likely to focus on the profit from the whole range rather than that on each single product. Take, for example, the use of loss leaders: a very low price for one product is intended to make consumers buy other products in the range which carry higher profit margins. Loss leaders also attract customers into retail stores where they will usually buy normally priced products as well as the loss leaders.

Activity 10

Try to think of some examples of a low-priced product 'locking in' a consumer to higher-priced products.

3.11 Sensitivity

Price decisions are often seen as highly sensitive and as such may involve top management more clearly than other marketing decisions. As already noted, price has a very obvious and direct relationship with profit. Ethical considerations are a further factor: whether or not to exploit short-term shortages through higher prices; illustrative of this dilemma is the outcry surrounding the series of petrol price rises following the outbreak of the Gulf Crisis in 1990.

Once the firm's overall pricing policy has been determined, pricing strategies must be formulated in keeping with the marketing strategy for each brand.

4 PRICE SETTING STRATEGIES

Pricing strategies must take into account marketing objectives.

Market penetration objective: here the organisation sets a relatively low price for the product or service in order to stimulate growth of the market and/or to obtain a large share of it. This strategy was used by Japanese motor cycle manufacturers to enter the UK market. It worked famously: UK productive capacity was virtually eliminated and the imported Japanese machines could then be sold at a much higher price and still dominate the market.

Sales maximising objectives are favoured when:

- Unit costs will fall with increased output (economies of scale)

- The market is price sensitive and relatively low prices will attract additional sales

- Low prices will discourage any new competitors

Market skimming objective: in many ways an opposite objective to market penetration. Skimming involves setting a high initial price for a new product in order to take advantage of those buyers who are ready to pay a much higher price for a product. A typical strategy would be initially to command a premium price and then gradually to reduce the price to attract more price sensitive segments of the market. This strategy is really an example of price discrimination over time.

This strategy is favoured when:

- There is insufficient market capacity and competitors cannot increase capacity

- Buyers are relatively insensitive to price increases

- High price is perceived as high quality (interaction in marketing mix)

- There is the danger of encouraging firms to enter the market

Early cash recovery objective: an alternative pricing objective is to recover the investment in a new product or service as quickly as possible, to achieve a minimum payback period. The price is set so as to facilitate this objective. This objective would tend to be used in conditions where:

- The business is high risk
- Rapid changes in fashion or technology are expected
- The innovator is short of cash

Product line promotion objective: here, management of the pricing function is likely to focus on profit from the range of products which the organisation produces rather than to treat each product as a separate entity. The product line promotion objective will take account of the constitution of the whole range in terms of:

- The interaction of the marketing mix
- Monitoring returns to ensure that net contribution is worthwhile

Intermediate customers: some companies set a price to distributors and allow them to set whatever final price they wish. A variant involves publishing an inflated recommended retail price so that retailers can offer large promotional discounts.

Cost-plus pricing: a firm may set its initial price by marking up its unit costs by a certain percentage or fixed amount, as already discussed.

(a) It conforms to internal company rules for 'satisfactory' return on investment.

(b) It takes no account of risk. In fact, riskier product lines should make higher returns.

(c) It cannot ultimately avoid market pressures: if 'overpriced', stocks will build up or if 'underpriced', excess demand will be created exceeding the firm's capacity and encouraging market entrants.

Target pricing: a variant on cost-plus where the company tries to determine the price that gives a specified rate of return for a given output. This is widely used by large American manufacturers, such as General Motors and Boeing.

Price discrimination (or differential pricing): offering different prices to different classes of buyer. The danger is that price cuts to one buyer may be used as a negotiating lever by another buyer. To avoid such leverage:

- Buyers must be in clearly defined segments, such as overseas and home, or students' concessionary fares
- Own branding where packaging is changed for that of a supermarket is a variation on this
- Bulk buying discounts and aggregated rebate schemes can favour large buyers

Going rate pricing: try to keep in line with industry norm for prices. Don't 'rock the boat' if everybody is charging relatively high near-monopolistic prices.

(a) This is typical behaviour of a mature oligopoly, akin to a cartel.

(b) Suppliers engage in less damaging competition than price cutting, such as advertising campaigns and post-sales service.

(c) This is often technically illegal but this does not stop individual firms accepting the role of price leaders in an industry.

Quantum price: in retail selling the concept of a 'quantum point' is often referred to. When the price of an item is increased from, say, £9.65 to £9.95, sales may not be affected

NOTES

because the consumers do not notice the price change. However, if the price is increased from £9.95 to £10.05 a major fall in sales may occur, £10 acting as a quantum point which can be approached but not passed if the price is not to deter would-be purchasers.

Odd number pricing: sometimes referred to as 'psychological pricing', in fact the odd number pricing syndrome (pricing at £1.95, £2.95 etc rather than £2, £3 etc) is said to have originated not as a marketing concept but in department stores in order to ensure the honesty of sales assistants. The customer has to wait for change from £1.95 when, as is usual, they offer, say, £2 in payment, so the assistant has to use the till. If the price was £2 and the customer need not wait for the change, there was thought to be a greater temptation to shop assistants to pocket the money and not to enter it into the till!

One coin purchase: confectionery firms have used another psychologically based concept of a 'one coin purchase' in pricing tactics. Rather than change price to reflect cost changes, such firms often alter the quantity in the unit of the product and keep the same price. This is a case of 'price-minus' pricing. The firm determines what the market will bear and works backwards, planning to produce and market a brand which will be profitable to them, selling at the nominated retail price.

Gift purchases: gift purchasing is often founded on the idea of price which is taken to reflect quality. Thus if a gift is to be purchased in an unfamiliar product category, a price level is often fixed by the buyer and a choice made from the brands available at that price. Cosmetics are often priced at £4.99 and £9.99 to appeal to gift purchasers at the £5 and £10 price level. Importantly, packaging is a major part of the appeal and must reflect a quality brand image, an important part of the psychology of gift choice.

4.1 Product line pricing

When a firm sells a range of related products, or a product line, its theoretical pricing strategy should be to set prices for each product in order to maximise the profitability of the line as a whole. A firm may therefore have a pricing strategy for an entire product line.

(a) There may be a brand name which the manufacturer wishes to associate with high quality but high price, or reasonable quality and low price and so forth. All items in the line will be priced accordingly. For example, all major supermarket chains have an 'own brand' label which is used to sell goods at a slightly lower price than the major named brands.

(b) If two or more products in the line are complementary, one may be priced as a loss leader in order to attract more demand for all of the related products.

(c) If two or more products in the line share joint production costs (joint products), prices of the products will be considered as a single decision. For example, if a common production process makes one unit of joint product A for each one unit of joint product B, a price for A which achieves a demand of, say, 17,000 units, will be inappropriate if associated with a price for product B which would only sell, say, 10,000 units. 7,000 units of B would be unsold and wasted.

4.2 Price changes caused by cost changes in the firm

During the prolonged period of high inflation in the 1970s, price increases generated by increased costs to the manufacturer were a common experience. The effect of inflation on price decisions was very noticeable and different organisations reacted in different ways.

(a)   Some firms raised their prices regularly.

(b)   Other firms gave advance warning of price rises, especially in an industrial market. Customers might then be persuaded to buy early in order to avoid paying the higher price at a later date.

(c)   A firm which did not raise its prices was in effect reducing its prices in real terms.

4.3   Competitive pricing

It is in the field of competition that price is the most potent element in the marketing mix. Professor Corey of the Harvard Business School summarised the role of price in competitive gameplaying.

The struggle for market share focuses critically on price. Pricing strategies of competing firms are highly interdependent. The price one competitor sets is a function not only of what the market will pay but also of what other firms charge. Prices set by individual firms respond to those of competitors; they also are intended often to influence competitors' pricing behaviour. Pricing is an art, a game played for high stakes; and for marketing strategists it is the 'moment of truth'. All of marketing comes to focus in the pricing decision.

4.4   Competitive price changes

A firm may lower its prices to try to increase its market share; on the other hand, a firm may raise its prices in the hope that competitors will quickly do the same (that is, in the expectation of tacit price collusion). The purpose of such competitive initiatives will presumably be to raise either profits or the firm's market share. In established industries dominated by a few major firms, however, it is generally accepted that a price initiative by one firm will be countered by a price reaction by competitors. Here, prices tend to be fairly stable, unless pushed upwards by inflation or strong growth in demand. Consequently, in industries such as breakfast cereals (dominated in Britain by Kellogg's, Nabisco and Quaker) or canned soups (Heinz, Crosse & Blackwell and Campbells) a certain price stability might be expected without too many competitive price initiatives, except when cost inflation pushes up the price of one firm's products with other firms soon following.

Activity 11

If your competitor cuts his prices in the expectation of increasing market share, what are your possible responses?

4.5   Price leadership

Given that price competition can have disastrous consequences in conditions of oligopoly, it is not unusual to find that large corporations emerge as price leaders. Price leadership here brings about relative price stability in otherwise unstable price dynamic oligopolies.

A price leader will dominate price levels for a class of products; increases or decreases by the price leader provide a direction to market price patterns. The price-dominant firm may lead without moving at all. This would be the case if other firms sought to raise prices and the leader did not follow, then the upward move in prices will be halted. The price leader generally has a large, if not necessarily the largest, market share. The company will usually be an efficient low-cost producer that has a reputation for technical competence.

The role of price leader is based on a track record of having initiated price moves that have been accepted by both competitors and customers. Often, this is associated with a mature well established management group.

Any dramatic changes in industry competition, (a new entrant, or changes in the board room) may endanger the price leadership role.

Activity 12

Are luxury products necessarily expensive?

Chapter roundup

- Pricing is the only element of the marketing mix which generates revenue rather than creating costs. Pricing decisions may have two main objectives: maximising profits or gaining market share.

- You should appreciate the concept of price elasticity, but realise that basic economic theory gives only a limited, simplified view of the real world.

- Setting prices in practice may be based on costs (cost-plus pricing, full cost pricing), competition or demand.

- Pricing policy will depend on price sensitivity, price perception, intermediaries' objectives, competitors' and suppliers' actions and reactions, income effects and a variety of other factors.

- Companies may undertake any of a variety of pricing strategies, depending on their motives, the industry they operate in and so on. These include market penetration pricing, market skimming, price discrimination and others. Where competition is fierce price may become the most important element in the marketing mix.

Quick quiz

1   What roles does price fulfil other than generating a desired level of income?

2   Why is cost plus pricing popular?

3   List four bases for price discrimination.

4   What is the difference between price sensitivity and price perception?

5   What is a loss leader?

6   What is market skimming?

7   What is a quantum point?

8   What options are there for pricing when a firm sells a range of related products?

Answers to activities

1 You might have identified a number of different factors here. Perhaps the most important general point to make is that price is particularly important if the other elements in the marketing mix are relatively similar across a range of competing products. For example, there is a very wide variety of toothpastes on the market, most of them not much differentiated from the others. The price of a particular toothpaste may be a crucial factor in its sales success.

2 The result was that every major carrier recorded losses on its transatlantic business. These losses were only alleviated when Laker himself went out of business. The issue is confused by alleged 'dirty tricks' against Laker. Virgin has similarly eaten into the revenue of other airlines, and has been subject to less than reputable retaliation, but the modern market is rather more favourable for Richard Branson.

There are plenty of other examples. You might have mentioned the oil/petrol industry where 'forecourt price wars' hit the headlines from time to time. Another example in recent years has been the High Street banks' attempts to attract customers by offering free banking, subject to certain conditions, or the free service provision offered by Internet service providers such as Freeserve.

3 The main problem is that unless very detailed research has been carried out the price elasticity of a particular product or service is likely to be unknown. As a theoretical concept, it is useful in gaining an understanding of the effects of price changes; but it is of little use as a practical tool in determining prices.

4 Many possible reasons could be given; the ones below are identified in a study by Lanzilotti.

   (a) Planning and use of scarce capital resources are easier

   (b) Easier assessment of divisional performance

   (c) Emulation of successful large companies

   (d) Belief by management in a 'fair return' policy

   (e) Fear of government action against 'excessive' profits

   (f) Tradition of production orientation rather than marketing orientation in many organisations

   (g) Tacit collusion in industry to avoid competition

   (h) Adequate profits for shareholders are already made, giving no incentive to maximise profits

   (i) Easier administration of cost-based pricing strategies based on internal data

   (j) Stability of pricing, production and employment produced by cost-based pricing over time

   (k) Social equability

5 We don't know the answer, but a suggestion is that the cost of the product was established (to make sure of breaking even), VAT added since it makes a significant difference for the customer, and comparisons were made with items of similar quality and rarity on the market. A range of possible prices, based on this data, might then have been presented to potential customers to see how they reacted to them. Data may also

PUBLISHING

NOTES

have been collected about the results of similar exercises by other watchmakers (or the like) in the past.

If you cheated and just read this solution without thinking for yourself, ask yourself how Swatch made the decision to produce no more than 12,999 watches. At what stage would the decision to go ahead and manufacture the watches be made?

6 The industry referred to is the mortgage industry. When economic factors cause alterations in interest rates (one of the main 'costs' borne by lenders, because of their interest payments to investors), the lenders reduce or increase their lending rates (the 'price' of their mortgage products). It is usual to see one of the larger mortgage providers leading the way, after which the others fall into line.

7 The obvious example is off-peak travel bargains. Rail companies are successful price discriminators, charging more to rush hour rail commuters whose demand for the service is inelastic at certain times of the day.

8 Your interpretation will say something about you, so we don't give an answer.

9 One distinctive feature of many Marks & Spencer suppliers is that they are 'tied', in the sense that Marks & Spencer are able, by virtue of their immense purchasing power, to dictate the prices charged. If the supplier is not happy with the price, and tries to raise it, he runs the risk of losing a potentially enormous volume of business. The recent troubles of M&S have led to it cancelling contracts with some suppliers, with disastrous consequences for these companies.

10 A simple example might be a low-priced razor, with a high price charged on the corresponding razor blades. Another might be a low-priced compact disc player – the price of compact discs themselves is often criticised as being unfairly high relative to the prices of records or audio tapes. (Not all CD player manufacturers also make CDs, however).

11 (a) You might maintain your existing prices if the expectation is that only a small market share would be lost, so that it is more profitable to keep prices at their existing level. Eventually, the rival firm may drop out of the market or be forced to raise its prices.

   (b) You might maintain your prices but respond with a non-price counter-attack. This is a more positive response, because you will be securing or justifying your current prices with a product change, advertising, or better back-up services etc.

   (c) You might reduce your prices. This should protect your market share so that the main beneficiary from the price reduction will be the consumer

   (d) You might raise your prices and respond with a non-price counter-attack. The extra revenue from the higher prices might be used to finance an advertising campaign or product design changes. A price increase would be based on a campaign to emphasise the quality difference between your own product and the rival's product.

12 Not necessarily, as this extract illustrates:

'Now ... people are looking for much greater value in what they buy whether it's a $30,000 car or at the supermarket. Value has become the new watch word in the luxury market, and nowhere is this truer than in car sales, where high priced European cars have taken a beating from new Japanese competitors. ... Mercedes, BMW and Audi are fighting back with marketing campaigns emphasising engineering excellence and safety rather than status. But market analysts say the struggle is uphill because the Japanese have succeeded in redefining luxury cars as those that have superb performance, looks and feel without a giddy price.' (Financial Times).

Mercedes and Ford have recently announced price cuts for certain models in the UK.

Further question practice

Now try the following practice questions at the end of this text.

Multiple Choice Questions: 61–70

Exam Style Question: 10

Chapter 9 :
PROMOTION

Introduction

'Promotion' is concerned with communication between the seller and the buyer (an increasingly widely used alternative name is marketing communications). Consequently it is the most visible aspect of marketing and, arguably, the most interesting. Promotion builds brands and we shall take a detailed look at branding in this chapter.

Promotion includes advertising, sales promotion activities, publicity or public relations, and the activities of the sales force. The fastest growing area, in the age of computers and telecommunications, is personal marketing. However, your first job if you choose marketing as a career may well be in the field of personal selling. All these topics are covered extensively below.

Firms will use a combination of promotion methods and the optimal communications mix will depend on the nature of the product, the market and the customer. A manufacturer of industrial goods may rely more heavily on personal selling and sales literature, whereas a consumer goods manufacturer will use advertising and sales promotion.

Your objectives

In this chapter you will learn about the following.

(a) The communication process

(b) The purpose and objectives of advertising, the six stages of an advertising campaign, when advertising is likely to be successful and the advantages of using agencies

(c) The importance of branding

(d) Examples of sales promotion activities and the meaning of merchandising

(e) The ways in which publicity may be used for promotion

(f) What is meant by direct marketing and why it is growing in importance, and the techniques of direct mail and telemarketing

(g) The tasks and process of personal selling, how a sales force might be organised and the value of after-sales service

1 PROMOTION AND COMMUNICATING WITH CUSTOMERS

1.1 Communicating with customers: the selling function

Figure 9.1 Marketing communications

Communication with customers involves many aspects of the marketing mix, but promotion is paramount.

Personal selling is not the only communication medium available to the organisation. In firms with a co-ordinated promotional strategy the activity of the sales team will be supported and supplemented by a combination of other communication tools. This combination is referred to as the **promotional mix**.

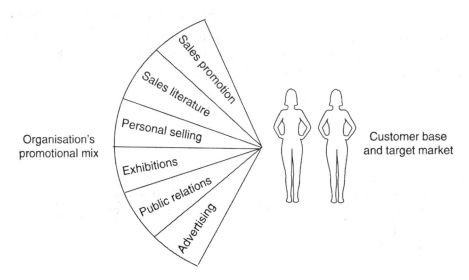

Figure 9.2 The promotional mix

These other communication tools are used to increase the efficiency and effectiveness of the sales effort. In combination, these represent the entire external communications activity of the organisation.

It is possible to use the same model of the communication process to describe one-to-one communication between friends, or a major multinational organisation communicating with its market place.

Effective communication requires several elements.

- A sender
- A receiver
- A message
- A communication channel or medium
- A feedback mechanism

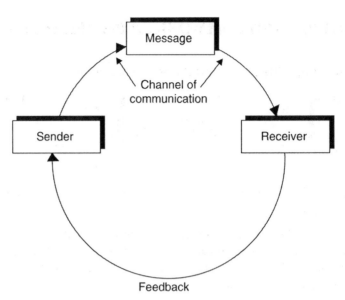

Figure 9.3 A simple model of communication

This simple model of communication can also be used to show where failures in the process can cause communication to be less effective. In this diagram we have looked at the model as though the sender was the salesperson.

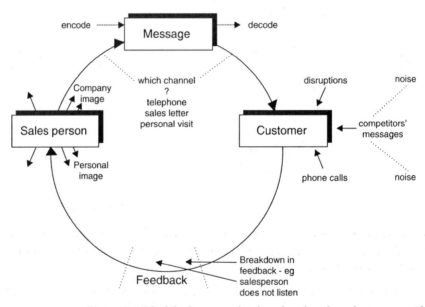

Figure 9.4 Model of communication showing the salesperson as the sender

The following table expands on the above diagram.

BPP
PUBLISHING

Element in process	How it can go wrong in personal selling
Sender	The salesperson transmits a personal and personified company image. The dress, the language used, and the car they drive creates that image. If it is inconsistent with the sales message or the customer's perceptions, communication can be adversely effected.
Message	The message has to be encoded and accurately decoded if it is to be effective. The words and pictures used can help or hinder this process. Using technical jargon to a non-specialist customer, or not having visual support aids and leaflets are examples of hindrances.
Channel	Choosing the wrong channel to transmit the sales message: an intrusive personal visit, instead of a phone call, or a phone call instead of a more effective personal visit.
Receiver	Much sales time and effort can be wasted talking to the wrong person. Ensuring the market has been correctly targeted and the decision making unit (DMU) identified, is essential to the selling process. Even when face to face with the decision maker, there will be distractions, or noise. This can include disruptions to a sales presentation like phone calls, or the impact of competitors' sales messages.
Feedback	The strength of personal selling lies in its ability to modify the message in response to customer feedback. If the feedback mechanism fails to work, selling loses its distinct advantage as a communication tool. A salesperson who fails to 'listen' to the customer and does not pick up body language cues will be not an effective salesperson.

The salesperson has to be aware that as a communicator it is not just 'what is said' which has an impact. 'How it is said', also 'speaks volumes'. How something is said directly communicates the salesperson's attitude to customers and reflects the degree to which customer care is meant. The 'how' of external communication is transmitted not by the spoken word, but through the unspoken signals of body language and the physical clues which we broadcast to those we meet.

We shall be discussing personal selling in more detail in the final part of this chapter.

Activity 1

You have no doubt been browsing in a shop and found that you are constantly bothered by sales assistants wondering whether they can help you. You have also no doubt been ready to buy something in a shop and been infuriated that you cannot find anyone to help you.

How can this situation be analysed in terms of the communication process?

1.2 'Push' and 'pull' effects

The promotional mix is often described in terms of 'push' and 'pull' effects.

(a) A 'pull' effect is when customers ask for the brand by name, inducing retailers or distributors to stock up with the company's goods.

(b) A 'push' effect is targeted on getting the company's goods into the distribution network. This could be by giving a special discount on volume to ensure that wholesalers stock up with products that the company is promoting.

Perhaps the most obvious way in which the marketer can communicate with large numbers of potential customers is advertising. One of the aims of advertising is to create the 'pull' effect described above.

2   ADVERTISING

Definition

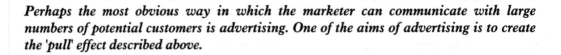

Advertising is defined by the American Marketing Association as:

any paid form of non-personal presentation and promotion of ideas, goods or services by an identifiable sponsor.

This definition clearly distinguishes advertising from personal selling and publicity (which is often not paid for and, even if it is, the sponsor does not openly present ideas or products).

Promotion, especially advertising, can be seen as attempting to move consumers along a continuum stretching from complete unawareness of the product to regular usage (brand loyalty). The AIDA model postulated by Strong in 1925 is a simple example of this approach known as the 'hierarchy of effects' model.

Awareness → Interest → Desire → Action

These models assume that customers formulate a behavioural intention which then leads to actual purchasing behaviour.

2.2   The purpose of advertising

Advertising is 'purposive communication' to a target market. It assists in selling by drawing attention to the characteristics of a product which will appeal to the buying motives (conscious or subconscious) of customers in the target segment of the market. It does not necessarily instruct or inform about all the characteristics of a product; its function is to identify an exploitable characteristic (that is, one which distinguishes it from other products) and to suggest that this characteristic gives it a special value for potential customers. If the product does not have a distinguishing characteristic, uniqueness is promoted by brand image.

Definition

The purpose of advertising is to enhance potential buyers' responses to the organisation and its offerings. It seeks to do this by providing information, by trying to channelise desires and by supplying reasons for preferring the particular organisation's offerings.   (Kotler)

Advertising is often classed under one of three headings.

(a)   **Informative advertising**. Conveying information and raising consumer awareness of the product. Common in the early stages of the lifecycle, or after modification.

(b)   **Persuasive advertising**. Concerned with creating a desire for the product and stimulating actual purchase. Used for well established products, often in the growth/maturity stages of the product life cycle. The most competitive form of advertising.

(c)   **Reminding advertising**. Reminding consumers about the product or organisation, reinforcing the knowledge held by potential consumers and reminding existing consumers of the benefits they are receiving from their purchase.

2.3   Brand versus generic advertising

It will only be worthwhile for an individual firm to advertise if it can differentiate its brands from competitors' in the eyes of the consumer. In the absence of product differentiation all advertising purchased by an individual firm would be generic, benefiting all producers equally at the firm's expense. This is a particular danger for commodity goods such as flour and sugar.

2.4   Above-the-line and below-the-line

The 'line' is one in an advertising agency's accounts above which are shown earnings on a commission basis and below which are shown earnings on a fee basis.

(a)   Above-the-line advertising refers to adverts in media such as the press, radio, TV and cinema.

(b)   Below-the-line advertising media include direct mail, exhibitions, package design, merchandising and so on. This term is sometimes regarded as synonymous with sales promotion.

2.5   The objectives of advertising

The objectives of advertising may be any of the following.

(a)   To ensure a certain exposure for the advertised product or service

(b)   To create awareness of new products, or developments to existing products

(c)   To improve customer attitudes towards the product or the firm

(d)   To increase sales (although it is difficult to relate advertising to sales volumes) and profits: for a non-profit-making organisation, the equivalent purpose will be to increase response to the product or service

(e)   To generate enquiries from potential customers

(f)   To change the attitudes and habits of people

Advertising is also a means of protecting the longer-term position of a company, by building a strong, established image.

The objectives of advertising which were listed above are rather general. The more specific targets of a particular advertising campaign might be as follows.

(a)   To communicate certain information about a product. This is perhaps the most important objective.

(b)   To highlight specific features of a product which make it different from the competitors'. The concept of the unique selling proposition (USP) is that by emphasising a unique feature which appeals to a customer need, customers will be influenced to buy the product.

NOTES

Business Basics: Marketing

(c) To build up a 'brand image' or a 'company image' through corporate advertising.

(d) To reinforce customer behaviour.

(e) Influencing dealers and resellers to stock the items (on as much shelf-space as possible).

(f) In the case of government advertising, to achieve a policy objective.

Activity 2

Look through a magazine or watch commercial TV for a while (neither task should be terribly demanding!) and see if you can spot examples of each of these types of campaign.

2.6 The role of advertising in industrial marketing

The principal aims of advertising targeted at industrial rather than consumer markets are as follows.

(a) **Awareness building**. If the prospect is not aware of the company or product, he or she may refuse to see the salesperson, or the salesperson may have to use up a lot of time in introducing himself and his company.

(b) **Comprehension building**. If the product represents a new concept, some of the burden of explaining it can be effectively carried on by advertising.

(c) **Efficient reminding**. If the prospects know about the product but are not ready to buy, an advertisement reminding them of the product would be much cheaper than numerous sales calls.

(d) **Lead generation**. Advertisements carrying return coupons are an effective way to generate sales leads for sales staff.

(e) **Legitimisation**. Company sales staff can use tear sheets of the company's advertisements to show prospects in order to demonstrate that their company and products are not fly-by-night but respectable and sufficiently financially sound to run an advertising campaign.

(f) **Reassurance**. Advertising can remind customers how to use the product and reassure them about their purchase.

Having decided that an advertising campaign will be the best way of communicating with potential customers, the marketing manager needs to consider the most effective way to launch a campaign. This may well involve appointing an advertising agency.

3 SUCCESSFUL ADVERTISING

The content of an advertisement is determined largely by the objective of the advertising and the motivation of the potential customer. An advertisement should present information which leads to a greater awareness of the product. It should be an attention-getter and may excite amusement or emotions such as fear, but inciting these feelings should not be allowed to be the only effect of the advertisement.

PUBLISHING

Advertising will be most successful if the following conditions apply.

(a)   The product should have characteristics which lend themselves to advertising.

     (i)   It should be distinctive and identifiable (if it is not, a distinctive brand should be created).

     (ii)   It should stimulate emotional buying (emotive products such as medicine, insurance, cosmetics and products which can be made to arouse social instincts, such as cars, alcohol, cigarettes and household appliances, can be advertised with great effectiveness).

     (iii)   If at the point of sale a customer can refute an advertising claim simply by inspecting the product, advertising will achieve no sales at all.

(b)   There should be consistency throughout the sales operation. Advertising, the activities of salespeople and dealers, branding, packaging and pricing should all promote the same product image.

(c)   There should be co-operation between advertising staff and all other activities in the company. Product design, production, distribution, selling and financial operations should all combine to achieve customer orientation and maximum selling efficiency.

3.1 Advertising agencies

Most large scale advertising involves not just an advertiser and the media owners, but also an advertising agency. An advertising agency advises its client on the planning of a campaign and buys advertising 'space' in various media on behalf of its client.

An advertising agency is appointed by clients to conduct an advertising campaign on their behalf. In the UK they receive a commission (of 10% or 15%) from the owners of the media with whom they place the advertisements.

Large or medium sized agencies may be creative agencies (specialising in originating creative ideas, which are necessary for, say, TV advertising) or media buyers (whose specialist skills are in buying media space and air time). Advertising of industrial goods is usually handled by smaller 'industrial agencies' which have the accounts of chemical, transportation and engineering firms. Most of their work is in the sphere of sales promotions, direct mail, exhibitions and public relations.

3.2 Advantages of agencies

The advantages of advertising agencies are as follows.

(a)   From the media owner's point of view

     (i)   They reduce the number of organisations with whom they have to deal

     (ii)   Agencies are bound to conform to the British Code of Advertising Practice in order to obtain their commission.

(b)   From the advertiser's point of view

     (i)   An agency's specialised services are likely to be cheaper than an internal advertising department

     (ii)   An agency will have broader contacts with ancillary services such as printers and photographers

(iii) The advertiser receives expert advice (for example, from the agency's account executive) free of charge

(iv) Agency employees have a broad experience in the field of advertising

3.3 The advertiser and the agency

To take full advantage of the agency's services, the advertisement manager of the advertising company must:

(a) Have a working knowledge of advertising

(b) Be able to negotiate with the agency so that the proposed campaign will achieve the marketing aims of the organisation

(c) Transmit whatever information is necessary to the agency which may be of value in furthering the advertising campaign in the best interests of the organisation (for example, the annual report and accounts, copies of all the news releases and house journals, changes in products, packaging or distribution methods and news about R & D).

Activity 3

The trade journal of the advertising industry is Campaign. This is targeted at people working in ad agencies but, although a lot of the gossip about individuals will go over your head, reading Campaign will give you a very strong flavour of the industry and some fascinating insights into what goes on behind the scenes. You will also become familiar with the industry's jargon and find articles that are directly relevant to your studies.

Your task, then, is to buy (and read) a copy of Campaign from time to time.

Once objectives are agreed between client and agency, the advertising campaign can be planned in detail. This will involve much collaboration between the two parties.

4 PLANNING AN ADVERTISING CAMPAIGN

There are six distinct stages in an advertising campaign.

Step 1: Identify the target audience

Step 2: Specify the promotional message

Step 3: Select media

Step 4: Schedule media

Step 5: Set the promotional budget

Step 6: Evaluate promotional effectiveness

4.1 Step 1: Identify the target audience

A list of dimensions which could be of use in identifying the target audience, depending on the type of product, is given below.

The target audience will be defined in terms of the segmentation variables described in Chapter 6. The psychographics approach enables campaigns to be planned which emphasise how the brand has relevance for the lifestyle of the target audience. Creativity is used to emphasise mood, atmosphere and environment for brand usage, usually relying on non-verbal communication such as background setting for an advertisement (indoor/outdoor, relaxed or tense environment, type of music, style of furniture, use of colour schemes, appearance of models etc).

These factors are particularly relevant when the aim of the campaign involves persuasion of the audience. Various research projects have been conducted which have attempted to identify relevant correlates of persuasibility. On balance the evidence is not conclusive. However, much advertising aims to accomplish very precise and limited changes in awareness of, or perceptions of, product attributes (repositioning).

For industrial goods the social and socio-psychological variables are still valid but are perhaps not as important as economic factors. Factors affecting behaviour include:

- Size of company (turnover, number of employees, profit levels)
- Production process
- Type of business activity
- Location
- Centralisation of buying
- Buying process
- Interdepartmental rivalries

4.2 Step 2: Specify the promotional message

People are very specific about the advertisements to which they pay attention. Most of us have the opportunity to see many hundreds of advertisements in many media each day, and cannot give our attention to each and every one.

The essence of specifying the promotional message lies in identifying the intended function of the campaign.

- To convey information
- To alter perceptions
- To stimulate desires
- To produce conviction
- To direct action
- To provide reassurance

Each function can suggest an appropriate form for, and content of, the message. Messages are usually tested before use in 'qualitative' group discussions with potential consumers.

Much research has been directed at how far the content of the message is likely to be influential in effecting attitude change. In particular, studies have been concerned with the varying effects of persuasive messages, some of which are assumed to have greater influence because they play upon the emotions of an audience, whilst others rely on a rational approach to intelligence and good sense. Both the rational and emotional appeal approaches have strong supporters.

The conclusion from various studies appears to be that a strong emotional appeal induces considerable anxiety but is unlikely to change attitudes. A restrained appeal may well change attitudes (resulting, for example, in purchase of a new brand of toothpaste) and such attitudes are likely to last longer.

4.3 Step 3: Select media

'Media advertising' means advertising through the media. Each medium provides access to a certain type of audience.

- National newspapers
- Regional newspapers
- Magazines and trade press
- Television
- Commercial radio
- Posters and transport advertising
- Cinema

The criterion governing the choice of medium for conveying a persuasive message to a potential market is that the medium used should be the one which will have the lowest cost-per-head of potential customers contacted. The choice of medium will depend on who the advertiser wishes to reach with the advertising message. If the advertiser wishes to sell to a particular market segment, advertising through a national medium might not be cost effective.

The choice of medium begins with a study of the target audience's media habits. The audience for particular media will be analysed and the media which are most used by customers in the potential market will be chosen for advertising.

(a) Television is watched by viewers from all social groupings and is an ideal medium for advertising mass consumer goods.

(b) A particular medium may reach audiences with special characteristics.

   (i) The cinema is visited mainly by young couples

   (ii) Many magazines and local newspapers are read predominantly by women

   (iii) There are magazines for qualified marketers, magazines for data processing managers and so on.

(c) The size of circulation or audience for a particular medium is important, but there is no value in reaching a wide audience if they are not potential customers for the product being advertised.

(d) It may be too expensive to try and reach an entire potential market with an advertising campaign; too wide a choice of media will probably bring diminishing returns on the money spent.

Activity 4

Where should the following businesses advertise to reach the right audience?

(a) Expensive camera equipment supplier
(b) High street butcher
(c) Industrial goods manufacturer

The advertiser will want reliable information about the audiences for each medium in order to help in the choice of media for an advertising campaign. Research into audiences is provided by the following:

(a) For major newspapers and magazines, the National Readership Survey or JICNARS (the Joint Industry Committee for National Readership Surveys)

(b) For television, BARB (British Audience Research Bureau)

(c) For radio, RAJAR (Radio Joint Audience Research)

(d) For poster audiences, JICPAS (Joint Industry Committee for Poster Audience Surveys)

(e) For the cinema, the Screen Advertisers' Association.

Another important consideration is cost.

- The cost of producing the advertisements
- The cost of exposure in the media

The costs of exposure are perhaps ten times the cost of production in consumer goods advertising.

The cost of a medium is measured by the 'cost per thousand' criterion. If a full page advertisement in a national newspaper circulating to 2 million readers is £7,000, the cost per thousand is £3.50.

Activity 5

Cost per thousand is a very simple measure, which should be interpreted with caution. Why?

4.4 Step 4: Schedule media

An advertiser will not restrict his campaign to one advertisement in a single newspaper or one appearance of an advertisement on television.

(a) An advertisement must be repeated because many members of the target audience will miss it the first time it appears.

(b) It has been found that a larger target audience is reached by advertising in several newspapers instead of just one, and in several media instead of just one.

The theoretical optimal level of advertising

It is generally undisputed that it is necessary to advertise. The problem facing management is just how much advertising maximises profits. This cannot be based on relations between advertising expenditure and sales figures because exogenous influences such as the marketing activities of competitors mask any underlying relationship between advertising spend and profits.

4.5 Step 5: Set the promotional budget

In an ideal world the budget for a campaign would be determined by a consideration of the four steps discussed so far. The budget needed is that which meets the objectives using the chosen media to convey the required message. In reality the constraint of what the organisation can afford is commonly paramount.

The promotional budget is often linked to sales.

- A percentage of last period sales
- A percentage of expected (target) sales
- A percentage of past (or target) profit

4.6 Step 6: Evaluate promotional effectiveness

An advertising campaign can only be termed successful if it generates profit for the company. However, it is almost impossible to measure the effect on sales and profits by any direct means. The problem is that advertising never takes place in a vacuum and other events in the market place, such as competitors' actions, changing attitudes and relative price changes, swamp the advertising effect. It is therefore necessary to observe changes earlier on in the buying process, the assumption being that favourable changes in awareness and attitude will result in higher sales and profits.

There is a paradox involved in trying to measure the effectiveness of advertising. The early stages in the process by which advertising generates sales are easy to measure (for example, exposure by readership and/or viewer surveys) but are of little direct importance. The real effect that is of interest is obviously the net increase in sales. However, the sales effect can at best be estimated.

This diagram indicates some measures of effectiveness.

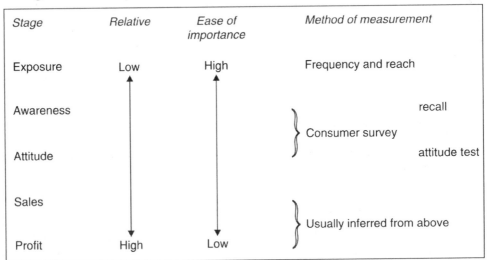

Figure 9.5 Measures of promotional effectiveness

Effective advertising often depends on giving a product a recognisable identity in the market place. 'Branding' is the name given to this process of creating identity.

5 BRANDING

Expenditure on promotion gives rise to brands.

Definition

> A 'brand' is a name, term, sign, symbol or design intended to identify the product of a seller and to differentiate it from those of competitors.

EXAMPLE

The new owners of Rover Cars, the Phoenix consortium, will face the challenge, among others, of deciding what the Rover brand does (or should) stand for.

- Niche or volume?
- Premium or middle market?
- Global or domestic?

You may have your own perceptions of the Rover brand. Knowing what the brand stands for is crucial for car manufaturers as it can help determine new product strategies, distribution strategies and investment decisions.

Not long ago (and this is still the case in many less developed countries) most products were sold unbranded from barrels and bins. Today in developed and even developing countries hardly anything goes unbranded. Even salt, oranges, nuts and screws are often branded. There has however been a limited return recently in some developed countries to 'generics'. These are cheap, unbranded products, packaged plainly and not heavily advertised.

Branding is a very general term covering brand names, designs, trademarks, symbols, jingles and the like. A brand name refers strictly to letters, words or groups of words which can be spoken. A brand image distinguishes a company's product from competing products in the eyes of the user.

A brand identity may begin with a name, such as 'Kleenex' or 'Ariel', but extends to a range of visual features which should assist in stimulating demand for the particular product. The additional features include typography, colour, package design and slogans.

Often brand names suggest desired product characteristics. For example, 'Fairy' gives impressions of gentleness and hence mildness.

Activity 6

What characteristics do the following brand names suggest to you?

(a) (i) Brillo (scouring pads)
(ii) Pampers (baby nappies)
(iii) Cussons Imperial Leather (soap)
(iv) Kerrygold (butter)
(v) Hush Puppies (shoes)

(b) A publishing firm is considering producing a range of books to rival BPP's Business Basics series. They are calling them the 'I Can't Believe I Made It To University' series. Can you foresee any problems with this brand?

The reasons for branding are as follows.

(a) It is a form of product differentiation, conveying a lot of information very quickly and concisely. This helps customers to identify the goods or services readily and thereby helps to create a customer loyalty to the brand. It is therefore a means of increasing or maintaining sales.

(b) Advertising needs a brand name to sell to customers so advertising and branding are very closely related aspects of promotion; the more similar a product (whether an industrial good or consumer good) is to competing goods, the more branding is necessary to create a separate product identity.

239

(c) Branding leads to a readier acceptance of a manufacturer's goods by wholesalers and retailers.

(d) It facilitates self-selection of goods in self-service stores and also makes it easier for a manufacturer to obtain display space in shops and stores.

(e) It reduces the importance of price differentials between goods.

(f) Brand loyalty in customers gives a manufacturer more control over marketing strategy and of choice of channels of distribution.

(g) Other products can be introduced into brand range to 'piggy back' on the articles already known to the customer (but ill-will as well as goodwill for one product in a branded range will be transferred to all other products in the range). Adding products to an existing brand range is known as brand extension strategy.

(h) It eases the task of personal selling (face-to-face selling by sales representatives).

(i) Branding makes market segmentation easier. Different brands of similar products may be developed to meet specific needs of different categories of users.

The relevance of branding does not apply equally to all products. The cost of intensive brand advertising to project a brand image nationally may be prohibitively high. Goods which are sold in large numbers, on the other hand, promote a brand name by their existence and circulation.

Where a brand image promotes an idea of quality, customers will be disappointed if their experience of a product fails to live up to expectations. Quality control is therefore an important element in branding policy. It is especially a problem for service industries such as hotels, airlines and retail stores, where there is less possibility than in a manufacturing industry of detecting and rejecting the work of an operator before it reaches the customer. Bad behaviour by an employee in a face-to-face encounter with a customer will reflect on the entire company and possibly deter the customer from using any of the company's services again.

The decision as to whether a brand name should be given to a range of products or whether products should be branded individually depends on quality factors.

(a) If the brand name is associated with quality, all goods in the range must be of that standard. An example of a successful promotion of a brand name to a wide product range is Kellogg's use of their family brand name to promote their cereal products.

(b) If a company produces different quality (and price) goods for different market segments, it would be unwise to give the same brand name to the higher and the lower quality goods because this would deter buyers in the high quality/price market segment.

5.1 Branding strategies

Branding strategy	Description	Implication
Family branding	The power of the family name to help products	Image of family brand applicable across a range of goods
Brand extension	New flavours, sizes etc to existing brand	High consumer loyalty
Multi-branding	Different names for similar goods serving similar consumer tastes	Consumers make random purchases across brands

Brand extension denotes the introduction of new flavours, sizes etc. New additions to the product range are beneficial for two main reasons.

(a)   They require a lower level of marketing investment (part of the 'image' already being known).

(b)   The extension of the brand presents less risk to consumers who might be worried about trying something new. (Particularly important in consumer durables with relatively large 'investment' such as a car, stereo system or the like.) Examples include the introduction of Persil washing up liquid and Mars ice cream.

Multi-branding: the introduction of a number of brands that all satisfy very similar product characteristics.

(a)   This can be used where little or no brand loyalty is noted, the rationale being to run a large number of brands to pick up buyers who are constantly changing brands.

(b)   The best example is washing detergents. The two majors, Lever Brothers and Procter & Gamble, have created a barrier to fresh competition as a new company would have to launch several brands at once in order to achieve sufficient market share.

Family branding: the power of the 'family' name to assist all products is being used more and more by large companies, such as Heinz. In part this is a response to retailers' own-label goods. It is also an attempt to consolidate highly expensive television advertising behind just one message rather than fragmenting it across the promotion of numerous individual items. Individual lines can be promoted more cheaply and effectively by other means such as direct marketing and sales promotions.

5.2   Trademarks

A trademark is a legal term covering words and symbols. A legally protected mark can be a very valuable asset.

(a)   The legal protection can continue after patent protection runs out

(b)   Competitors will be prevented from using a market leader's branding as a generic term for a class of products (as has happened with aspirin and cellophane)

However, even with trademark protection the impact of a market leader's branding may be weakened by consumers who perceive the brand name as a generic term.

•   How many people 'hoover' with an Electrolux machine?
•   Have you ever 'xeroxed' on a photocopier not made by Rank?

The Trademarks Act 1994 has expanded the range of items that can be registered to include smells, musical sounds and the shape of goods or their packaging, in addition to the existing list of: devices (such as the Mercedes three-pointed star), names, words (such as Kodak), letters (such as BP) and numerals (such as '4711').

Activity 7

Think of some more examples on the same lines as Hoover and Xerox.

5.3   To brand or not to brand?

The advantages of branding include the following.

(a) Branding facilitates memory recall, thus contributing to self-selection and improving customer loyalty.

(b) In many cultures branding is preferred, particularly in the distribution channel.

(c) Branding is a way of obtaining legal protection for product features.

(d) It helps with market segmentation. (Take toothpaste for example: Crest is marketed to a health conscious segment, Ultrabrite is marketed for its cosmetic qualities.)

(e) It helps build a strong and positive corporate image, especially if the brand name used is the company name (for example, Kellogg's, Heinz). It is not so important if the company name is not used (for example, Procter & Gamble).

(f) Branding makes it easier to link advertising to other marketing communications programmes.

(g) Display space is more easily obtained and point-of-sale promotions are more practicable.

(h) If branding is successful, other associated products can be introduced.

(i) The need for expensive personal selling/persuasion may be reduced.

Branding is not relevant to all products, only those:

(a) that can achieve **mass sales** – this is because of the high cost of branding and the subsequent advertising (this is particularly important if global branding is sought) and

(b) whose **attributes can be evaluated** by consumers.

5.4 Success criteria for branding

Branding should be a central and strategic part of both product and promotional planning. It should not be a casual afterthought. It therefore requires research in all the markets in which the brand is planned to be marketed. For international companies name research can avoid possible faux pas because of cultural and language differences.

World-wide research suggests that the beneficial qualities of a brand name are that it should:

(a) Suggest benefits, for example, Ultrabrite toothpaste, Slimline tonic

(b) Suggest qualities such as action or colour, (for example, Shake 'n Vac)

(c) Be easy to pronounce, recognise and remember (that is, be short and punchy)

(d) Be acceptable in all markets both linguistically and culturally

(e) Be distinctive, for example, Kodak

(f) Be meaningful. When Procter & Gamble wished to launch 'Crest Tartar Control' into South American countries, research found that there was no recognised Spanish translation for dental tartar.

5.5 Global brand decisions

For the international company marketing products which can be branded there are two further policy decisions to be made.

(a)   If and how to protect the company's brands (and associated trademarks)

(b)   Whether there should be one global brand or many different national brands for a given product.

The major argument in favour of a single global brand is the economies of scale that it produces, both in production and promotion. But whether a global brand is the best policy or even possible depends on a number of factors.

5.6   Legal considerations for branding

(a)   Legal constraints may limit the possibilities for a global brand, for instance where the brand name has already been registered in a foreign country.

(b)   Protection of the brand name will often be needed, but internationally is hard to achieve.

- In some countries registration is difficult
- Brand imitation and piracy are rife in certain parts of the world

There are many examples of imitation in international branding, with products such as cigarettes (USA), and denim jeans.

Worse still is the problem of piracy where a well known brand name is counterfeited. It is illegal in most parts of the world but in many countries there is little if any enforcement of the law. (Levis is one of the most pirated brand names).

Activity 8

The following are all names of copy-cat products that have been taken to court by the owners of the original brands.

Johnny Black

Raylas

Marabou

Zia Marina

M & B

(a)   See if you can name the original brand.

(b)   Why should the makers of the original sue the counterfeiters and what advantage is there for the counterfeiters in what they do?

5.7   Cultural aspects of branding

Even if a firm has no legal difficulties with branding globally, there may be cultural problems, such as unpronounceable names, names with other meanings (undesirable or even obscene).

There are many examples of problems in global branding, for example Maxwell House is Maxwell Kaffee in Germany, Legal in France and Monky in Spain. But sometimes a minor spelling change is all that is needed, such as Wrigley Speermint in Germany.

5.8   Other marketing considerations

Many other influences affect the global branding decision, including the following.

Askham Bryan College
LIBRARY BOOK

(a) Differences between the firm's major brand and its secondary brands. The major brand is more likely to be branded globally than secondary brands.

(b) The importance of brand to the product sale. Where price, for example, is a more important factor, then it may not be worth the heavy expenditure needed to establish and maintain a global brand in each country; a series of national brands may be more effective.

(c) The problem of how to brand a product arising from acquisition or joint venture. Should the multinational company keep the name it has acquired?

Whether the product is to be advertised or not, other forms of communication with potential customers will be necessary. This communication often takes the form of sales promotion.

6 SALES PROMOTION

Definition

> Sales promotions are 'those marketing activities other than personal selling, advertising and publicity, that stimulate consumer purchasing and dealer effectiveness, such as displays, shows and exhibitions, demonstrations and various non-recurrent selling efforts not in the ordinary routine.

As we have seen, sales promotions are also called 'below-the-line' activities, distinguishing them from advertising, personal selling and publicity, which are 'above-the-line' activities.

Sales promotions are used extensively, because there is often a direct link between the promotion and short-term sales volume. For example, the offer of a free gift or a reduced price 'bargain' will be made dependent on the purchase of the product. A promotion offer might be a free gift if the consumer sends in three packet tops of the product; or a competition entry form might be printed on the product's packaging.

Sales promotional techniques have a more direct effect on usage than does advertising. As such sales promotions can be particularly useful in inducing trials by consumers of rival products, the three for the price of two offer being a sufficient inducement to wean the consumer away from purchasing their usual brand.

Examples of sales promotion activities are as follows.

(a) **Consumer promotions**

   (i) Free samples

   (ii) Coupon offers (money-off offers)

   (iii) Price reductions as sales promotions

   (iv) Competitions

   (v) Free gifts (in exchange for, say, packet tops – these are known as 'free sendaway premiums')

   (vi) Combination pack offers (two for the price of one)

   (vii) Off-price labels

   (viii) Trading stamps

(ix)   Samples

       (x)   Exhibitions and demonstrations (such as the Motor Show or Ideal Home Exhibition)

       (xi)   Catalogues (notably the large mail order catalogues of mail order firms)

       (xii)   On-pack offers (that is, free gifts which come with the product. This is sometimes used for first editions of new magazines)

(b)   **Retailer or middleman promotions as a 'push policy'**

       (i)   Extended credit

       (ii)   Merchandising facilities

       (iii)   Contests for retailers or shop assistants

       (iv)   Consumer promotions and advertising act as a 'pull policy' to attract dealer attention by means of consumer demand

(c)   **Sales force promotions**

       (i)   Bonuses
       (ii)   Contests between sales staff (based on volumes of sale)
       (iii)   Sales motivators: gifts linked to sales

(d)   **Industrial promotions**

       (i)   Sales literature and catalogues

       (ii)   Special discounts

       (iii)   Events, say invitations to customers to visit the Wimbledon Tennis Championships or the Open Golf Championship

       (iv)   Trade-in allowances

       (v)   Inducements (such as diaries and calendars)

Activity 9

Which one of these methods do you think is the most effective?

Sales promotions are essentially short-term sales measures and an advertiser planning a campaign should not be tempted to sacrifice long-term prospects (for example, brand image built up through media advertising) in order to spend too much on short-term promotions. Although sales promotion is short-term in its effects, its objectives are broadly similar to those of above-the-line advertising.

- To increase sales revenue by generating extra interest
- To attract new customers
- To encourage resellers to stock the item or increase their stocks
- To stimulate slow moving lines
- To clear out stocks
- To counter the moves of a competitor
- To launch a new product
- To encourage the sales force to greater effort

6.1 Merchandising

A manufacturer of consumer goods usually relies on reseller organisations (rather than direct selling) to bring the goods to the point of sale with the consumer. This dependence on resellers for the sales volume of a product will be unsatisfactory to the manufacturer who may therefore try to take on some of the job of selling to the consumers. Manufacturer involvement in selling to consumers is achieved by advertising, packaging design or sales promotion offers. Another way of extending manufacturer involvement in selling is by means of merchandising.

Merchandising is a method by which the manufacturer tries to ensure that a retailer sells as many of his products as quickly as possible. The manufacturer therefore gives advice to the retailer, either from the sales force or from full time merchandising specialists.

Merchandising is concerned with putting the manufacturer's goods in the right place at the right time.

(a) In the right place. The right place means not just the stores and shops with the highest turnover, but also the best locations within the store. In self-service stores, some shelves are in 'strategic' positions which attract greater customer attention, and merchandising staff attempt to secure these strategic positions for the manufacturer's products. Due to the costs of merchandising work, these efforts will usually be restricted to the larger, more profitable stores with a high turnover.

(b) At the right time. In most stores, there are some days when demand is at a peak. Merchandising staff should try to ensure that if a strategic location is only available for a limited time, then this time should include a period of peak demand. Similarly, it is important to ensure that seasonal goods (Christmas items or Easter eggs) receive prominent display at the right time of year.

As an aspect of sales promotion activity, merchandising is designed to give a short term boost to sales. Inevitably, the retailer will later move the product away from prime locations, or give it a reduced amount of shelf space.

Other items associated with merchandising activities are point of sale material. The point of sale is the shop where goods are sold, and point of sale material is used in sales promotion.

- Posters (for example, holiday posters in travel agents' offices)

- Showcards (for example, dispensers from which customers can take the product)

- Mobiles (display items suspended from the ceiling of, say, a supermarket)

- Dump bins or dumpers: a product is dumped into a bin, suggesting a bargain offer

- Dummy packs

- Metal or plastic stands (to display the birthday cards of one manufacturer, say)

- Plastic shopping bags

- 'Crowners' – the price tags or slogans slipped over the neck of a bottle

Activity 10

Everything that you have read about advertising, branding and sales promotion will sound very familiar, but would you have examples at your fingertips in an examination? Pick some products that you buy regularly or are interested in and make a point of tracking their advertising and promotion over a period of several months. Note how posters and shop displays back up TV campaigns, and see whether the campaign attracts any 'free' publicity in the form of press coverage, or references by public figures like TV comedians. Is the promotion talked about at work or in the pub? Has the slogan caught on and fallen into general usage?

The more you look, the more you will see.

The customer recognises sales promotion and advertising messages as coming direct from the manufacturer or service provider. More subtle communication techniques are possible; together these are known as publicity.

7 PUBLICITY

Publicity is defined as being any form of non-paid, non-personal communication, and like advertising, it involves dealing with a mass audience. Although some components are 'paid for', we can also include public relations under this general heading since it is concerned more generally with building and maintaining an understanding between the organisation and the general public.

Good publicity offers a number of benefits to the organisation. It has no major time costs, it provides access to a large audience and the message is considered to have a high degree of credibility. The information is seen as coming from an independent or quasi-independent source as opposed to from the company itself.

Traditionally, publicity and public relations were concerned with producing regular, informative press releases and building up good contacts with journalists. As a consequence, their importance has often been underestimated. However, with increasing pressure on advertising space, time and costs, the importance of publicity seems likely to increase.

7.1 Sponsorship

In marketing terms, sponsorship is a form of marketing communication. It stands alongside media advertising, personal selling, public relations and other forms of sales promotion as a method by which companies can communicate with potential customers. There are many other influences on sales, and it is extremely difficult to isolate the effects of specific marketing activity on them. There are, however, several other potential advantages of sponsorship, besides awareness creation in a wider audience than could be reached cost-effectively by other forms of advertising and the media coverage generated by the sponsored events. These include the following.

(a) Distributor and customer relations.

(b) The impact of sponsoring 'worthy' events can have a wide positive effect on the attitude of potential customers toward the company's services.

(c) Sponsorship has wider implications in public relations terms. It demonstrates good corporate citizenship and it may also have a positive impact on the company's employees.

EXAMPLE: SPONSORSHIP AND THE SYDNEY OLYMPICS

Were the Sydney Olympics too 'corporate'? Mike Bushell, general manager of SOCOG (Sydney Organising Committee for the Olympic Games) says that without sponsors there would be no Games at all.

These sponsors were sold to the Australian public as 'Australia's dream team to help deliver the Olympic Games'. Also known as the 'Team Millennium Olympic Partners', they committed products, people, finance and services to every Olympic athlete and event. For example, Australia's largest telecommunications firm, Telstra, laid the cables and managed the infrastructure needed for broadcast networks. General Motors Holden supplied athletes' transport.

7.2 Exhibitions and trade fairs

Britain has been fairly backward in its use of exhibitions and trade fairs and even the Birmingham National Exhibition Centre does not rival the foreign exhibition centres of Hanover or Geneva.

The advantages of exhibitions

- (a) The products can be viewed and demonstrated
- (b) A wide range of up to date products can be seen in one place and expert assistance is available for answering queries
- (c) They attract many visitors who are potential customers; prospective customers are met quickly and cheaply
- (d) They are a valuable public relations exercise
- (e) They are useful for launching a new product, or testing a market
- (f) They sell the product

Disadvantages of exhibitions

- (a) They are costly to prepare and operate
- (b) They take sales people away from normal selling duties because exhibition stands must be permanently staffed

Exhibitions are more naturally suited to some products than to others. Where demonstrations are particularly valuable to the prospective customer (for agricultural equipment, for example) or at least visual inspection and expert information are required (for example, motor cars) exhibitions are a valuable means of sales promotion.

In all communication methods discussed so far, the customer is aware of being addressed impersonally. Some may feel that the message is 'not for them'. It is possible for marketers to communicate personally with prospective customers, via direct marketing techniques.

8 DIRECT MARKETING

The aims of direct marketing are to acquire and retain customers. Here are two definitions.

Definitions

Direct marketing is 'the planned recording, analysis and tracking of customer behaviour to develop relational marketing strategies'.

Institute of Direct Marketing (UK)

Direct marketing is 'an interactive system of marketing which uses one or more advertising media to effect a measurable response and/or transaction at any location'. Direct Marketing Association (US)

It is worth studying these definitions and noting some key words and phases.

   (a) **Response**: direct marketing is about getting people to send in coupons, or make telephone calls in response to invitations and offers.

   (b) **Interactive**: it is a two-way process, involving the supplier and the customer.

   (c) **Relationship**: it is in many instances an on-going process of selling again and again to the same customer.

   (d) **Recording and analysis**: response data are collected and analysed so that the most cost-effective procedures may be arrived at. Direct marketing has been called 'marketing with numbers'. It aims to take the waste out of marketing.

   (e) **Strategy**: direct marketing should not be seen merely as a 'quick fix' or a 'one-off mailing'. It should be seen as a part of a comprehensive plan stemming from clearly formulated objectives.

Direct marketing creates and develops a direct relationship between you and your prospect, between the consumer and the company on an individual basis. It is a form of direct supply, embracing both a variety of alternative media channels (like direct mail), and a choice of distribution channels (like mail order). Because direct marketing removes all channel intermediaries apart from the advertising medium and the delivery medium, there are no resellers, therefore avoiding loss of control and loss of revenue.

8.1   Components of direct marketing

Direct marketing encompasses a wide range of media and distribution opportunities which include television, radio, direct mail, direct response advertising, telemarketing, 'statement stuffers', inserts, 'take-ones', electronic media, door to door, mail order, computerised home shopping, and home shopping networks. In developing a comprehensive direct marketing strategy, organisations will often use a range of different yet complementary techniques.

8.2   The growth of direct marketing

Between 1988 and 1992 there was a major increase in the amount spent on direct marketing activities. A number of factors have contributed to this growth and will undoubtedly play a significant part in the future.

The mainstay of UK society, the nuclear family, is no longer the dominant group within the population. Single parent families and cohabitants now form over 35% of the households in the UK. Consequently, advertisers aiming at the traditional family unit via TV run the risk of communicating with a high proportion of non-nuclear families, so the wastage rate is potentially very high. A continuance of this trend will lead to the emergence of new customer groups with a diverse range of needs, which will require a more individualistic marketing strategy.

Retailers within the UK have now become the custodians of that most important marketing tool, information. Not only has this further strengthened their hand in the manufacturer-retailer war, but it enables them to build up a much clearer customer profile and gives them the ability to use this in launching and targeting new goods and services more effectively. Financial services, especially banks, are more active than most in using direct marketing. For banks it is not just a tool for improving targeting; it is also helping them to dismantle their branch networks in favour of a more cost-effective distribution system.

The continued growth in acceptance and use of credit cards has provided financial institutions, multiple retailers and mail order companies with a plethora of personal information which, when merged with other data sources, transforms the art of marketing into a scientific skill. It has never been easier to target tightly-defined customer groups.

Activity 11

In the light of these comments, how effective do you think your bank is at targeting you and your personal financial needs?

There has been a significant rise in the real cost of television advertising. Whilst audiences have diminished, advertising rates have increased, pushing up the real cost of what is already a very expensive medium. The advent of satellite and cable television will further fragment the potential audience, and unless advertising rates adequately reflect the changing structure of the market, then advertisers will seek to pursue other more cost-effective forms of advertising.

The development of global markets and the breaking down of cultural boundaries has opened up an entire new world of experience in terms of consumers who are more adventurous in their choice of goods and services. In the UK it is now easier to locate a Chinese, Italian or Indian restaurant than an English one, and even the biggest food retail superstores are finding it increasingly difficult to stock the entire range of food and drink products which we now demand. Communicating with each and every one of these new markets requires a more highly targeted and sophisticated approach than can be offered by traditional mass media techniques.

Consumers are becoming more educated in terms of what they are purchasing and, as a consequence, are much more likely to try out alternatives. Own label brands have grown in significance, as consumers appreciate the parity, in terms of value, with major brands. The shift away from habitual brand loyalty coupled with a constant array of new products in the market place, reinforces the need to address the factors which will determine long-term customer loyalty to a particular product and/or company. Relationships have to be identified, established and developed as part of the direct marketing strategy.

The vast majority of UK households now own a telephone, which has improved their accessibility for the direct marketers. Direct Line, the insurance company, have turned the motor insurance industry on its head through their ability to by-pass the traditional brokers and offer the average consumer not only a cheaper form of insurance but a high degree of service.

Finally, and above all, the ubiquitous power of the computer has transformed the processes by which marketers relate to their customers. Improvements in technology and the reductions in the cost of computer systems now provide the opportunity for the smallest operations to develop and benefit from the information era.

Most direct marketing approaches are made via direct mail, so we shall now look at that in some detail.

9 DIRECT MAIL

Direct mail has a number of strengths as a direct response medium.

(a) The advertiser can target down to individual level.

(b) The communication can be personalised. Known data about the individual can be used and parts of a letter can be altered to accommodate this.

(c) The medium is good for reinforcing interest stimulated by other media such as TV. It can supply the response mechanism (a coupon).

(d) The opportunity to use different creative formats is almost unlimited.

(e) Testing potential is sophisticated: a limited number of items can be sent out to a 'test' cell and the results can be evaluated. As success is achieved, so the mailing campaign can be rolled out.

(f) What you do is less visible to your competitors than other forms of media.

There are, however, a number of weaknesses with this medium.

(a) It does not offer sound or movement, although it is possible for advertisers to send out audio or video tapes, and even working models or samples.

(b) There is obvious concern over the negative association with junk mail and the prerogative of individuals to exercise their right to privacy.

(c) Lead times may be considerable when taking into consideration the creative organisation, finished artwork, printing, proofing, inserting material into envelopes where necessary and finally the mailing.

(d) The most important barrier to direct mail is that it can be very expensive on a per capita basis. A delivered insert can be 24 to 32 times more expensive than a full page colour advert in a magazine. It therefore follows that the mailshot must be very powerful and, above all, well targeted to overcome such a cost penalty. (In many cases, though, this is possible.)

Activity 12

How long do you think people take, on average, to decide whether a piece of direct mail is worth reading?

EXAMPLE: DIRECT MAIL AND THE INTERNET

The website of the Royal Mail (www.royalmail.co.uk) contains advice and tips for businesses on generating cutomer loyalty and exploiting the internet and e-commerce to build relationships. Perhaps not surprisingly, it champions direct mail as an "extremely

PUBLISHING

accountable medium" which can be used in conjunction with a company website when targetting customers. To quote from the website:

> "You can compare the volume of site visits you get when you do and don't have a mailshot out in the market place.
>
> You can select different groups from your customer and prospect files to test different offers or types of messages, and analyse how it affects your response.
>
> You can even find out the value of other types of communications, such as radio ads/ press ads/mailshots by giving each one a slightly different website address and comparing their performance.
>
> Companies who use direct mail quickly build up massive amounts of information not only about their customers and prospects but also about the most effective and efficient ways to reach them. The key is to make sure that all of the data you collect can be used to improve your communications, helping you say the right things at the right time to the right people."

The cornerstone upon which the direct mailing is based is the mailing list. It is by far the most important element in the list of variables, which also include the offer, timing and creative content.

9.1 Building the database

We first looked at databases in Chapter 6. A database is a collection of available information on past and current customers together with future prospects, structured to allow for the implementation of effective marketing strategies. Database marketing is a customer-oriented approach to marketing, and its special power lies in the techniques it uses to harness the capabilities of computer and telecommunications technology. Building accurate and up-to-date profiles of existing customers enables the company to achieve the following.

    (a)   To extend help to a company's target audience

    (b)   To stimulate further demand

    (c)   To stay close to them. Recording and keeping an electronic database memory of customers and prospects and of all communications and commercial contacts helps to improve all future contacts

The database may be used to meet a variety of objectives with numerous advantages over traditional marketing methods.

- Focusing on prime prospects
- Evaluating new prospects
- Cross-selling related products
- Launching new products to potential prospects
- Identifying new distribution channels
- Building customer loyalty
- Converting occasional users to regular users
- Generating enquiries and follow-up sales
- Targeting niche markets

The database should not be seen as a tool simply to generate the one-off sale, requiring the marketing effort to be re-engaged time and time again. The reason for this is simple: it is four times more expensive to win a new customer than it is to retain an existing one.

The type of information required for a marketing database to operate can easily be obtained from both internal and external sources. This will typically include customer, market and competitor information. A large amount of this data is often already collected for invoicing or control purposes, but is frequently not in a format suitable for use by the marketing department.

Information on the firm's existing customers will form the core of the database, with the sales invoice being perhaps the most valuable input. While the invoice is created for financial purposes, it contains a considerable amount of customer data which can be made immediately available to marketers. A typical selection of data recorded on a sales invoice is shown below.

Information	Marketing use
Customer title	Sex, job description
Customer first name	Sex coding, discriminates households
Customer surname	Ethnic coding
Customer address	Geodemographic profiling and census data
Date of sale	Tracking of purchase rates, repurchase identification
Items ordered	Benefit/need analysis, product clusters
Quantities ordered	Heavy/light/medium use
Price	Life time value of customer
Terms and conditions	Customer service needs

The specific information held may vary by type of market. For example, an industrial database will hold data on key purchases, influencers and decision makers, organisational structure, Standard Industrial Classification (SIC codes, as used by the government for classifying and analysing industry), and business size.

A sophisticated consumer database may use postcodes to overlay specialist geodemographic data, or include lifestyle information allowing customer profiles to be developed.

The information held in a marketing database is potentially an invaluable aid in decision making. However, a database built for marketing purposes must, like the marketing function itself, be future orientated. It must be possible to exploit the database to drive future marketing programmes and database marketing provides a strategy to do this.

In order that the marketing specialists are able to make clear and informed marketing decisions, the marketing information must be comprehensive, accurate, and simple to use.

9.2 Buying lists from elsewhere

The sources of data available to an organisation from its own database are finite and will diminish over time as customers cease to trade with the organisation. Therefore, it is necessary to go outside to other sources. These may include the following.

(a) List owners and managers. They may rent direct, through a broker or not at all. They may also swap lists.

(b) List brokers who are independent and operate various lists. According to Lists and Data Sources, there are over 3,800 lists of names available for purchase or rental in the UK. The most comprehensive consumer or household list is the National Census. New census data are constantly being combined with demographic databases, of which the most important are considered to be the geodemographic and lifestyle selectors.

(c)   List compilers, who then manage and rent them directly.

(d)   Directories (telephone and commercial).

(e)   Exhibition organisers.

(f)   Publishers.

(g)   Associations and clubs.

(h)   Professional organisations.

Some of the best lists to use will be those which are noted as 'mail responsive'. It is a proven fact that people who have responded by mail or telephone to anything in the past, will be more likely to do so again. Therefore, mail responsive lists are better then 'compiled' lists, which are made up from sources such as members of societies and business directories.

In the process of evaluating lists, the following are some of the questions to which answers will be needed.

- What is the source?
- Who is the owner?
- Are there names as well as addresses?
- Is it mail responsive or compiled?
- How active are the names?
- How up-to-date are the addresses?
- Are they buyers or enquirers?
- How frequently do they buy?
- How much do they spend?
- How did they pay?
- How often are they mailed?
- Who uses the list successfully?
- What selections are available?
- Will the list owner endorse you?

Possibly the major problem with any list, is the task of keeping it up to date. Every year a proportion of the people on the list will move house or change jobs. Therefore, a list bought in from outside may have to be checked for its recentness and accuracy.

While not as extensively used as direct mail, the telephone is becoming increasingly important as a tool of direct marketing

10   TELEMARKETING

Definition

> Telemarketing is the planned and controlled use of the telephone for sales and marketing opportunities. Unlike all other forms of direct marketing it allows for immediate two-way communication.

Telemarketing is a quick, accurate and flexible tool for gathering, maintaining and helping to exploit relevant up-to-date information about customers and prospects. It can be used at all stages, from building highly targeted mailing lists through to screening respondents to determine the best type to follow up, and then to supporting the salesforce in maximising customers' value throughout their lifetime.

10.1 Benefits of telemarketing

(a)   Targeted – the recipient of the call can be identified every time and the message appropriately tailored

(b)   Personal – telemarketers can determine and respond immediately to the specific needs of individuals, building long-term personal and profitable relationships

(c)   Interactive – since the dialogue is live, you can guide the conversation to achieve the desired results; the client's representative is in control

(d)   Immediate – every outbound call achieves an immediate result, even if it is a wrong number or 'not interested'. Customers and prospects can be given 24 hour constant access to the company

(e)   High quality – minimum amounts of information can be gathered accurately, kept up-to-date and used to select and prioritise leads for follow-up calls

(f)   Flexible – conversations can be tailored spontaneously as the representative responds to the contact's needs; there are no geographical constraints on calls which can be timed to suit the contact, providing the opportunity for maximum response levels

(g)   Accountable – results and effectiveness can be checked continuously

(h)   Experimental – campaign variables can be tested quickly, and changes made while the campaign is in progress

(i)   Cost effective – when used professionally in the right application, all the above combine to create a highly effective marketing tool

10.2 Problems with telemarketing

Despite the many attractions offered by telemarketing, there are a number of disadvantages. First, it can be costly. There are few economies of scale associated with telemarketing, and techniques such as direct mail and media advertising can be cheaper. Labour overheads are potentially high, although this can be counterbalanced by operating the business from a central point.

A telemarketer can only contact around 30 to 40 customers in a day, whereas media advertising can reach a mass audience in a single strike. However, media advertising married with telemarketing can be a very powerful combination.

If poorly handled, telemarketing may be interpreted by the customer or prospect as intrusive. This may alienate the customer and lead to lost sales opportunities.

Activity 13

How else could poor telemarketing lose business?

10.3 The roles of telemarketing

When combined within the marketing and selling functions, telemarketing plays an important role in the following areas.

(a) Building, maintaining, cleaning and updating databases. The telephone allows for accurate data-gathering by compiling relevant information on customers and prospects, and selecting appropriate target groups for specific product offerings.

(b) Market evaluation and test marketing. Almost any feature of a market can be measured and tested by telephone. Feedback is immediate so response can be targeted quickly to exploit market knowledge.

(c) Dealer support. Leads can be passed on to the nearest dealer who is provided with full details.

(d) Traffic generation. The telephone, combined with postal invitations, is the most cost-effective way of screening leads and encouraging attendance at promotional events.

(e) Direct sales and account servicing. The telephone can be used at all stages of the relationship with the prospects and customers. This includes lead generation, establishing buying potential for appropriate follow-up and defining the decision-making process.

(f) Customer care and loyalty building. Every telephone contact opportunity can demonstrate to customers that they are valued.

(g) Crisis management. If, for example, there is a consumer scare, immediate action is essential to minimise commercial damage. A dedicated hotline number can be advertised to provide information and advice.

There are still many instances when marketing communications are best conveyed face-to-face, in a personal meeting between seller and potential buyer. This is the role of personal selling.

11 PERSONAL SELLING

The sales force is an important part of the communication mix. It engages in 'personal' selling, as compared with the 'non-personal' selling of advertising and sales promotion activities.

Each individual probably has his or her own ideas of the 'typical' personal sales representative, but it is interesting to consider the wide range of face-to-face sales activities which exist.

(a) Delivery staff who also sell (the classic example being a milkman)

(b) Sales staff within the premises of the sales organisation (such as a shop assistant)

(c) Travelling sales representatives, who require limited technical knowledge (for example, soap, food and drink)

(d) Sales staff who need technical expertise to sell their product, probably selling to a small number of potential industrial customers (for example, salespeople of computer hardware or software systems)

(e) Sales staff who need to create a sale through their selling methods where an established market does not exist (for example, door-to-door selling of encyclopaedias and insurance policies)

To be an effective salesperson, it is necessary to recognise the problems of potential customers and to offer help in solving them. The buyer-seller relationship is critical, and it is the immediacy of this relationship of face-to-face selling that helps to 'make a sale'.

Given that the term 'salesperson' covers a wide range of selling activities, it may be apparent that the desirable personality of the sales person is likely to vary from one type of selling to the next.

(a) Shop assistants are expected to conform to the shop's norms for appearance (so that, for example, Harrods staff should look smart and conventional), easily recognisable (for example, because they wear a uniform or stand behind a counter), and polite and pleasant.

(b) Travelling sales representatives must be able to strike up an instant rapport with potential customers. Shopkeepers welcome fast talkers and sales reps who bring news and gossip to accompany their sales 'patter'.

(c) A travelling sales representative dealing in consumer goods might also need to be able to convince shopkeepers and managers of the advantages of a sales promotion, in order to win more shelf space or a prominent display position in a store or supermarket. Sales promotion skills are therefore essential.

(d) A sales representative for industrial goods will expect to sell his or her product on its technical merits (or other comparative advantage). Persuading the customer by rational suggestions will require technical expertise, pamphlets and reference to other industrial users. Customers may be 'persuaded' over a business lunch. This style of selling, because of its special nature, is probably well suited to a more sober personality.

Recruitment and training programmes should operate to ensure that the right type of person is employed to do the job of selling.

The salesperson is, from the customer's perspective, a personification of the company. The quality of their appearance, the company car they drive, their social confidence, and organisational competence all reflect directly on the company. These aspects therefore need to be recognised and considered by sales management and the salesperson.

The role of training is also critical if the company is to feel confident in the sales force's command of both the what and the how of communication. Customer care training is fundamental for anyone in direct contact with the external customer.

11.1 The task of selling

The task of selling involves the following.

(a) Communicating the advantages of a product to the customer, to develop the target customer's 'product and market knowledge'

(b) Securing a sale

(c) Prospecting for additional customers. This involves searching for prospective customers, perhaps visiting them several times, and then making a sales 'pitch'

(d) After-sales service. Queries and complaints will arise and must be dealt with to the customer's satisfaction, in order to win repeat sales

(e) Gathering information about what the customer wants

The selling tasks above are those of the travelling sales representative. Selling tasks of the sales department may include:

- Product delivery (remember the milkman)
- Order taking inside the seller's store
- Order taking 'outside' by a field sales force
- Order taking by telephone

- Building up goodwill (such as by merchandising work)
- The provision of technical or engineering advice to customers
- 'Creative' selling of tangible products
- 'Creative' selling of intangible products such as banking or insurance

Liaison and feedback

The salesperson must think of his or her role as being that of the spokesperson for the rest of the organisation, with a clear responsibility to provide feedback to the company.

The sales force can make an important contribution to the management information system. Feedback and market intelligence gathered by the sales team are a valuable by-product of the sales process.

Management must provide systems and opportunities to encourage this information. The sales team on their part need to recognise their contribution in providing such market knowledge and take a positive and proactive approach to it. A proactive approach involves not only taking positive steps to bring information to management's attention, but also actively looking out for changes and developments in the market place.

Management is likely to be particularly interested in customer feedback covering a number of key areas.

- The product/service
- Promotional activities
- Pricing and credit
- Delivery and service queries
- The sales activity.

11.2 Personal and non-personal selling

Since the work of the sales force is only one element in the sales mix, greater dependence on advertising and sales promotion will mean a lesser dependence on personal selling. At one extreme, direct mail firms do not need any sales force. It is unlikely, however, that sales staff – even shop assistants – could sell without some advertising or sales promotion back-up.

Personal and non-personal selling should be co-ordinated using a sales plan or budget, so that:

- The sales staff have sufficient sales literature to show to prospective customers

- Their task is aided by a sales promotion activity

- Advertising campaigns are used to prepare the ground for sales effort

Activity 14

The number of buyers in a market, and the extent of their geographical dispersion, are influences on the optimum mix of personal and non-personal selling. State how, in your opinion, the mix will vary as a result of these factors.

Although the emphasis of the above is the co-ordination of elements in the sales mix, the marketing effort as a whole will call for a co-ordination of all the elements in the marketing mix: product, price and place as well as promotion. Indeed, one of the tasks of a manufacturer's sales force might be to extend the reseller network by obtaining new reseller customers, so that the selling effort would be directed towards improving the 'place' in the marketing mix. Another example of co-ordinating the mix is the need to ensure that the sales force has a product to sell, so that stocks must be available and delivery dates promised should be adhered to!

11.3 Size of the sales force

An important problem is to decide the optimum size of the sales force. Provided that an organisation has sufficient resources to increase its output and distribution, the sales force could be increased up to the point where the marginal costs of extra sales effort begins to exceed the marginal revenue from the incremental sales. Effectively, however, the overall size of the sales organisation is restricted by the resources available to the company and by company policy, and by the balance in the sales mix between personal and non-personal selling.

Differing views exist as to whether sales staff should be given an equal workload (which relates to the number of calls and the size of customer) or whether they should be given territories of equal sales potential (regardless of geographical area) in order to optimise their efficiency. There are practical considerations here: the sales rep asked to cover South-East London will have less travelling to do between calls than the rep asked to cover the North of Scotland. The fact that these areas may have the same sales potential is less relevant.

Every organisation will have some idea about what it can afford to spend on selling. In practice 'rules of thumb' are usually applied. If it is decided that selling expenses should not exceed, say, 10% of sales and if a sales representative, with selling expenses and commission, costs, say, £30,000 per annum, turnover of £300,000 per annum would then be required to support each representative. So, if a company budgets annual turnover of, say, £6 million, then the total sales force could then not exceed 20 staff.

The figures above are hypothetical, but should indicate how a rule of thumb judgement can be made about the maximum economic size of a sales force, based on annual turnover and selling costs. A complex sales force organisation would be inappropriate for a firm with only a relatively low sales turnover.

Activity 15

The power of direct selling and the qualities that make a good salesperson seem to exert a fascination over businessmen, academics and even the general public. Next time you are in a bookshop notice how many books there are with titles like Getting to Yes, Clinching the Deal and so on.

11.4 Communicating with the sales force

The role of management in maintaining not just routine communication, but informative, supportive, persuasive and effective communication, is key to successful sales operations. It is fair to say that ideally all management need to be equally rigorous in their communications with any staff. The sales job is peculiar: it is often isolated and difficult, yet performance can be measured and monitored by the success or not of yesterday's sales calls.

Commonly used methods of communicating with the sales force are sales manuals, sales bulletins and sales meetings or conferences.

(a) Sales manuals can be useful reference documents for the sales team, providing detailed information about products and procedures. However, these should be used to support other forms of staff briefing and training.

(b) Sales bulletins can be seen as more immediate communication, useful when staff are not in regular contact with managers. They provide a means of keeping staff up to date on relevant issues between sales meetings. Information on product availability, promotional activity or price changes can all be communicated quickly in this way.

Written communications should be used in support of other kinds of communications. They should be kept factual and functional.

(c) Sales meetings or sales conferences have the advantage of offering two-way communication opportunities. Feedback allows managers to assess attitude and monitor responses from their teams.

Effective meetings are those which are called for a specific reason; they have a clear objective. There can be many reasons or objectives for a sales meeting ranging from motivating to informing, from planning and training to discussing and reporting.

Venues, times and frequency of meetings need careful consideration to minimise disruption to other sales activities and to ensure maximum support. Objectives need to be translated into a clear agenda, with plenty of opportunity for participation from all those attending. Results need to be reviewed and analysed. Training inputs may need to be repeated and messages reinforced in other ways.

11.5 The selling organisation

The most suitable type of selling organisation will be influenced by various factors.

(a) Intensity of competition, and possibly the structure of a competitor's selling organisation, will affect a company's own sales organisation structure. If, for example, specialisation appears to give a marketing advantage to a rival product, a company might need to use specialised selling itself.

(b) If it is decided that personal selling by sales representatives is the most efficient way to sell, the quantity and quality of the sales force will reflect this decision (so low dependence on advertising may result in a greater reliance on personal selling).

(c) Whenever possible, specialisation of the sales force should be introduced (whether by function, product, type of customer, outlet or market).

(d) The extent to which dealers are used will affect the sales organisation. If a company sells only to a limited number of multiple stores and wholesalers, a small sales organisation will be sufficient.

(e) Generally, direct selling is appropriate for industrial goods but sales are often confined to a few customers, so that the number of orders is small but their value high.

11.6 The personal sales process

Many guides have been written on ways of improving the performance of personal selling. In this section, the main stages of the personal sales process are highlighted with some common guidelines for each stage.

Stage 1: prerequisites

Before a salesperson begins work, a number of prerequisites should have been met.

    (a)   The salesperson should have a good knowledge of the company and its products and service.

    (b)   The salesperson should know the limits of negotiation within which the deal can be made regarding price, delivery terms, volume and cash discounts, credit and other relevant items.

    (c)   The salesperson should feel that he or she has top management support.

Stage 2: gain the customer's attention

Here the aim is to define the customer's need by identifying the problem which the customer is buying the product or service to solve. A good salesperson should aim to follow these eight steps to attract and keep the customer's attention.

    (a)   Don't mention the product until the need is identified

    (b)   Try to identify how the decision is to be made (such as by consideration of alternatives)

    (c)   Gain attention quickly before the client loses interest

    (d)   Have a good first sentence

    (e)   Show he or she can solve the problem

    (f)   Ask positive questions (Have you? Can you? Are you?)

    (g)   Avoid external distractions (TV, telephone, other people)

    (h)   Maintain eye contact.

Stage 3: create interest

This stage involves making the prospect interested in the product. At this stage, a good salesperson tries to match the product to the needs of the customer.

    (a)   Demonstrate the product or service to let the prospect see how it works

    (b)   Get information from the prospect about his or her needs

    (c)   Involve him or her in conversation

    (d)   Do not simply let the prospect look at brochures and so lose his or her attention, enabling the prospect to say 'I'll read it and come back later'.

Activity 16

See if you can sell something that you have to your flatmates or fellow students. Take some time to prepare by following through the stages described above and below – gaining attention, creating interest, stimulating desire and so on. If they are not marketing students, for example, you could try to persuade them that it would be useful to go out and buy a copy of this book, since any future employers are likely to be marketing-oriented organisations.

Stage 4: stimulate the desire to buy

Here the salesperson should be seeking proof that the product matches the customer's needs. The customer's acceptance of this is the proof which is being sought. The salesperson should:

(a) Sell the idea or problem solution, not the product itself

(b) Get the customer to decide on principles and sort out the details later

(c) Involve the customer in the process

(d) Remember that repetition can reinforce

(e) Try to satisfy the customer's special requests; this involves him more closely and makes him feel special

(f) Anticipate events – talk as though the sale is concluded and discuss after-sales issues (but do not write out the order until he agrees to buy)

(g) Show that the purchase is seen as inevitable, because radiating conviction can induce the prospect to buy

(h) Invite the client to spell out remaining objections and then clear them up

(i) If no decision is made, if appropriate keep in touch with the prospect and try to make a further appointment (which should always be kept)

Stage 5: conclude the sale

The final part of the process can be the most difficult: the client must make the final decision. The salesperson should:

(a) Ask questions that require positive answers while making sure that negative answers allow the sale to continue

(b) Know what to say whatever the response of the prospect

(c) Offer alternatives which are positive ('would you prefer this one or that one?')

(d) Invite the prospect to agree several times, moving closer to the sale each time.

These sales stages are bound to be generalisations and tend to imply a non-specialist buyer. Selling to a specialist buyer (such as an organisational buyer) is a more sophisticated process although similar principles can be of some use.

Activity 17

Can you think of some of the differences in attitude and approach between an organisational buyer on the one hand and an individual consumer on the other?

11.7 Sales force organisation

A sales force may be organised in several different ways.

(a) Territorial design

(b) A specialised structure of the sales force with sales staff specialising in

- Types of product
- Types of outlet (which is a form of specialisation by customer)

Many companies use a combination of these different types of sales force organisation.

It has already been suggested that design of the sales territory will influence selling efficiency.

(a) A salesperson needs an area of adequate sales potential.

(b) A salesperson should not be given a sales area which is beyond his or her workload capabilities; equally, there must be sufficient sales potential in the area to motivate the salesperson.

(c) The lower costs of territorial organisation should be considered against the possible loss of custom which might result as a failure to specialise. A sales force structured by type of customer or by product may cost more than a simple territorially based sales force, but it could be capable of winning many more sales.

A further aspect of sales territory design is sales call planning. Given that a sales area must have adequate sales potential and workload, it should be possible to plan the number of calls sales staff should be able to make over a period of time. 'Standards' should exist for the average number of calls per day, or average miles travelled per day; and by planning the sales staff's workload, it should be possible to prevent time lost through inefficient routing, or spending too long with difficult or reluctant customers.

11.8 Territorial design

Eventually, all large sales organisations involve a territorial breakdown. Where there is no specialisation, the sales organisation may be based entirely on geographical divisions.

(a) There may be a pyramid organisation structure with top management at head office, sales supervisors controlling the sales force in a region and a salesperson or sales force for each territory in a region.

(b) The span of control of a sales supervisor is influenced by:

  (i) The amount of work to be done

  (ii) The physical conditions under which it is done (such as how much travelling is involved)

(c) The amount of supervision required depends on two factors.

  (i) The initiative which individual sales staff are allowed (if they can arrange delivery dates, price and production possibilities, they must have easy communication access back to their immediate superiors).

  (ii) The size of sales commission will determine how much sales staff are willing to work without the need to be supervised.

(d) The size of each sales territory should be such that the amount of time wasted by sales staff in travelling is not excessive; there should be a good 'frequency of call' rate.

It is most suited, therefore, to the sale of products in an homogeneous range (because it is important for the sales staff to know their products as well as their customers). If the range of products is wide, and technically complex, it is unlikely that an individual salesperson will be able to learn enough about them to sell them effectively.

NOTES

The size of the sales area will depend on the expected workload for each sales person, or the sales potential of any area.

Activity 18

What might be the administrative and logistical benefits of a territorial structure?

11.9 Specialised structures

Specialisation may be introduced into a sales organisation, and may take any of the following forms (or combination of several).

(a) **Specialisation by function**: for example, advertising group, market research group, new production group, sales/production liaison group, sales training and personnel section. This type of specialisation is more relevant to the marketing and selling department as a whole rather than to the sales force itself.

(b) **Specialisation by the nature of goods**: the more complex the nature of the goods to be sold and the more knowledgeable the customer, the more it is necessary to employ sales staff with a skilled knowledge of the product.

(c) **Specialisation by the range of goods**

(i) If a company manufactures a range of goods, its sales staff may specialise in a section of the range; for example, in the sale of a range of office equipment some sales staff may specialise in calculators and others in document copiers.

(ii) It is also possible to employ product managers who specialise in a product or range of products and who advise the sales force who sell the entire range without specialising. This type of organisation has drawbacks because it may be difficult to decide to what extent product managers should simply be advisers and how much authority they should be allowed over sales executives.

(iii) Sales staff must know their products; therefore if the company's product range is broad and complex, product specialisation may be desirable. Several sales staff would be required to cover the same sales area.

Disadvantages of product specialisation

(i) Travelling time and expenses are higher than with a territorial sales organisation

(ii) One customer buying two different products from the same company might have to deal with two different salespeople

(d) **Specialisation by range of market**

- Home and overseas sales
- Industrial and non-industrial sales
- Male and female markets (for example, clothiers)

The advantage of market specialisation is that sales staff get to know the needs of a particular market segment.

The disadvantages of market specialisation

(i)   Travelling time and costs

(ii)   Potential problems for product designers when different market segments begin to show differing requirements

(iii) The potentially complex organisation structure, such as possible problems of identifying boundaries between one segment of the market and another, especially when new market segments are evolving

(e) Specialisation by range of customers: in selling industrial goods, a specialised sales force should be organised so that each salesperson deals with a small number of potential customers in order to foster a better understanding of the motivation of the customers. This could be vital for securing large or valuable industrial orders.

The advantages of specialisation by types of customer

(i)   The sales force will be more alert to the specific needs of each type of customer

(ii)   In selling industrial goods, knowledge about the customer's industry and needs might be crucial in winning sales over the bids of competitors

(f) Specialisation by range of outlets: with changing patterns of consumer and wholesale buying, such as the growth of multiple stores and superstores, specialisation by sales staff in dealing with different types of outlet may improve a manufacturer's selling efficiency.

A combination of these different types of sales force designs can be used. For example, sales staff might specialise in a type of customer or type of product within a sales area or in a type of product for a restricted number of potential customers.

11.10 Evaluation of sales force performance

The sales function as a whole and individual sales personnel should be evaluated. Performance should be measured against objectives which may be quantifiable such as the number of new accounts, or more qualitative such as customer satisfaction.

11.11 After-sales service

After-sales service is especially important in industrial markets where technical service may be required long after purchase.

Activity 19

Try to list some of the purposes of good after-sales service. Some are fairly obvious, but others need a little thought. Answers are given in the paragraphs that follow.

Much of the work on after-sales service involves producing instruction manuals and the like. The overall product offering (including heavy industrial manufacturing equipment) has a service element included. This can be pre-sale (for example, design and installation services) or post-sale (for example, maintenance and training services). After-sales service is one way in which organisations can build a competitive advantage and is increasingly valued by the customer. An increased awareness of developing service quality can lead to important benefits.

(a) **Greater customer retention rates and customer loyalty**. If customers are satisfied with the service the supplier provides, they are less likely to switch to another supplier.

(b) **Attraction of new customers from word of mouth recommendation**. Customers are more likely to recommend a high quality service than a poor one to their friends, family and business colleagues. Such recommendations are much more potent than other forms of promotion because the customer is seen as an objective judge.

(c) **Greater market share**. This advantage flows from the first two. If maintained, higher levels of customer care can lead to greater market share. Higher levels of service quality are more difficult for competitors to copy.

(d) **Improved employee morale**. Higher service quality means fewer customer complaints and higher levels of satisfaction with the service. Service personnel are more likely to gain job satisfaction if not faced by a constant stream of complaints and abuse. Employees are thus more likely to have positive attitudes to their jobs, to feel more professional and to be more committed to their organisation. As a result staff turnover is likely to be lower and fewer mistakes are likely to be made; both of these in turn lead to higher service quality and lower costs (in training, for example).

(e) **Insulation from price competition**. If customers evaluate suppliers in terms of value for money rather than purely in cost terms then service quality is more difficult for competitors to copy.

(f) **Lower advertising and promotion costs**. As noted above, word of mouth recommendation is much more potent than paid for advertising in gaining new business; it is also free.

(g) **Lower operating costs**. Cost can be saved in a number of ways.

- From reduced staff turnover
- In training and retraining costs
- In rectifying transaction mistakes
- In administrative costs
- From customer complaints being reduced

(h) **Increased productivity** should flow from these advantages and should lead to increased financial performance and profitability.

Personal selling is still the most important element in the sales mix for the selling of industrial goods and for sales to government markets. Similarly, personal selling plays an influential role in sales to reseller markets. However, the rapid increase in labour costs inevitably turned management attention to the cost effectiveness of sales staff, with the following results.

(a) In many shops, there has been a switch to self-service displays and a reduction in the selling role of shop assistants.

(b) Advertising is used in advance of a sales campaign, so that sales staff do not have to start 'cold' with prospective customers.

(c) Selling by telephone (or at least, obtaining initial customer reactions by telephone, with a follow-up personal visit if a sale might be in prospect) is a way of cutting down travelling time and selling costs. Sales staff can reach

BPP PUBLISHING

NOTES

more prospective customers by telephone than by personal visits – even if they work in a very restricted geographical area.

(d) Sales managers pay more attention to sales call planning and sales territory design. Sales call planning should help to reduce the average cost per call, and efficient sales territory design should enable a higher average sales value per call to be achieved.

(e) The growth of large retail chains (notably supermarket chains) with a central buying department has meant that the manufacturer must now sell to a small group of purchasing managers instead of a large number of individual stores. Although personal selling is an important feature of selling to these retail chains, the number of salespeople required to do the job is much less than in selling to individual shops.

Personal selling is probably one of the most expensive forms of promotion in terms of cost per person contacted. The extent to which sales staff are used varies with different products and different markets, but there are few occasions when some element of personal selling is not needed. The use of personal selling is probably most extensive in industrial markets where the number of buyers is small, the value of the account potentially large and there is often a demand for a specialised or customised product. A particular strength is that personal selling allows for feedback in the communication process.

12 THE INTERNET

A new medium for marketing communications is the Internet, an interlinked network of computers. The **World Wide Web** enables people to access different sites quite easily, with **hypertext connections** between different documents.

Connections or sites on the Internet are growing rapidly in number. The advantage to marketers generally is that people who 'visit' Internet sites via computers generally **want** to do so. Hypertext enables advertisers to offer a much greater volume of information in the ad, and to provide pathways where the enquirer can find answers to any questions raised by the ad.

Advertising on the Web

The multimedia capability of the Web allows advertising to be more colourful and entertaining and to reach many more people for the cost of an advertisement in a magazine. In addition, Web users tend to be from higher socio economic groups.

Public relations

The Internet can be used for a variety of functions, such as posting of product notices and press releases, sponsorship and on-line publications.

Direct sales

Concerns about security are being dispelled and there is more and more on-line ordering and product information. Books, music and travel are particularly strongly represented, but there has also been an explosion in on-line share dealing.

The limitations of the Internet as an advertising medium are these.

Chapter 9: Promotion

267

(a) For international marketers, whilst Internet use is high in countries such as the US and the UK, in countries with poor telecommunications or a low level of computerisation, the Internet is useless.

(b) Anecdotal evidence suggests that many Internet users are young and male. Advertisers wishing to reach affluent older people might be wasting their time.

(c) Designing good websites is a skill in short supply.

The Internet is valuable in **business to business** marketing, perhaps for small businesses, as it avoids the expense of an international advertising campaign.

It is increasingly likely though that, in the future, organisations will have to use high speed communications channels in order to stay in touch with their markets and stay competitive. The three areas of organisational knowledge, integration of business processes and use of efficient commerce links are fundamental.

EXAMPLE

The UK retail giant Sainsbury has an e-commerce system linking 1,000 of its smallest suppliers using Internet technology. This replaced an old fax-based ordering system and enables two way communication with suppliers, thus extending the company's supply chain across the world and reducing inaccuracies and delays.

Chapter roundup

- Promotion comprises advertising, sales promotion, publicity and the sales force's activities. Firms use varying combinations of these activities depending on the nature of their business.

- Promotional activity may have either a pull effect (whereby consumers ask distributors for the product) or a push effect (whereby distributors decide to stock it) or both.

- The AIDA model suggests that promotion moves consumers from Awareness to Interest to Desire to Action. Advertising may be informative, persuasive or reminding. It must be able to differentiate the advertised product rather than advertise the generic product class.

- The six steps in an advertising campaign are: identifying the target audience; specifying the promotional message; selecting media; scheduling media; setting the promotional budget and evaluating promotional effectiveness. You should be able to discuss each of these steps, in particular the factors involved in selecting media, the factors affecting the promotional message and the difficulty of determining the optional amount of, and the effect of, advertising.

- Promotional expenditure creates brands. Branding is used to differentiate products and so build consumer and distributor loyalty. It is most relevant in marketing mass market items in competition with very similar generic products.

- Sales promotion activities have a more direct but possibly shorter term effect on sales than does advertising. There are many techniques, which you should be able to list and discuss. Merchandising is a particularly important one.

- Promotion includes public relations exercises, including sponsorship, exhibitions and trade fairs. The purpose of this type of activity is not directly to increase sales but to increase and improve the profile of the firm and its products, particularly in its target market. PR in the form of media coverage of 'newsworthy' products/actions can be highly cost-effective. It can also be highly damaging in the wrong circumstances.

- Direct marketing is the fastest growing area in promotion because of factors such as the disintegration of the nuclear family, the cost of TV advertising, and the impact of telecommunications and the computer. Direct mail has many advantages. It entails building a database, and buying and refining lists. Telemarketing is a quick, accurate and flexible tool for maintaining and exploiting relevant and up-to-date information about customers.

- Personal selling embraces a variety of activities including prospecting for new customers and providing after-sales service. The process of personal selling entails preparation, gaining the customer's attention, creating interest, stimulating desire, and concluding the sale. Sales forces may be organised territorially or in some form of specialised structure.

Quick quiz

1 What communication techniques might you expect to be used as part of the promotional mix?

2   In what way could poor encoding of a sales message impair sales performance?

3   What is a push effect, in promotional terms?

4   Distinguish between advertising and sales promotion.

5   What does AIDA stand for?

6   List three main types of advertising.

7   What is the role of advertising in industrial markets?

8   Which organisation measures radio audiences?

9   What are 'frequency' and 'reach'?

10   List the conditions for successful advertising.

11   What are the reasons for branding?

12   What legal matters are relevant to branding?

13   Give examples of sales promotion activities aimed at

(i)   the retailer;
(ii)   the sales force.

14   What is merchandising?

15   Give examples of point of sale material.

16   Give reasons for engaging in sponsorship.

17   What are the strengths of direct mail?

18   How can a customer database be used?

19   How can a salesperson stimulate the desire to buy?

20   What are the benefits of good after-sales service?

Answers to activities

1   You could answer in considerable detail, but briefly, in the first case you are sending out messages that you do not want to be bothered, but the sales assistant is either insensitive to them or deliberately misreads them. In the second case the organisation that you want to buy from fails to decode your message. Put from the other point of view you are taking in the shop's messages in the form of sales display and giving feedback in the form of your response to the goods. The channel is mainly body language.

4   (a)   Photography magazines (small, specialist readership).
(b)   Locally, for example in local newspapers.
(c)   Trade magazine.

5   (a)   The advertisement might be reaching many people who will not be affected by it. Males might account for half the readership of a newspaper, so there is relatively little value in advertising female fashions to male readers.

(b)   Not all users of the medium will see the advertisement. Many TV viewers will leave the room during a commercial break; magazine and newspaper readers will not look at every advertisement.

6   As examples:

    (a)   (i)   Shine, brilliance
           (ii)   Comfort, care
           (iii) Luxury, tradition
           (iv) Irish farms, happy cows, quality
           (v)   Comfort, soft leather

    (b)   The brand may alienate customers who had every confidence of gaining a university place. They may perceive the product as being aimed at dunces.

7   The most successful examples of world-wide branding occur where the brand has become synonymous with the generic product: Cellophane, Sellotape, Aspirin, Kleenex, Filofax, Xerox. This can eventually, however, carry its own dangers. When the brand name has been adopted as the description of the generic product (such as Thermos for a vacuum flask) the manufacturer of the brand can find it difficult to convey the specific product advantages of the brand.

8   (a)   Raylas is the probably the most difficult. This was an imitation of Bailey's Irish Cream. The others were pretending to be Johnnie Walker, Malibu, Tia Maria, and J & B whisky.

    (b)   The legal director of International Distillers and Vintners puts it like this.

        'Brands are our most important assets. Through them we communicate the quality of our products to consumers. They represent a huge investment of time, effort, and money, that can be diluted, weakened, even destroyed by those who copy them.

        Counterfeits or imitations can be sold cheaper. Their producers do not have to spend on advertising and marketing. Nor do they have to bother about the quality of the drink or the packaging.'

9   In an article on the launch of the soap powder Persil Power the *Financial Times* reported that 'There is evidence that, for consumers, sampling is rated above all other forms of marketing communication ... "Sampling is the only form of unsolicited communication which is received without suspicion or annoyance. Psychologically, sampling creates an unusual climate in these days of the cynical consumer, who prides herself on seeing through all the wiles of the advertiser. The sample appears more in the nature of a gift – something for nothing – and the recipient seems to feel a more personal gratitude and pleasure than is inspired by most other forms of media activity." '

11   One way of measuring is to see how much of what your bank sends you ends up in the bin! Arguably, the UK High Street banks are better at collecting information than at using it intelligently, though this is gradually changing.

12   Research into how people read direct mail has identified 'fixing points' (places where the eye will momentarily alight to absorb information). The eye rests on each fixing point for just two-tenths of a second. The tolerance level of an A4 sheet is about 10 fixing points. This means that a piece of direct mail that doesn't catch the attention may well be destined for the bin within about two seconds.

13   Businesses greatly overestimate the resistance among consumers to the telephone, according to a report in the *Financial Times*. Nearly three-quarters of users say that getting an immediate answer is top of their list

of priorities, yet businesses continue to make customers hang on, subject them to unwanted music or automated systems, or ping-pong them between departments. Studies have indicated that in the financial services sector alone as many as 30 million calls a year are abandoned by customers who get fed up with waiting or who are answered by unhelpful staff.

14   The number of buyers, particularly if they are close geographically, can favour personal selling. With many buyers, scattered over a wide area, the importance of advertising increases.

17   The subject of buyer behaviour was, of course, covered in Chapter 4. How much can you remember now?

18   The benefits of a territorial sales force

- To reduce travelling time and costs

- To enable the sales staff to get to know their customers and sales areas

- To motivate sales staff by giving them autonomy over their area

- To give staff an equal workload or equal sales potential

- To keep the organisation and administration simple

Further question practice

Now try the following practice questions at the end of this text.

Multiple Choice Questions: 71–80

Exam Style Questions: 11–12

Chapter 10:
PLACE

Introduction

This component of the marketing mix is essentially concerned with the processes by which the product is made available to the consumer in a particular place. Other commonly used terms for 'place' include distribution, delivery systems and marketing channels. (It is perhaps more helpful to think of 'place' as a noun rather than a verb.) Although place is often treated as the last element in the list of marketing mix variables, its importance should not be underestimated, especially in the provision of services. Marketing effort will be futile if the product is not actually in the right place at the right time so that a purchase can be made. Furthermore, effective and efficient distribution can be a crucial source of competitive advantage.

Distribution is often seen as the Cinderella of the marketing mix. In companies where distribution involves the physical transport of goods and stores, a lack of co-ordination often results in inadequate control over the distribution function. However, the choice of a particular distribution policy, such as whether or not to use wholesalers, may result in the company delegating to intermediaries much of its marketing function, such as selling to the end user.

A profound influence on distribution in recent years has been the introduction of Just-in-Time (JIT) production and purchasing (this is linked to Total Quality Management.) We shall consider the impact of JIT in the final section of this chapter.

Your objectives

In this chapter you will learn about the following.

- (a)   A variety of distributors
- (b)   How distribution channels are chosen and set up
- (c)   The problems of international distribution
- (d)   The role of specialised logistics managers
- (e)   The significance for marketing of Just-in-Time systems

NOTES

1 WHAT ARE DISTRIBUTION CHANNELS?

In order for a product to be distributed a number of basic functions usually need to be fulfilled.

(a) **Transport**

This function may be provided by the supplier or the distributor or may be sub-contracted to a specialist. For some products, such as perishable goods, transport planning is vital. The 'rent or buy' decision on transport is important and has both financial and operational consequences.

(b) **Stock holding and storage**

For production planning purposes an uninterrupted flow of production is often essential, so stocks of raw materials and components accumulate and need to be stored, incurring significant costs and risks.

For consumer goods, holding stock at the point of sale is very costly; the overheads for city centre retail locations is prohibitive. A good stock control system is essential, designed to avoid stockouts whilst keeping stockholding costs low.

(c) **Local knowledge**

As production has tended to become centralised in pursuit of economies of scale, the need to understand local markets has grown, particularly when international marketing takes place. The intricacies and idiosyncrasies of local markets represent key marketing information. Whilst it is possible to buy specialist market research help, the local distributor with day-to-day customer contact also has a vital role.

(d) **Promotion**

While major promotional campaigns for national products are likely to be carried out by the supplier, the translation of the campaign to local level is usually the responsibility of the local distributor, often as a joint venture. Hence the advertising agency of the supplier will produce local advertising material which leaves space for the local distributor's name to be added. National press campaigns can feature lists of local stockists.

(e) **Display**

Presentation of the product at the local level is often a function of the local distributor. Again, specialist help from merchandisers can be bought in but decisions on layout and display need to be taken by local distributors, often following patterns produced centrally.

Independently owned and operated distributors may well have their own objectives, strategies and plans. In their decision making processes, these are likely to take precedence over those of the manufacturer or supplier with whom they are dealing. This can lead to conflict. Suppliers may solve the problem by buying their own distribution route or by distributing direct to their customers. Direct distribution is common for many industrial and/or customised systems suppliers. In some consumer markets direct distribution is also common, for instance for service industries such as double glazing and Avon cosmetics.

Activity 1

For many types of goods, producers invariably use retailers as middlemen in getting the product to the customer. Try to think of some of the disadvantages of doing this, from the producer's point of view.

1.1 Points in the chain of distribution

Distributors include the following.

(a) **Retailers.** These are traders operating outlets which sell directly to households. They may be classified by:

(i)   Type of goods sold (such as hardware, furniture)

(ii)   Type of service (for example, self-service, counter service)

(iii) Size

(iv)   Location (rural, city-centre, suburban shopping mall, out-of-town shopping centre)

Another classification, overlapping with the first, is:

(i)   **Independent retailers** (including the local corner shop, although independents are not always as small as this)

(ii)   **Multiple chains.** Some of these are associated with one class of product; others are 'variety' chains, holding a wide range of different stocks; still others are voluntary groups of independents, usually grocers.

Activity 2

Think of at least one example of each of these categories of multiple chains.

(b) **Wholesalers.** These are intermediaries who stock a range of products from competing manufacturers to sell on to other organisations such as retailers. Many wholesalers specialise in particular products. Most deal in consumer goods, but some specialise in industrial goods (for example, steel stockholders and builders' merchants).

(c) **Distributors and dealers.** These are organisations which contract to buy a manufacturer's goods and sell them to customers. Their function is similar to that of wholesalers, but they usually offer a narrower product range, sometimes (as in the case of most car dealers) the products of a single manufacturer. In addition to selling on the manufacturer's product, distributors often promote the products and provide after-sales service.

(d) **Agents.** Agents differ from distributors in the following ways.

(i)   Distributors buy the manufacturer's goods and re-sell them at a profit.

(ii)   Agents do not purchase the manufacturer's goods, but earn a commission on whatever sales they make.

(e) **Franchisees.** These are independent organisations which in exchange for an initial fee and (usually) a share of sales revenue are allowed to trade under the name of a parent organisation. For example, few of the Kall Kwik chain of High Street print shops are actually owned by Kall Kwik – most are run by franchisees.

Activity 3

Some very well known businesses are run partly or wholly on a franchise basis. Can you think of any? What are the advantages of such an arrangement to the franchiser?

(f) **Multiple stores** (such as supermarkets) buy goods for retailing direct from the producer, many of them under their 'own label' brand name.

(g) **Direct selling**

- Mail order

- Telephone selling

- Door-to-door selling

- Personal selling in the case of industrial goods

- Computer-shopping or TV shopping

The marketer must choose a distribution channel appropriate for the particular goods or services being sold. We now look at the criteria for making this choice.

2 THE CHOICE OF DISTRIBUTION CHANNEL

Choosing distribution channels is important for any organisation, because once a set of channels has been established, subsequent changes are likely to be costly and slow to implement. Distribution channels fall into one of two categories: direct and indirect channels.

Direct distribution means the product going directly from producer to consumer without the use of a specific intermediary. These methods are often described as active since they typically involve the supplier making the first approach to a potential customer. Direct distribution methods generally fall into two categories: those using media such as the press, leaflets and telephones to invite response and purchase by the consumer and those using a sales force to contact consumers face to face.

Indirect distribution refers to systems of distribution, common among manufactured goods, which make use of an intermediary; a wholesaler, retailer or perhaps both. In contrast to direct distribution, these methods are often thought of as being passive in the sense that they rely on consumers to make the first approach by entering the relevant retail outlet.

Activity 4

One factor influencing the choice between direct and indirect methods is the average order size for a product. State what you think the relationship might be between average order size and the occurrence (or non-occurrence) of direct distribution.

2.1   General principles

Marketing involves certain basic processes.

- Bringing buyers and sellers into contact

- Offering a sufficient choice of goods to meet the needs of buyers

- Persuading customers to develop a favourable opinion of a particular product.

- Distributing goods from the manufacturing point to retail outlets

- Maintaining an adequate level of sales

- Providing appropriate services (for example, credit, after-sales service)

- Maintaining an acceptable price

The choice of channels of distribution will depend on how far a manufacturing company wishes to carry out these processes itself, and how far it decides to delegate them to other organisations: there is a range of choice between direct selling and selling through independent outlets.

In building up efficient channels of distribution, a manufacturer must consider several questions.

(a)   How many intermediate stages should be used? There could be zero, one, two or three intermediate stages of selling. In addition, it will be necessary to decide how many dealers at each stage should be used: how many agents should be used, or how many wholesalers should be asked to sell the manufacturer's products, and even then 'what should be the size of the direct sales force be?'

(b)   What kind of support should the manufacturer give to the dealers? It may be necessary to provide an efficient after-sales and repair service, or to agree to an immediate exchange of faulty products returned by a retailer's customers, and to regularly visit (weekly, bi-weekly or monthly) retailers' stores. To help selling, the manufacturer might need to consider advertising or sales promotion support, including merchandising.

(c)   To what extent does the manufacturer wish to 'dominate' a channel of distribution? A market leader might wish to ensure that its market share of sales is maintained, so that it might, for example, wish to offer exclusive distribution contracts to major retailers.

(d)   To what extent does the manufacturer wish to integrate its marketing effort up to the point of sale with the consumer? Combined promotions with retailers, for example, would only be possible if the manufacturer dealt directly with the retailer (and did not sell to the retailer through a wholesaler).

Activity 5

The use of intermediaries has a dramatic effect on the number of distribution channels. Suppose a product is available from 30 suppliers and purchased for re-sale by 200 retailers. How many channels of distribution does this represent? Now suppose that all sales/purchases are transmitted through a single wholesaler, taking product from all 30 suppliers and selling to all 200 retailers. How many channels are there now?

PUBLISHING

2.2 Channel design decisions

In setting up a channel of distribution, the supplier has to take the following into account.

- Customers
- Product characteristics
- Distribution characteristics
- The channel chosen by competitors
- The supplier's own characteristics

Customers

The number of potential customers, their buying habits and their geographical locations are key influences. The use of mail order for those with limited mobility (rural location, illness) is an example of the influence of customers on channel design. Marketing industrial components to the car industry needs to take account of location of the car industry in the UK. Selling to supermarket chains in the UK is now very difficult as the concentration of grocery retailing into a few large chains has increased the power of the buyers: specialist centralised buyers can extract highly favourable terms from suppliers. Unless the supplier is successful in selling to the big chains, the product will only be available to small numbers of shoppers each week.

Product characteristics

Some product characteristics have an important effect on design of the channel of distribution.

(a) **Perishability**

Fresh fruit and newspapers must be distributed very quickly or they become worthless. Speed of delivery is therefore a key factor in the design of the distribution system for such products.

(b) **Customisation**

Customised products tend to be distributed direct. When a wide range of options is available, sales may be made using demonstration units, with customised delivery to follow.

(c) **After-sales service/technical advice**

Extent and cost must be carefully considered, staff training given and quality control systems set up. Training programmes are often provided for distributors by suppliers. Exclusive area franchises giving guaranteed custom can be allocated, to ensure distributor co-operation; the disadvantage of this is that a poor distributor may cost a supplier dearly in a particular area.

(d) **Franchising**

Franchising has become an increasingly popular means of growth both for suppliers like the Body Shop and for franchisees who carry the set-up costs and licence fees. The supplier gains more outlets more quickly and exerts more control than is usual in distribution.

> **Activity 6**
>
> This is not an exhaustive list of the ways in which product characteristics influence channel choices. Try to add to it.

Distributor characteristics

The capability of the distributor to take on the distributive functions already discussed above is obviously an important influence on the supplier's choice.

Competitors' channel choice

For many consumer goods, a supplier's brand will sit alongside its competitors' products and there is little the supplier can do about it. For other products, distributors may stock one name brand only (for example, in car distribution) and in return be given an exclusive area. In this case new suppliers may face difficulties in breaking into a market if all the best distribution outlets have been taken up.

Supplier characteristics

A strong financial base gives the supplier the option of buying and operating their own distribution channel: Boots the Chemist is a prime example. The market position of the supplier is also important: distributors are keen to be associated with the market leader but the third, fourth or fifth brand in a market is likely to find more distribution problems.

2.3 Making the channel decision

Producers have to decide the following.

(a) What types of distributor are to be used (wholesalers, retailers, agents)?

(b) How many of each type will be used? The answer to this depends on what degree of market exposure will be sought.

- Intensive – blanket coverage
- Exclusive – appointed agents for exclusive areas
- Selective – some but not all in each area

(c) Who will carry out specific marketing tasks?

- Credit provision
- Delivery
- After-sales service
- Training (sales and product)
- Display

(d) How will performance of distributors be evaluated?

- In terms of cost?
- In terms of sales levels?
- According to the degree of control achieved?
- By the amount of conflict that arises?

To sum up, to develop an integrated system of distribution, the supplier must consider all the factors influencing distribution combined with a knowledge of the relative merits of the different types of channel available.

2.4 Factors favouring the use of direct selling

(a) The need for an expert sales force to demonstrate products, explain product characteristics and provide after-sales service. Publishers, for example, use sales reps to keep booksellers up to date with new titles, to arrange for the return of unsold books and so on.

(b) Intermediaries may be unwilling or unable to sell the product.

(c) Existing channels may be linked to other producers, reluctant to carry new product lines.

(d) The intermediaries willing to sell the product may be too costly, or they may not be maximising potential sales.

(e) If specialised transport requirements are involved, intermediaries may not be able to deliver goods to the final customer.

(f) Where potential buyers are geographically concentrated the supplier's own sales force can easily reach them (typically an industrial market). One example is the financial services market centred on the City of London.

Activity 7

(a) Again, the list above is far from complete. Try to add to it.

(b) Why do you think the Direct Line insurance company has been so successful?

2.5 Factors favouring the use of intermediaries

These are as follows.

(a) Insufficient resources to finance a large sales force

(b) A policy decision to invest in increased productive capacity rather than extra marketing effort

(c) The supplier may have insufficient in-house marketing 'know-how' in selling to retail stores

(d) The assortment of products may be insufficient for a sales force to carry. A wholesaler can complement a limited range and make more efficient use of the sales force

(e) Intermediaries can market small lots as part of a range of goods. The supplier would incur a heavy sales overhead if its own sales force took 'small' individual orders

(f) Large numbers of potential buyers spread over a wide geographical area (typically consumer markets)

2.6 Multi-channel decisions

A producer serving both industrial and consumer markets may decide to use intermediaries for his or her consumer division and direct selling for the industrial division. For example, a detergent manufacturer might employ sales staff to sell to wholesalers and large retail groups in their consumer division. It would not be efficient for the sales force to approach small retailers directly.

The distribution channels appropriate for industrial markets may not be suitable for consumer markets.

2.7 Industrial and consumer distribution channels

Industrial markets may be characterised as having fewer, larger customers purchasing expensive products which may be custom built. It is owing to these characteristics that industrial distribution channels tend to be more direct and shorter than for consumer markets. It has to be remembered, however, that the most appropriate distribution channels will depend specifically on the objectives of the company regarding market exposure. There are specialist distributors in the industrial sector which may be used as well as, or instead of, selling directly to the companies within this sector.

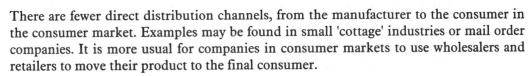

Activity 8

Given the obvious advantages of direct selling in industrial markets, why might the use of distributors sometimes be preferable?

There are fewer direct distribution channels, from the manufacturer to the consumer in the consumer market. Examples may be found in small 'cottage' industries or mail order companies. It is more usual for companies in consumer markets to use wholesalers and retailers to move their product to the final consumer.

(a) Wholesalers break down the bulk from manufacturers and pass products on to retailers. They take on some of the supplier's risks by funding stock. Recently in the UK there has been a reduction in importance of this type of intermediary.

(b) Retailers sell to the final consumers. They may give consumers added benefits by providing services such as credit, delivery and a wide variety of goods. In the UK, retailers have increased in power while wholesalers have declined. Retailing has also become more concentrated with increased dominance of large multiples.

2.8 Distribution strategy

There are three main strategies.

(a) **Intensive distribution** involves concentrating on a segment of the total market, such as choosing limited geographical distribution rather than national distribution.

(b) Using **selective distribution,** the producer selects a group of retail outlets from amongst all retail outlets on grounds of the brand image ('quality' outlets), or related to the retailers' capacity to provide after-sales service.

(c) **Exclusive distribution** is an extension of selective distribution. Particular outlets are granted exclusive handling rights within a prescribed geographical area. Sometimes exclusive distribution or franchise rights are coupled with making special financial arrangements for land, buildings or equipment, as in the case of petrol station agreements.

Selective and exclusive distribution have been criticised by the European Commission as being restraints on competition. Criticisms of the brewers' 'tied house' system, a form of exclusive distribution, led to a requirement that the numbers of 'tied' outlets be cut drastically to improve consumer choice.

Activity 9

In comparison with exclusive and selective distribution, the intensive strategy involves high costs for the producer. List some of the reasons for this.

2.9 Channel dynamics

Channels are subject to conflicts between members. This need not be destructive as long as it remains manageable. Manufacturers may have little influence on how their product is presented to the public. Conflicts are usually resolved by arbitration rather than judicial means.

(a) A distribution system with a central core organising marketing throughout the channel is termed a vertical marketing system. Vertical marketing systems provide channel role specification and co-ordination between members.

(b) In corporate marketing systems the stages in production and distribution are owned by a single corporation. This common ownership permits close integration and therefore the corporation controls activities along the distribution chain.

(c) Contractual marketing systems involve agreement over aspects of distribution marketing. One example of a contractual marketing system that has become popular over the last decade is franchising.

(d) If a plan is drawn up between channel members to help reduce conflict this is often termed an administered marketing system.

Channel leadership gives power to the member of the channel with whom it lies. We considered earlier in this section the changing power relationship between manufacturers and retailers in consumer goods markets. In industrial markets where channel lengths are generally shorter (more direct) then power often lies with manufacturers of products rather than 'middlemen'.

Activity 10

One of the fastest growing forms of selling in the US over the past decade has been the factory outlet centres. Discount factory shops, often situated on factory premises, from which manufacturers sell off overmakes, slight seconds, or retailers' returns are already well-established in the UK, but in the US developers have grouped such outlets together in purpose-built malls.

What would you suggest are the advantages of this method of distribution for customers and manufacturers?

2.10 Disintermediation and the Internet

This term refers to the process of 'removing the **middleman**', giving the consumer **direct access** to information that would otherwise require an intermediary, such as a salesperson or a retail channel. The new technology of the **Internet and e-commerce** gives consumers the power to find product information directly, either removing the need for the salesperson altogether, or at least changing the relationship between buyer and seller.

Customers can increasingly collect information for themselves by searching the world wide web. This can be advantageous for new entrants into the competitive marketplace, though it may also be a liability if their offerings are unsatisfactory. It is particularly important for new entrants to ensure that their first customers are pleased with what they get, so that positive rumours begin to spread. The position is further complicated by the fact that new entrants inevitably have a very small market share, so opinions about their product reliability can be shaped through the feedback from a very small number of customers (bearing in mind, too, that it is the dissatisfied customers who are more likely to make a noise).

EXAMPLE

The potential of the Internet to serve as a channel for products and services is a real challenge for many brand-name 'bricks and mortar' companies. Traditional bookshops find themselves challenged by companies such as Amazon or BOL. Stockbroking firms are seeing a tidal wave of on-line 'home investors' using vehicles such as Charles Schwab's on-line dealing service. These comparatively young internet ventures have a culture of risk-taking that threatens to leave traditional companies behind. As a result, more and more companies are looking for Internet distribution expertise. For example, The New York Times invested $15 million is TheStreet.com, a financial news service.

The primary advantage of Internet retailing rests on the fact that Internet retailers do not usually hold **stocks**. For example, a company called Valley Media Inc fulfils CD orders for Amazon in the US. When a customer order comes in, the e-tailer (Amazon) takes the order and the **distributor** (Valley Media) fills it. Distributors such as Valley Media are themselves a new kind of middleman.

On-line travel sites are another manifestation of disintermediation. Internet based search agents can now locate flights and fares and book them on-line. Eventually, the Internet service may even generate the tickets themselves. Airlines have been moved to lower the fees that they pay to travel agencies, in part because customers can now make purchases without using local agents.

In an article in *The Financial Times* (Value Chain: Exposed links in the established chain', 14 October 1998), Peter Martin discusses the specific case of **electricity supply**. Until recently, electricity was generated, transmitted and distributed by monopolies. Changes in regulation have meant that these monopolies are now split into separate generation, transmission and distribution companies. The next change - which, significantly, could not have occurred without the possibilities implied through electronic commerce - is the further split between distribution and supply. This means that one company may own the cables over which electricity travels, whilst another supplies the electricity to customers, having bought it in the first place from the generators.

Another issue concerns the degree to which customers are prepared to **rely on a single supplier** (albeit a trusted one) for a range of apparently unrelated products and services. Many are **reluctant** to do so in case it makes them excessively **dependent**. With this in mind, John Hagel of McKinsey envisages the creation of 'infomediaries', businesses that make money by 'capturing customer information and developing detailed profiles of individual customers for use by selected third-party vendors.'

These developments reflect the growing importance of **digital information**. Increasing the number of people using it costs nothing, but adds hugely to its value: this is why crucial pieces of Internet software have been provided free of charge.

As with other aspects of global marketing, there are special considerations to take into account when choosing distribution channels for goods to be sold abroad.

3 INTERNATIONAL CHANNELS

The cost of physically transporting goods between countries has been estimated to be as high as 25% of the landed price of an item (more typically 15%), and thus represents a significant part of the cost structure of the item involved. But international logistics provide services to the customer in terms of availability, speed of delivery and convenience, which provide significant added value to the goods themselves.

In international marketing the longer distances involved and the problem of dealing with other cultures means that the time between placing an order and its delivery can be quite considerable when compared to locally sourced supplies, and result in significantly higher cost.

A key concept in the management of international logistics is that of customer service. Customer service involves defining adequate levels of performance.

- Order cycle time (order to delivery)
- Accuracy of order processing
- Delivered quality of goods

It is thus concerned with getting the right goods to the right person, at the right time, at a reasonable cost.

3.1 Transportation

Transport between markets is often the easier part of the problem, with good transport systems and infrastructure (roads, ports, airports, railheads and so on) between nations. Within a particular country, however, both the transport systems and the infrastructure may vary in quality considerably. Generally the more developed nations have reasonably efficient transport facilities internally but, in the lesser developed countries, the quality of communications, availability of transport facilities, and the physical infrastructure may pose significant problems to the international marketer.

3.2 Modes of transport

The international marketer has not only to take into account the cost of transport between countries, but also the cost within the country. This applies regardless of the nature of the contract (that is, who pays for it) as it affects the competitive nature of the offer.

Temporary storage and handling form a significant part of the overall cost of transport. Thus methods of transport which minimise them tend to be more competitive. The development of container systems for road, rail, sea and air has reduced the amount of labour involved in transferring goods between types of transport. The preference is therefore to use a mode of transport which, wherever possible, provides a 'through delivery' to the customer.

Road transport has a major advantage in its ability to deliver directly to the customer's premises, thus minimising both delay and handling. Since other forms of transport (rail, air, water) normally use road transport at the beginning and end of the journey, they require handling on the transfer from one form of transport to another. Per tonne-mile road transport is more expensive than rail due to the upper size limit on vehicle loads in most countries, and is generally slower on long journeys than air, even taking handling transfer into account. Nevertheless, where good land borders, or short sea ferry services exist, the use of road transport for loads up to, say, 40 tonnes, and distances of up to, say, 1500 km, allied with the flexibility and lack of intermode transfer, gives it the advantage.

Where physical conditions permit, the use of rail transport has significant advantages over its main inland rival, road, in that it can carry much larger quantities over long distances. Per tonne-mile, rail is far superior to road in cost over distances exceeding 1500 km. Over shorter distances the advantages of the load capacity are outweighed by the transfer costs on and off the rail network. Rail is not economical for short journeys. Bulky, low unit value items such as raw materials are more economically moved by rail where circumstances permit.

For bulk transfer of items, water transport has similar advantages to rail, and is widely used where geography allows. Where a suitable network of rivers and canals exists, inland waterways can bring the load nearer to the customer. Again the problem of transfer and handling may make this approach expensive but its bulk carrying capacity does provide significant cost advantages over long distances.

Air transport is probably the most expensive of all four options for short journeys. The economics of air transport, together with handling costs, make air uncompetitive both in time and cost over short distances. The advantage of air transport lies in speed rather than cost, and this can be most effective over longer distances. The load carrying capacity and fuel costs do not make sense for bulky, low unit value loads, but where high value, small unit size loads are being considered, air transport may be viable.

In particular, where early speedy delivery to a market can give significant price advantages (for example, early flowers and vegetables can command a 10-fold price advantage over maincrop in many cases) air transport costs can be justified because of the high unit value of the goods. Similarly where the customer is willing to pay a premium for speedy delivery, for example a spare part for a manufacturing plant, air transport can be justified. It is widely used for high value, low volume, perishable items such as pharmaceutical drugs.

The advantage of air transport, speed, can however be lost if delays at the airport in forwarding to the customer erode the time saving.

Activity 11

In respect of the criteria listed below, try to decide which method of transport (rail, water, road or air) is best and which is worst.

(a)   Speed of delivery from door to door
(b)   Cost of delivery
(c)   Reliability in meeting schedules
(d)   Variety of goods carried
(e)   Number of locations served

We now look briefly at the practical aspects of handling large consignments of goods over long distances to a variety of destinations.

4   LOGISTICS MANAGEMENT

Logistics management involves physical distribution and materials management encompassing the inflow of raw materials and goods and the outflow of finished products. Logistics management has developed because of an increased awareness of the following factors.

(a) Customer benefits that can be incorporated into the overall product offering because of efficient logistics management

(b) The cost savings that can be made when a logistics approach is undertaken

(c) Trends in industrial purchasing that necessarily mean closer links between buyers and sellers, for example Just-in-Time purchasing and computerised purchasing

Logistics managers organise inventories, warehouses, purchasing and packaging to produce an efficient and effective overall system. There are benefits to consumers from products that are produced by companies with good logistics management. There is less likelihood of goods being out of stock, delivery should be efficient and overall service quality should be higher.

EXAMPLE: THE LOGISTICS INDUSTRY

Contracted-out distribution services require enormous trust, especially in the food business. Sensitive information must be exchanged between the retailer or manufacturer and the distribution company and responsibility for food safety and hygiene must be shared. However, contracting out offers benefits in terms of flexibility and the elimination of the need for costly capital investment: hence the success of specialist distribution companies such as NFC, Christian Salvesen and Hays.

Activity 12

Consider the following extract from an article in the Financial Times.

'British Steel is aware of the stiff competition it faces in its planned assault on European mainland markets. Physical distribution is an important plank in its campaign and the costs and efficiency of the service will help determine the success or failure of the venture.

High on the agenda for discussion is the setting up of regional distribution centres closer to customers and the development of world class information technology (IT) links between production plants, distribution operators and customers.

Meanwhile, the company spends some £375m a year on shipping products to mainland Europe and tends to deal direct with transport operators and suppliers rather than go through forwarding agents.

Its sales in Europe represent about 2.5 per cent of the total European market and the objective is to achieve significant increases.

Its main European destinations are Italy, Germany and Spain, followed by France, Greece and the Netherlands.'

If you were the marketing manager of a small business contemplating the opportunities of the Single European Market would you be encouraged or discouraged by this article?

NOTES

The great challenge to the 'Place' component of the marketing mix is to have the product available when required by the customer whilst avoiding expensive overstocking. The Just-in-Time philosophy was developed in response to this.

5 JUST-IN-TIME

5.1 Creative use of availability as a source of competitive advantage

That availability is a critical factor in the formulation of the marketing mix cannot be seriously doubted. Increasingly, logistics management has been recognised for the advantages in terms of customer benefits which such an approach brings, along with saving in costs and improved company image. A more profound impact has been proposed, however, with the use of more creative and sophisticated systems bringing in not just new possibilities of improved delivery systems, but also higher quality and increased profitability and efficiency.

Distribution is a key issue for the paper industry in Europe. Logistics here are viewed as a way of reducing costs and increasing efficiency, since there is a great problem from declining demand and the market penetration of low cost, low quality products from overseas competitors. Here, the buyer dominates the market and manufacturers look to their distribution specialists to implement supply systems which protect the product, and deliver in a form which involves minimum waste and keeps stockholding costs at ground level. Customers often require delivery of orders within 24 hours and to accomplish this suppliers are establishing warehouses which are adjacent to the markets they seek to supply, in order to satisfy these time constraints. Margins are becoming squeezed and there are new techniques available to cope with these pressures, but also to provide creative means to accomplish new market opportunities.

5.2 The challenges of the new market

Customers have an ever growing choice of companies striving to satisfy their needs. As a consequence, they have become more discriminating and competition has increased. Product differentiation and the identification and satisfaction of the precise needs of clearly targeted market segments means that companies must not only be aware of their customer needs but place them at the heart of their corporate thinking.

These needs can, and increasingly do, change very rapidly. Tom Peters has referred to this complex mix of factors as the 'chaos' of the modern marketplace. To compete in this marketplace, a company must be aware not just of its customers but of competitors' strategies, the pace and scope of the market, and the technology available within it.

EXAMPLE

Tom Peters illustrates this with a personal story. He goes out to buy a laptop computer, and returns feeling pleased with his new acquisition – less than three months on the market, with the standard software and hardware, at a bargain price. He shows it proudly to his teenage son, who eyes it expertly. 'Oh,' he sniffs, 'I see you bought another antique ...'.

The computer market has seen an unprecedented rate of competition and innovation throughout the eighties and early nineties. Even IBM has found the pace too fast, in a market situation where competitor numbers have grown from single figures to around 5,000. 'Big Blue' has been forced to radically restructure in the face of markets where flexibility is all, and margins have been cut drastically.

5.3 Just in Time: a creative competitive tool

Just In Time (JIT) is a system of inventory control invented by the Japanese. The benefit is that it allows 'pull' in the market, in contrast to the traditional system of 'just in case'.

Definition

> JIT is:
>
> an inventory control system which delivers input to its production or distribution site only at the rate and time it is needed. Thus it reduces inventories whether it is used within the firm or as a mechanism regulating the flow of products between adjacent firms in the distribution system channel. It is a pull system which replaces buffer inventories with channel member co-operation.

JIT aims to produce instantaneously, with perfect quality and minimum waste.

Synchronisation is an essential component of such systems. A successful channel will require precise synchronisation between suppliers, through the production units to retailers and finally suppliers. This depends crucially on information being freely passed back and forth between channel members; suppliers need to be informed about raw material deliveries, and also the components delivered to manufacturers. For their part, manufacturers must be confident that their deliveries will arrive on time.

In the Japanese system, this exchange of information can be supplied throughout the production process by 'Kanban'. This is a very simple 'pull' system which operates at the local level and is very effective for avoiding stockpiles.

Customers need to be treated in a new way; loyalty is no longer to be taken for granted. Indeed, as consumers more and more realise the power they wield, and become more sophisticated in the criteria they apply when evaluating and choosing products, manufacturers find that they must become responsive to these needs and also be able to adjust themselves rapidly in order to satisfy them. The keyword of the modern marketplace is flexibility, and this is coupled with profitability.

This flexibility is now the key element in:

- The company meeting customer requirements
- The production process
- The company's organisation

Manufacturing and marketing systems need to be programmable, above all else. Manufacturing and marketing must be able to re-tool and re-formulate systems rapidly so that new requirements can be identified and formulated into new products, and those products constructed and made available when they are needed.

Lean production

New production processes which aim to meet these requirements have been called 'lean production', and combine efficiency, quality and flexibility with a capacity to innovate.

The 'lean' firm is involved in producing products which are:

(a) Profitable – with an emphasis on productivity and cost effectiveness

(b) High quality – deriving from the need to compete not just on price, but standards

(c) Matched to market needs – which requires the firm to employ production processes which are flexible, involving teams of multiskilled workers producing small batches of varied, diversified products

(d) Responsive to change – the firm must be customer-orientated, and able to produce products which match rapidly changing and highly individual customer requirements

Time lags are critical in these processes. Reducing times taken for the product to get from the design stage to the market place is critical for success.

Marketing, and the need to be aware of customer needs and respond to them, have now been recognised as the difference between success and failure, and as a consequence have been propagated throughout the modern organisation. One of the key areas which this philosophy has affected is the distribution process. Success nowadays, some commentators have argued, depends on the ability of the company to perform simultaneously rather than sequentially in the processes involved in product development through to product release. Lower investment in goods within this process and faster response to customer needs means reduced costs, better value for customers and increased benefits for other channel members within the distributive process, enabling everyone within the channel to compete more effectively.

Activity 13

A system called ShopperTrak has been developed that tracks people entering and leaving stores, where they go when inside and the average amount of time spent there. It can distinguish adults from children. The system uses infra-red sensors at strategic points linked to the retailer's tills or electronic point of sales systems.

What might be the uses of such a system?

Organisational resources form a pool which can be used to counter the challenges of change in competitive markets. Every aspect of the company policy is critical in this effort to maximise competitive capability. At the heart of this is the system by which product and service are made available to the customer.

The role of the supplier

If this synchronisation is effectively organised, a JIT system can meet consumer demand while at the same time profits may be maintained or enhanced, because stockpiles and inventory levels (and consequently, the costs of capital tied up unproductively in materials or products which are not being used) are cut dramatically. The supplier/manufacturer interface is, however, crucial to the success of these changes, and a close relationship must be built up. The changes mean that increasing numbers of component parts will be bought from outside the organisation, rather than being manufactured internally.

When this system is instituted suppliers become important to the planning process in manufacturing and may well be brought into production forecasts, schedules and even the design stage. When decisions related to these are being made, the capacities of and constraints on suppliers are critical. In fact, liaison becomes an important function; their salespeople may well spend less time selling and become intermediaries, conveying information and mediating between the buyer and their own production management.

Finding new customers becomes less important than sustaining and improving relations with existing patrons.

JIT, it can be argued, even improves product quality. If suppliers are being provided with minimum resources and required to focus on using them to maximum effect, then it becomes even more important to get it 'right first time', since there is very little leeway in the amounts available to do it again. Right first time and just in time go together very well indeed!

Disadvantages of JIT

However, problems with JIT have been identified, according to some commentators. These include the following.

(a) Conflicts over customers. Suppliers will often have commitments to other customers and this may well cause expensive and disruptive delays.

(b) Conflicts with the workforce. Excellent industrial relations are vital to the success of this system, as are flexible, sometimes multiskilled workforces with a willingness to accept varying work routines and hours, so that management can vary manning arrangements.

(c) Problems over timescales. These systems take a very long time to develop. Toyota took 20 years to develop theirs!

JIT, then, is expanding as lean production becomes more important. Focusing as it does on consumer choice, company profit and strong company-supplier relations, this concept fits comfortably alongside other managerial developments such as TQM and accelerating change in product markets.

Activity 14

A large company has just installed a JIT system. One of its suppliers has had a history of poor labour relations. What consequences does this have for the company?

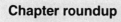

Chapter roundup

- Without an efficient distribution system goods may not reach the target customers. The options open to companies are vast and are more complicated if the company decides to export goods.

- Each way in which goods are distributed has advantages and disadvantages, although often this comes down to 'control' aspects. The longer the length of the distribution chain, the greater the loss of control over how the product is delivered.

- You should be able to define different types of distribution channel; channel design decisions and channel dynamics.

- Just-in-Time (JIT) is a relatively new development, based on Japanese methods.

Quick quiz

1   Give examples of direct distribution in consumer markets.

2   What effect do product characteristics have on channel design?

3   Why use direct selling?

4   List the factors favouring the use of intermediaries.

5   Distinguish between intensive, selective and exclusive distribution.

6   What is a vertical marketing system?

7   To which type of marketing system does franchising belong?

8   Why has logistics management developed?

9   Define Just-in-Time (JIT).

10 What problems have been identified with JIT?

Answers to activities

1   Your answers might include some of the following points.

 (a)   The middleman of course has to take his 'cut', reducing the revenue available to the producer.

 (b)   The producer needs an infrastructure for looking after the retailers – keeping them informed, keeping them well stocked – which might not be necessary in, say, a mail order business.

 (c)   The producer loses some part of his or her control over the marketing of the product. The power of some retailers (for example, W H Smith in the world of book publishing) is so great that they are able to dictate marketing policy to their suppliers.

2   Stores associated with one class of product: Boots, Sainsbury's etc (though you may have noted the trend towards diversification in both of these).'Variety' chains: Littlewoods, Woolworth's. Voluntary groups of independents: Spar.

3   Apart from the example quoted (Kall Kwik), you might have thought of Wimpy, McDonalds, Body Shop, or others. From the franchiser's point of view, the arrangement is excellent in terms of cash flow. The franchisee pays in a substantial amount up front, finances his or her own working capital and pays a regular revenue share to the franchiser.

4   Other things being equal, if the order pattern is a small number of high-value orders, then direct distribution is more likely to occur. If there are numerous low-value orders, then the cost of fulfilling them promptly will be high and the use of intermediaries is likely.

5   To begin with, there are 6,000 channels. The introduction of a wholesaler reduces this to 230 (30 into the wholesaler and 200 out).

6   (a)   Some types of groceries can only be sold to outlets having a freezer room.

 (b)   Many specialised products (such as motor cars) can only be sold through dealers with the requisite specialised skills and knowledge.

 (c)   Bulky products (such as fridges or lawnmowers) can only be sold through outlets with ample display and storage space.

Direct selling through the Internet is changing this to some extent. For example, Comet, the UK electrical retailer, sells its goods via its website for UK mainland delivery and installation.

7   (a)   (i)   The producer gets closer to his ultimate consumer, which improves his market knowledge.

           (ii)   Order sizes from retailers will be few and large (which means they can be serviced relatively cheaply), particularly where the product is one that consumers are accustomed to buying through large stores.

           (iii)   Selling direct to retailers may give producers some say in how their products are displayed and sold.

     (b)   Part of the reason is because Direct Line only accepts very safe bets – average value cars whose drivers have good records – but the company is able to charge very competitive premiums because of the money it saves by not having branch offices and selling through brokers. The little red telephone is very memorable, too!

8   One important factor is the stockholding cost. If the product is large and expensive, or again if a wide variety of brands must be produced (for example, in the case of small machine tools), the producer may prefer to shift the stockholding cost to the distributor.

9   (a)   It is more costly to fulfil a large number of small orders than a small number of large orders.

     (b)   The wide geographical dispersion of potential outlets will add to costs.

     (c)   The whole of the advertising/promotional costs fall on the producer, because outlets will be reluctant to share such costs if the benefit (of attracting a sale) may go to some other outlet nearby.

10   Prices are up to 50% below conventional retail outlets and shoppers can choose from a wide range of branded goods that they otherwise might not be able to afford. They can also turn a shopping trip into a day out, as factory outlet centres are designed as 'destination' shopping venues, offering facilities such as playgrounds and restaurants.

Manufacturers enjoy the ability to sell surplus stock at a profit in a controlled way that does not damage the brand image. They have also turned the shops into a powerful marketing tool for test-marketing products before their high street launch, and selling avant-garde designs that have not caught on in the main retail market.

11   (a)   Water is usually slowest. Air travel is fastest over long distances, but for shorter distances rail or road may be quicker door to door.

     (b)   Water is usually cheapest, air the most expensive.

     (c)   Air and rail tend to be more reliable than roads and water.

     (d)   The widest range of goods is probably carried by rail and water, with roads and air next (in that order).

     (e)   Road transport can penetrate just about everywhere. Rail is probably next best. Water and air transport are severely restricted by the need for port or airport facilities.

12   Initially you might be discouraged. It is more difficult to identify target markets in a foreign culture and there are language barriers and

BPP PUBLISHING

problems of control to be overcome. The cost of overseas representation (people/offices or both) may be prohibitive.

On the other hand most of these barriers are psychological rather than real. A relationship with an agent could be established. Costly investment in high tech systems may be unnecessary for the smaller business, especially if products are specialised, high value items. The potential for obtaining a share of the total European market as opposed to restricting operations to the domestic market must be a temptation.

13   The main idea is to cut down long waits in check-out queues and weary searches by customers for staff. The system enables managers to adjust staffing to demand and so increase purchases per visit, encourage return visits and to lift 'conversion rates' – the percentage of people entering the stores who actually buy something. The system also provides information to improve the quality and style of service and enables stores to be designed and laid out more effectively.

14   If there is a strike at the suppliers', the company's operations will come to a halt quickly as it has no stock. JIT, therefore, requires good industrial relations.

Further question practice

Now try the following practice questions at the end of this text.

Multiple Choice Questions: 81–90

Exam Style Questions: 13–14

Chapter 11:
COMBINING THE MARKETING MIX

Introduction

The purpose of this final chapter is to recap and pull together all that you have been learning about marketing. In the first few sections of the chapter we revisit the product life cycle concept – it is a very useful form of analysis in spite of its limitations – and look at its implications in terms of each of the four Ps. In the final part we consider how different elements of the marketing mix may assume different levels of importance depending upon the market, most especially when marketing takes place at an international level.

Your objectives

In this chapter you will learn about the following.

(a)   Marketing mix decisions that may arise at different stages of a product's life

(b)   The importance of the different elements of the marketing mix in different settings

(c)   You will also be reminded briefly of many topics that arose in previous chapters.

1 THE PRODUCT LIFE CYCLE REVISITED

Activity 1

To make a start, consider for yourself what, in terms of the four Ps, are the implications for a product of being in, say, its growth stage. We shall make some suggestions in a few pages' time, but if you have a go at this now you will realise how much you have learned about marketing.

1.1 Stages of the life cycle

According to the theory of the product life cycle, each of the stages (introduction, growth, maturity, decline) involves different market conditions. When the product has been newly introduced, for instance, consumer awareness will be extremely limited and it will be necessary for promotion to be geared towards telling an identified target group that the product exists, and communicating a selling proposition to them, involving the needs the product can fulfil and the satisfactions it offers. Prices may need to be adjusted to take account of the unresponsiveness and initial lack of demand within the marketplace; distribution channels may be very limited because there is not yet a proven market for this product, and so on. Later these policies will need to be adjusted as the product becomes first established and later, hopefully, successful. The marketing mix, then, will have to be varied according to the stage of the life cycle at which the product has arrived.

When do stages begin and end?

The points at which these stages begin and end are somewhat vague. The duration of the stages (and consequently the profile of the demand curve which is associated with these stages) is likely to vary a great deal, according to product type and market conditions, since how the 'life' of the product develops is affected by the consumer world into which it is 'born', how it is received and how competitive products behave.

The product life cycle concept and its mix implications

	Introduction	**Growth**	**Maturity**	**Decline**
Product	Initially poor quality. Product design and development key to success. No standard product and frequent design changes.	Competitors' products have marked quality differences and technical differences. Quality improves. Product reliability may be important.	Products become more standardised and differences between products less distinct.	Products even less differentiated. Quality becomes more variable.
Customers	Initial customers willing to pay high prices need to be convinced about buying.	Increasing numbers.	Mass market saturation. Repeat buying becomes significant. Brand image also important.	Customers are sophisticated buyers of a product they know and understand well,
Marketing Mix– promotion– place	High advertising and sales promotion costs.	High advertising costs still, but as a % of sales these are falling.	Markets become more segmented. Segmentation and maturity of the life cycle can be key strategies.	Less money spent on advertising and sales promotion.
Prices (and profits)	High prices possible, but high fixed costs too.	High price, high contribution margins and increasing profit margins.	Falling prices but good profit margins due to high sales volume. High prices in some markets.	Still low prices but falling profits as sales volume falls, since total contribution falls towards the level of fixed costs. Some increases in price may occur in the late decline stage.

2 MARKETING MIX DECISIONS RELATED TO THE STAGES OF THE LIFE CYCLE

Thus at every stage of the life cycle of the product, each component of the marketing mix involves distinctive problems and necessitates particular kinds of policies, according to the strategic objectives of the company.

2.1 Introduction stage of the product life cycle

Here, failure risks (and actual product failures) are high. Although business and initial sales may be slow there is, in many cases of new product introduction, little or no competition, since at least some new products are innovative. Purchasers at this stage are innovators and are a small proportion of the total marketplace, with different tastes and behaviour from the rest of the population. Profit margins may well be small (because of low sales and the need to recover start-up costs). All marketing expenditure, at this stage, will be very heavy. Strategically, companies will be aiming to recover these costs in the medium or long term. All aspects of the mix are involved, however, and a number of factors may necessitate choosing between a number of strategic alternatives.

Product

Quality may be problematic. Production processes and the performance of the product in the field are still naturally discovering flaws and problems which may have been unsuspected during the product development programme. Quality problems may also occur in the process of delivery and in responses to customer complaints. A high failure rate is general in almost all product areas. Few competitive products, if any, are around when a product is newly launched. The risk element is still predominant and until there are apparent profits to be made from the concept, competitors will stay off the bandwagon!

Place

Distribution is limited but growing during the introductory stage. For many companies, dealerships and space on shelves have to be fought for, with special deals and intensive personal selling.

Price

The distinctiveness of a product, or 'product differentiation factor' will be a key consideration in the formulation of a pricing policy. Products which have a very strong differentiation from potential competitors, which is likely to be sustained over the medium or long term, will have different pricing options than products which are likely to attract 'me too' competitors very quickly.

Most products have two options in pricing decisions.

(a)   Skimming involves asking a high price of a small group of consumers (early adopters) and is used when a product is unusually distinctive and demand is inelastic (that is, unlikely to be strongly affected by price changes). When price reductions occur, they are often related to careful identification and targeting of new groups of consumers.

(b)   Penetration is used as a pricing strategy when demand is elastic, competition is fierce and product differentiation will not provide a lasting competitive edge. Prices are set low in order to attract the largest number of consumers at an early stage of the life cycle and acquire market share.

These are not, in either case, strategies aiming at short-term profit maximisation, but are rather looking to short-term survival and development, and the long-term and medium-term achievement of profitability and success, building the brand into a profit-making line.

Promotion

Directed at creating product awareness, promotion here may involve relatively high spending and the heavy use of personal selling in order to generate interest and commitment both from end consumers and intermediaries in the distribution process. For consumer goods, advertising expenditure will be very high, relative to other costs and returns.

Between introduction and growth stages there occurs what marketers refer to as the 'shake-out', when products and even companies disappear from the scene. Which products survive has a strong impact on the ways in which the strategies of other products in the market place are formulated.

Business Basics: Marketing

Activity 2

Here is a newspaper article about the launch of a new product.

Hewlett-Packard to launch new desk-top range

By Louise Kehoe in San Francisco

Hewlett-Packard will today launch two product lines to expand in the corporate computing market.

HP will announce an enterprise desktop computer combining the high performance of a scientific workstation with the lower cost and software standards of personal computers. The company will introduce a line of network servers, priced to compete with PC servers but offering performance that competes with mini-computers.

The new computers, based on a low-cost version of HP's PA-Risc microprocessor chip, are aggressively priced. The desktop machines, which start at $3,995, will compete with high-end PCs. The new HP servers, which range in price from $7,569 to $14,919, outperform PC servers while undercutting the price of mini-computers, such as the IBM AS/400.

HP's new computers are aimed at companies adopting the client server networked computing model.

"These are the machine needed by companies that are re-engineering their businesses," says Mr Willem Roelants, general manager of HP's computer systems operations. "The fundamental idea of re-engineering is to give employees tools so that one person can complete a job, such as a customer transaction, without having to pass it on to several different people in different departments."

Sales of enterprise workstations are rising sharply according to a market report issued last week by Frost and Sullivan, the US market research group. World sales were expected to reach $25bn per year.

HP's challenge in the enterprise workstation market is to displace high-end PCs. To do so, it will offer compatibility with programs designed for the Microsoft Windows environment as well as UNIX applications. HP will introduce multi media programs for video and voice applications.

HP has designed its new desktop and server computers so that they can run Microsoft's new Windows NT operating system.

Lotus Development, Applix and Clarity have developed programs for the new HP desk-top machines.

The new HP desktop computers will run standard PC programs and UNIX application programs.

Analyse this *Financial Times* article in terms of the four Ps (and indeed any other aspect of marketing that you are now familiar with).

2.2 Growth stage of the life cycle

Those products which survive the introduction phase will find that during growth competition will increase and competitive 'copy-cat' or 'me too' products will try to capture part of what has proved to be a viable market. The product will face a struggle to retain distinctiveness and rising sales are linked to increasing profitability. This may well attract the attention of larger and more powerful companies, who may try to take over the company or the product which has proved successful.

Product

The line becomes established during this phase as important attributes are identified and consolidated, and the product developments and 'tweaking' which was still going on in the introductory stage are left behind. Product quality has improved and reliability is also important to the growing volume of consumers.

Place

Distribution is an important aspect of the fight to establish a particular brand within an increasingly competitive section of the marketplace. Dealership and distribution outlets are the key to many markets which are served by a smaller number of retail chains (as for instance in parts of the UK retail sector, where a small number of supermarket chains account for a very large proportion of grocer sales). Gaining space on the shelves of these outlets is life or death for many types of product, since fast moving consumer goods (FMCGs) are bought by consumers who are spending less time on shopping and visiting smaller numbers of shops than they used to do in the past. To miss out on one supermarket chain will close off a large section of the possible buying public. For makers of certain products gaining shelf space with one particular retailer may be the difference between great success and almost certain failure. In the case of prepared meal products, for instance, Marks & Spencer gained 60% of total sales in the UK market at one stage, although they accounted for only 6% of the total grocery trade. Gaining acceptance by them was clearly important for any manufacturer of non-branded prepared meals selling to the own-label sector. Other stores like Tesco and Sainsbury have now eroded the M&S dominance of the prepared meal market, and have become new customers for the manufacturers.

Price

It is during this phase, probably towards the end, that maximum profitability is achieved by the brand. Brand shares will have achieved their 'ambient' level and become stable, and competitors within the same market have accepted the way in which the market is divided, by and large. As a consequence prices stabilise and some profit taking can happen, while prices may well fall towards the end of this stage, to gather in a few more prospects.

Promotion

As in the preceding stage, advertising and promotion feature heavily here and are a significant part of marketing budgets. Since consumers are now aware of the existence of this product type, however, the messages involved seek to generate awareness and appreciation of a brand or trade name. In addition it is now more important for the product to be generating profit, so that expenditures are not allowed to reach the same levels which were found during the introductory phase. When a large company is thinking in terms of a long-term strategy of market dominance, however, gaining very large proportions of the available market and building up consumer loyalty may yet outweigh immediate profit.

The end of the growth stage inevitably involves the beginning of either stabilisation or decline.

2.3 Maturity stage of the life cycle

At any one time, most markets are dominated by mature products. The most successful products, as we can see by looking around us, persist, and have been earning large profits for the major companies who control them for many years. Marketing strategy in the maturity stage is a major preoccupation of decision-makers. This stage is longer than any other and it is the stage, according to the theory of the life cycle, when the bulk of profits are realised. Sales may be continuing to grow, but the rapid increases of the growth stage are left behind; new ways to increase profits are sought.

Problems of strategy are a product of the success of products. Competition increases and crowds the marketplace, so maintaining competitive edge through differentiation

PUBLISHING

becomes difficult. This is further complicated by 'wearout' effects, as customer needs and preferences may shift, and by environmental changes such as increased costs for raw materials, production processes or new entrants in the market as a consequence of, for example, more open trade policies bringing in low-cost 'me-too' competition.

This is what happened to Timex, who dominated the low price end of the US market for watches until the 1970s when imported digital watches and shifts in consumer tastes towards more fashion-related and prestigious brands, cut swathes through its market share.

Changes may also provide the opportunity to use the mix as a means to increase profits and open up new markets. Product improvements are a regular consequence of increased competition and market conditions may also provide the opportunity for growth.

Activity 3

Gold Blend is a mature product. A recent Nescafé Gold Blend promotion included three mini-packs of After Eight with a jar of coffee.

Why does this represent the producers of Nescafé taking advantage of new opportunities?

Products

Market shares for the product have typically stabilised during the growth stage, and with market growth fairly limited, products are often modified or used as the basis for extension lines; for example, new colours or styles for a car, new flavours or basic ingredients (vegetable kievs, curried beans) in the case of food products. Differentiation is difficult to achieve at this stage. Since the product is well established and familiar, many consumers may be strongly attached to the product in this form and changing a winning recipe or a familiar appearance can be dangerous!

A number of ways in which product differentiation can take place relate to the improvement of product and service quality. Market leaders may choose to analyse their market and invest in product development to retain a competitive edge, particularly where active technological development is still going on, and the market looks likely to expand strongly for some time (for instance, information technology markets).

Defending a market share may best be accomplished by emphasising superior quality or service or by maintaining a low cost or value for money approach.

Dimensions of differentiation may relate to the following.

Product quality differentiators	Service quality differentiators
Functional performance, eg speed, economy, comfort, handling for automobiles	Tangibles – appearance of facilities, equipment, personnel, communications materials
Durability or safety	Reliability
Absence of defects ('conformance')	Responsiveness: willingness to help, speed
Variety of features: standard and optional	Assurance: knowledge and courtesy of employees and their ability to convey trust and confidence
Reliability: consistency over a number of purchases or continued delivery of promised attributes	Empathy: caring, individualised attention
Serviceability: speed of repairing	
Fit and finish, reputation of brand name	

Place

Distribution is an important aspect of the fight to establish a particular brand within an increasingly competitive section of the marketplace. Dealership and distribution outlets are the key to many markets which are served by a smaller number of retail chains (as for instance in parts of the UK retail sector, where a small number of supermarket chains account for a very large proportion of grocer sales). Gaining space on the shelves of these outlets is life or death for many types of product, since fast moving consumer goods (FMCGs) are bought by consumers who are spending less time on shopping and visiting smaller numbers of shops than they used to do in the past. To miss out on one supermarket chain will close off a large section of the possible buying public. For makers of certain products gaining shelf space with one particular retailer may be the difference between great success and almost certain failure. In the case of prepared meal products, for instance, Marks & Spencer gained 60% of total sales in the UK market at one stage, although they accounted for only 6% of the total grocery trade. Gaining acceptance by them was clearly important for any manufacturer of non-branded prepared meals selling to the own-label sector. Other stores like Tesco and Sainsbury have now eroded the M&S dominance of the prepared meal market, and have become new customers for the manufacturers.

Price

It is during this phase, probably towards the end, that maximum profitability is achieved by the brand. Brand shares will have achieved their 'ambient' level and become stable, and competitors within the same market have accepted the way in which the market is divided, by and large. As a consequence prices stabilise and some profit taking can happen, while prices may well fall towards the end of this stage, to gather in a few more prospects.

Promotion

As in the preceding stage, advertising and promotion feature heavily here and are a significant part of marketing budgets. Since consumers are now aware of the existence of this product type, however, the messages involved seek to generate awareness and appreciation of a brand or trade name. In addition it is now more important for the product to be generating profit, so that expenditures are not allowed to reach the same levels which were found during the introductory phase. When a large company is thinking in terms of a long-term strategy of market dominance, however, gaining very large proportions of the available market and building up consumer loyalty may yet outweigh immediate profit.

The end of the growth stage inevitably involves the beginning of either stabilisation or decline.

2.3 Maturity stage of the life cycle

At any one time, most markets are dominated by mature products. The most successful products, as we can see by looking around us, persist, and have been earning large profits for the major companies who control them for many years. Marketing strategy in the maturity stage is a major preoccupation of decision-makers. This stage is longer than any other and it is the stage, according to the theory of the life cycle, when the bulk of profits are realised. Sales may be continuing to grow, but the rapid increases of the growth stage are left behind; new ways to increase profits are sought.

Problems of strategy are a product of the success of products. Competition increases and crowds the marketplace, so maintaining competitive edge through differentiation becomes difficult. This is further complicated by 'wearout' effects, as customer needs and preferences may shift, and by environmental changes such as increased costs for raw materials, production processes or new entrants in the market as a consequence of, for example, more open trade policies bringing in low-cost 'me-too' competition.

This is what happened to Timex, who dominated the low price end of the US market for watches until the 1970s when imported digital watches and shifts in consumer tastes towards more fashion-related and prestigious brands, cut swathes through its market share.

Changes may also provide the opportunity to use the mix as a means to increase profits and open up new markets. Product improvements are a regular consequence of increased competition and market conditions may also provide the opportunity for growth.

Activity 3

Gold Blend is a mature product. A recent Nescafé Gold Blend promotion included three mini-packs of After Eight with a jar of coffee.

Why does this represent the producers of Nescafé taking advantage of new opportunities?

Products

Market shares for the product have typically stabilised during the growth stage, and with market growth fairly limited, products are often modified or used as the basis for extension lines; for example, new colours or styles for a car, new flavours or basic ingredients (vegetable kievs, curried beans) in the case of food products. Differentiation is difficult to achieve at this stage. Since the product is well established and familiar, many consumers may be strongly attached to the product in this form and changing a winning recipe or a familiar appearance can be dangerous!

A number of ways in which product differentiation can take place relate to the improvement of product and service quality. Market leaders may choose to analyse their market and invest in product development to retain a competitive edge, particularly where active technological development is still going on, and the market looks likely to expand strongly for some time (for instance, information technology markets).

Defending a market share may best be accomplished by emphasising superior quality or service or by maintaining a low cost or value for money approach.

Dimensions of differentiation may relate to the following.

Product quality differentiators	Service quality differentiators
Functional performance, eg speed, economy, comfort, handling for automobiles	Tangibles – appearance of facilities, equipment, personnel, communications materials
Durability or safety	Reliability
Absence of defects ('conformance')	Responsiveness: willingness to help, speed
Variety of features: standard and optional	Assurance: knowledge and courtesy of employees and their ability to convey trust and confidence
Reliability: consistency over a number of purchases or continued delivery of promised attributes	Empathy: caring, individualised attention
Serviceability: speed of repairing	
Fit and finish, reputation of brand name	

(David A Aaker Strategic Marketing Management, 1988 and Zelthaml,
Parasuraman and Berry Delivering Quality Service: Balancing
Customer Perceptions and Expectations, 1990)

Quality was discussed in more detail in Chapter 3.

Place

Distribution here poses its own problems. When the popularity of products falls, it may be difficult to retain their place within retail outlets and there is a fair amount of 'rationalisation' and the replacement of products which cannot compete for their space on the shelf with other, more profitable lines. These 'shakeouts' in the transition from growth to maturity are becoming much more common, as the number of products proliferates within many markets.

When distribution costs are a high proportion of the total delivered cost of a product, alternative low-cost channels are an effective option. This often involves the limitation, or shifting to the customer, of functions performed by traditional channels to achieve a lower price. For example, in PC hardware and software industries, mail order discounters can offer lower prices because they have fewer fixed costs than retail stores. This means dispensing with customer support services such as technical advice and post-sale service, however.

Price

Prices are beginning to fall, largely as a consequence of battles between established products for market share. This may well involve falling profits too, since the need to promote the product is likely to remain strong. Nevertheless, a low-cost position such as one of the following can be an effective strategy at this stage of the life cycle.

(a)   A no-frills approach, developing a basic product without the extras

(b)   Innovative product design, simplified with standardised components

(c)   Cheaper raw materials, compressed fibre rather than 'natural wood', for example

(d)   Innovate production processes, such as CAD-CAM, transfer to low labour cost locations

(e)   Low-cost distribution, such as mail order, direct marketing

(f)   Reducing overheads, by downsizing labour and upgrading plant

Promotion

This can be crucially important for the success of a number of different mature market strategies. Growth extension strategies, for example, rely heavily on effective advertising and promotion. If it is decided to increase penetration, this involves targeting present non-users with a view to converting them into users. This requires an extensive promotional programme to communicate the benefits of the product to non-user targets.

- Advertising through appropriate media
- Sales promotions aimed at stimulating trial
- Sales effort redirected to new account generation

If the strategic objective is to extend use, to increase frequency of use, or to encourage a wider variety of uses, this will require consumer promotions to offer quantity discounts, multipack purchase, flier programmes and reminder advertising, or the communication of new product uses through information packs, in-store presentations, sales promotions or tie-ins with complementary products.

A market expansion strategy, in which a product is re-positioned or re-differentiated to focus on untapped or underdeveloped market segments, will often require new advertising, personal selling, packaging and sales promotion campaigns related to the specific interests and concerns of potential customers in these new markets.

2.4 Decline stage of the product life cycle

Since markets may well remain in the mature stage for decades (although there are some indications that the life cycle of many product types is becoming shorter), milking or harvesting mature product markets by minimising short run profits makes little sense in the majority of cases. Pursuing this kind of objective usually means substantial cuts in marketing and R&D expenses. That may lead, in turn, to premature losses of volume and market share, and lower profits in the longer term. During the early years of maturity, the main objective should be to maximise the flow of profits over the remaining life of the product market. Critically, this requires the manager to maintain and protect the business's market share. If few new customers buy the product for the first time in a mature market, a business must continue to win its share of repeat purchases from existing customers.

Even though products are in decline they may still be profitable. Even when, for example, the number of potential customers is declining (for demographic reasons, perhaps), if the company is prepared for the change and adopts appropriate strategies, the market will still remain profitable for years to come.

Three factors are crucial in determining the attractiveness of declining markets.

- Conditions of demand
- Rivalry determination
- Exit barriers

Demand may decline swiftly (as when a product becomes overtaken by superior technology which is rapidly accepted by the markets) or relatively slowly (when new technology does not offer sufficient extra benefit to existing users to make switching cost effective). Slow decline is more likely to promise continuing profit. This is also likely to be associated with 'pockets' of enduring demand, with consumers who are brand loyal (who have invested effort and time into 'learning' about a product, for example) and with stable prices, which do not threaten premiums or actually fail to recover costs.

Activity 4

Suppose you have a large number of very good quality black and white television sets. You find that your market has dried up. What can you do with the TVs?

Exit barriers, representing the ease or trouble involved in weaker competitors leaving a product market, can create very inhospitable conditions within a declining market. If weak competitors find it hard to leave a product market as demand falls (because, for example, their brand generates a large proportion of their profits, or the plant involved in producing the product represents heavy investment) excess capacity develops, and firms engage in aggressive pricing wars or mount promotional efforts aiming to prop up their volume and hold down unit costs. Whether this is likely to create problems within the market can be assessed by looking at needs for reinvestment, excess capacity within the market, the age of assets, their resale value, amounts of shared facilities, the degree of vertical integration and the amount of single product competition.

The intensity of potential future rivalry is also important. Even if there are large pockets of continuing demand available, if rivalry is likely to be intense it may not be wise to remain within the market. This is likely to be influenced by the size and bargaining power of remaining customers, their ability to switch to substitute products or alternative suppliers (how safe is their loyalty to this product?) and potential diseconomies of scale which may be involved in pursuing this declining group of consumers.

Five options are open to the firm in the decline stage of the life cycle. These are as follows.

(a) **Divestment or liquidation**: recovering some of the investment by selling the business in the earliest possible stages of decline.

(b) **Harvesting**: maximising short-term cash flow; maintaining or increasing margins, even if this generates quicker decline in market share.

(c) **Maintenance**: when the product line is important to the firm, but the future is uncertain. This is a short-term strategy to maintain market share even at the cost of declining margins.

(d) **Profitable survivor**: aims to increase his or her share of the declining market, with a view to future gains, usually when weaker competitors are leaving the market.

(e) **Niche**: identifying a small number of segments and concentrating activity into those areas. Again, this is a longer-term strategy.

For all the mix variables at the decline stage, policies vary according to the strategy selected. For most, reduction in cost is the major issue. Divestment or liquidation will obviously preclude contemplation of the other options.

Product

(a) Harvesting. R&D expenditure is eliminated, along with capital investment related to the product in question. The product is not being developed.

(b) Maintenance. Product and process expenditures are maintained, at least for the short term. Product quality may even be improved.

(c) Profitable survivor. Product and process expenditures are maintained, as part of a process of pursuing increased market share. Link up with 'private' (own brand) labels.

(d) Niche. Continued product and process R&D aiming at product improvements or modifications to appeal to target segments; extend production into private labels.

Place

(a) Harvesting. Focus on maintaining existing channels, to retain present customers.

(b) Maintenance. Trade promotion focuses on maintaining existing channels and distribution coverage.

(c) Profitable survivor. Maintaining existing distribution channels. Own label distribution may be considered.

(d) Niche. Maintain distribution channels appropriate for reaching the desired target segment. Try to develop unique channel arrangements to reach targeted customers better.

Price

(a) Harvesting. Across the board cost cutting in all areas. Price may well be raised to maintain margins.

(b) Maintenance. Lower prices, if necessary, to maintain market share. Reduced margins are acceptable under this strategy.

(c) Profitable survivor. Lower prices as appropriate to increase market share, even with much lower margins.

(d) Niche. Prices tied to the nature of the segment targeted. Unit costs are critical, and the means of holding them down (through, for instance, expanding production into private labels) may be part of this strategy.

Promotion

(a) Harvesting. Sales and marketing budgets are slashed under this strategy. Advertising is reduced or eliminated, trade promotions are cut to the minimum level necessary to prevent rapid loss of distribution coverage, and sales force efforts are concentrated simply on getting repeat orders from existing customers.

(b) Maintenance. Maintenance levels of advertising and sales promotion are continued here, while trade promotions are sustained at a level sufficient to prevent any erosion of existing coverage. The sales force seeks repeat purchases from current users.

(c) Profitable survivor. This strategy requires that a signal be sent out to competitors that the firm intends to remain in this market, and increase its share of the market. Advertising and promotion are increased or at least maintained, whilst increased distribution coverage is sought by strong trade promotions. Attempts are made by the sales force to get competitors' customers to switch.

(d) Niche. Advertising, sales promotion and personal selling campaigns are all focused on customers in the target segment(s) with appeals carefully identified and targeted precisely at these new customers.

Having considered the practical implications of the product life cycle concept for the marketing mix, we need to look at the assumptions which underpin the concept and the limitations to its application.

3 ASSUMPTIONS AND LIMITATIONS OF THE PRODUCT LIFE CYCLE CONCEPT

We have already indicated that the PLC concept has a number of problems associated with its use, as well as obvious benefits in the analysis and formulation of marketing mix strategies. These arise partly because the PLC rests on a number of key, and interrelated, assumptions about how product markets develop and what factors are important in their profitability. Key assumptions of the PLC concept are as follows.

Assumption	But... ?
Products have finite life spans.	When is it over? Many seem to go on and on. Many die very early, too.
Strategic objectives and marketing strategy should match the market growth rates.	Strategy also influences and generates growth.
For most mass produced products, costs of production are closely matched to experience (volume) – unit costs go down as production volume increases.	Many markets are never going to reap the benefits of 'economies of scale' – product may require specialised techniques which can only be carried out by a skilled craftsman. Many markets are too small to warrant large production runs.
Expenditures are directly related to rates of growth – products in growth markets will use more resources than products in mature markets.	When do the stages begin and end? The most important shortcoming of the concept is the difficulty of saying when 'growth' finishes and 'maturity' begins.
Margins and the cash generated are positively related to the share of the market. Products with high relative share of their market will be more profitable than products with a low share.	(a) Leadership is not the only way to profitability. (b) Not every product can be, or wants to be, a market leader!
At the maturity stage, products with high market share generate a stream of cash greater than that needed to sustain them in the market. This cash is available for investment in other products or in research and development to create new products.	Whether this is what the company actually does depends on a whole raft of issues (market conditions, technical change, competitor activity and so on) rather than simply 'life cycle' stage. Acceptance of 'mature' status denies the possibility of relaunch or reposition which can happen right into the 'decline' stage!

The PLC provides a framework for planning and not a rigid predictive device. The span of the curve involved, the onset of stages, progression through stages – all these are subject to strategic action by managers and influences from the environment which may override the 'logic' of life cycle development; for instance, catastrophic economic recession, or revolutionary technological change, such as the growth of the Internet.

Product lives go on and on. Nylon, as Levitt points out, has been endlessly extended because endless new uses have been found for the generic product. New users can be found, or the product can be re-positioned. Hellman's mayonnaise was a mature product, in terms of the life cycle, until it was re-launched with promotion targeting it at a younger, broader mass market as a 'fun' product. Market share went from around 10% to 50% in a very short time. In some ways, the new image and the new marketing message created a 'new' product. Certainly, if considering the product to be the end result of a value-adding process, including the symbolic values added by promotion (fun, in the case of Hellman's mayonnaise) and the satisfactions which promotion adds to the product concept, then it is a new product.

The importance of the product life cycle should not be underestimated. It has been extended and incorporated into a number of other tools for strategic analysis and decision making, such as the Boston Consulting Group Portfolio Analysis method, the General Electric Matrix and the Barksdale and Harris model, all of which highlight additional issues.

Barksdale and Harris, for instance, place great emphasis on differentiating products within life cycle stages, so that pioneering new products, 'infants', may require a distinct strategy, while for products in declining markets, how profitable they are (whether they are war-horses, having high market share or 'dodos' having low share) – will determine how decisions are taken. This approach is based on the idea that the introduction and decline stages are also important, whereas, it is claimed, use of the life cycle alone tends to lead to other stages being emphasised.

> **Activity 5**
>
> Try to apply some of your knowledge of the product life cycle to hi-fi equipment over the past decade.

Nor should business-to-business marketing, non-profit organisations and service marketing be forgotten.

These were dealt with in more detail in Chapter 7, but it is important to remember how different elements of the marketing mix will assume different levels of importance depending upon the market.

3.1 Business-to-business

This used to be known as the industrial goods market. Business-to-business markets exhibit many variations in buying behaviour and the variety of product just as consumer markets do. However, business buyers have some special attributes.

- Buyers are not spending their own money

- The buying decision making unit (DMU) may involve many people

- Decision making may take a long time

- The customer base is often small and easy to identify

- Average order values and quantities are higher than in consumer markets

- Personal contacts and relationships are often a key part of the buying decision

3.2 The marketing mix for services

Definition

> A service is any activity or benefit offered by one party to another which is essentially intangible and does not result in the ownership of anything physical. An example is a seat on an aircraft, which the customer uses for the duration of the flight but does not own.

In addition to the four elements in the marketing mix for tangible products, there are three more ingredients in the mix for services. These are process, physical evidence and people.

Process

User-friendly systems for selling and buying are essential. Not only should it be easy for organisations to operate efficiently, but customers should not face any unnecessary bureaucracy or delay. Information technology and the widespread use of computers to take the drudgery out of form filling, the ordering of goods and the maintenance of accurate customer records have greatly aided the move to more customer-friendly systems.

EXAMPLE: INSURANCE OVER THE PHONE

Let us look at an example. Do you like filling in forms? You can now buy car insurance over the telephone or the Internet. You give a certain amount of information and with the use of a computer you can get a firm quotation. Driver and vehicle details then have to be confirmed by you. One company may send these details on a computer-generated listing together with a blank form for you to complete. Another company may send a form that had already been completed by the computer. You simply have to check the entries on the form and sign to show that the information is correct. The second company has the advantage, because it has made life easier for you.

Physical evidence

Services tend to suffer from the intangible nature of the offering. The services provided by a breakdown company like the RAC is a sense of security which only becomes a reality when you have to make use of it. The sense of security tends to fade when you do not make any use of it and then you start to question the fee. Organisations in the service sector are increasingly using devices such as newsletters to maintain the customer's desire to have the service. A plastic membership card is issued as a reminder of the service and its provider. The patrolmen drive vehicles with distinctive logos and they wear uniforms as a permanent display of the quality of the service.

People

For most services, a key element is the people who are an integral part of the process. If the staff who deal with customers are poorly motivated or badly trained, this can greatly affect the quality of the service. Banks can design products and encourage customer interest but if their staff fail to deliver the service in the way intended, for example by misrepresenting the product, business will suffer. Many people in organisations come into direct customer contact, not just those whose jobs are staffing counters or in other sale positions, but also others in backroom roles such as accounts and stores may have contact with customers. How they treat customers will greatly impact upon the business. Any problems that arise can be largely overcome by training in interpersonal skills, setting standards of conduct and dress and creating customer service teams. It is important that internal communication is effective to ensure that customers are dealt with properly.

3.3 The reasons for starting to market internationally

Firms may be pushed into international marketing (IM) by domestic adversity or pulled into IM by attractive opportunities abroad. More specifically, some of the reasons firms enter into IM are the following.

(a)   Chance. A company executive may recognise an opportunity while on a foreign trip or the firm may receive chance orders or requests for information from foreign potential customers.

(b)   Mature or declining home market. IM may provide for sales growth since products are often in different stages of the product life cycle in different countries.

(c)   Intense competition in the domestic market sometimes induces firms to seek markets overseas where rivalry is less keen. This was a major reason in

NOTES

Business Basics: Marketing

Gillette's decision to begin marketing razor blades outside its US home markets.

(d)   Many companies enter into IM to diversify away from an over-dependence on a single domestic market.

(e)   Technological factors may be such that a large volume is needed either to cover the high costs of plant, equipment, R&D and personnel or to exploit a large potential for economies of scale and/or experience. For these reasons firms in the aviation, ethical drugs, computer and automobile industries are often obliged to enter several countries.

(f)   IM can facilitate the disposal of discontinued products and seconds since these can be sold abroad without spoiling the home market.

(g)   Many firms are attracted into IM by favourable opportunities such as the development of lucrative Middle Eastern markets, marked depreciation in their domestic currency values, corporate tax benefits offered by particular countries and the lowering of import barriers abroad.

3.4   Some differences between domestic and international marketing

Sound marketing principles are generally applicable universally. However, there are major environment differences between home and overseas markets and therefore marketing principles need to be adapted accordingly.

	Domestic	International
Cultural factors	National price	Diverse national prices
	Usually no language problems	Many language barriers
	Relatively homogeneous market	Fragmented, diverse markets
	'Rules of the game' understood	Rules diverse, changeable and unclear
	Similar purchasing habits	Diverse purchasing habits
Economic factors	Uniform financial climate	Variety of financial climates, ranging from very conservative to highly inflationary
	Single currency	Currencies differing in stability and real value
	Stable business environment	Multiple business environments, some unstable
Competitive factors	Data available, usually accurate and easy to collect.	Formidable data collection problems
	Competitor's products, prices, costs and plans usually known	Many more competitors, but little information about their strategies
Legal factors	Relative freedom from government interference	Involvement in national economic plans
		Government influence on business decisions
	Political factors relatively unimportant	Political factors often significant
Technological factors	Use of standard production and measurement systems	Training of foreign personnel to operate and maintain equipment
		Adaptation of parts and equipment
		Different measuring systems

We turn next to a consideration of how the mix is influenced by where products are marketed; how the mix may vary in different settings.

308

4 THE MIX IN DIFFERENT MARKETPLACES AND INTERNATIONALLY

Marketers may find that, within a single country, mix variables assume different degrees of importance. For instance, the same media may not be appropriate, effective or available in different regions. Radio may be more effective at reaching certain segments of the market in some places than others. For example, ethnic minorities are more important market segments and larger sections of the population in some parts of the UK, France, Germany, Australia and the USA, and media provision varies accordingly. Spanish language TV and radio in parts of the south west of the USA reaches a very large market segment. Hindi and Gujarati-speakers are better catered for on the radio stations in the Midlands than they are in, for example, Scotland. Marketers aiming for these segments cannot rely on the same 'reach' in other areas, so that promotion may well have to be varied.

The other elements of the mix will vary too. Competition, local tastes or differences in levels of disposable income will make price variations necessary. In the UK, for example, many brewers provide 'bands' of prices for the same product within different areas of the same locality, but allow the licensee of the public house to adjust the price up or down to achieve certain kinds of advantage for the premises in question: special low prices at certain times ('happy hour') or special offers on certain products.

Distribution costs, of course, will vary greatly within the same country, although these are usually absorbed equitably across the different regions, so that the most distant from a manufacturer is not disadvantaged. One of the main exceptions occurs where postal costs are a significant part of the total outlay for the distributor; in many mail order businesses postal charges have to be varied according to the cost to the business.

Products generally remain very similar within national boundaries, although local variations in taste and tradition (particular local delicacies or specialities incorporated into a range of foodstuffs) or local conditions (the kinds of fuel which can be burned by a stove, or the size of dish required by a satellite TV receiver) may be incorporated into the product portfolio.

Major variations in the marketing mix are likely to be necessary across national boundaries, however, and we next turn to a consideration of how the mix varies in international marketing.

4.1 The marketing mix within international marketing practice

Most of the considerations detailed previously within this book are also, of course, relevant in the practice of international marketing. There are some factors, however, which have a special significance.

In developing an international marketing mix, the key considerations to be borne in mind when we decide which aspects can be standardised and which must be related to local conditions are particularly important.

4.2 Product

The international marketing mix in relation to product strategy involves the following possible approaches.

(a) Marketing the same product to all countries (a global product) is possible when the products are not culture-sensitive and when economies of scale are significant. It assumes that consumer needs are very similar everywhere or that low prices will prove attractive enough to overcome differences.

(b) Adapting the product to local conditions. Keeping the physical form essentially the same but changing its promotion is very attractive, for obvious reasons, but faces certain dangers.

(c) Developing a country-specific product may be necessary. The physical form of the product is specifically altered for one of a number of different reasons.

Products developed and successfully marketed within one country cannot necessarily be moved tout court into an alien market without problems. Since a product is composed of physical dimensions such as its shape, colour, smell and so on and also symbolic and psychological aspects such as the image or personality of the product, the associations and meanings involved, entry often entails dealing with a different set of cultural, religious, economic, social and political factors.

Activity 6

You have probably noticed differences in products that are available both at home and abroad when you have been on holiday. Pool your knowledge with classmates and generate a list of examples.

Standardisation

Target marketing and segmentation suggest that the way to maximise sales is to identify specific consumer needs and to tailor promotional appeals specifically to those needs (that is, to adapt a product for a new foreign market). It is less costly to produce a standardised product for a larger market segment.

Arguments in favour of product standardisation include the following.

(a) **Economies of scale** in the following.

(i) **Production**

(1) Plant probably confined to one country rather than duplicated.

(2) Plant expansion may attract 'home' government's grants or other support.

(3) Plant used to maximum capacity offers best return on its costs.

(4) Exporting is easier rather than difficult licensing deals.

(ii) **Research and development**

Product modification, such as that needed to tailor products to specific foreign markets, is costly and time consuming in an area where resources are always jealously husbanded.

(iii) **Marketing**

Promotion which can use the same images and themes in advertising is clearly more cost effective. If distribution systems, sales force training, after-sales provision and other aspects of the product mix can be standardised, this also saves a great deal of money.

(b) **Consumer mobility**. Often the same people will have come across products in different countries, as a result of holidays, or because of living and working abroad. Differences may not be as great as they appear.

(c) **Technological complexity**. It may not be easy to modify some products to suit the special requirements or conditions found in the foreign marketplace. For example, some computer software may be difficult to programme into certain kinds of languages easily. The costs of developing a special version of a word-processor or a spreadsheet for a particular, comparatively small group of language speakers may be disproportionate to the potential profit involved.

Country-specific products

Arguments in favour of country-specific products include the following.

(a) Greater sales where this also means greater profitability – which it may not!

(b) Varied conditions of product use which may force a company to modify its product.

(i) Climatic variations (corrosion in cars produced for drier climates)

(ii) Literacy or skill levels of users (languages which can be used on a computer)

(iii) Cultural, social or religious factors (religious or cultural requirements for food products, for example Halal slaughtering of New Zealand lamb for Middle Eastern markets, or dolphin-friendly tuna catching methods for Europe and the USA).

(c) Variation in market factors. Consumer needs are in their nature idiosyncratic and there are likely to be distinctive requirements for each group not met by a standard product.

(d) Governmental or political influence. Political factors may force a company to produce a local product through taxation legislation, or pressure of public opinion.

(e) Local competition may be particularly effective because of sensitivity to the particular needs of local markets, so that the business is forced to adapt its product to local conditions in order to compete at all.

Conditions of entry are also particularly important and bear heavily on the mix which is arrived at for local conditions.

4.3 Place

Distribution channels are a key issue for entrants to foreign markets. Getting the product to the consumer is a major hurdle and presents problems quite different in range and scale from those faced by marketers within a domestic setting. Major alternative methods of entry would divide into the following approaches.

(a) Export goods manufactured outside the target country.

(b) Transfer the technology and skills necessary to produce and market the goods to an organisation in the foreign country through licensing/contractual arrangements.

(c) Transfer manufacturing and marketing resources by direct investment in a foreign country.

Major entry modes are as follows.

Export entry modes	Indirect
	Direct agent/distributor
Contractual entry modes	Licensing
	Franchising
	Technical agreements
	Service contracts
	Management contracts
	Turnkey construction contracts
	Contract manufacture
	Co-productive agreements
Investment entry modes	Sole venture: new establishment
	Sole venture: acquisition
	Joint venture: new establishment acquisition

Simple exporting

This is often based on the need to dispose of excess production for a domestic market and is the commonest form of export activity. Minimal financial risk is involved and it is often viewed as an 'opportunity' rather than long-term project. It may, however, involve an intermediary (a company 'selling on' to export, after purchasing from manufacturer) and it may be direct or indirect.

Indirect exporting involves less risk, less investment. The firm makes no investment in an overseas sales force and relies on the expertise of domestic international middlemen such as export merchants, export agents and co-operative organisations.

Direct exporting is used when there are enough business opportunities abroad to warrant investing in marketing activities. This involves using foreign based distributors/agents or setting up operating units in the foreign country in the shape of branches or subsidiaries.

In general, exporting (as opposed to more involved methods of market entry such as overseas manufacture) is suited to:

- Small firms with limited resources
- Markets where there is political risk (such as of civil war, nationalisation)
- Small overseas markets
- Overseas markets where there is no pressure for local manufacture

Activity 7

What would you suggest is the major danger in exporting?

Contractual entry modes

Non-equity contractual arrangements involve the transfer of technology and/or human skills to an entity in a foreign market.

Licensing involves a firm offering the right to use its intangible asset (technology, know-how, patents, company name, trade marks) in exchange for royalties or some other form of payment.

This is less flexible than exporting, with less control than when the company is doing its own manufacturing and then exporting. A small capital outlay is required, however, and it is particularly appropriate when the market is unstable and the licensing firm would have financial and marketing problems in penetrating the foreign market. Favoured by small and medium-sized companies, it is the least profitable method of entry but has the least associated risks. A positive approach to export decision making and planning is required.

Franchising differs from licensing.

- Motivation is different
- Services are rendered
- Duration is specified

Franchising grants the right to use the company's name, trademarks and technology. Typically the franchisee receives help in setting up. Service firms are particularly appropriate franchisees (for example, fast food businesses).

This is a low cost option which combines local knowledge with entrepreneurial spirit.

Contract manufacturing involves sourcing a product from a manufacturer located in a foreign country for sale there or elsewhere. It is attractive when:

- The local market is small
- Export entry is blocked
- A quality licensee is not available

Various forms exist. **Turnkey construction contracts** require that the contractor makes the project operational before releasing it to the owner, or in some cases providing the services, such as worker training, when the project is completed. High risks are involved. **Management contracts** give a company the right to manage the day-to-day operations of a local company and are used mainly in conjunction with turnkey or joint venture agreements. Countries may only allow contractual arrangements when unable to service an industry with home personnel (for example when an industry has been taken over). Circumstances usually dictate the choice, or the solution is sometimes forced upon a company making a strategic decision about methods of entry.

Industrial co-operation agreements are contractual arrangements between a western company and an organisation in what used to be communist/eastern bloc countries. They are usually licensing technical assistance agreements and turnkey projects. They can also take the form of co-production agreements, which involve western companies providing the technological know-how and components in return for a share of the output that it agrees to market in the west. Obviously these arrangements have lost most of their raison d'être with the fall of the communist system, and the opening up of eastern European markets to both western companies and western capital.

This sector is nonetheless very important. Under the old arrangements this involved around 10% of all world trade. Up to 350 arrangements had been completed by 1989; the situation is obviously very different now and it seems likely that new challenges will be involved because of ex-eastern bloc destabilisation and fragmentation, coupled with political and economic instability.

Investment overseas

Investment overseas can take one of two forms.

Joint ventures involve collaboration with one or more foreign firms to produce/market goods in the foreign market. The degree of ownership for the 'home' partner can vary from small to 50%, but this approach is increasing in popularity: it avoids quotas and import taxes and satisfies government demands for local production. The outstanding examples are Japanese companies such as Nissan, Mitsubishi and Toyota, which have

313

established joint venture motor manufacturing in the UK and the USA. Globalisation of certain markets requires alliances because:

(a) Costs of technological competition are too high for any but the largest companies

(b) Change from a variable to a fixed cost environment is involved

(c) Increasing numbers of giant multinational competitors are in the marketplace

(d) There is a growing convergence of consumer needs

This approach is subject to changes in the market position of the partners and suffers from a lack of flexibility. There are reduced economic and political risks, however, and the advantage of a partner's 'ready made' distribution system. Access is the critical factor; this may be the only way to gain entry to particular foreign markets.

Sole ownership involves establishing a manufacturing facility in a host country which then makes its own operating decisions. The parent company provides finance, R&D, product specifications and product technology and retains complete control: there is no shared management. A high level of commitment and high risks are involved. At a macro-economic level, a total country may be affected, while at a micro-economic level only one economic sector may be involved. It is only justified by very heavy demand.

(a) Advantages

- Lower labour costs
- Avoidance of import taxes
- Lower transport costs

(b) Disadvantages

- Significant commitment
- Higher involvement levels
- Higher levels of risk

4.4 Promotion

Aside from the size and location of the target market, one of the major considerations in the selection of advertising media relates to the logistics of the communication process. Many different factors can lead to decreased profitability or even failure. These include the following.

(a) **Cultural factors**. Language, social systems and religious differences may well cause severe problems in marketing a product for reasons unsuspected by a marketer used to a single, culturally homogeneous market. For instance, when Ever Ready were marketing a standard radio across the whole of Africa just before World War II, their research determined that the only colour which would be acceptable across the various cultural boundaries involved was blue.

(b) **Customs** can also be an important consideration. For instance, it may be important that goods which are used by wives are actually bought by (and consequently initially promoted to) husbands.

(c) **Geographical remoteness**. Can the media actually penetrate to the areas in question?

Activity 8

TV programmes like those of Chris Tarrant have popularised what, to UK viewers, are some of the perceived absurdities in advertising in other countries.

Your task is to take note, when you are watching programmes such as these, of any examples that may be useful for essays or exams.

If possible, international marketers would wish to use essentially the same advertising in as many different countries as possible. There are some factors which encourage this.

- The widespread international ownership of TV sets
- The growing importance of satellite and cable systems

But there are many more tending towards local adaptation.

- Very localised tastes (for example, in food and drink)

- Differences in the availability of media

- Problems in translating advertising messages (an English ad runs 15% longer in French, 50% longer in German)

The general response is to use broadly the same approach but give a 'twist' which customises the campaign for specific audiences.

Media problems

Media problems are likely to relate specifically to the following.

(a) **Availability**. Particular media may be more important and effective in some countries than in others (for instance, cinema in India, radio in the USA) while there may be a lack of specific media in others.

  (i) Newspapers may not be widely available because of low levels of literacy, or even specific policies on the part of the government.

  (ii) Magazines, which are so important for specialist products such as industrial machinery, may be very restricted.

  (iii) TV commercials are restricted, or even banned, in many countries. For instance, advertising specifically directed at children is banned in some Scandinavian countries. It is also sometimes very difficult to gauge effectiveness because of missing market research data.

  (iv) Billboards, direct mail and other forms of promotion may be unfamiliar or ineffective (for example, very limited use of billboards in some formerly Communist countries).

(b) **Financial aspects**. Costs may be very difficult to estimate in many countries, since negotiation and the influence of intermediaries is likely to be much greater. There may also be expectations of gift giving in the negotiation process.

(c) **Coverage of media** (or 'reach' of advertising message). This relates to the forms of media employed as well as the physical characteristics of the country. Inaccessible areas may rule out the use of direct mail or posters, scarcity of telephones may rule out this form of advertising promotion. It may also be difficult to monitor advertising effectiveness.

(d)   **Lack of information** on the characteristics of the target markets. Often there is little information on the differences between groups within the population towards which advertising and promotion are being targeted. This is critical for decisions about the mix to be employed and decisions such as standardisation/ adaptation.

As we can see, developing a marketing mix for international markets is a challenging and complex business. Product, promotional and place decisions are, in themselves, radically different from those involved in domestic marketing, with complex environmental and strategic factors at play.

4.5   Price

Pricing decisions are equally complex, with such considerations as exchange rates, fluctuations in the currency markets and rapid economic changes within overseas markets which may make it very difficult to establish appropriate levels of pricing. Famously, in countries suffering from hyperinflation, stores are busiest in the early mornings. Often workers are paid daily and the value of the currency may change several times in the course of a few hours, so that there is a rush to buy goods in the early morning in order to maximise purchasing power!

These matters bear heavily on the calculation about method of entry.

When choices are made, the quality of the marketing manager and his or her capacity to use marketing tools for effective decision-making are not simply a matter of whether he or she can engage in academic debate about one or other method of describing or analysing the market, or selecting a strategy: good decisions lead to commercial success; bad decisions lead to failure.

Chapter roundup

- We looked at various aspects of the product life cycle earlier in this book. Here, we have brought together the various threads of discussion.

- We have looked at what marketing mix decisions are taken in relation to the product life cycle at each stage.

- We have also looked at the assumptions underlying the PLC concept, and limitations and criticisms of the concept.

- Finally, we considered key considerations in developing an international marketing mix such as product standardisation, adaptation or modification, exporting versus licensing, franchising or overseas investment, media problems, exchange rate fluctuations and so on.

Quick quiz

1   In the introduction phase of the PLC, describe skimming and penetration as pricing strategies.

2   Why is 'place' so important in the growth stage of the life cycle?

3   In the maturity stage, how can low costs be used to offset prices falling?

4   How do exit barriers affect weaker competitors in the decline stage?

5   How does 'harvesting' in the decline stage affect promotion?

6   List the key assumptions of the PLC concept.

7   What are the possible approaches to product strategy in international marketing mix?

8   What are the arguments in favour of product standardisation?

9   List the different types of contractual entry modes to foreign markets.

10   What extra factors affect promotion strategy in foreign markets?

Answers to activities

2   One point that you may have missed is that the article itself, which appeared in the Financial Times, is a fine piece of promotion in the form of public relations: it sounds as if it is taken verbatim from HP's press release. There are numerous other more obvious points to make about products satisfying needs, marketing strategy, pricing and so on.

3   Because Nestlé, who make Nescafé, had recently taken over Rowntree, who make After Eight. Both the coffee and the mini-packs were being promoted, of course.

        Watch out for other examples of novel ways of marketing products that are very familiar to you.

4   The UK market may have dried up but there are plenty of countries less advanced than the UK that would be glad of your TVs. Failing this, perhaps the best option is to break them up and sell or re-use any components that are suitable. Other possibilities are selling them at such a cheap price that they are seen as a bargain spare set, in case the main family set goes wrong; dressing them up in, say, a 1950s casing so that they can be sold as novelty nostalgia items; perhaps marketing them as a package with a series of classic black and white films on video (though you would be pushing your luck here). You may have had other ideas.

5   The compact disc player demonstrates the product life cycle. Initial high prices meant that it took a while to be accepted, but its benefits have led to a considerable growth in sales. CD players have come down considerably in price and the market is reaching maturity. Consequently vinyl records are virtually extinct and hi-fi systems have shrunk in size: nowadays they only need to be as wide as a CD is. The market for Digital Versatile Discs (DVD) is now on the increase.

7   The main problem for most companies is collecting the debts of their foreign customers. There is however a sophisticated system of export credit guarantee insurance that can be purchased, and certainly should be if exporting is to become a regular activity.

Further question practice

Now try the following practice questions at the end of this text.

Multiple Choice Questions: 91–100

Exam Style Questions: 15–17

GLOSSARY

Tutorial note. In this subject, it is not always easy to arrive at exact definitions of certain words, as different authors use them in different ways. So treat this brief glossary as a memory jogger, not as the definite answer to your query. If in any doubt after you have used this glossary, consult the index and go back to the relevant section of this Study Guide.

ACORN A Categorisation of Residential Neighbourhoods.

Adoption process Similar to buyer behaviour ie the process of deciding to buy a product. Adopter categories can indicate the extent to which people are prepared to innovate and try out new products.

Agent A person authorised to act for another (the principal) and bring that other into legal relations with a third party.

AIDA Acronym denoting elements of a marketing communications strategy (to generate awareness, arouse interest, stir up desire and trigger action).

Ansoff Matrix Shows the four main growth strategies that are open to most organisations.

Attitude A relatively consistent, learned predisposition to behave in a certain way in response to a given object.

Attribution theory Theory that individuals attribute motives and qualities to themselves and other people.

Boston consulting Group Matrix Used to analyse product mix performance, combining market share and market growth.

Brand A name, term, symbol or design (or combination) which is intended to signify the goods or services of one seller or group of sellers and to differentiate them from those of competitors. Also, a particular make of a product form.

Business cycle (or trade cycle) The periodic fluctuation of levels of economic activity, for example output and employment.

Causal models Equations used to explain the relationship between a dependent variable (the one being forecast) and a number of independent variables.

Competitive advantage Factor which enables a firm to compete successfully with competitors on a sustained basis.

Competitor analysis Analysis of competitors' strengths and weaknesses, strategies, assumptions, market positioning, etc from all available sources of information in order to identify suitable strategies.

Consistency theories Theories of decision making which assume that an individual seeks consistency between his or her values, ideas and behaviour.

Consumer goods Goods made for the household consumer, which can be used without any further commercial processing. Convenience goods are generally purchased in small units or low value (eg milk). Shopping goods have higher unit values and are bought less frequently (eg clothes, furniture). Speciality goods are those of high value which a customer will know by name and go out of his or her way to purchase. These distinctions are broad and blurry; there is no point in logic-chopping.

Consumer panels A representative cross-section of consumers who have agreed to give information about their attitudes or buying habits (through personal visits or mail questionnaires or data transferred from a home recording computer by modem) at regular intervals which go beyond contractual or legal requirements.

BPP PUBLISHING

Consumer The end user of a product service. May or may not be the customer.

Consumerism An organised movement of members of the public and government to improve the rights and powers of consumers.

Corporate culture Culture residing in an organisation; influenced by the organisation's founder, history, structure and systems leadership and management style.

Corporate objectives Objectives for the firm as a whole.

Corporate strategy Strategy for the business as a whole (Johnson and Scholes).

Correlation The degree to which change in one variable is related to change in another. The interdependence between variables.

Culture The sum total of beliefs, knowledge, attitudes of mind and custom to which people are exposed in their social conditioning.

Customer care A fundamental approach to the standards of service quality. It covers every aspect of a company's operations, from the design of a product or service to how it is packaged, delivered and serviced (Clutterbuck).

Customer The purchaser of a product/service. May or may not be the consumer.

Decline Stage of the product life cycle characterised by declining sales volumes and profits.

Deming System based on the improvement of products and services by reducing uncertainty and variability in the design and manufacturing processes through an unceasing cycle of product design, manufacture, test and sales, followed by market surveys to gain feedback, after which the cycle begins again with re-design.

Demography The study of the population.

Desk research The collection of secondary data in marketing research.

Differentiated marketing Introduce several versions of a product, each tailored to a particular segment.

Direct distribution Supply of goods to customers without an intermediary (eg direct sales, mail order in some cases).

Direct exporting Exporting to overseas customers, who might be wholesalers, retailers or users, without the use of export houses etc. See also indirect exporting.

Direct mail Means of promotion, whereby selected customers are sent advertising material addressed specifically to them (eg by post and/or fax).

Direct selling The use of a salesperson to sell a product, as opposed to advertising etc.

Dissonance The tension that exists when there is a perceived gap between a person's current situation and the situation they would prefer to be in.

Distribution channel Means of getting the goods to the consumer.

DMU Decision-making unit ie the people in a business who decide whether to buy a product.

Exit barriers These make it difficult for firms to withdraw from an industry.

External green Ps An addition to the marketing mix's 4 Ps to cover environmental factors outside the business: Paying customers, Providers, Politicians, Pressure groups, Problems, Predictions, Partners.

Family life cycle (FLC) A summary of demographic variables, combining the effects of age, marital status, career status (income) and presence/absence of children.

BPP PUBLISHING

Field research The collection of primary data in market research.

Forecasting 'The identification of factors and quantification of their effect on an entity, as a basis for planning' (CIMA).

Franchising Popular in retail and service industries, the franchisee supplies capital and the franchiser supplies expertise, a brand name and national promotion.

Gap analysis involves focusing on the potential gaps between identification, interpretation, specification, delivery and reaction to services. Customer satisfaction – satisfying the customer's needs in the delivery of a quality product or service – occurs when these are matched, and the gaps are minimised. Dissatisfaction (a poor quality product or service) occurs when these gaps are broad.

Growth Stage of product life cycle characterised by increasing sales volumes, profitability and competition.

Habituation The phenomenon of the absolute threshold – a stimulus which becomes familiar is no longer perceived

Indirect distribution The use of intermediaries, such as wholesalers and retailers, to supply a product to the customer.

Indirect exporting Use of intermediaries such as export houses, specialist export management firms, complementary exporting (ie using other companies' products to pull your own into an overseas market); ie the outsourcing of the exporting function to a third party.

Industrial markets Business-to-business market (eg the sale of machine tools, consultancy advice etc).

Innovation The process by which new products are brought to market.

Interest group Pressure group, or defensive group (eg trade union) promoting the interests of a group in society.

Interest rate The percentage of a sum lent which the borrower pays to the lender: in other words, the price of money.

Internal green Ps An extension of the marketing mix's 4 Ps to include environmental matters. The 8 Ps are: Product, Promotion, Place, Price, Providing information, Processes, Policies, People.

Introduction Stage of the product life cycle; sometimes referred to as launch. Product sells in small volumes, and sales promotion is expensive.

JIT (just in time) A technique for the organisation of work flows to allow rapid, high quality, flexible production whilst minimising manufacturing waste and stock levels. An item should not be made or purchased until it is needed by the customer or as input to the production process.

Joint venture An arrangement of two or more firms to develop and/or market a product or service; each firm provides a share of the funding and has a say in management.

Licensing An alternative to foreign direct investment by which overseas producers are given rights to use the licensor's production process in return for royalty payments.

Macroeconomics The study of the economy as a whole.

Market A group of consumers who share some particular characteristic which affects their needs or wants, and which makes them potential buyers of a product (Economist Pocket Marketing).

Market A situation in which potential buyers and potential seller of a good or service come together for the purpose of exchange.

Market economy An economy in which economic decisions are made by consumers, producers and owners of factors of production.

Market environment All aspects of a market which affect the company's relationship with its customers and the patterns of competition.

Market forecast The assessment of environmental factors, outside the organisation's control, which will affect the demand for its products/services.

Market management A variant on the product management structure. Instead of individual managers taking responsibility for particular products they take responsibility for particular markets.

Market positioning 'The attempt by marketers to give the product a distinct identity or image so that it will be perceived to have distinctive features or benefits relative to competing products' (Economist Pocket Marketing).

Market research Sometimes used synonymously with marketing research; strictly speaking, however, it refers to the acquisition of primary data about customers and customer attitudes, for example, by asking a sample of individuals to complete a questionnaire.

Market segmentation See segmentation.

Market share One entity's sales of a product or service in a specified market expressed as a percentage of total sales by all entities offering that product or service. A planning tool and a performance assessment ratio.

Marketing audit Part of the position audit which reviews the organisation's products, markets, customers and market environment: 'a comprehensive, systematic, independent and periodic examination of a company's or business unit's marketing environment, objectives, strategies and activities with a view to determining problem areas and opportunities and recommending a plan of action to improve the company's marketing performance' (Kotler)'

Marketing The management process which identifies, anticipates and supplies customer requirements efficiently and profitably.

Marketing mix The set of controllable variables and their levels that the firm uses to influence the target market. The mix comprises product, place, price, promotion (the 4 Ps). In service industries, this can be expanded to include people, processes, and physical evidence.

Marketing orientation A commitment to the needs of customers; 'marketing (focuses) on the idea of satisfying the needs of the customer by means of the product and the whole cluster of things associated with creating, delivering and finally consuming it' (Levitt).

Marketing research The objective gathering, recording and analysing of all facts about problems relating to the transfer and sales of goods and services from producer to consumer or user. Includes market research, price research etc. Marketing research involves the use of secondary data (eg government surveys) in desk research as well as field research (which the firm undertakes itself) to acquire primary data.

Matrix management can be thought of as an integration of the product and market management approaches.

Matrix organisation Organisation in which unity of command is sacrificed to coordination across business functions, eg projects; or in which people report both to product managers and area managers.

Maturity Stage of product life cycle characterised by relatively stable sales volumes and profitability.

Media Non-personal means of communication (eg TV, newspapers etc).

Microeconomics The study of the behaviour of individual economic units, particularly consumers and firms.

Mission An organisation's rationale for existing at all and/or its long-term strategic direction and/or its values; basic function in society in terms of the products and services an organisation produces for its clients.

Mission statement Document in which the mission is formally stated.

MKIS Marketing information system.

Monopoly A market with only one supplier of a product.

Motivation The sum total of the influences which make us do something.

Motives These sit between needs and action. A need motivates a person to take action.

Non-profit marketing Marketing activities undertaken by non-profit making organisations such as charities, government departments etc.

Norms are the values or standards most frequently found in a given society or culture.

Observation A form of qualitative marketing research in which phenomena are observed and recorded.

Oligopoly A market dominated by a few suppliers.

Opinion leader A person who influences the decisions of others.

Perception The process by which data is selected, sorted, organised and interpreted in order to form a meaningful and coherent 'picture' of the world.

Personal selling The presentation of goods or services in person by a sales representative.

PEST factors Factors in an organisation's environment (political-legal, economic, social-cultural, technological).

Pilot test A trial undertaken on a modest scale in order to test the feasibility of something much bigger (Economist Pocket Marketing).

Place Element of the marketing mix detailing how the product/service is supplied to the customer (distribution).

Planning The establishment of objectives, and the formulation, evaluation and selection of the policies, strategies, tactics and action required to achieve them. Planning comprises long-term/strategic planning, and short-term operation planning. The latter is usually for a period of one year.

Positioning See market positioning.

Pressure group Group of people who have got together to promote a particular cause (eg nuclear disarmament). Sometimes called a cause group. However, also used to mean any interest group.

Price This can be defined as a measure of the value exchanged by the buyer for the value offered by the seller.

Price discrimination The practice of charging different prices for a product to different groups of consumers, or to the same consumer for different units of the product. For price discrimination to succeed, segmentation of the market and prevention of resale between segments must both be possible.

Price elasticity of demand A measure of the responsiveness of demand to changes in price: the percentage change in the quantity of a good demanded, divided by the percentage change in its price.

Primary data In market research, this is data collected specifically for the study under consideration (eg by questionnaire).

Product Element of the marketing mix: Anything that can be offered to a market that might satisfy a need or a want. It may be an object, a service, a place, an organisation, or an ideal (Economist Pocket Marketing.)

Product class Broad category of product (eg cars).

Product life cycle A model which suggests that sales of a product grow and mature and then decline as the product becomes obsolete and customer demands change. Applicable in some cases (eg horse-drawn transportation) but perhaps less so in others (eg corn flakes); use with caution. It is defined in the CIMA Official Terminology as 'the pattern of demand for a product over time'.

Product mix (or product assortment or portfolio) All the product lines and items that the company offers for sale.

Promotion Element of the marketing mix which includes all communications with the customer, thus including advertising, publicity, PR, sales promotion etc.

Psychographics, or life style segmentation. This seeks to classify people according to their values, opinions, personality characteristics and interests.

Qualitative research The gathering of data in the form of impressions and narrative.

Quality The totality of features and characteristics of a product or service which bears on its ability to meet stated or implied needs; fitness for use.

Quantitative research The gathering of data in number form.

Questionnaire The primary tool of market research, a device for delivering questions to respondents and recording their answers (Economist Pocket Marketing).

Quota sampling Sampling individuals in a population as they turn up, without looking for specific individuals. Individuals in the quota are selected purely on the basis of meeting some pre-defined criteria: for example, women over 50, male smokers under 25. This is often used in street surveys.

Random sample A sample in which every member of a population has an equal chance of being selected.

Regression A method of predicting values of one variable given values for another variable.

Risk (perceived) The uncertainty that consumers face when they cannot foresee the consequences of their purchase decisions.

Sales promotions Those marketing activities other than personal selling, advertising and publicity, that stimulate consumer purchasing and dealer effectiveness, such as displays, shows and exhibitions, demonstrations and various non-recurrent selling efforts not in the ordinary routine.

Sampling (random) Selecting a sample in such a way that every member of the population has an equal chance of being included.

Sampling (systematic) Selecting every nth item after a random start.

Sampling Taking a limited number of a large population so that by studying the part something may be learnt about the whole. The 'population' is all those people who have the characteristics in which the researcher is interested (Economist Pocket Marketing).

Secondary data In marketing research, data neither collected directly by the user nor specifically for the user, often under conditions not known to the user. Examples include government reports.

Segmentation (market segmentation) The subdividing of the market into distinct and increasingly homogeneous subgroups of customers, where any subgroup can be selected as a target market to be met with a distinct marketing mix.

Services Distinguished from products because they are generally produced as they are consumed, and cannot be stored or taken away. For example, a bus is a product which is used to provide a service (transportation); the service is provided as you are consuming it (ie your trip from A to B). Also the standard of service differs each time it is produced (eg one bus driver may be a better or faster driver than another).

Social responsibility Accepting responsibilities to the various publics of an organisation.

Socialisation The process by which individuals become accustomed to the norms expected of them by society.

Stakeholder Person or group with an interest in organisational activities (eg shareholders, employees, customers, government etc).

Strategy 'A course of action, including the specification of resources required, to achieve a desired objective' (CIMA). Note that different authors use the word to mean different things.

Sub-culture Cultural group within a wider culture (eg UK youth culture). A useful means of segmenting a market.

Substitute A good which can be substituted for another good, or an input which can be substituted for another input.

Sustainability Developing strategies so that the business or entity only uses resources at a rate which allows them to be replenished in order to ensure that they will continue to be available.

Target market Market, or market segment to which an organisation offers goods/services; one or more segments selected for special attention by a business.

Technology The knowledge which allows people to make and do things. Such knowledge often comes from scientific research and can be 'high tech', for example, the use of micro chips. However, technology can also be 'low tech', for example, childproof tops on medicine bottles.

Test marketing Samples of a proposed new product are tried out in areas which are supposed to be representative of the market as a whole.

Time series forecasts Historical (past) data is analysed and trends or patterns are projected into the future.

TQM (Total quality management) An approach to production, and also management, aimed to prevent defective manufacture and to promote continuous improvement. CIMA defines it as 'the continuous improvement in quality, productivity and effectiveness obtained by establishing management responsibility for processes as well as outputs. In this, every process has a process owner and every person in an entity operates within a process and contributes to its improvement'.

Trade/retail audits Marketing research technique, where inspectors are sent to selected shops/outlets to count stock and deliveries, hence to estimate throughput.

Undifferentiated marketing Hope as many people as possible will buy the product, therefore do not segment.

Unique selling proposition (USP) The idea that a product should have at least one unique feature that differentiates it from all its competitors, and that can be easily communicated to customers through advertising (Economist Pocket Marketing).

Utility The value put on what can be purchased with available income.

Variable costs Costs which vary with the level of output produced by a firm.

Wholesaler Intermediary between manufacturers and retailers.

World class manufacturing Term covering diverse issues such as JIT, TQM, human resources management, etc.

World trade organisation (WTO) Set up under the 1993 GATT agreement, the WTO is a body which adjudicates between countries who have disputes over trade.

MULTIPLE CHOICE QUESTIONS

Chapter 1

1   Which of the following activities are 'marketing'?

    1   A 'Retailer of the Year' competition as an incentive to retail outlets to stock and display the company's product.

    2   Keeping abreast of technology in related product areas.

    3   Budgeting for expenditure on advertising.

    4   After-sales service and repair

    A   Activity 1 only
    B   Activities 1, 3 and 4 only
    C   Activities 1, 2 and 3 only
    D   Activities 1, 2, 3 and 4

2   Which of the following products could be identified as the fruit of a 'marketing orientation' to business?

    A   The Sinclair C5
    B   Concorde
    C   The personal stereo
    D   Double glazing

3   The environment of organisations consists of several aspects.

    1   Political/legal environment
    2   Economic/commercial environment
    3   Social/ethical environment
    4   Technological environment

An organisation's policy on Health and Safety at work, for example, would be affected by:

    A   Aspect 3 only
    B   Aspects 1 and 3 only
    C   Aspects 1, 2 and 3 only
    D   Aspects 1, 2, 3 and 4

4   A market oriented firm is one which plans its activities on the principle that

    A   consumers know (and buy) a 'good thing' when they see it

    B   a 'good thing' is by definition one that consumers will want to buy

    C   consumers will buy whatever the sales function tells them is a 'good thing'

    D   consumers will not know (or buy) a 'good thing' without being told by the sales function

BPP
PUBLISHING

5   Which of the following are involved in marketing management?

    1   Planning
    2   Selling
    3   Control
    4   Analysis

    A   2 only
    B   1, 2 and 3 only
    C   1, 3 and 4 only
    D   1, 2, 3 and 4

6   Marketing activities are primarily aimed at:

    A   distributing 'something of value' to buyers and sellers
    B   facilitating and expediting satisfying exchanges
    C   producing a product
    D   exploring consumer behaviour

7   Which of the following are the three 'C's?

    1   Communication
    2   Competition
    3   Customer
    4   Company

    A   1, 2 and 3
    B   2, 3 and 4
    C   1, 3 and 4
    D   1, 2 and 4

8   What are the additional 3 'P's which are said to exist?

    1   Processes
    2   Production
    3   People
    4   Physical evidence

    A   1, 3 and 4
    B   1, 2 and 4
    C   2, 3 and 4
    D   1, 2 and 3

9   Matrix management is:

    A   the separation of product groups into divisions
    B   an integration of product and market management approaches
    C   managers being responsible for particular markets
    D   managers being responsible for particular products

10 'Place' is one element of the marketing mix. Which of the following is a component of 'place'?

    A   Packaging
    B   Merchandising
    C   Allowances
    D   Stockholding

Chapter 2

11 Fairly Green plc has just sent its senior managers on a training course, where they have heard about the 'societal marketing concept'. They have now to look at a set of proposals for:

    1   a new factory – to be carefully landscaped on reclaimed land;

    2   a price rise on several of their ranges of bottled drinks;

    3   a new product: an easy-to-open medicine bottle;

    4   an extension of their soft drink ranges to include low-calorie and caffeine-free varieties

The societal marketing concept might make them think twice about:

    A   proposal 1 only
    B   proposal 3 only
    C   proposals 2 and 3 only
    D   proposals 1, 2 and 4 only

12 Which of the following factors would not generally impose social responsibility on organisations?

    A   The need for new products
    B   Organisational ethics
    C   The organisation's self-interest
    D   Membership of a professional body

13 A marketing audit:

    A   assesses the sales figures
    B   focuses on the marketing budget
    C   checks marketing expenses
    D   focuses on all the relevant marketing activities

14 Demography is a:

    A   study of economic trends
    B   study of cultural trends and values
    C   study of social attitudes
    D   study of population characteristics and trends

Chapter 3

15 Which of the following are environmental issues which will impact upon marketing practices?

1 Ethics
2 Genetic diversity
3 Noise pollution
4 Culture

A 1, 2 and 3
B 2, 3 and 4
C 2 and 3
D All of these

16 Which of the following are considered to be external green Ps'?

1 Partners
2 Paying customers
3 Promotion
4 Price

A 2 and 4
B 1 and 2
C 2, 3 and 4
D 1, 2 and 4

17 A successful Green marketer needs:

A to charge higher prices
B to match price to consumer demand
C to ensure constant advertising
D to ensure complete 'greening' of manufacture

18 Successful quality programmes include the following key characteristics.

1 Customer orientation
2 All products checked before going to consumer (on completion)
3 Total involvement
4 Company decides quality

A 1 and 3
B 2 and 3
C 2, 3 and 4
D 1, 2 and 4

19 Why would employees put pressure on their employer to consider environmental issues?

A To increase sales
B To ensure the survival of the company
C For their own safety
D To ensure higher profits

BPP PUBLISHING

20   Many large companies use political lobbyists. Why is this so?

A   To encourage MPs to sponsor the company
B   To advertise their company to people who matter
C   To ensure money donated to political parties is spent wisely
D   To put their point of view and persuade politicians to do things

Chapter 4

21   Which of the following sales promotions techniques would you expect to be most frequently used in industrial markets?

A   Exhibitions
B   Point of sale display
C   Sponsorship
D   Consumer incentives

22   The subdivision of a market into identifiable buyer groups, or sub-markets, with the aim of reaching such groups with a particular marketing mix, is:

A   marketing fragmentation
B   market segmentation
C   product positioning
D   quota sampling

23   There are two main types of classification of needs. Physiological needs are one type. Which of the following is a physiological need?

A   affection
B   food and drink
C   belonging
D   acceptance

24   Complete the following sentence. 'Culture represents ....'

A   regions
B   language differences
C   religion
D   a group's common interests

25   The ACORN system is:

A   a socio-economic group classification
B   a family structure classification
C   a cultural group classification
D   a sociological grouping

26   Is the Howard-Sheth model:

A   a black box model
B   a personal variable model
C   a theoretical model; or
D   a socio-economic model?

BPP
PUBLISHING

27 Which are the types of organisational buyer behaviour identified by Howard and O'Shaughnessy?

1   Non-problem solving
2   Routinised buyer behaviour
3   Limited problem solving
4   Non-routinised buyer behaviour

A   1 and 2
B   3 and 4
C   2 and 3
D   1 and 4

28 Global marketing strategy stresses the:

A   diversity and uniqueness of consumers in different national cultures
B   similarity and shared nature of consumers worldwide
C   difference in distribution of tastes of consumers
D   diversity of language and customs

29 What is the term used by Kotler to identify the person who suggests a purchase?

A   Influencer
B   Initiator
C   Decider
D   Buyer

30 The 'user' is the person who

A   purchases the product
B   decides on the purchase
C   owns the product
D   consumes the product

Chapter 5

Data for questions 31–33

Delphi Coracles (small boat builders) have identified the following as features of their business.

Features

1   The yard has just been refitted with more space and new machinery

2   The area is being redeveloped as a coastal holiday resort

3   The founder and senior executive, the charismatic Mr Delphi, is approaching retirement, with no obvious successor.

31 Feature 1 is:

A   a strength
B   a weakness
C   an opportunity
D   a threat

32   Feature 2 is:

    A   a strength
    B   a weakness
    C   an opportunity
    D   a threat

33   Feature 3 is:

    A   a strength
    B   a weakness
    C   an opportunity
    D   a threat

34   The profitability of an industry depends, among others, on two of the following features.

    1   Threat of entry
    2   High pricing policy
    3   Bargaining power of suppliers
    4   High sales

    A   1 and 4
    B   2 and 3
    C   1 and 3
    D   2 and 4

Data for questions 35 and 36

	Existing products		*New products*
Existing markets	Consolidation	X	Product development
New markets	Market development		Y

Ansoff's product-market matrix

35   Product-market strategy X is:

    A   market development
    B   market penetration
    C   market segmentation
    D   diversification

36   Product-market strategy Y is:

    A   product positioning
    B   market penetration
    C   market segmentation
    D   diversification

37   Which is the 'odd one out' among the following market strategies?

    A   Segment-specific marketing strategy
    B   Niche marketing strategy
    C   Differentiated marketing strategy
    D   Product-market strategy

38   Backer de Laurie Ltd sells household goods of consistent medium quality at consistently low prices. Their price-quality strategy might be called:

A   an average price-quality strategy
B   a value for money strategy
C   a cheap goods strategy
D   a penetration strategy

39   An estimation of a product's performance (expressed as sale volume revenue and profit) in a future period, at a given price and using a stated method of promotion is:

A   a sales forecast
B   a market forecast
C   the marketing mix
D   the promotional mix

40   Setting an advertising budget is based on the theory of ....

A   percentages
B   estimated capacity
C   diminishing returns
D   sales returns

Chapter 6

41   'The objective gathering, recording and analysing of all facts about problems relating to the transfer and sale of goods and services from producer to consumer or user' (British Institute of Marketing), is a definition of:

A   product research
B   distribution
C   market research
D   marketing research

42   Which of the following is one of the stages in marketing research procedure?

A   Assessment of risk
B   Presentation of a report
C   Presentation of financial information
D   Post-testing

43   Which of the following is not a source of information from the government?

A   Economic trends (monthly)
B   Census of population
C   British business (weekly)
D   Society of Motor Manufacturers and Trades (SMMT)

44   The collection of secondary data is often described as:

    A   field research
    B   primary research
    C   desk research
    D   analysis research

45   Interviewing certain numbers of people in the 16–25 age group is an example of

    A   stratified sampling
    B   quota sampling
    C   systematic sampling
    D   specific sampling

46   The 'funnelling' techniques may be applied when:

    A   designing questionnaires
    B   pilot-testing questionnaires
    C   classifying questionnaires
    D   analysing questionnaires

47   Database marketing relies heavily on the theories underlying

    A   demographic segmentation
    B   psychographic segmentation
    C   geographic segmentation
    D   ACORN and JICNAR groupings

48   Which of the following characterises a marketing information system?

    A   An orderly gathering of information that is not supplied through routine reporting systems such as sales reports.

    B   Conducted on a special-project basis when needed.

    C   Provides a flow of information about such things as distribution costs, prices, sales and advertising expenses.

    D   Has to be computerised to be effective.

49   Attitudes are measured by means of attitude scales and one common type used in marketing research is:

    A   Likert
    B   statistical significance test
    C   discriminant analysis
    D   EPOS

50   Post-testing is used to:

    A   check on advertising copy
    B   check on the success of test marketing
    C   check on test panel's viewpoints
    D   check on the communication effect of advertisements

BPP PUBLISHING

Chapter 7

51 Pro-Duct Mick's has diversified. It uses its metal-tube technology to manufacture bicycles. The Pro-Duct Cycle has many rivals in a mass market. Management's objective is to defend the existing market share of the product. Distribution is intensive. Sales are growing slowly and cash in-flow is high. The marketing budget is aimed mainly at fostering brand loyalty. Profits are actually declining, as the price of the Cycle is lower this year than last and bigger discounts are being given to retailers. R & D are looking into the possibility of modifying the style as a 'BMX'-style model.

What state of the product life cycle has this bike reached?

A Introduction
B Growth
C Maturity
D Decline

52 Based on the Boston Consulting Group matrix of market growth rate/market share, a 'cash cow' is a product where there is:

A low market-growth rate, high market share
B high market-growth rate, high market share
C low market-growth rate, low market share
D high market-growth rate, low market share

53 Which of the following would not be true of a 'question mark' or 'problem child' product?

A A question mark is a low market share activity in high growth markets.

B Question marks consume finance supplied by cash cows.

C A question mark that fails to fulfil its potential becomes a cash cow.

D A question mark may be developed into a star by increasing market share.

54 Market penetration involves:

A marketing existing products into new markets
B entering new markets with new products
C developing new products for existing markets
D increasing market share for existing products in existing markets

55 In product portfolio planning, width describes:

A the closeness of items in the range in terms of marketing
B the number of product lines the company carries
C the total number of items carried divided by the number of product lines
D the closeness of items in the range in terms of production

56   Which step in developing new products involves determining whether the product idea is compatible with company objectives, needs and resources?

A   Product development
B   Evaluation of competitor's efforts
C   Screening
D   Business analysis

57   Which of the following characteristics make marketing services distinctive from the marketing of goods?

1   Ownership
2   Inseparability
3   Perishability
4   Intangibility

A   All these
B   1 and 3
C   1, 3 and 4
D   2 and 4

58   Which of the following would be considered a manufacturer's brand?

A   Sainsbury
B   Tesco
C   St Michael
D   Nissan

59   An example of a convenience good is:

A   a hi-fi unit
B   a newspaper
C   a motorcycle
D   a bicycle

60   A company's product mix is best described as:

A   all products offered by a firm

B   product, distribution, promotion and price

C   all products of a particular type

D   a group of closely related products that are considered a unit because of market, technical and end-use considerations

Chapter 8

61   What is price elasticity?

A   The change in price caused by changes in demand
B   The extent to which a change in price will alter demand
C   The movement of prices in the market place
D   The extent to which a change in supply will alter price

BPP PUBLISHING

62 The price elasticity of demand would be inelastic if:

    A   a decrease in price resulted in an increase in total revenue
    B   an increase in price resulted in a fall in total revenue
    C   revenue remains the same regardless of price
    D   an increase in price resulted in an increase in total revenue

63 A train company charges £65.00 return from Glasgow to London, but the fare from London to Glasgow return is £45.00. This is an example of:

    A   going-rate pricing
    B   cost-plus pricing
    C   price discrimination
    D   full-cost pricing

64 Market skimming when setting prices involves:

    A   setting a low initial price for a new product
    B   matching competitors' prices for a new product
    C   setting a high initial price for a new product
    D   adding a percentage mark-up to costs

65 An oligopoly is where:

    A   relatively small numbers of competitive companies dominate the market
    B   one seller dominates many buyers
    C   there are many buyers and many sellers dealing with identical products
    D   one buyer dominates many sellers

66 A quantum point is:

    A   the pricing at £1.99, £3.99 etc rather than £2, £4

    B   the point a price is kept at to stay around the industry norm

    C   the point at which a price is varied for price discrimination

    D   the price which may be approached but not passed if the price is not to deter consumers

67 Why might a customer react to a price increase by buying more?

    A   They do not really notice prices.
    B   They assume the quality has increased.
    C   They assume the product is very popular.
    D   They have more disposable income.

68 Many firms base price on cost-plus rules. This means:

    A   the average cost of production and allocation of overheads plus a conventional profit margin

    B   adding a fixed margin to the buying-in price

    C   adding a fixed margin to the buying-in price plus a percentage mark-up

    D   the estimated cost plus a profit margin

69   Why may cost-based pricing reflect missed opportunities?

    A   It does not take into account what consumers are willing to pay.
    B   It does not take competitor prices into account.
    C   It de-stabilises prices.
    D   It does not allow for variations in supply.

70   The strategy taken by certain companies in order to ensure investments are recovered as quickly as possible tends to be used when:

    A   competitors cannot increase capacity
    B   the company wants to ensure the contribution is worthwhile
    C   the products are low priced, fast moving
    D   rapid changes in fashion are expected

Chapter 9

71   The primary role of promotion is:

    A   information
    B   manipulation
    C   communication
    D   interpretation

72   What source of information is usually effective for moving many people into the awareness stage of the product adoption process?

    A   Salespeople
    B   Mass communication
    C   Personal sources
    D   Consumer advocates

73   Which communication ingredient costs considerably more than advertising to reach one person, but can provide more immediate feedback?

    A   Publicity
    B   Sales promotion
    C   Personal selling
    D   Public relations

74   Which of the following would not be a 'trade description' under the Trades Description Act 1968, section 2?

    A   The British Standard 'Kite Mark'
    B   £6.95
    C   Solid silver
    D   Only one previous owner

75   Sloe Cellar Ltd is a gin manufacturer. It has just done an appraisal of its advertising. Expressed as 'cost per thousand people reached by the medium', it's doing rather well. Audience research has also shown that people who have seen the advertisement have a good recall of it: they even talk about the advertising campaign in conversation. Sloe Cellar's market share is growing. The only snag is that it is costing them a fortune, and eating into profits badly. The campaign obviously has a problem with:

A   reach
B   frequency
C   wastage
D   impact

Data for questions 76 and 77

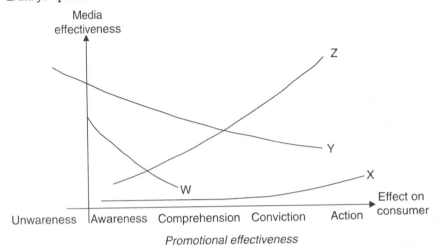

76   Advertising may be represented by:

A   W
B   X
C   Y
D   Z

77   Personal selling may be represented by:

A   W
B   X
C   Y
D   Z

78   Hugh Needsham & Son has two main elements in its promotional mix. It advertises in the national newspapers (through an agency), and it sponsors a football club (through Hugh's personal friendship with the chairman). Which of these activities is a 'below-the-line' method of promotion?

A   The advertising only
B   The sponsorship only
C   Both
D   Neither

79   Telemarketing is:

A   use of the telephone for sales and marketing opportunities
B   use of editorial on television for marketing
C   telephone numbers for customers to call to place an order
D   use of the television for marketing opportunities

80   Pro-Duct Mick's is a popular drain manufacturer. The management team decides to sell more heavily through agents and trade distributors. It will reduce its own sales force. At the same time, it will increase its advertising expenditure to reach small trade users as well as personal 'DIY' consumers. These plans will directly affect the marketing mix through:

    A   promotion only
    B   promotion and place only
    C   promotion, place and price only
    D   promotion, place, price and product

Chapter 10

81   Old Crocks Ltd sells pottery items, through mail order catalogues, advertising (with product-description and order form) in local newspapers and 'mailshot' letters and brochures through the post. This is a form of:

    A   merchant supply
    B   direct supply
    C   short channel supply
    D   long channel distribution

82   A channel network which has more than one outlet but fewer than the total number of intermediaries who could/would like to carry the manufacturers' product offers adequate market coverage, with control and cost advantage. This is called:

    A   short channel distribution
    B   intensive distribution
    C   exclusive distribution
    D   selective distribution

83   Just In Time (JIT) techniques of production management operate on the principle that stocks should be kept to a minimum so as to avoid the various costs of stockholding and tying up resources in idle assets. Three elements of JIT are:

    1   prompt delivery of materials and components from suppliers
    2   scheduling production runs to meet specific customer orders
    3   low stockholding of finished goods items

For JIT systems to operate efficiently, it will be important to have:

    A   a large number of raw materials and component suppliers for each material or component item

    B   centralised management of production operations

    C   a fairly limited product range, to facilitate stock control

    D   a high quality of raw materials and components, and high quality of production

Askham Bryan College
LIBRARY BOOK

84   The traditional channel for distributing consumer products is producer to:

    A   wholesaler to retailer to consumer
    B   retailer to consumer
    C   wholesaler to consumer
    D   retailer to wholesaler to consumer

85   In the chain of distribution, agents:

    A   earn commission on sales they make
    B   act as intermediaries stocking a range of goods
    C   purchase and re-sell the manufacturers' goods at a profit
    D   pay an initial fee and a share of sales revenue

86   In certain circumstances direct selling is the preferred channel of distribution. This may be because:

    1   intermediaries may be too expensive
    2   it may involve specialised transport to final customer
    3   potential buyers are geographically concentrated
    4   the assortment of products may be insufficient.

    A   1 and 3
    B   all of these
    C   1, 2 and 3
    D   2 and 4

87   Why have selective and exclusive distribution been criticised by the European commission?

    A   As monopolistic.
    B   As increasing consumer costs.
    C   As being too dealer oriented.
    D   As a restraint on competition.

88   When might rail transport be chosen as the mode of transport?

    A   for bulky loads over short distances
    B   for bulky loads over long distances
    C   for high value, small unit loads
    D   for high value, low volume loads

89   An essential component of JIT systems is:

    A   emphasis on error detection
    B   multiple suppliers
    C   synchronisation
    D   algorithmically derived schedules

90   The 'lean' firm is involved in producing products which are:

1   responsive to change
2   standardised
3   profitable
4   produced in large quantities

A   1 and 3
B   1, 2 and 3
C   2 and 4
D   2, 3 and 4

Chapter 11

91   When a product is in the growth phase of the product life cycle it has the following effect on price and profit.

A   High prices and high fixed costs, so low profits
B   High prices and increasing profit margins
C   Falling prices and high profit margins
D   Low prices and falling profits

92   Marketers refer to the 'shakeout' which is:

A   at the final decline stage where products are dropped

B   between R & D and introduction when products never make it at all

C   the dropping of products when competitors enter the market

D   between introduction and growth stages of the PLC when products disappear from the scene

93   Arguments in favour of product standardisation include:

1   consumer mobility
2   varied conditions of use
3   greater sales
4   technological complexity

A   1, 3 and 4
B   1 and 4
C   2 and 3
D   2, 3 and 4

94   Which stage of the product life cycle is said to last longer than any other?

A   Decline
B   Growth
C   Maturity
D   Introduction

BPP PUBLISHING

95   How may a company best defend its market share?

    A   By constantly cutting prices.
    B   By changing the product's appearance.
    C   By changing the product's name.
    D   By emphasising superior quality.

96   In a declining market, a competitor cannot easily leave the product market as their brand generates a high proportion of their profits. This means your company may find itself involved in:

    A   the raising of prices
    B   a price war
    C   spending less on promotion
    D   higher purchases

97   Which of the following are assumptions of the PLC concept?

1   Products have finite life spans

2   Many markets never reap the benefits of economies of scale

3   Unit costs fall as production volume increases

4   Products with a high market share will be more profitable than those with a low share

    A   1, 3 and 4
    B   1, 2 and 3
    C   1, 2 and 4
    D   all of these

98   Marketing the same product to all countries is possible when:

1   the company is well known world-wide
2   the products are not culture sensitive
3   the product is completely new
4   economies of scale are significant

    A   1, 2 and 3
    B   2, 3 and 4
    C   1, 2 and 4
    D   2 and 4

99   Which major entry made to a foreign market does franchising belong to?

    A   Investment entry
    B   Contractual entry
    C   Export entry
    D   Direct entry

100 Which of the following are advantages of the sole ownership form of investment overseas?

1   Lower level of commitment
2   Lower labour costs
3   Avoidance of import taxes
4   Lower transport costs

A   all of these
B   1, 3 and 4
C   2, 3 and 4
D   1, 2 and 4

BPP
PUBLISHING

EXAM STYLE
QUESTIONS

Chapter 1

1 UNNECESSARY NEEDS

It has been commonly said that marketing is satisfying customer needs at a profit. Yet critics of marketing have said that marketing creates unnecessary needs and wants. How would you attempt to explain these apparently contradictory views?

Chapter 2

2 SOCIAL TRENDS

(a) What is the significance of the social environment for the marketer?

(b) Select two significant social trends and discuss their marketing implications for either a grocery retailer or a bank.

(c) Provide an annotated bibliography or relevant data sources on social trends.

Chapter 3

3 CHANGING VALUES

(a) In what ways can pressure groups be said to represent the changing values of society?

(b) In what ways can businesses respond to pressure groups?

Guidance note

It is too simplistic to say that pressure groups represent the values of society as a whole. It is necessary to analyse the different types of pressure groups in order to understand the different constituencies of interest that they represent.

Chapter 4

4 INDIVIDUAL AND INDUSTRIAL CUSTOMERS

Many textbooks suggest that customer behaviour, when the customer is an organisation, is quite different from customer behaviour when the customer is an individual consumer. How far do you agree? To what extent is it possible to discern similarities? How would your approach differ if you were responsible for marketing any one of the following products or services to both individual and industrial customers?

(a) Window-cleaning services
(b) Mobile telephones
(c) Floor-coverings

5 PASSIVE BUSINESS BUYERS

You have just read a newspaper article which is highly critical of many industrial/organisational buyers because they are too passive and simply react to the supplier's marketing mix. Compose a 'Letter to the Editor' in which you assess the accuracy of the criticism and identify the features of a more accurate model for industrial buying.

Chapter 5

6 SEGMENTATION APPROACHES

You are working for a newly-appointed senior manager who has never had anything to do with marketing before: he has already expressed scepticism about the time and effort involved in classifying market segments for your business. Generate a document which seeks to justify the benefits and uses of market segmentation in general terms; illustrate your argument by showing (with reasons) what kind of segmentation approach could be appropriate for any two of the following:

(a)   bottled mineral water
(b)   a hotel chain
(c)   toothpaste
(d)   personal computers.

7 APPROACHES TO SEGMENTATION

Approaches to segmentation can be classified as follows.

(a)   A priori segmentation – ie segments are identified prior to any market research being undertaken, or post hoc segmentation, where customers are grouped into segments on the basis of research findings.

(b)   Segmentation according to objective variables (like quantity purchase, frequency of purchases etc) or subjective variables (such as degree of brand loyalty, life-style, etc).

If you were a marketing consultant, which approach or combination of approaches would you recommend, and why, for segmenting the actual/potential market for either an airline or a bicycle manufacturer?

Write your answer in the form of a report addressed to your client's board of directors.

Chapter 6

8 SAMPLING AND STATISTICS

Sampling and Statistics by Paul Hague and Paul Harris (London: Kogan Page, 1993) claims that 'Quality market research is the result of care and attention to four vital aspects of the process':

(a)   Asking the right question
(b)   Finding the right person
(c)   Analysing the data
(d)   Interpreting the data

Produce a short guide, written as if it were friendly advice to your marketing colleagues, showing what can go wrong in each of these four aspects, and including some positive guidance on precautions which can minimise the likelihood of mistakes.

BPP PUBLISHING

Chapter 7

9   PP TELEVISION LTD

PP Television Ltd (PPT) has been a manufacturer of television sets since its inception. It prospered greatly during the years in which demand exceeded supply and the ownership (including hire and rentals), of black and white TV sets rose from 0% to over 90% of all UK households.

Today the television set market in the UK could be said to be saturated and the product to be in the decline stage of its PLC. Nevertheless PPT still have a profitable business and say they have achieved this by anticipating and pre-empting market changes.

How might PPT have changed their marketing mix at different stages of the PLC to meet the needs of different market places?

Chapter 8

10   PRICING NEW PRODUCTS

Write a report to your marketing manager identifying the factors which should be taken into consideration when establishing prices for an innovative line of products your company has recently developed for the computer software industry.

Chapter 9

11   CIM RADIO TRENT TOUR

CIM RADIO TRENT TOUR

Wednesday 18 January 1995

Following a successful visit to the New 96 Trent FM last May, we are repeating this exciting event especially for you.

Commercial radio is a very important part of the local advertising scene and is very effective in what it does. The new style Trent has proved to local people how successful a radio station it is by providing listeners with what they want to hear.

The CIM Nottingham branch has organised a presentation and tour on Wednesday 18 January at 6.30 pm. Paul Cranwell, Sales Manager at the station, will be hosting the evening. He will take us on a tour of the station showing the internal workings of a live commercial radio station. We will be looking at live studios and the recording studios and some lucky people will be given the opportunity to record a script for a commercial.

As last year, we are very limited to places due to the tight conditions at Radio Trent, so please only apply if you are seriously considering attending. Please apply early as tickets will be given on a first come, first served basis and only one application is allowed per form.

The cost of the event is £3.00 per person and this includes a buffet.

Above is an actual extract from a CIM Branch circular. Explain how this event and the surrounding publicity successfully uses and integrates various elements of the promotional mix in achieving the aims of both the CIM Branch and the commercial radio station concerned.

12 ADVERTISING AND SELLING

Your company's sales manager has presented a report to the marketing director complaining that the money spent on advertising and sales promotion would be better spent on the sales force.

Your marketing director has now asked you to prepare notes that he can use in his reply to explain how advertising and sales promotional activity actually help the sales force in their selling tasks.

Chapter 10

13 LOGISTICS

What is the role and function of physical distribution management in connecting products to consumers?

14 JIT QUICK

Your company supplies components for the automotive industry. Your largest customer has recently announced that it is moving towards a lean manufacturing system which will adopt within one year 'just in time' principles of component delivery.

Write a report to your marketing director stating the implications of this announcement and suggesting what your company should do in order to be prepared for this change within one year.

Chapter 11

15 PLC MODIFICATION

Using a product of your choice, explain the changes in emphasis that occur in the promotional strategy at each stage of the product life cycle.

16 BETTER BANANAS

Improved bananas with a wider range of flavours and a longer shelf-life have been developed by scientists.

'We have now developed bananas with an in-built resistance to diseases having looked at 1,000 varieties of seeds to find those with natural anti-fungal properties', said a leading researcher, *'the result has been that we have identified the relevant genes and are now able to add them to the banana's genetic make-up'.*

Bananas are currently harvested while still green and ripening is induced artificially by the importers after transportation. Although a number of different varieties of bananas are cultivated, no attempt is currently made to differentiate them in the market place in terms of flavour – despite the fact that flavours are quite distinctive ranging from small, hard texture, bitter tasting 'jungle' bananas to large, soft, sweet tasting plantation cultivated bananas. Growers tend to be

BPP PUBLISHING

relatively small and importers very large, two actually owning and operating their own fleets of specially constructed ships. Growers contract with the importer to sell their crops at a price which is determined before the growing season begins.

The genetically improved varieties now being developed which can ripen naturally, will taste better and have a longer shelf-life. By the year 2002 it is expected that most commercially grown bananas throughout the world will be grown in this way.

Assume that the above scenario is exactly as anticipated by the year 2002.

(a)   How might the marketing mix for bananas have changed from the point of view of:

    (i)   Growers
    (ii)   Importers
    (iii)   Retailers?

(b)   How do you feel these changes might have influenced customers' needs?

17   EXPORTING SUCCESS

(a)   As marketing advisor to a medium sized company, provide the board, in note form, with an outline of the factors they should consider before marketing internationally for the first time.

(b)   What steps would you advise the company to take in order to ensure exporting success?

ANSWERS TO MULTIPLE CHOICE QUESTIONS

NOTES

1	D		39	A
2	C		40	C
3	D		41	D
4	B		42	B
5	C		43	D
6	B		44	C
7	B		45	B
8	A		46	A
9	B		47	B
10	D		48	C
11	B		49	A
12	A		50	D
13	D		51	C
14	D		52	A
15	C		53	C
16	B		54	D
17	B		55	B
18	A		56	C
19	C		57	A
20	D		58	D
21	A		59	B
22	B		60	A
23	B		61	B
24	D		62	D
25	A		63	C
26	C		64	C
27	C		65	A
28	B		66	D
29	B		67	B
30	D		68	D
31	A		69	A
32	C		70	D
33	B		71	C
34	C		72	B
35	B		73	C
36	D		74	B
37	D		75	C
38	B		76	C

77	D		89	C
78	B		90	A
79	A		91	B
80	D		92	D
81	B		93	B
82	D		94	C
83	D		95	D
84	A		96	B
85	A		97	A
86	C		98	D
87	D		99	B
88	B		100	C

ANSWERS TO EXAM STYLE QUESTIONS

1   **UNNECESSARY NEEDS**

Effective marketing takes the approach that the customer is the most important person to the company. Its success is based on satisfying the needs and wants of customers through offering products and services that marketing research has proved they demand.

This basic principle of marketing confirms that marketing satisfies customer needs and does not create unnecessary ones. The structure of a marketing department emphasises the importance of marketing research, which plays the role of gathering information required to identify marketing problems and opportunities. A large amount of this research is gathered from customers' ideas on:

(a)   products on sale;
(b)   performance of products;
(c)   problems in performance;
(d)   development of products; and
(e)   new products customers would like to see on the market.

Analysis of collected data allows organisations to identify market trends, forecast sales and achieve or maintain a competitive advantage.

Customers' wants and needs, when recognised, are put to product research for the generation of new product ideas that satisfy demands.

Organisations are in business fundamentally to maximise profits through satisfying customer needs. It is not feasible to create products/services that would be extremely profitable if there is doubt that customers would purchase them. That propensity to purchase has to be proved through research as the product that consumers want to buy. The risks are too high in creating a product and then unnecessarily trying to create a need through marketing tactics. Any company which purposely practises this approach can expect major problems. No amount of advertising and promotion can make a person buy something they really do not want to purchase.

Understanding the buying behaviour of customers is complex. Organisations that have a full understanding of why customers purchase will have added advantage over less aware competitors.

Marketing strategies do have the ability to affect buyer behaviour. An example of this would be marketeers offering a product mix that gave the customer more choice and range, a situation that may have an effect on the buying process. Marketing communication and image, for example, can often affect the consumers' decision. Marketing strategies aimed at influencing customers may lead to a motivation on the part of the consumer to become more aware of or even to purchase the product; however the first stimulation of the consumer's needs or wants is not due to marketing activity but to the individual's thoughts. Marketing then aims to raise awareness and offer satisfactions to the wants and needs. This type of influence is far from the view of critics that marketing creates unnecessary needs and wants.

If we now concentrate on individual influences on behaviour towards buying, we will understand that unnecessary needs cannot be created by marketing.

Factors that have a major influence on consumers' individual wants and buying behaviour are as follows.

(a)   Psychological factors – attitude, personality and perception influence the basic behaviour of individuals' interpretation and subconscious selection.

(b)   Lifestyle variables – needs and wants are influenced by individuals' attitudes, interests and opinions and the environment in which they live.

(c)   Demographic variables – age, gender, income, education and occupational factors have a bearing on the types of products consumers want to purchase.

(d)   Economic situation – however much marketing influences needs, the individual's economic buying power will be the deciding factor as to whether the purchase will be made or not.

These individual influences provide strong evidence that marketing does not create unnecessary needs and wants. Organisational strategies aim to satisfy customer needs; if they perform this successfully then profits will be maximised (the company's overall objective) as without profits they will cease trading.

Although it is an understandable statement that marketing creates unnecessary needs and wants, it is not justifiable. It is evident that marketing can influence buyer behaviour but the customer's decision that he or she needs or wants a product or service is created by individual influences and not marketing.

2   SOCIAL TRENDS

(a)   The social environment comprises the cultural and social influences in a society which impinge on an individual's attitudes and behaviour. It is important for markets to understand the social environment in order to understand the complex factors which influence an individual's purchase decisions. The social environment is constantly changing and differs between countries. For example, family sizes, participation in leisure activities and attitudes towards marriage have all changed over time and affect the marketing of products differently in different countries.

(b)   Two social trends are considered here: (i) the greater importance attached to quality, and (ii) the growing importance of instant gratification.

(i)   Growing importance of quality. As societies become wealthier, their members are no longer prepared to accept mediocre standards of goods or services. This is reflected in retailing in the following ways:

(1)   a desire for better quality products, in terms of the percentage which are faulty

(2)   a requirement for a range of products which can be described as 'premium'

(3)   better quality service provision, for example in the manner in which staff serve customers

(4)   extended warranties for consumer durable goods

(ii)   Increasing desire for instant gratification. Many observers have noted that buyers in Western countries seek satisfaction of their needs immediately rather than at some time in the future. Retailers have identified this social trend and have responded in the following ways.

(1)   Greater availability of goods on demand, without the need to order in advance. This has been facilitated by the development of 'just-in-time' distribution systems.

(2)   Instant credit facilities, which avoid the need for customers to wait until they can pay cash for a product.

(3)   Faster service in stores, for example many supermarkets give guarantees that additional check-outs will be opened if queues develop.

(c)   Bibliography of data on social trends

Social Trends: an annual summary of government statistics which lists a range of indicators of social trends.

Family Expenditure Survey: an annual report of government research into consumer expenditure.

Target Group Index: an annual report of research into a panel of consumers which analyses their attitudes and spending patterns.

ICD National Consumer Database. The ICD is one of a number of companies which regularly collects information about spending patterns and attitudes and can provide data tailored to the requirements of individual companies.

3   CHANGING VALUES

(a)   To address this question, we should consider the different types of pressure groups. Pressure groups can be divided into sectional groups and promotional groups.

Sectional groups exist to promote the common interests of their members over a wide range of issues. Trades unions and employers associations fall into this category: they represent their members' views to government on a wide range of issues such as proposals for new employment legislation, import controls which may threaten their members' interests, and Sunday trading laws. This type of pressure group frequently offers other benefits to its members such as legal representation for individual members, the dissemination of information through newsletters and specially negotiated discounts on members' purchases from various organisations.

Promotional groups on the other hand, represent a specific issue rather than a specific group of people. The issue could be nuclear disarmament (represented by the CND), protection of the environment (Friends of the Earth) or more road building (the British Roads Federation). Some promotional groups are permanently fighting for a general cause, whereas others are set up to achieve a specific objective and are dissolved when this objective is met (for example, a pressure group set up to fight a specific new road scheme).

Sectional groups tend to pursue policies which are of general acceptability to their members, although doubts are still often raised about the extent to which the stated policy of the group is representative of the membership at large. For example, although trade unions generally campaign for broadly socialist policies, they generally include in their memberships significant numbers of Conservative Party voters. By contrast, promotional groups enjoy much stronger support from their members, who are attracted to the group because of the single cause which it stands for. However, although such groups may achieve significant media publicity, it must be remembered that they often represent the interests of a small minority of active members of the population, rather than the population as a whole.

(b)   Businesses can respond to pressure groups in a number of ways, which can be seen in terms of enlightened self-interest.

(i)   One simple way in which a business can react is not to respond at all, ignoring the existence of a pressure group. This may be quite appropriate for some fringe pressure groups with little popular support. However, if the group is mounting a well organised campaign for a widely recognised cause, this can be a dangerous strategy.

(ii) Businesses may choose to consult with pressure groups. Not only is this good as a public relations exercise, companies can pick up a lot of valuable information from pressure groups. Information gained can include new technical developments, as well as being able to monitor public attitudes towards a cause.

(iii) Businesses may extend consultation to the point where it becomes co-operation. For example, car manufacturers may co-operate with environmental pressure groups to monitor the effects of vehicle exhaust emissions.

(iv) Businesses may formally involve pressure groups in their planning processes. A company seeking to build a new factory on a green field site may involve a nature conservation group in the planning of the factory. By allowing early involvement, the company could avoid expensive problems at a later stage. Environmentally sensitive solutions might be developed more cheaply at the planning stage than if it were left to a public planning enquiry. There is also the public relations benefit to the company of having been seen to involve a pressure group in its new development.

(v)   Companies can accommodate the concerns of a pressure group by incorporating suggested improvements in its business practices. An example would be where a company stops including a harmful substance in its packaging materials, following a pressure group's revelation of health risks involved.

(vi) Finally, businesses may negotiate with a pressure group. This may be appropriate where the pressure has significant power. For example, the pressure group CAMRA is in a powerful position to influence its members' choice of drinking establishments.

4   INDIVIDUAL AND INDUSTRIAL CUSTOMERS

Introduction

As with many aspects of behaviour, it is overly simplistic to say that customer behaviour is different when considering individuals and organisations. There are areas of difference and areas of similarity. These will be considered first, then the application to the marketing of window cleaning services will be compared and contrasted in the two situations.

Areas of difference

The marketing approach is different when marketing products/services to individuals. The individual customer may be very much more easily emotionally swayed than the industrial customer, as there is likely to be less formalisation about the purchasing decision process. One can appeal to the individual's emotional personality which is affected by things such as sexuality, ego, status and general appeal. In contrast, the industrial customer is often claimed to be very rational, looking for quality, value for money, ease of use and durability.

Other areas of difference lie in the significantly smaller market for organisations (there are many fewer organisations than individuals), the existence of reciprocal buying agreements and the possibility that the organisational buyer may have enormous purchasing power which may allow them to play one supplier off against another.

Areas of similarity

On the other hand, both situations involve people making buying decisions. The organisation has a formalised Decision Making Unit (DMU) with roles allocated to paid individuals who perform the roles of initiator, gatekeeper, influencer, decider, buyer, and so on. At first sight this may appear to look like a difference between the two situations, but individuals are commonly influenced by their own DMU (usually called the family and friends) so both are open to group pressures and influences. Both situations normally operate under limited budgets, so both involve decisions about value for money, and both tend to have purchasing areas where inertia is a significant determinant. In the organisational setting this may be dealing with a single paper supplier as a matter of habit, while the individual may buy 'own brand' baked beans without thought in the course of the weekly one-stop supermarket shopping expedition.

Marketing window cleaning services

If window cleaning services were to be marketed to an individual the window cleaner could appeal to an individual's emotional side by promoting benefits of having 'nice clean' windows regularly, even in the cold weather when the customers may find the idea of washing them themselves very unappealing. If the window cleaner were selling the service to an industry he may promote the value for money the industry was receiving – a good quality service, regular and reliable and cheap in relation to this.

Marketers must aim to keep the differences in customer behaviour in mind when promoting services, as an organisational buyer may not view the benefits in the same way as an individual. In particular, there is a need to be aware that in the individual's case the customer and user are likely to be the same person (or members of the same family group – implicitly very small) whereas the organisational customer (payer) is not the sole user. It may therefore be more important to impress the purchasing officer with promises of regularity of visits, low cost etc than the individual who may be more directly concerned with the cleanliness of the windows!

5   PASSIVE BUSINESS BUYERS

J Bloggs
1 The Common
Xton

5 October 2000

The Editor

Xton Times

Dear Sir,

I write in response to the article you carried in 'The Times' last week regarding organisational buyers. In the article criticisms were levelled at these persons that would appear to be rather one-sided and somewhat lacking in accuracy and completeness.

Your article accused them of being passive and of reacting 'simply to the suppliers' marketing mix'. Historically there may have been a degree of truth in such an accusation, especially where the purchaser was facing a situation where there was a high degree of demand for products and services. We have also experienced in the past phases where the relationship between organisational buyer and supplier was far from co-operative with both sides attempting to 'put one over the opposition'.

Nowadays we live in a very different economy which is highly competitive. This has led many organisations to review their relationships with suppliers and to actively seek joint, long-term solutions to problems, minimising the distortions caused by fluctuations in the future market. At first sight this could appear to be passive to an outsider but it makes a great deal of sense to ensure future supplies and reduce the chance of being 'held to ransom'. Thus long-term advantages accrue to both parties and it becomes a 'win-win game'.

Some may argue that this could be at the expense of the final consumer – but the gains made by such approaches as Total Quality Management or Just in Time are passed on to the consumer directly in terms of improved reliability, quality and cost.

Examples of highly successful collaborations between suppliers and buyers include The Body Shop, Toyota, Tesco – none of which can be viewed as 'passive and reactive' laggards in the competitive marketplace.

A further objection to the article is the implication that the buyer acts alone on behalf of the organisation. Few things could be further from the truth as the buyer is only one part of what is usually called the Decision Making Unit (DMU). This will also comprise 'gatekeepers' (who control the flow of data and access), 'influencers' (specialists who will advise and evaluate), 'users' (the people who actually process the bought material), and 'deciders' (who exercise the real power, often accountants or senior executives). It is not uncommon for there to be 'differences of opinion' between members of the DMU so the situation may be analogous to the swan: serenity on the surface disguising frantic activity below the waterline!

Additionally, a buyer may be responsible for the purchase of a huge range of goods and materials: it could range from multi-million pound items to lavatory paper! In the interests of common sense and sanity, some of these may be undertaken as a 'routine re-buy' decision.

One popular model to illuminate the organisational buyer's role has been put forward by the American Marketing Association. It is usually displayed diagrammatically.

Within the
organisation

Cell 1: Purchasing agent   Cell 2: The Buying Centre

Buying department ———————————|——————————— Other departments

Cell 3: Professionalism   Cell 4: Organisational environment

Outside the
organisation

This representation emphasises some of the complexities of the buying role and it can encompass many of the issues with which organisational buying is concerned: cost, continuity of supply, after-sales service, all operating within limitations set by organisational policy and the legal and moral framework. In addition, technology is changing the marketplace on a daily basis.

Be fair! Organisational buyers do a difficult job brilliantly well: the real measure of their success is to be seen every time we go out shopping!

Yours faithfully,

J Bloggs

6 SEGMENTATION APPROACHES

To: Mr A Manager, Chief Executive

From: Andrew Student

Date: 2 October 2000

Subject: Market Segmentation

The market is a highly competitive place where companies seek to gain competitive advantage by getting closer to their customers and getting to know them. This is done through market research. In some cases, it is possible to interview/research every person or body that you deal with, for example in a census, but in others, it is necessary to segment people or bodies into different groups that can then be researched, analysed, marketed to and sold to.

Market segmentation is therefore an essential approach to make our marketing messages more effective communications. It is a device which allows us to do all of the following.

(a)   Develop products specifically for different segments of the market.

(b)   Identify market areas which may be ripe for expansion/development/ exploitation.

(c)   Improve our chances of market penetration.

(d)   Diversify profitably into new market areas.

In order for a segmentation system to be useful it should split the population up into sections which are large and substantial enough to warrant attention. The segments should also be measurable, stable and accessible.

There are a number of well-tried approaches to segmentation which have proved to be of use in the marketing area – primarily for consumer (non-industrial) products.

(a)   Geographical – where is your market?
(b)   Demographic – what are they like?
(c)   Psychographic – what are their interests, attitudes, opinions?
(d)   Socio-economical – what is their social class (A,B,C1,C2,D,E)?
(e)   'Loyalty set' – do they know your product?
(f)   Residential – what type of property do they live in (for example, ACORN)?

Examples

(a)   Bottled mineral water

       In the case of a firm bottling mineral water, certain qualities of the product mix will appeal to certain sections of the population, as not everybody buys/uses it. In classifying your market segment and identifying your customers, it is possible for you to 'target market' your product, thus saving time, money, and resources by not having to appeal (or attempting to appeal) to a mass market.

Your research might show that your market is largely southern based, bought/used by 20–45 year olds, ABC's, who know the product and identify with its health image, who live in terraced housing (ACORN Class 4) and who are usually female.

Thus by segmenting you can gain a profile of your market and tailor promotional material to that segment. Alternatively we could modify the product and target other segments – such as older, health-conscious customers.

(b)   Personal computers

In this case you can target both a consumer market (individuals) and a business one. At the moment personal computers are relatively cheap (hence the Christmas advertising on TV). However, people who buy them are a specific section of the population. Through your research, you may find that your segmentation techniques discover that PC users are social class BC, based in cities, have 'economic consumer' profiles, read into the subject, know what they are buying, are male, aged 18–30, and may even be 'yuppies' (young, urban professionals), and home owners.

You may be able to sell your PCs to an industrial market. SIC (Standard Industrial Classification) codes all industries: for example, food, drink and tobacco manufacturing is found under 'Other manufacturing' class 41/42, division 4. You may segment your market by its size, for example large/small industry by its buying nature (credit, cash), by its DMU (decision making unit; for example how many people there are involved).

Thus by segmenting your market and finding out exactly what type of customer you have, you can pinpoint or 'target' your marketing mix to suit. Advertising and marketing is now regarded as a science.

7   APPROACHES TO SEGMENTATION

From: C Boardman

To: Squarewheels Cycle Company

Date: 23 November 2000

Subject: Segmentation of markets

Introduction

Segmentation is the process of breaking down a broad and varied market into groups. Successful segmentation results in sub-groups which differ significantly from each other in their requirements, but which are large enough to make it profitable to develop separate marketing or product offerings. In a successful segmentation exercise the sub-groups should also be accessible and identifiable as well as being measurable and stable.

The idea of segmenting the bicycle market is of prime importance to an organisation seeking to target customers. Your market is made up of many different kinds of customers and it is important for you to know who these customers are and how to sell the products to them. Segmentation holds the key for you and successful bicycle sales.

A priori or post hoc segmentation?

In a priori segmentation segments are identified in advance of any market research while in post hoc segmentation the segments are determined following research and based upon it.

Advantages of a priori segmentation

The advantages of this approach are that it is relatively cheap and quick. We sit down in advance and decide which groups we are going to target – in the case of the cycle market we might decide to 'go for' segments based on age (children, adult commuters, adult off-roaders) and as you can see such a decision could be made very swiftly.

Disadvantages of a priori segmentation

The great weakness of this approach is the danger that we get the segment wrong – or, even more likely, fall into the trap of assuming that, for example, all off-roaders are the same. In other words a priori segmentation is limited by the imagination and knowledge of the people making the a priori decision.

Advantages of post hoc segmentation

Post hoc segmentation has the advantages of starting with a relatively clear sheet and a relative absence of preconceptions. It is possible to undertake research specifically to identify groups which satisfy the characteristics of successful segments as listed above (that is, different, sizeable, identifiable, measurable, accessible and stable).

Disadvantages of post hoc segmentation

It is likely to be time-consuming, expensive and may not identify any segments which were not evident to experienced observers of the market already.

Segmentation by objective or subjective variables?

This classification draws a distinction between segments based on hard, objective data such as purchasing patterns derived from existing sales figures, and subjective variables based on less tangible aspects such as lifestyle or benefit derived from purchase.

Advantages of objective segmentation

The main benefit of objective segmentation is its relative certainty – if we are operating by age or purchasing pattern we are dealing with known variables.

Disadvantages of objective segmentation

The objective data may not be relevant. In the case of bicycles it is unlikely that there will be any significant pattern of bicycle purchase as most people buy bikes rarely. We may also have to consider the fact that many or even most purchasers of children's bikes are parents or adults and hence the picture can become even more confused.

Advantages of subjective segmentation

This acknowledges that the motivation of purchasers may be emotional and varied. In the case of cycles the benefit sought could be a number of different types – some seek fitness, others want cheap transport, some wish to pose while yet others may wish for an excuse to wear lycra shorts in public.

Disadvantages of subjective segmentation

The notion of lifestyle may prove difficult to isolate and target in segmentation terms.

Conclusion

In the context of the cycle industry I would recommend a mixture of a priori and subjective segmentation. The a priori approach will encompass a degree of objective analysis – age, socio-economic grouping, postcode and so on while the subjective will concentrate on the crucial lifestyle aspect which is likely to prove the most potent segmentation tool of all. This should ensure the most effective coverage of the significant sections of the bicycle buying public without engaging in expensive and time-consuming research to establish who might be worth targeting with lifestyle analysis. Hence we obtain the most useful analysis at least cost.

8   SAMPLING AND STATISTICS

A SHORT GUIDE TO RECOGNISING AND AVOIDING MISTAKES IN SAMPLING AND STATISTICS

Introduction

Market research is an essential requirement of modern business practice. It enables the business to get close to its customers, to find out their needs and wants, to tailor and develop products to their requirements and to establish an appropriate marketing mix. It gives the company a competitive advantage by being able to 'sell products that don't come back to people that do'. It helps to give the company a unique selling proposition (USP) and ultimately an advantage over all other competitors in the market. Therefore market research, or to be more precise, quality market research is vital to a company's growth and success. This care and attention must at all times be taken to ensure that the research bears beneficial results. Bias in any stage of research can render the whole, expensive process useless. Equally, poor or shoddy (wrong) analysis of data can lead to faulty interpretations and hence bad business decisions.

So, what can go wrong in the four vital aspects of quality market research?

(a)   Asking the right question

The first thing you must do with all research is to define your objectives: what do you want to know?

Without defining your objectives at the start you may go through costly research and come up with the right answer – but to a question which you didn't need to ask in the first place. The best way to ask the right question is to audit and assess your position: where are you now? where do you want to go? how can you get there? Having defined the objective we come to the equally important issue of the way in which you ask the questions.

In qualitative research open-ended questions yield important information about attitudes, motivation and values. Open questions can be very useful early in the process to make sure no relevant themes or issues are missed. However, open questions can give rise to woolly answers – you also need to analyse the essentials in order to use them in a measurable way.

Questions can be structured to give answers which are easy to handle and analyse by using closed (yes/no) questions. A development is to use dichotomous questions (good/bad; tasty/dull) and, taking the idea still further, you can use multiple choice which allows the respondent to make more subtle judgements such as very good, good, ok, poor, bad. Similarly attitudes can be elicited using Likert scales (strongly agree, agree, maybe, disagree, strongly disagree). All these approaches allow you to obtain relevant information which is fairly easily useable.

Irrespective of the question form used:

(i)   avoid ambiguity – test the question out in a pilot study;

(ii)   avoid bias and leading – don't let them know what the 'right' answer is;

(iii)   use language the respondent can understand;

(iv)   keep it focused on the objectives.

(b)   Finding the right person

It is a waste of time to ask the right question only to find it was the wrong sample – all findings then become useless. You must first decide who you want/need to ask. Who can give the information you need? Who will be representative of the group you are considering?

Many sources are available and it is essential that you target the right ones to avoid wasting money and effort. If you are trying to improve a soap powder, ask the buyers and users. It is pointless to ask people who have no experience or no part to play in the purchase decision. Sometimes this may be a problem, for example if you are investigating toys for tiny children you may find they cannot answer your questions, however you choose to ask them! So you may have to settle for the parents (who may, of course, be the customer rather than the user).

The size of the sample is vital. Too small a sample makes the results less valid and reliable as the sample will be prone to bias; too large and you are wasting time and effort. Decide on how to choose your sample – stratified, cluster, quota and multilayered are all types of random sample which may be appropriate. If in doubt come and ask one of the market research planners – they will advise.

If you decide to use a questionnaire do be careful – the response rate may be a factor which distorts the value of any results.

Whatever sample you use remember the previous section and tailor the questions to the group.

(c)   Analysing the data

Many mistakes can be made with data; first the data can be wrong before it even arrives to be assessed. Thus care and attention in the field are essential for accurate research. Percentages can too easily be wrongly calculated, or decimal points put in the wrong place and so on.

Some steps you can take to minimise the problem:

(i)   order the data to be analysed;
(ii)   group it for processing;
(iii)   carry out random quality checks to ensure reliable coding;
(iv)   check the logic and any formulae used.

(d) Interpreting the data

Any research can be misinterpreted and it can mislead. It is therefore important that both honesty and accuracy are your key concerns at the interpretation stage. In particular:

(i) ensure that meaningful classifications are created and used;

(ii) make sure that the statistics are properly represented (without loading to make a predefined conclusion look more reasonable);

(iii) avoid spurious correlations, 'gee whiz' graphs and other such dubious practices.

Finally, exercise caution in the claims you make – do not overstate your case!!

Conclusion

One of the best ways to ensure accuracy is to carry out a pilot survey on a small number of respondents. In this way you are doing market research on your market research. Your pilot respondents can also give valuable feedback on the efficiency/ease of use of your interview or questionnaires. Piloting will also allow you to run through the analysis process to ensure that there are no gremlins in the system.

Finally, if there is one single thing to keep in mind it is this: be clear about what you are trying to do!

9 PP TELEVISION LTD

From the launch of a new product the PLC could be said to go through four major stages.

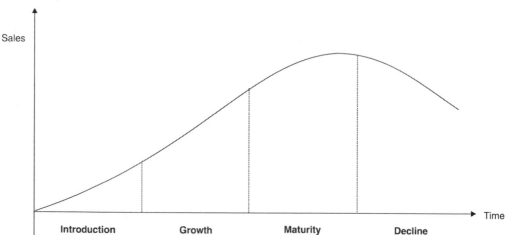

(a) Introduction stage. At this stage when the technology was new and demand exceeded supply PPT would have been able to charge higher prices to recover the cost of product development as quickly as possible, and to earn sufficient surplus to invest in keeping up with rapid changes in technology. Promotional spend would be largely aimed at creating favourable awareness of the PPT brand and gaining maximum penetration of the market in terms of distribution outlets. In order to overcome price resistance in lower income households, PPT will have traded increasingly with multiple outlets offering hire purchase and/or rental services.

(b) Growth stage. As favourable awareness grew, PPT will have been able to take advantage of economies of scale and the learning curve to reduce costs and prices. With an elastic demand, this will have further increased volume sales. Product design was likely to have been dominated by reliability and maintenance considerations so as to build up brand loyalty and word-of-mouth recommendation. Mass distribution outlets will have been courted by PPT during this stage. Advertising will then have changed from building awareness to promoting reliability and service aspects.

(c) Maturity stage. As growth began to slow, PPT along with other manufacturers will have sought to persuade the market to change their TV sets for ones with larger screens, better looking cabinets, lighter and slimmer sets etc. This was the strategy of product modification. PPT will also have promoted the purchase of more than one black and white TV as prices continued to reduce and affordability increased. The wealthier households were persuaded to buy extra sets for the bedroom or for the children etc, to stretch the market.

The technological breakthrough of colour TV will have brought a new surge in demand and a new growth stage. People will have bought colour TV sets to supplement black and white. Premium pricing will have been re-applied during this new introduction stage and initial distribution will have been through the more upmarket channels. Colour TV's advent will have accelerated the decline of black and white sets.

(d) Decline stage. PPT will have reduced brand advertising of the TVs in favour of sales push and dealer incentives. Product guarantees and maintenance package deals will also have featured strongly in the marketing mix. PPT will no doubt have offered a range of accessories such as remote control units, to enlarge the size of purchase and to cushion falling prices on TV sets.

PPT will be working hard to develop new technologies such as three-dimensional TV, wall screens, interactive units etc so as to engender another growth stage.

10 PRICING NEW PRODUCTS

REPORT

To: Marketing manager

From: A student

Date: XX.X.XX

Subject: Establishing prices for innovative computer software

Introduction

There are a number of internal and external factors which have to be taken into account when determining a price for a product. Our products are particularly innovative and therefore our pricing strategy must reflect this while taking into account the competitive environment we are operating in. This report will consider the range of factors we need to consider when setting our prices.

The market

The computer software market is highly competitive but growing. While the pace of technological change is rapid and many innovative products are being introduced, opportunities do exist for our company to launch innovative new software. Our pricing strategy will be determined by the market segments we target, our positioning and the degree of differentiation in our software. Is our market volume or niche? Are we targeting specialist or general applications? We also need to consider how we wish our software to be distributed as this will impact upon our price levels.

Competition

We need to consider our competitors' pricing strategies in terms of what they are charging for similar products and in which market segments they are placed. We also need to consider their possible reaction to our new software. To avoid a price war we must strongly differentiate our product and offer additional benefits to the user. This would give us the option of pricing our software above the competition.

The environment

We must consider the broad external factors that impact upon consumer behaviour, in particular the impact of current economic policies such as tax and interest rate changes, the level of credit and the overall 'feel good factor'. We must also consider the impact of demographic change particularly the reduction in size of the number of 16/24 year olds. Technological factors will obviously impact upon our pricing strategy as major developments are occurring, particularly in the field of multimedia.

The consumer

As indicated above, the extent to which our software meets the needs of the consumer will be a major determinant of the price we set. The ability and willingness of the consumer to pay, the perceived value of our software and their attitudes towards and general knowledge of our products are all important. Their degree of price sensitivity and the extent to which they are influenced by branding and marketing communications will also impact upon price.

The company

We need to consider the prices we set in relation to our overall objectives and strategy, in particular how we wish to be perceived as a company and our long-term corporate aims. We must also consider the volume of sales we require and our manufacturing capability. Closely linked to this is the level of production costs involved, both fixed and variable. If the new software has not incurred substantial developmental costs this will enable more flexibility in our price setting.

The product

As indicated above, the extent to which our software is differentiated and the added value it offers our consumers are important factors to be considered when setting price, as is the extent to which we offer other factors that augment the product (free help line, technical support and so on) which will influence the perceived value of the product. The strength of our brand in relation to competitive brands and the relative position of the brand in the market are important considerations. Finally, because this is a new and innovative product we will need to consider the length and projected course of the product's life cycle, when determining the price at which we launch the product, that is, the price for the introduction stage of the life cycle.

Conclusion

As you can see from the above, a range of factors should be taken into account when setting the price for our new software. The weighting of these factors will depend upon their relative importance. Should you require any further information I would be happy to develop this further.

11   CIM RADIO TRENT TOUR

The elements of the promotional mix could be said to be advertising, sales promotion, public relations and personal selling. Sales promotion has its own particular sub-mix comprising mailshots, exhibitions, point-of-sale display material, dealer/consumer/salesforce incentives, sales literature, packaging, merchandising etc.

It is just as important to achieve the right balance between elements of the promotional mix as it is to harmonise the marketing mix itself. All promotional elements need to sing the same tune.

We shall take first the commercial radio station which is concerned with maximising listenership and advertising revenue. For this station the tour is a piece of public relations aimed at favourably impressing a specialised group of people among whom will be some spenders on advertising for their companies. Others will be influencers on the advertising spend. Other young marketers in the tour group will be future marketing managers. It would be very time-consuming and costly for Radio Trent to communicate individually with such an audience. The hands-on opportunity to record a script for a commercial is designed to reduce fear, to familiarise and to create a sense of ownership – in the same way as an experienced salesperson will hand you the product (or a sample) to hold and to feel, rather than simply demonstrate it to you.

The talk by the Sales Manager will capitalise upon the goodwill generated by the tour. Sales literature and business cards (sales promotion) will, no doubt, be liberally available. It is a form of personal selling.

The in-house tour and talk can be seen to employ the elements of PR, sales promotion and personal selling in an harmonious and integrated way. This event could also be said to be advertising in that it has appeared in the medium of the CIM Branch circular.

Such events are, for the host, very cost-effective and instrumental in developing good personal relations with customers and prospective clients.

From the CIM Branch viewpoint it is of course using a mailshot to communicate this event to its members. By getting members together in a relaxed atmosphere, it is also providing social benefits and indulging in a form of PR. The circular is advertising a previous successful visit and playing upon the limited availability of place so as to create demand and gain further favourable publicity. CIM Branch officials will no doubt be doing a personal sell at the end of the talk on the next Branch event. The opportunity to record a script for a commercial is, from the CIM's point of view, a consumer incentive.

When analysing this event from these two standpoints, it can be seen to comprise all the major elements of the promotional mix and to integrate these in a synergistic way.

12   ADVERTISING AND SELLING

Advertising, sales promotion and the sales force are all methods of effecting marketing communication with potential and existing consumers.

Marketing theory stresses that a range of tactics is more successful than 'putting all your eggs in one basket'. It would seem more feasible to have advertising, sales promotion and the sales force working in unison with each other to produce more effective marketing. Some of the following notes may explain how advertising and sales promotion actually help the sales force.

We must recognise some objectives of advertising and sales promotion and then consider whether they enhance the sales force's position.

(a)   Advertising's fundamental objectives are to:

    (i)   influence attitudes;
    (ii)   create awareness of products/services;
    (iii)   increase knowledge;
    (iv)   act as a reminder;
    (v)   motivate enquiries; and
    (vi)   provide leads for the sales force.

(b)   Sales promotion objectives are:

    (i)   to encourage product trial;
    (ii)   to encourage greater use;
    (iii)   to attract non-users;
    (iv)   to stimulate larger orders; and
    (v)   to encourage brand switching.

From the above list, the sales force will recognise objectives that apply to them as well. The sales force aims:

(a)   to inform about new products;
(b)   to demonstrate products;
(c)   to provide after-sales service;
(d)   to effectively display products; and
(e)   to provide training for use of the product.

Many of the above objectives rely on earlier awareness from advertising and sales promotion.

Advertising and sales promotion can actually assist the sales force with their job performance. If the sales force were expected to start with introducing the product and raising awareness before being able to concentrate on achieving their objectives, there would need to be considerably more sellers. Starting with cold calling is a much more difficult position to be in and proportions of sales to customers visited would be much lower.

If the sales force were to work independently, there would be a large amount of time wasted on potential customers who are not interested in buying the product at all. If the advertising and sales promotion could raise initial awareness of genuinely interested parties then the job of the sales force would be considerably more effective.

Advertising is effective at building an image for the sales force to promote. Sales promotion can provide physical incentives for consumers which the sales force can then introduce, explain and promote to the potential consumers. In this situation, elements of communication are likely to boost the sales forces' capabilities.

Advertising and sales promotion can also benefit the sales force through confirming the product's image and capabilities. The marketing mix will support the sales force's selling process and again help to maximise profits – the overall objective of all elements of the marketing mix.

All the points we have noted confirm that money spent on advertising and sales promotion would not be better spent on the sales force. It can be seen that communication elements actually complement each other and work towards a more effective marketing mix.

Advertising and sales promotion fundamentally raise awareness and knowledge, remind and provide leads for the sales force to turn into measurable sales. Surely their job would be less effective without the synergistic ability that the communication elements have when they work in conjunction with each other.

13   LOGISTICS

In order that goods move from producer to consumer efficiently and effectively the movement of these goods needs to be managed. To get products to the right place at the right time in the right quantities takes a good deal of management skill. The physical flow of goods and materials coming into the company and going out of the company to the final consumer is usually termed 'logistics management'. Logistics management comprises materials management and physical distribution. Materials management is the flow of goods and materials into the company. This includes all the raw materials that go into the production of the final goods. Physical distribution on the other hand concerns the movement of finished goods to the customers.

The output of a distribution system is a level of customer service. Physical distribution managers have to balance the desired level of service with their decisions on transport, warehousing and inventory management.

There has recently been an upsurge in interest in physical distribution because it has been recognised that this area offers some potential for achieving a competitive edge and thus for achieving customer loyalty due to a product being available when it is required.

Inventory management involves finding a balance between keeping inventory costs as a whole as low as possible and providing customers with a good service. Costs come from the holding of inventories, ordering inventory and the risks that stocks will run out. So the main management roles concerning inventory management are to decide how many goods to order, when to order and how to balance keeping adequate stocks against the costs of stockholding. How much to order can be assessed using specific formulae and/or the skill and experience of management. Sales forecasts can be used in order to ascertain when to reorder stocks. Sales forecasts are subject to some amount of error. If this was not so there would never be occasion to run out of goods. An estimate of this error can be used to provide the company with a buffer stock to be used if demand is greater than expected.

Recent advances in information technology and the use of it (particularly in retailing) has allowed companies to become much more accurate in their sales forecasts and thus to reduce their stockholding. Just in Time (JIT) has been introduced in many areas where a product is made available just before it is required. This minimises stock holding and thus reduces costs.

Physical distribution management is often thought of in simple transportation terms. Although there is much more to this management task, transportation is still a very important aspect. If transportation is not handled efficiently then stocks can build up and inventory costs soar, in addition to the adverse effects on customer service. There are many ways in which goods can be transported from one place to another. Management must choose the most suitable method for the product in question according to:

Askham Bryan College
LIBRARY BOOK

BPP PUBLISHING

(a) speed;
(b) dependability;
(c) availability;
(d) frequency;
(e) capability; and
(f) cost.

There are five main transportation methods available to management: rail, road, sea, air and pipeline. Each of these can be assessed according to the six criteria outline above. The 'best' method of transporting goods will depend on the product characteristics. For example, oil is suitable for pipeline transportation while coal is suitable for transport by rail, road or sea.

In conclusion, successful physical distribution management is a key factor in the success of a company. It is one of the most obvious ways in which marketing management can build a high level of customer service into their product offering as it concerns the actual delivery of the product to the consumer. The desired level of customer service needs to be balanced against the costs of the physical distribution management. An effective physical distribution system should be developed by management and incorporated into the overall logistics management of the business.

14   JIT QUICK

To: Marketing Director

From: A Student

Date: XX.XX.XX

Subject: Implications of 'Just in time' manufacturing in our largest customer

Introduction

'Just in time' was pioneered by Toyota in the 1950s. The system works on the basis that components are supplied direct to the production line just as they are needed. The system reduces the manufacturer's stock requirements to nil, frees up space for other 'more productive' functions and increases the company's efficiency and profitability. The need for close partnerships and for supplies which are prompt and reliable means that local suppliers are often preferred. The implementation of such a system by one of our major customers has important implications for our company's operations.

Implications for us

Our customer will no longer accept the need to hold stock and will therefore require frequent, prompt and flexible delivery of small quantities of our products. We can no longer work on the basis of offering delivery dates and being unreliable in meeting our delivery promises.

JIT requires supplies of good quality. Our customer will not accept material of insufficient or variable quality. Such a situation would result in them not being able to run their lean manufacturing system. If we cannot meet this requirement then it is likely our customer will source its supplies from elsewhere.

The customer will require close relationships with suppliers and those suppliers must ensure that such relationships pervade the whole organisation. This may well require a significant culture change in our organisation, particularly in the way we perceive and act towards our customers.

Actions required

To ensure that our company can respond to these requirements it will be necessary for the following actions to be implemented.

(a)   An effective planning system.

(b)   A sophisticated marketing information system to provide timely and accurate data to management. This information should cover parts, products, production flows, buying information and costs.

(c)   A Total Quality Management programme to ensure that our internal systems strive towards the goal of zero defects. To achieve this it may be necessary to implement quality circles and multifunctional teams. It will also require a change in management style and relationships with employees. Staff must be empowered to take more responsibility in ensuring our service goals are achieved.

(d)   'Just in time' principles with our own suppliers to ensure we can deliver the required service to our customer.

(e)   A flexible manufacturing system.

(f)   An analysis and appreciation of the financial effects of the customer reducing its buffer stock to zero over the coming year.

Conclusions

While the implications of our customer's decision are serious and the actions we are required to take extensive, the long-term benefits outweigh any short-term gain we might make in not proceeding with investing in the changes outlined above. Other companies are likely to adopt these principles including our competitors so we will end up in the position where we lose more and more of our customers.

15   PLC MODIFICATION

Introduction phase

The wide screen TV is in the introductory phase of its product life cycle. The prime promotional strategy at this time is to create awareness of the existence of wide screen TVs and their benefits. The main method that should be used to generate awareness is through heavy spend on above-the-line media such as TV, magazines and newspapers. To obtain publicity, specialist journalists should be sent details of the new product and its benefits.

Sales promotion should be geared to getting customers to try the product, thus special offers such as free 30 day in-home trial could be used.

It is essential that retailing sales personnel are well versed in the advantages of the product and thus a training support package should be made available.

The competitive position is that few manufacturers are offering this product widely.

It is important not to confuse the customers nor sales staff. They are at the start of the learning curve as well as the life cycle. Few versions of the TV should be offered, or even only one, as customers and sales staff have to be familiarised with the concept.

The retailer does not need to sell at wafer-thin margins, but has to price the product so that the customer feels he or she is getting good value, and so that the retailer is getting a return for the trouble it has taken in stocking and selling this new and complex type of product.

Customers who are early adopters of innovative products often like to feel that the product is not widely available. They want a considerable degree of individual attention and like to feel exclusive and select. Likewise, the manufacturer will not want to go to the expense of training staff in all possible retailers for a new TV product which may well have only very limited appeal. Thus distribution will be selective.

Growth stage

If this product does grow, then the manufacturer should change promotional strategy to:

(a) establish strong branding in the minds of both sales staff and the (existing and potential) customers;

(b) prepare for some aggressive competition (with this particular product we can expect competition from several but not all TV manufacturers);

Promotional strategy will dictate high spending to match the competition and create product differentiation.

Maturity stage

The firm's promotional objective will be to maintain/strengthen loyalty.

(a) The competitive position will feature some firms doing well but others squeezed out of the market.

(b) Marketing intelligence should be used to seek product improvements, broaden the market and introduce new promotional theme(s).

Thus the role of advertising will be to differentiate the product from the competition and to encourage brand loyalty, ie to ensure existing customers buy the same brand again as a replacement or second TV set.

Decline stage

If the manufacturer still has not withdrawn, the main objective will be to extract profit against low promotional expenditure.

There will be fewer competitors, with little if anything to choose between them. The intelligence efforts will be directed towards determining when to stop marketing and selling these products.

Alternatively attempts can be made to extend the PLC by product line extensions or targeting a new segment. In these cases promotional support would be required.

16 BETTER BANANAS

(a) The development of genetically produced bananas with the subsequent improvement in shelf-life of the product and wider range of flavours will have a major impact upon the nature of the marketing environment for the three groups under discussion. The development has been possible through improved technology but its implications for the means by which the banana is marketed will impact upon all elements of the marketing mix.

Current situation

Pricing. The relationship between growers and importers has traditionally been one of importer dominance. Due to the large number of small growers the price for bananas has been determined by market forces. With numerous suppliers, few buyers and a product that can deteriorate rapidly, the need for using the services of the importer is paramount. It is likely that under these circumstances growers have to accept a competitive market price at the beginning of the growing season at low profit margins and rely on good harvests to ensure good profits. A bad harvest will not enable the grower to renegotiate the price which was set at the beginning of the growing season. Dominant wholesaler and retailer groups will negotiate prices direct with the importers and will also determine the retail selling price at which they sell the bananas to the consumer. This price will vary according to the nature of the retail outlet and the quality of the product.

Product. Despite the fact that flavours and textures of bananas tend to vary, no attempt has been made by growers to differentiate their product. Similarly, limited branding has occurred and the consumer is probably unaware of the country of origin. The majority of bananas imported will be the cultivated soft, sweet bananas to which the UK consumer is accustomed. The major problem with the banana in the current situation is its rapid rate of deterioration.

Distribution. As indicated above, the growers are reliant upon the importers to distribute the product to the retailer, often via wholesalers. No direct distribution to retailers can occur due to the small size and large number of growers. The case study does not indicate any form of producer association that could have acted as a representative of the growers when negotiating distribution. The supply of bananas direct from grower to wholesalers in the country of origin is also not available due to volume of supply and the need for appropriate transportation. The benefit to the growers is that high volumes of bananas can be exported via the importers but growers have no control over the distribution system. Retailers will not want to hold large stocks of bananas due to the problem of deterioration, therefore regular daily supplies of product will be required.

Promotion. The growers have limited ability to promote the products or the brand name that they produce. The importers will be negotiating directly with UK wholesaler and retailer buyers. Trade marketing will be the dominant form of communication between the importers and the UK wholesalers and retailers.

Genetically improved banana

Pricing. The new genetically improved varieties of banana will lengthen the shelf-life of the product, stabilise supply due to the increased resistance to disease and enable the grower to develop unique flavours which can be targeted at specific groups and usage occasions. The potential for differential pricing becomes possible as the quality and nature of the product can be better controlled. In the early stages of the product's life cycle, either a premium pricing or penetration pricing strategy could be pursued: premium pricing because of the product's uniqueness and improved quality; or penetration pricing because of the lower costs incurred in producing the product (ie less wastage).

Product. There are now opportunities for differentiation via branding, packaging and range of flavours, due to the improved shelf-life of this product and the ability of the grower to control product design and quality. This will enable the growers to target and position their products at specific market segments. Product development is possible with opportunities for enhancing the range of bananas available. Retailers may be offered the opportunity for branded or own brand products and can specify requirements.

Distribution. The improved shelf-life of the genetically produced banana will reduce the reliance the growers have on the importers. New means of distribution could be identified without the need for specialised transportation. Wastage will be reduced at the growing, stocking and transportation stages. Retailers will be able to hold stocks longer therefore reducing the number of deliveries required. Larger order quantities will be possible which will reduce distribution costs further. The importers will have to adapt the methods of distribution currently offered including cheaper services, alternative distribution methods and the opportunity to enable growers to supply direct to retailers. The new banana will reduce the need for the function of the middleman who traditionally acted as a wholesaler.

Promotion. The growers will have the option of supplying retailers directly. Direct marketing could replace the traditional trade marketing strategies offered by the importer. Branding of products will be possible and therefore growers may adopt traditional brand-building promotional techniques. It is possible that the new banana could be promoted by the retailer in the same way as traditional FMCG branded products, with attention being given to design and packaging alongside brand building advertising and sales promotion.

(b)   Influence on customer needs

The impact of these changes upon customer needs is likely to occur in stages. As with the introduction of all new products there is likely to be a cycle of adoption of innovations. Many consumers may need to be educated as to the desirability of such genetically produced products. By 2002, it is likely that many other products will have been launched on to the market using such technology. Therefore, the rate of adoption may be quicker.

Purchase behaviour

Consumer perception of the product is unlikely to change dramatically. However purchase behaviour may alter in that the product offers higher quality and flavours that might appeal to specific market segments. The impact of improved packaging and branding will also influence consumer's behaviour as the banana will be positioned not just against alternative fruits but also against other brands of bananas (differentiation).

Customer needs

Consumer needs vary from wanting to be healthy to wanting self esteem. The traditional banana has predominantly satisfied needs of hunger, health and convenience. Its wide availability throughout the year has meant it has no prestige value. It is unlikely that the wide availability of genetically produced bananas will change these fundamental needs. However, changing perceptions of the improved product and improved targeting to appeal to individual tastes may well influence consumers to purchase the banana instead of alternative products.

17 EXPORTING SUCCESS

(a)   Outline of factors to be considered before entering international markets

Your company may have operated very successfully at home and expansion to overseas markets may represent a logical business development. However, you should consider a number of key issues when deciding to enter overseas markets, which can be very different to the ones you are familiar with at home.

Issues to be raised in analysing an overseas marketing environment are examined under the overlapping headings of the political, economic, social and technological environments.

The political environment

(i)   We may take political stability for granted in our own country, but will this be the case overseas? While radical change rarely results from political upheaval in most Western countries, the instability of many Eastern European governments leads to uncertainty about future market opportunities.

(ii)   Licensing systems may be applied by governments in an attempt to protect domestic producers, putting you at a competitive disadvantage.

(iii)   Regulations governing product standards may require you to expensively re-configure your products to meet local regulations (this is becoming less of an issue in the single European market).

(iv)   Controls can be used to restrict the import of manufactured goods, requiring you to create a local source of supply, leading to possible problems in maintaining consistent quality standards and also possibly losing economies of scale.

(v)   Restrictions on currency movements may make it difficult for you to repatriate profits earned from an overseas operation.

The economic environment

(i)   In assessing overseas markets, you should consider their economic attractiveness. A generally accepted measure of the economic attractiveness of an overseas market is the level of GDP per capita.

(ii)   More importantly, you should place great emphasis on the expected future economic performance of a country and the stage which a country has reached in its economic development. While many Western developed economies face saturated markets for many products, less developed economies may be just emerging.

(iii)   A crucial part of the analysis of an overseas market focuses on the level of competition within that market. While many markets for your products in Western Europe may be saturated, relatively new and less competitive markets to aim at may occur in many developing economies of the Pacific Rim, allowing better margins to be achieved.

The social and cultural environment

Although you may understand the buying and consumption patterns of your products at home, you will need to understand differences which may occur in overseas markets, for example as follows.

(i) Buying processes vary between different cultures. For example, in some cultures, women may be the usual purchasers of a product which is routinely bought by men in our culture.

(ii) Some categories of your products may be rendered obsolete by different types of social structure. For example, extended family structures common in some countries have the ability to produce themselves a wide range of products which you sell.

(iii) Some of your products which are taken for granted at home may be seen as socially unacceptable in an overseas market.

(iv) What is deemed to be an unacceptable activity in procuring sales at home may be considered essential overseas. In some countries a bribe to a public official may be considered essential.

The technological environment

Under this heading you need to consider the availability of technical facilities to provide adequate pre- and after-sales support to your product. You may also need good telephone facilities to support your market entry. These may be lacking in some countries.

(b) How can you ensure export marketing success? Here are a few tips to reduce the risks of exporting and maximise your profitability from exporting.

(i) You must ensure that you base export decisions on adequate information. You can start by employing a UK based consultancy to evaluate worldwide market opportunities for your product. You can follow this up by employing a local consultant in the export market of your choice.

(ii) Having decided to enter an overseas market, you must make marketing mix decisions which will allow you to successfully penetrate that market. To be successful, you may need to adapt your product to meet the differing needs of overseas buyers. Also consider whether the promotional messages and media which you are successfully using at home will need adapting to overseas markets.

(iii) You should try to minimise your risk by test marketing, and gradually committing more resources to a market once you understand more about the risks and opportunities involved.

(iv) You need to consider whether you should enter the market on your own, or in collaboration with a partner. Where you have little knowledge of an overseas market, it may make sense to work with a local joint venture partner or to appoint a sole import agent to distribute your products. These can share their knowledge of the expert market, but you will lose some control over your operations.

INDEX

NOTES

ORDER FORM

Any books from our Business Basics range can be ordered in one of the following ways:

- Telephone us on **020 8740 2211**

- Send this page to our **Freepost** address

- Fax this page on **020 8740 1184**

- Email us at **publishing@bpp.com**

- Go to our website: **www.bpp.com**

We aim to deliver to all UK addresses inside 5 working days. Orders to all EU addresses should be delivered within 6 working days. All other orders to overseas addresses should be delivered within 8 working days.

BPP Publishing Ltd
Aldine House
Aldine Place
London W12 8AW
Tel: 020 8740 2211
Fax: 020 8740 1184
Email: publishing@bpp.com

Full name: _____

Day-time delivery address: _____

_____

_____ Postcode _____

Day-time telephone (for queries only): _____

Please send me the following quantities of books:

	No. of copies	Price	Total
Accounting		£13.95	
Law		£13.95	
Quantitative Methods		£13.95	
Information Technology		£13.95	
Economics		£13.95	
Marketing		£13.95	
Human Resource Management		£13.95	
Organisational Behaviour		£13.95	

	Sub Total	£

Postage & Packaging

UK : £3.00 for first plus £2.00 for each extra	£
Europe : (inc. ROI) £5.00 for first plus £4.00 for each extra	£
Rest of the world : £20.00 for first plus £10.00 for each extra	£

	Grand Total	£

I enclose a cheque for £_____ (cheque to BPP Publishing Ltd) or charge to Access/VISA/Switch

Card number: ⬜⬜⬜⬜⬜⬜⬜⬜⬜⬜⬜⬜⬜⬜⬜⬜⬜⬜⬜

Issues number (Switch only): _____

Start date: _____ Expiry date: _____

Signature _____

REVIEW FORM & FREE PRIZE DRAW

We are constantly reviewing, updating and improving our publications. We would be grateful for any comments or thoughts you have on this book. Cut out and send this page to our Freepost address and you will be automatically entered in a £50 prize draw.

Jed Cope
Business Basics Range Manager
BPP Publishing Ltd, FREEPOST, London W12 8BR

Full name: _____

Address: _____

_____

_____ Postcode _____

Where are you studying?

Where did you find out about BPP books?

Why did you decide to buy this book?

Have you used any other BPP products in your studies?

What thoughts do you have on our:

- Introductory pages

- Topic coverage

- Summary diagrams, icons, chapter roundups and quick quizzes

- Activities, case studies and questions

The other side of this form is left blank for any further comments you wish to make.

Please give any further comments and suggestions (with page number if necessary) below.

FREE PRIZE DRAW RULES

1   Closing date for 31 January 2001 draw is 31 December 2000. Closing date for 31 July 2001 draw is 30 June 2001.

2   Restricted to entries with UK and Eire addresses only. BPP employees, their families and business associates are excluded.

3   No purchase necessary. Entry forms are available upon request from BPP Publishing. No more than one entry per title, per person. Draw restricted to persons aged 16 and over.

4   Winners will be notified by post and receive their cheques not later than 6 weeks after the relevant draw date.

5   The decision of the promoter in all matters is final and binding. No correspondence will be entered into.

Askham Bryan College
LIBRARY BOOK